PASSAGE OF DARKNESS

CW00952233

PASSAGE

OF

DARKNESS

The Ethnobiology of the Haitian Zombie

by Wade Davis

The University of North Carolina Press
Chapel Hill & London

The paper in this book meets the
guidelines for permanence and
durability of the
Committee on Production Guidelines
for Book Longevity of
the Council on Library Resources.

03   02   01   00   99   9   8   7   6   5

Library of Congress Cataloging-in-Publication Data

Davis, Wade.

Passage of darkness.

Bibliography: p.

Includes index.

1. Zombiism—Haiti. 2. Bizango (Cult)
3. Tetrodotoxin—Physiological effect. 4. Haiti—
Religious life and customs. 5. Haiti—Social life and
customs. 6. Davis, Wade. I. Title.

BL2530.H3D37   1988   299'.65   87-40537

ISBN 0-8078-1776-7 (alk. paper)

ISBN 0-8078-4210-9 (pbk.: alk. paper)

Portions of this book appeared in essentially the same form in
The Serpent and the Rainbow, © 1985 by Wade Davis, published by
Simon and Schuster. The University of North Carolina Press gratefully
acknowledges the permission of the publisher to use this material.

For my father

I am the scorn of all my adversaries,
a horror to my neighbors,
an object of dread to my acquaintances;
those who see me in the street flee from me

I have passed out of mind like one who is dead;
I have become like a broken vessel.

Yea, I hear the whispering of many—
terror on every side!—
as they scheme together against me,
as they plot to take my life.

—Psalm 31:11–13

CONTENTS

FOREWORD

by Robert Farris Thompson

While in Haiti in the summer of 1961, I saw my first zombie. It was not the actual phenomenon, as explained in this book. Instead I was viewing a performance in a small outdoor theater in Port-au-Prince. Nevertheless, the scene was impressive: a person playing the role of bokor, or negative priest, cracked a long whip over the body of a zombified person, who moved dully in his shroud.

The skit was oddly familiar. It brought to life a traditional image of mystic punishment from one of the early paintings of the Haitian Renaissance—*The Zombi*, by Fernand Pierre—published in 1948 by Selden Rodman in his *Renaissance in Haiti: Popular Painters in the Black Republic*. Pierre shows a cemetery alive with ritual notations. There is an altar for Baron Samedi, the god of cemeteries, a whip draped upon a cross, mystic fronds deliberately planted on tombs, and so forth. The bokor looms in front of that spectral backdrop with a tallness suggestive of his powers. He controls a zombie, shown with corpse-swath still tied about his jaws in Haitian funereal fashion, by cracking a whip and leading him away by a length of rope tied to the hapless being's hands. In 1974 Rodman published another book on Haitian painting, *The Miracle of Haitian Art*. That volume, too, includes a painting on the zombie theme: Hector Hypollite's *An Avan, An Avan! (Go Forward, Go Forward!)*, dated circa 1947. The bokor here has a monstrous right hand, in which he holds a power-bottle probably used to activate the spirit, Baron Samedi; he leads two zombies by a length of rope to an unknown destiny.

Several years after I saw that first performance, I learned in Kongo that the whip in the bokor's hand was not, as so many in Haiti insisted, merely a relic of the days of slavery—the argument being that the bokor played the role of the old plantation overseer, cracking his whip on the backs of slaves. Actually, in the classical religion of Kongo, ritual experts sometimes activate a *mfimbu* (whip), cracking it loudly to lend energy to a charm or to chase away a spirit of ill-will from a cemetery. The latter ritual is termed *kuma mpeeve zambi* (chasing the wind of [an evil] soul), according to Fu-Kiau Bunseki, a leading theoretician of the culture of his people.

In point of fact, the cracking of whips and the firing of *bizango* (guns) are used again and again in Kongo in contexts of ritual reconciliation or to protect a village from mystic sources of jealousy and envy in the night. Whip cracking, which has become part of the lore of the zombie in Haiti, is definitively used in Kongo as an acoustical door to the other world. Fu-Kiau continues: "My own father did this, he would go to the cemetery and crack a whip when someone was sick or mysteriously suffering in the village. He did this to control an offending ancestral spirit who was responsible for the bad luck."

It is very likely that the mystic usage of the whip in Kongo was reinforced by its use under the backbreaking conditions of Haitian slavery, but the point is that I would have never been steered in the right direction, taught to take the zombie phenomenon seriously as a social sanction of the greatest import, had I not come in contact with the research distilled in this volume by Wade Davis.

Speaking as an art historian focused in Afro-Atlantic visual happening, let me describe some of the things that make this book important. First, Davis makes scientific sense out of sensation. He suggests that zombie making, itself a very rare and carefully considered form of punishment (not at all the assembly-line process imagined by the press) is imposed by the Bizango societies of the night, an extraordinarily dramatic and effective guild that maintains order and ethical behavior in rural communities.

On 21 March 1975, in Port-au-Prince, I invited André Phonord, one of the most responsible of my informants in Haiti, to look at Hector Hypollite's depiction of two zombies with a bokor, *An Avan, An Avan!*, and comment. He responded: "These men [the zombies] must have done something terrible to their families." I asked the obvious follow-up question. Phonord replied: "You know, they took their jobs away from them, or stole their wives, or let them be in misery while they were rich. . . . See that skull [a human skull, in the painting, is shown deliberately deposited before a cross of Baron Samedi, along with a ritual feast

for the lord of the cemetery].... [It represents] someone who
had done terrible things to his people. [In revenge] they went to
Baron Samedi, three Fridays straight, each time at midnight, in
the cemetery, and asked help in getting the zombie of the man."
Phonord concluded his fascinating exegesis with this observation: "Regard those zombies; they can't lift their heads. Zombies
cannot look up, they only look down."

In March 1975 I also visited, near Léogane, a locally famous
healer-diviner named Alvarès. Although blind, he lived in a compound bristling with images and drums and stones and bead-
wrapped swords and chromolithographs of the saints—all in
service of the *loa*, the gods of West Africa and the ancestral spirits
and animate charms of Kongo, alive in Haiti. He told me that
anyone going to Baron Samedi and the persons of the night,
asking zombification of a person, had best carry a special guard
or passport, for example a wine bottle filled with a special "Baron
drink" and appropriately wrapped in crimson cloth. Even better
was to present a Baron bottle not only covered with red cloth but
also cabalistically emblazoned with a pair of scissors, open and
bound to the bottle with insistent windings of wire. Otherwise,
Alvarès warned, "if you go into a cemetery and call Baron and
you are not strong, he is going to kill you." And then, he too,
made the point that zombiism, as such, was an extraordinary
form of social punishment. As a parting gift, Alvarès let me paste
into my field notebook a sprig of *mo levé*. With a grin, he assured
me that this herb, mixed with "other things," had the power to
"raise the dead." He implied that I was leaving with part of the
antidote to zombification.

In any event, I left Haiti that spring with the eerie sensation
that I had been given testimony about zombies on the basis of
actual observation as opposed to mere citation of Haiti's extraordinarily rich oral literature. If my informants had not actually
seen zombies or been witness to their making—and curing,
even—their colleagues had. But I lacked the evidence to pursue
this private hunch. Nevertheless, from that moment on, when-
ever I lectured about paintings showing zombies I took care to
cut through the lurid to the essential social point: such persons
had been punished for building their private gain on the insecu-
rity of their communities.

With the appearance of Davis's research the proof of what

Phonord and Alvarès were suggesting becomes complete. Vague intimations become brilliantly reported fact. Now, in this text, we have the full cultural and historical setting, studded with first-rate chapters on death, poison, and antidotes. Most important, I think, Davis elucidates how the zombie tradition works as a form of social control and the role of the Bizango societies at the heart of that deliberately intimidating process. Davis broke into that amazing world for the first time and what he found has, I think, possible transoceanic resonance. At least I would like to suggest a lead as to whence came this society of the night that holds the trial that decides whether the zombie dosage will be administered:

> In north Kongo if there is something wrong concerning conduct in a village, a society will come out, in the night, with guns, and fire them—*Kúbula bizongo*—to attack the village. Not to kill people, but to attack the village symbolically, firing salvoes in the air at 3 or 4 o'clock in the morning while people are sleeping. They deliberately shatter public peace to dramatize that something has gone wrong in village affairs, something quite serious (field notes from the Manianga area, summer 1985).

Is it possible the Kongo notion of seizing the soul (*nzambi*) of a socially dangerous person as moral punishment was blended together with notions, from the same area of tropical Africa, of nocturnal tribunals in the rise of the zombie/Bizango phenomenon in Haiti? Was this unique Creole blend deepened or reinforced by knowledge of a Yoruba ritual from what is now southwestern Nigeria, involving the carrying of indigo-coated skulls of felons and murderers on "trays of heaven" by moral inquisitors (*egúngún alateorun*), who were believed to have come from the dead to judge the living, morally intimidating them with their terrifying insignia? And was the Ki-Kongo term for socially allusive gunfire in the night, *bizango*, used as an appropriately based term for the new and emergent Haitian tradition?

Future research will test this hypothesis. But we would not be moved to ask these questions without the impetus of Davis's discoveries. He has written of one of the most fascinating and most misunderstood phenomena of all the Black Americas—in his own words, one "that has been used to denigrate an entire people. I find it extraordinary that when even an educated person in the West is called upon to list the great or significant religions of the world there is an entire subcontinent that is consistently left out of the calculus." To read this book, then, is to savor "an Antaean imperative," the renewal of contact with true sources of moral energy and spirit.

PREFACE

by Richard Evans Schultes

The interdisciplinary field of ethnobiology has grown fast during the past half-century. Extensive and intensive investigation, especially in ethnobotany, has come into its own and is now attracting the attention and efforts of well-trained research scientists. All this progress is indicated by the proliferation of courses in our universities and by the establishment of a number of journals devoted to the study of the appreciation, in primitive societies, of the value of their ambient flora and fauna.

But there are not yet enough botanists and anthropologists to cope with the ever more rapid erosion and disappearance of the knowledge of the properties of species—knowledge accumulated over millennia of experimentation by peoples in preliterate societies around the world. Their acquaintance with natural phenomena in the plant kingdom—of extraordinary academic and intellectual significance to social scientists and of great practical value to our modern societies—is disappearing much faster in many regions than the plants themselves. It is the inexorable advance of Western civilization and the resulting acculturation or annihilation of aboriginal societies that has doomed the perpetuation of native folklore. It is the frenetic road-building programs, increasing missionary efforts, commercial penetration, and even widening tourist and military activities that lead to this loss of ethnobotanical wealth. Often it takes only a single generation for much of this precious knowledge to be lost—to be forever entombed with the culture that gave it birth.

It should be our aim to train more ethnobiologists so that we may salvage this knowledge. It may not long be available to salvage, and its loss will be one of the greatest tragedies of this century.

The Botanical Museum of Harvard University has long been active in the development of economic botany and ethnobotany. Its academic interests in these fields goes back to its founding in

1854. The museum has primarily emphasized several aspects of the field: archaeoethnobotany, ethnomycology, ethnopharmacology, and ethnoecology. Most of its research has been located in tropical America.

Wade Davis is a product of the Botanical Museum's ethnobotanical program. As an undergraduate in Harvard College concentrating in anthropology, he became interested in ethnobotany through one of the museum's courses in economic botany, entitled Plants and Human Affairs. He decided at that time to devote his efforts towards ethnobotany, and he enrolled in the university as a graduate student in the department of biology, where he eventually took his Ph.D. degree. It was my good fortune to have had Wade as my undergraduate and graduate student.

Thoroughly dedicated to this field of research, he carried out during his undergraduate years ethnobotanical and botanical studies among Indians in British Columbia, his native region in Canada, and, alone or with colleagues, similar investigations in Bolivia, Brazil, Colombia, Ecuador, and Peru. Much of his field research has not yet been published, but he has produced a number of papers with outstanding contributions, including ethnobotanical studies among the remote Waorani Indians of Amazonian Ecuador and investigations of the botany and ethnobotany of the poorly known hallucinogenic cactus *Trichocereus pachanoi* in the Peruvian Andes.

Six or seven years ago a friend of mine, Nathan Kline, telephoned me requesting help in ascertaining the toxic plants and animals used in the several zombie preparations of Haiti. He was interested in the effects of these preparations from the medical point of view. Due to my ongoing research of forty years on the medicinal and toxic plants of the Amazonian part of Colombia, I was unable to undertake any new projects. Realizing that research into zombiism would demand an anthropological or sociological approach, I recommended that he meet with Wade. Following their discussions, Wade agreed to undertake the assignment. His successful prosecution of field studies lasted for many months and resulted eventually in his dissertation and this book.

By interest, academic training, field experience, breadth of outlook, and personality Wade has the exceptional set of qualifications that this interdisciplinary field requires. I hope that his success will encourage others to take up this important work.

ACKNOWLEDGMENTS

My research on the zombie phenomenon was undertaken with the support of the Social Science and Humanities Research Council of Canada. Direct financial support was also generously provided by the International Psychiatric Research Foundation, the Wenner-Gren Foundation for Anthropological Research, and the National Science Foundation. My botanical determinations were verified by R. A. Howard of the Arnold Arboretum, Harvard University. Zoological determinations were furnished by the staff of the Museum of Comparative Zoology, Harvard University; in particular I would like to thank Karsten Hartel, John Hunter, Jim Knight, Greg Mayer, Jose Rosado, Franklin Ross, and Ernest Williams. Complete sets of voucher specimens have been deposited at the M.C.Z. (animals) and at the Economic Herbarium of Oakes Ames in the Botanical Museum of Harvard University (plants).

Valuable bibliographical materials were provided by Bruce Halstead, Bo Holmstedt, C. Y. Kao, Richard Evans Schultes, Robert Shipp, M. G. Smith, and Noel Vietmeyer. The title and epigraph were suggested by Gail Percy. I owe special thanks to David Maybury-Lewis and Richard Evans Schultes for their support during my entire career, and to Irven DeVore, Leslie Garay, Bruce Halstead, John Hartung, M. G. Smith, Robert Farris Thompson, and Rolla Tryon for their intellectual contributions and encouragement on this project.

My understanding of Haitian history was informed by the excellent work of Gerald Murray, Michel Laguerre, and Jean Fouchard, an independent scholar in Port-au-Prince. I thank Lyall Watson for introducing me to the literature on premature burial and the problems of diagnosing death. My perspective on the interaction between psychoactive compounds and human societies grew directly from my understanding of the visionary work of Andrew T. Weil. The preliminary laboratory work was done by Leon Roizin of Columbia University. For other laboratory work and advice I am indebted to Laurent Rivier, James Cottrell, and John Hartung. The Zombie Project was born of the vision of three men: David Merrick, Heinz Lehmann, and the late Nathan S. Kline.

xx   The work in Haiti was made possible by the cooperation and active support of many individuals. Keith Hulse introduced me to valuable informants. Lamarque Douyon shared his insights concerning the medical aspects of zombification and introduced me to Clairvius Narcisse. Medical records and other documents were generously furnished by the BBC and by the staff of the Albert Schweitzer Hospital. In Port-au-Prince I was kindly received and assisted by Max Paul and his staff at the Institut National Haitien de la Culture et des Arts, Eleanor Snare at the Institut Haïtiano-Américain, and Lesly Conde at the National Office of Tourism. In rural Haiti I worked directly with several people who openly shared their knowledge. In particular I would like to thank Jean Baptiste, Jacques Belfort and Madame Jacques, Michel Bonnet, Andrés Cajuste, Andrés Celestin, Robert and Carmine Erie, Cesar Ferdinand, Ives François, La Bonté, Jean-Jacques Leophin, Miriatel, Jean Price-Mars, Marcel Pierre, and Solvis Silvaise. All of these individuals, some of whom are identified here by pseudonyms, were directly responsible for the success of the project. Finally, I would like to acknowledge Herard Simon and Max Beauvoir. Herard Simon and his wife Hélène are serviteurs of the most profound awareness. A great houngan, Herard offered me his protection, without which this project would never have been complete. Max Beauvoir and his wife Elizabeth offered me their home and generous hospitality. Their daughter, Rachel Beauvoir, worked first as my interpreter and later as my field assistant, and her help was invaluable. My debt to all the people of Haiti who received me so kindly is impossible to measure.

In France, where the bulk of the book was written, I was grateful for the warm hospitality of my friends, Jo and Rosemary Giausserand. My family has been behind me on all my projects, and without the support of my mother, Gwen Davis, and my beloved father, George Edmund, I would never have been able to obtain the education and experience upon which this work has been based. It was my profound wish that my father would see this work completed but, sadly, he died in the last months. It is to his memory that this book is dedicated. Finally, I would like to acknowledge Monique Giausserand, a dear friend and respected colleague, who assisted me profoundly not only on this project, but on all endeavors I have undertaken in recent years.

PASSAGE OF DARKNESS

INTRODUCTION

The Zombie Project began in the spring of 1982 when the Botanical Museum at Harvard was contacted by the late Nathan S. Kline, eminent psychopharmacologist and then director of the Rockland State Research Institute of New York. Kline had worked in Haiti for more than thirty years; he knew François Duvalier and had been instrumental in establishing the country's first and only modern psychiatric facility, the Centre de Psychiatrie et Neurologie Mars-Kline. The center's first director was Lamarque Douyon, a Haitian psychiatrist who had trained at McGill University, where his work had come to the attention of Heinz Lehmann, another psychopharmacologist and a close colleague of Nathan Kline's. Since assuming the directorship of the psychiatric institute in 1961, Douyon, in collaboration with both Kline and Lehmann, had been systematically investigating all popular reports of the appearance of zombies, the infamous living dead of Vodoun folklore. In 1980 their efforts were rewarded by the discovery of the extraordinary case of Clairvius Narcisse.

What made this case noteworthy was the fact that Narcisse had been pronounced dead in 1962 at the Albert Schweitzer Hospital, an American-directed philanthropic institution that maintains precise and accurate records. Therefore, in addition to the death certificate, Douyon was able to obtain a medical dossier outlining the history of the case and the particular symptoms suffered by the patient at the time of his demise. According to these records, Narcisse was pronounced dead on 2 May by two attending physicians—one an American, both American-trained—and his death and subsequent burial eight hours later were witnessed by family members. In 1980 a man claiming to be Narcisse returned to his village and introduced himself, by a boyhood nickname, to his sister. He stated that he had been made a zombie eighteen years before by his brother because of a land dispute.

The case was studied at length by Kline and Douyon. With the help of Narcisse's family, Douyon devised a series of questions concerning intimate aspects of the family past. These Narcisse answered correctly. Based on the results of this questionnaire, the testimony of villagers, family members, and physicians, forensic examination by Scotland Yard of the fingerprints on the death certificate, and the reasonable assumption that there was no social or economic incentive to perpetrate a fraud, Douyon and Kline concluded that the case was legitimate. In other words, they suggested that Clairvius Narcisse had been mistakenly diagnosed as dead, buried alive, and, having survived a period of time in the coffin, had been taken from the grave, presumably by the one who had perpetrated the deed.

If the case of Clairvius Narcisse was to be believed, there had to be a material explanation, and the attention of the medical team shifted to the possible existence of a folk toxin which had long been rumored to be involved in the process of zombification. It was, of course, theoretically possible that a folk preparation might exist which, if administered in the proper dosage, would lower the metabolic state of the victim to such a level that he or she would be considered dead. In fact, however, the recipient of the toxin would remain alive, and an antidote, properly administered, could then restore him or her at the appropriate time. The medical potential of such a drug, particularly in the field of anesthesia, could be significant, but no one had yet obtained its formula. Douyon sent one sample of the reputed powder to Kline's laboratory in New York, but it proved to be chemically inert. Moreover, Douyon was unable to observe the preparation of the powder, nor did he have an opportunity to collect voucher specimens of the crude ingredients. He reported merely that a toxic powder and its antidote existed by folk record, that the poison was placed on the ground in the form of a cross, and that the potential victim had merely to walk across it to succumb.

Nathan Kline, despite his high-level contacts and his thirty years' experience in the country, also failed in his attempts to identify the elusive toxin. Indeed, though the preparation of the poison is specifically referred to in the Haitian penal code and reports of its existence by both popular and ethnographic literature date back well into the nineteenth century, no researcher had managed to discover its ingredients. It was with this precise assignment of obtaining samples of the folk toxin—if in fact it existed—and documenting its preparation that I was asked to join the Zombie Project. This book is the result of my participation in the project, which spanned a two-year period between 1982 and 1984. In the end, the identity of the folk toxin was established, but perhaps more significantly, the interdisciplinary approach that led to its discovery and a glimpse at the process of zombification also suggested cultural aspects of great importance. Evidence suggests that zombification is a form of social sanction imposed by recognized corporate bodies—the poorly known and clandestine secret Bizango societies—as one means of maintaining order and control in local communities.

Any presentation of results, of course, reflects a logical progression of ideas that, to say the least, was not at all evident at the beginning of the project. When I was first asked to go to Haiti, my own notion of zombies, if indeed I had one, was infected with misconceptions derived from a slew of sensational films and pulp fiction. As I began the investigation it became clear that these misconceptions would not be contradicted or clarified by the ethnographic literature. Anthropologists on the whole had perfunctorily dismissed the phenomenon as superstition. Reported cases that had at least the veneer of legitimacy, and which collectively demanded explanation, were ignored. Although it was mentioned in many major ethnographic and popular publications, the folk toxin had never been systematically investigated. The entire notion of zombies was seen as little more than a symptom of the Haitian peasant's notorious instincts for the phantasmagoric. Indeed, for a phenomenon that had so electrified the rest of the world, and which had been used in an explicitly racist way to denigrate both a people and their religion, there was a glaring absence of serious academic research that might prove once and for all whether zombies of any form were to be found in Haiti.

Clearly the elusive poison was critical to both the Narcisse case and the zombie problem in general. Without it, one was obliged to consider the phenomenon as magical belief, the Narcisse case itself a fraud. Therefore, the initial phase of the project consisted of the formulation of a hypothesis by a careful consideration of the ethnopharmacological literature and the field testing of that hypothesis in Haiti. From preliminary reports, it appeared that the preparation had to be topically active, capable of inducing a prolonged psychotic state, and that the initial dosage had to bring on a deathlike stupor. The substance had to be extremely potent and, because both the toxin and its purported antidote were likely to be organically derived, their source had to be a plant or animal currently found in Haiti.

An obvious candidate was *Datura stramonium* L., a psychoactive plant known to induce stupor in high dosages, and which in Haitian Creole has the provocative name *concombre zombi*—the zombie's cucumber. The plant owes its activity to a series of tropane alkaloids and, interestingly, the recognized medical antidote for these compounds is derived from a West African liana, *Physostigma venenosum* Balf.—a plant employed in ritual context as an ordeal poison by precisely the indigenous groups that were sold into bondage to Saint Domingue.

During the spring and summer of 1982 I tested this hypothesis in the field in Haiti. It proved to be false. Neither in the modest national herbarium nor in extensive field surveys was any evidence found to suggest that *P. venenosum* had been naturalized in Haiti. Feral populations of the weedy *D. stramonium* were common, particularly in old fields, but no evidence suggested that the plant was an ingredient in the zombie preparations. Nevertheless, this initial period achieved several important research goals. Working first with Douyon and subsequently alone, I conducted extensive interviews with Clairvius Narcisse, his family, and a number of villagers, as well as with the family of Francina Illeus, a second reputed zombie who remained at the time in a catatonic state. These interviews added considerably to the body of information on Narcisse and Illeus and allowed me to introduce the cases into the technical ethnopharmacological literature (Davis 1983a).

Next, with the assistance of a prominent Port-au-Prince houngan, I was able to establish within a very short time extensive contacts with numerous sorcerers (*bokor*) and Vodoun priests (*houngan*). In April 1982, working through these contacts, I met an individual who was reputedly capable of preparing the zombie powder. After a complicated series of negotiations, I was able to purchase a sample of the powder and its "antidote" and observe their preparation, at the same time obtaining complete sets of voucher specimens of all the raw ingredients. Following this initial success, I attempted to obtain the preparation at other

localities throughout Haiti. Between April and November 1982,
I studied five other preparations in the communities of Saint
Marc, Gonaïves, Léogane, and Petite Rivière de Nippes. Oral
interviews at two other communities, Montrouis and Archaie,
verified the critical ingredients. This fieldwork, together with
subsequent collections made in the spring of 1984, produced a
total of eight preparations—a significant number by ethnobiological standards.

Although I have detailed elsewhere the complete process of
obtaining these preparations and the voucher specimens (Davis
1985), there are several important points to note here. First, the
preparation of the zombie powder is not the "dark secret" that
most of the literature has assumed it to be. For reasons that
will be discussed at length in chapter 6, the Vodounist believes
emically that the preparation is only a support of the magical
force of the sorcerer, and it is this power, not a poison, that
creates the zombie. However, like all the elements of the sorcerer's repertoire, the formula of the zombie powder is highly valued
and obtaining it necessitated a complex process of negotiation.
To be sure, it cost money, and there is an odd and unwarranted
sense among some ethnographic fieldworkers that data obtained
by financial remuneration is somehow tainted. This is, in general, an arrogant proposition, as it assumes that the informant has
nothing better to do than provide free information to a foreign
investigator. In Haiti, such an attitude is not only unjust but
counterproductive, for within the Vodoun society to do something for nothing is generally seen as "less a manifestation of
generosity than as a sign of gullibility, is less a virtue than a
weakness" (Murray 1977, 596). The Haitians themselves pay the
bokor for his knowledge and powders, and so should the ethnobiologist.

This does not mean that money should be thrown at a problem, or that financial payment alone would have obtained the
correct formula of the zombie powder. Those who have abra-
sively attempted to buy, bribe, or threaten the bokor in the past
have been unsuccessful. Indeed, in the process of successfully
obtaining any ethnographic information, there is an ineffable
quality to the interaction between researcher and informant,
impossible to quantify but often critical to the legitimacy of the
data and the overall value of the research. This quality is re-

flected in gesture, attitude, spontaneous repartee, and other moments that seldom find their way into print but whose importance is appreciated by all fieldworkers. Establishing a positive relationship with an entire network of houngan and bokor was the critical hidden element in the Zombie Project, and the character of that relationship, its positive and negative aspects, accounts directly for any successes or shortcomings in this study.

The second major phase of the Zombie Project began in the fall of 1982 upon my return to the Botanical Museum. Taxonomic identification of all the ingredients in the reputed poisons and antidotes, along with additional readings in the literature, revealed that:

1. The ingredients and composition of the various antidotes are completely inconsistent from one region to the next, and the constituents themselves are probably chemically inert or else are used in insufficient quantities to result in any pharmacological activity.
2. The poisons contain a plethora of ingredients. In general, these ingredients fall into three broad categories. First, human remains—dried viscera, shavings of skulls, tibia, etc.—are included for magical reasons in every preparation. Second, plants and animals known to be pharmacologically active are added. Third, all the preparations contain elements that severely irritate the skin—ground glass, plants with urticating trichomes or toxic resins—and the inclusion of these irritants, several of which may induce self-inflicted wounds, is related to the way the preparation is applied. The powders are administered topically to open wounds or abraded skin and may be applied more than once.
3. Among the various preparations, there is one consistent ingredient of great interest: various species of marine fish of the order Tetraodontiformes, which contain in their viscera tetrodotoxin, an extremely potent neurotoxin.

This discovery proved highly significant, for the effects of tetrodotoxin poisoning have been well documented, particularly in Japan where related toxic species have long been consumed as delicacies. With the assistance of the staff of the National Museum of Medicine in Washington, D.C., and with the active cooperation of Bruce Halstead, who helped me obtain translations of the early Japanese biomedical documents, I undertook an extensive review of the medical literature. By comparing the symptoms of tetrodotoxication as described in that literature with the constellation of symptoms recorded from the zombies, it became clear that tetrodotoxin offered a material basis for the zombie phenomenon. In brief, the toxin induces a state of complete peripheral paralysis, marked by imperceptibly low metabolic levels and the retention of consciousness on the part of the patient up until the moment of death. Correlation, for the first time, of this obscure literature with the case histories from Haiti suggested that the folk preparation, if administered in the proper dosage, could in fact bring on a state of apparent death that might allow an individual to be misdiagnosed and buried alive. Indeed, the literature reported instances in Japan and the South Pacific, completely unrelated to zombification, in which poison victims had in fact been mistaken for dead and placed in their coffins ready for burial.

Following the identification of the raw ingredients of the poison, the powder itself was tested on laboratory animals by Leon Roizin at Columbia Presbyterian Hospital in New York. A topical application of the powder to the abdominal surfaces of white rats produced shallow, faint breathing and decreased spontaneous activity. Within thirty minutes the rats lay immobilized; for three to six hours they displayed only mild response to corneal stimulation, pain, and sound and showed evidence of hypothermia. From six to nine hours after administration of the powder, they appeared comatose and showed no response at all to external stimuli. The electroencephalograph (EEG) continued to monitor central nervous system activity, and the hearts were not affected. Certain rats remained immobilized for twenty-four hours and then recovered with no apparent sign of injury. In a separate experiment, the powder was applied topically to the shaved belly of a rhesus monkey. After twenty minutes the monkey's usual aggressive behavior diminished and it retired to a corner of its cage and assumed a catatonic posture. The animal remained immobilized for nine hours. Recovery was complete (Leon Roizin, pers. comm., 1982).

These preliminary laboratory results, together with discoveries in the field and the biomedical literature, suggested strongly that there could be an ethnopharmacological basis to the zombie phenomenon. The consistent and critical ingredients in the poison appeared to be marine fish containing known toxins capable of inducing a physical state that could allow an individual to be misdiagnosed as dead. That Narcisse's symptoms are consistent with the known effects of tetrodotoxin suggests the possibility that he was exposed to the poison. If this does not prove that he was a zombie, it does, at least, substantiate his account.

The formula of the poison provides a possible means by which an individual might, under rare circumstances, be made to appear dead, but the physical constituents alone explain very little about the zombie phenomenon. Any psychoactive drug possesses a completely ambivalent potential. It induces a certain condition, but that condition is only raw material, which is then worked upon by particular cultural and psychological forces and expectations. Until those expectations are understood, one cannot claim to know anything about the zombie phenomenon.

Therefore, the third phase of the Zombie Project focused exclusively on the emic interpretation of zombification and involved a complete immersion in the closed system of spiritual and magical belief that typifies the Vodoun worldview. After extensive work in the field with numerous bokor, it became clear to me that their conception of zombification bears little resemblance to what has been reported in the ethnographic literature. In brief, the Vodounist believes that anyone who dies an unnatural death—one caused by the intervention of sorcery—may be claimed as a zombie. It is not a poison but the performance of a magical rite by the bokor that creates a zombie; zombification is perceived as strictly a magical process totally dependent on the special and esoteric powers of the bokor. The bokor gains power by capturing the victim's *ti bon ange*—that component of the Vodoun soul that creates personality, character, and willpower. A zombie appears cataleptic precisely because it has no *ti bon ange*. Robbed of the soul, the body is but an empty vessel subject to the commands of an alien force, the one who maintains control of the *ti bon ange*. It is the notion of external forces taking control of the individual that is so terrifying to the Vodounist. In splitting the sacred components of man, the bokor makes two kinds of zombies: the *zombi éfface* or *zombi astral*, which is a spirit; and the *zombi corps cadavre*, which is the zombie of the flesh. To the Vodounist both forms of zombification are equally real, but for the latter to exist one must discover an etic, or in this case pharmacological, cause. The application of the toxic preparation is, for the bokor, only one means of causing the prerequisite unnatural death. How the poisoning is done, and how the bokor manages to rationalize failures while emphatically emphasizing successes, will be discussed at length in chapter 6.

Yet, while the potency of the sorcerer's spell and the powder itself suggest a means by which both physical and spiritual zombies may be created, they nevertheless explain very little about the process of zombification within the context of Haitian traditional society. The peasant knows that the fate of the zombie is enslavement. Yet given the availability of cheap labor and the debilitated physical condition of the zombies, there is obviously no economic incentive to create a workforce of indentured labor. Instead, the concept of slavery implies that the victim of zombification suffers a fate worse than death—the loss of individual freedom implied by enslavement, and the sacrifice of individual identity and autonomy implied by the loss of the *ti bon ange*. It must be emphasized that the fear in Haiti is not *of* zombies, but rather of *becoming* a zombie. This fear is pervasive and has given rise to a complex body of folklore that continues to influence behavior. Both the threat and the fact of zombification confer on the bokor a potent means of social control if he chooses to use it. Under what circumstances, then, does the bokor invoke this power? Or, to rephrase the question, why is someone chosen to become a victim in the first place? These questions prompted the final and no doubt the most significant phase of the research project.

From extensive examination of the cases of Narcisse and other reputed zombies, it did not appear that the threat of zombification was invoked in either a criminal or a random way. Significantly, all of the reputed zombies were pariahs within their communities at the time of their demise. Moreover, the bokor who administer the spells and powders commonly live in the communities where the zombies are created; regardless of personal power, it is unlikely that a bokor who was not supported by the community could continue to create zombies for long, and for his own personal gain, with impunity. A more plausible view is that zombification is a social sanction administered by the bokor in complicity with, and in the services of, the members of his community. In fact, the authority to create a zombie may rest not solely with an individual bokor but with the secret society of which he is a member.

The last phase of the Zombie Project addressed the possible connection between the Bizango secret societies and zombification. With the assistance of established contacts, I was able to work directly among several Bizango societies for a four-month period in the spring and summer of 1984. The results of that effort are detailed in chapter 8, and they represent perhaps the only firsthand account of the structure and function of these clandestine societies ever to enter the ethnographic literature. In short, these contemporary secret societies constitute a force, if not an institution, parallel to the Vodoun temples headed by the houngan. They are polycephalous; each local hierarchical organization is headed by an *emperor*, who is attended by one or more *presidents* and *queens*. Members recognize each other by means of ritualized greetings learned at initiation, and by identification papers known as passports. The societies have their own drumbeats and body of songs and dances, and they are active by night. Like the secret societies of West Africa from which they are descended, the Bizango societies appear to be an important arbiter of social life among the peasantry. They constitute a force that protects community resources, particularly land, as they define the power boundaries of the village. Sorcery and poison are their traditional weapons, and there exists within the Bizango a complex judicial process by which those who violate the code of the society may be sanctioned. My research suggests that zombification represents the ultimate social sanction invoked by the societies. In addition, there is strong evidence, presented in chapter 8, that the secret societies may be the key to understanding recent Haitian political history—in particular, the meteoric rise of the *Tonton Macoute* under François Duvalier. There can be no doubt that the Bizango societies were critical to the Duvalier regime or that their failure to support his son, Jean-Claude, was in no small part responsible for the sudden collapse of his government.

The ethnobiological search for the Haitian zombie powder unveiled ethnographic and historical vistas of considerable importance. In offering a general theory to account for zombification, this research has also highlighted the sorcerer's remarkable knowledge of natural products, identified what may be the first verified zombies, and clarified the emic/etic confusion that has plagued previous research on the subject. The network of secret societies, with their elaborate judicial function, their sanctions, and their utilization of folk toxins, may be traced in a direct lineage to the maroon bands of colonial Saint Domingue and even beyond to the secret societies of West Africa. By tracing those connections, this book provides further evidence of the remarkable part that African institutions have played in the evolution of the Haitian amalgam.

Republic of Haiti

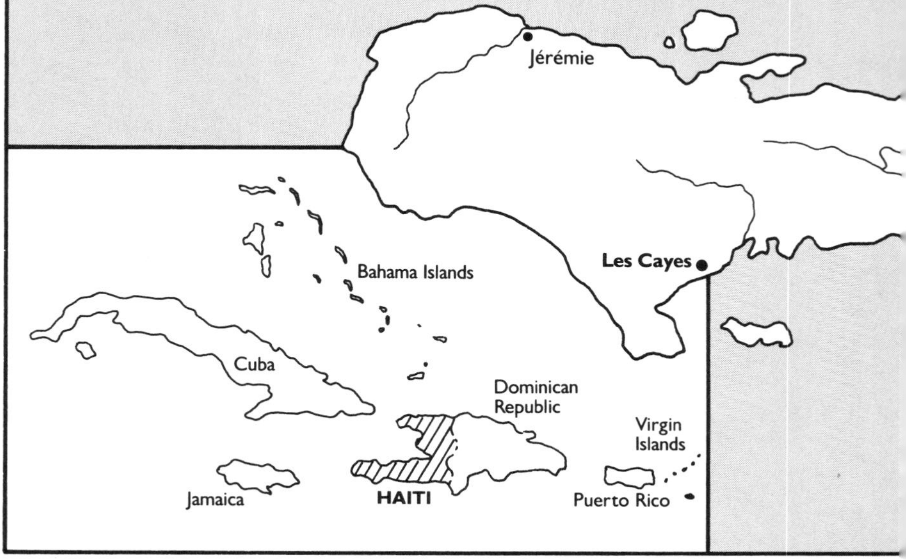

Jérémie

Les Cayes

Bahama Islands

Cuba

Dominican
Republic

Virgin
Islands

Jamaica

HAITI

Puerto Rico

Île de la Tortue

Atlantic Ocean

Port-de-Paix

e Saint-Nicolas

Limbé • Cap Haïtien

• Milot • Limonade
Plaisance

• Dondon

• Ennery

Gonaïves • St. Michele de l'Atalaye

Gulf of Gonave • L'Estere

HAITI

• Petite Rivière de
l'Artibonite

Saint-Marc

Artibonite River

• Montrouis

Ville Bonheur

Île de la Gonave • Arcahaie • Mirebalois

PLAINE
DU
CUL-DE-SAC

⭐ Port-au-Prince DOMINICAN

• Léogane • Pétionville REPUBLIC

• Miragoâne • Grand Goâve
opes Petit Goâve • Marbial

Jacmel

Caribbean Sea

0   10   20   30   40

Miles

CHAPTER ONE

THE HISTORICAL AND

CULTURAL SETTING

COLONIAL ORIGINS AND THE BIRTH
OF THE HAITIAN PEASANTRY

Following his first voyage, when asked by Isabella to describe the island of Hispaniola, Columbus took the nearest piece of paper, crumpled it in his hand, and threw it on the table. "That," he said, "is Hispaniola." Columbus had come to the land now known as Haiti by way of the island of San Salvador, his first landfall in the Americas, where the inhabitants had told enticing tales of a mountainous island where the rivers ran yellow with gold. The admiral found some gold, but to his greater excitement he also discovered a tropical paradise. In rapture, he wrote back to his queen that nowhere under the sun were there lands of such fertility, so void of pestilence, where the rivers were countless and the trees reached into the heavens.

The indigenous Arawaks he praised as generous and good, and he beseeched Isabella to take them under her protection. This she did. The Spaniards introduced all the elements of sixteenth-century European civilization to the island, and within fifteen years a combination of disease and wanton cruelty had reduced the native population from approximately half a million to sixty thousand (James 1963; Courlander and Bastien 1966). Although isolated communities of Indians may have survived in the interior as late as the seventeenth century, the fundamental patterns of European settlement on the island occurred, to a large extent, as if the land had never been inhabited (Mintz 1972). As a result, aboriginal patterns of social organization, land tenure, religious beliefs, and even the basic elements of the subsistence economy played a comparatively limited role in the evolution of the Haitian amalgam (Murray 1977).

The rugged, mountainous terrain of northern Haiti

As the original dreams of gold proved to be illusory, Spanish imperial interest turned to Mexico and South America; those Europeans who remained on Hispaniola supported themselves principally by raising livestock and exporting lumber. Throughout most of the sixteenth century the western half of the island that would eventually become Haiti, with its rugged mountainous terrain and dearth of navigable rivers, remained virtually deserted (Leyburn 1941).

Ironically, it was gold once again—but from a different source—that attracted the next wave of Europeans. In 1629 Norman and Breton pirates harrying the Spanish Main sought refuge on the small island of Tortuga, six miles off the northwestern coast of Hispaniola. From this haven, they crossed to Hispaniola to hunt wild cattle, smoking the meat to supply food for their predatory raids. They became known as the *boucaniers* (from the French *boucaner*, to smoke meat) and, together with a polyglot of European outcasts and adventurers, they systematically raided not only the returning Spanish galleons, but also the settlements in eastern Hispaniola and the British outposts in nearby Jamaica. Despite the concerted efforts of the Spanish and British fleets, the buccaneers, eventually supported by the

French crown, maintained their outpost and then spread to the mainland of Hispaniola.

Beginning around 1650 a wave of agriculturalists arrived, establishing small freeholdings dedicated principally to the cultivation of tobacco, which would be the colony's most important export for the next fifty years (Murray 1977). The growth of this yeoman population effectively secured the French presence in the nominally Spanish colony; French hegemony was officially established by the Treaty of Ryswick in 1697, which ceded the western half of Hispaniola to France (Leyburn 1941). The new colony was rechristened Saint Domingue.

The Treaty of Ryswick catalyzed a profound transformation in the agricultural base of the colony. Years before, in eastern Hispaniola, the Spanish had established a fledgling plantation economy based on the production of sugar and other export commodities. Labor shortages were a problem from the start, and as early as 1517 Charles V had authorized the importation of 15,000 black slaves to replace the dwindling stock of Indians—a race one prominent Spanish official had described at the time as "so weak that they can only be employed in tasks requiring little endurance" (Williams 1971, 53). One African, it was argued, was worth four Indians.

In the half of the island dominated by the French, by contrast, official policy had actually frowned on the planting of sugar, encouraging instead the growing of tobacco, which as late as 1689 remained the principal crop (Murray 1977). In 1684 the total population of Saint Domingue consisted of some 2,200 blacks, 1,421 colonists, and 1,565 indentured persons (Fouchard 1981); the ratio indicates that yeomen growing tobacco must have done much of the field labor themselves. The security afforded by the Treaty of Ryswick, however, brought a new sort of agriculturalist to the French colony—highly capitalized proprietors who could afford both the labor and the machinery necessary to produce plantation crops, particularly sugar. This shift in the agricultural base was recognized or perhaps even stimulated by an abrupt change in official policy that lifted restrictions on the cultivation of sugar and placed them instead on the production of tobacco. By 1716 sugar had become the colony's dominant export (Murray 1977), and its ascendancy set in motion a social, demographic, and economic transformation of staggering proportions. In 1697 there were three Europeans for every African in Saint Domingue; less than a hundred years later there were eleven blacks for every European, and on the plantations the blacks outnumbered the whites a hundred to one (Thompson 1983; Herskovits 1975; James 1963; Fouchard 1981).

By the closing decades of the eighteenth century the French colony of Saint Domingue had become the envy of all Europe. A mere 36,000 whites and an equal number of free mulattoes dominated a slave force of almost half a million and generated two-thirds of France's overseas trade—a productivity that easily surpassed that of the newly formed United States (James 1963) and actually outranked the total annual output of all the declining Spanish Indies combined (Leyburn 1941). In the single year 1789 the exports of cotton and indigo, coffee, cacao, tobacco, hides, and sugar filled the holds of over four thousand ships. On the eve of the French Revolution, Saint Domingue grew 60 percent of the world's coffee, more sugar than all the British Caribbean possessions combined, and over two-thirds of France's tropical produce (Rotberg 1971). Two-thirds of France's foreign commercial interests centered in the colony, which accounted for 40 percent of the country's foreign trade (Leyburn 1941). No other European colony contributed so much to the economic well-being of its mother country; in France no fewer than five million of the twenty-seven million citizens of the *ancien régime* depended economically on the trade from Saint Domingue (Rotberg 1971; Leyburn 1941). It was a tremendous concentration of wealth, and it readily cast Saint Domingue as the jewel of the French Empire and the most coveted colony of the age.

In 1791, two years after the French Revolution, the colony was shaken and then utterly destroyed by the only successful slave revolt in history. The resulting war lasted twelve years, as the newly freed slaves were called on to defeat the greatest powers of Europe. They faced first the remaining troops of the French monarchy, then a force of French republicans, and finally drove off a Spanish and then a British invasion. The British, in their attempt to conquer the slaves, lost more men than Wellington did some years later in the entire Peninsular Campaign against Napoleon (James 1963).

In December 1801, two years before the Louisiana Purchase,

*Haitian peasant cutting cane. In the late eighteenth century the
French colony of Saint Domingue exported some 163 million pounds
of sugar annually. Today sugar remains a dominant agricultural
product of Haiti.*

Napoleon, who was at the height of his power, dispatched the
largest expedition ever to have sailed from France. Its mission
was to take control of the Mississippi River, hem in the expand-
ing United States, and reestablish the French Empire in what
had become British North America. En route to Louisiana, the
expedition was to pass by Saint Domingue and quell the slave
revolt. The first wave of the invading force consisted of twenty
thousand troops under Bonaparte's ablest officers, commanded
by his own brother-in-law, Leclerc. So vast was the flotilla of
support vessels that, when it arrived in Haitian waters, the leaders of the revolt momentarily despaired, convinced that all of
France had appeared to overwhelm them (James 1963; Leyburn
1941).

Leclerc never did reach Louisiana. Within a year he was dead,
and of the 34,000 troops that landed with him, a mere 2,000
exhausted men remained in service. Following Leclerc's death,
French command in Haiti passed to the infamous Rochambeau,
who immediately declared a war of extermination against the
former slaves. Common prisoners were put to the torch; rebel
generals were chained to rocks and allowed to starve. The wife

and children of one prominent rebel were drowned before his eyes while French sailors nailed a pair of epaulettes into his naked shoulders. Fifteen hundred dogs were imported from Jamaica and taught to devour black prisoners in obscene public events housed in hastily built amphitheaters in Port-au-Prince. Yet despite this deliberate policy of torture and murder, Rochambeau failed to regain control of the island. A reinforcement of 20,000 men simply added to the casualty figures. At the end of November 1803, the French, having lost over 60,000 veteran troops, finally evacuated Saint Domingue (James 1963; Fouchard 1981; Leyburn 1941; Dorsainvil 1934).

That the revolutionary slaves of Saint Domingue defeated one of the strongest armies of Europe is a historical fact that, though often overlooked, has never been denied. How they did it, however, has usually been misinterpreted. There are two common explanations. One invokes the scourge of yellow fever and implies that the white troops did not die at the hands of the blacks, but from the wretched conditions of the tropical lands. Although doubtless many soldiers did succumb to fever, this supposition is contradicted by two facts: first, European armies had been triumphant in many parts of the world plagued by endemic fevers and pestilence; second, in Haiti the fevers began with the regularity of the seasons and did not start until the onset of the rains in April. Yet the French forces led by Leclerc landed in February 1802 and, before the beginning of the fever season, had suffered 10,000 casualties (James 1963).

The second explanation offered for the European defeat is that fanatic and insensate hordes of blacks rose as a single body to overwhelm the more "rational" white troops. It is true that in the early days of the revolt the slaves fought with few resources and extraordinary courage. Accounts of the time report that they went into battle armed only with knives and picks, or with sticks tipped in iron, and they charged bayonets and cannon led by the passionate belief that the spirits would protect them, and that their deaths, if realized, would lead them back to Guinée, the African homeland (Fouchard 1981; James 1963; Leyburn 1941). Indeed, the strength of their convictions is reflected in one of their battle songs of the war (cited in Laroche 1976, 54–55):

Grenadier à laso   Grenadiers to the assault
Sa ki mouri zafé à yo What is death?

Nan pouin maman	We have no mother
Nan pouin pitit	No child
Sa ki mouri zafé à yo	What is death?

Their fanaticism, however, sprang not only from spiritual conviction but also from a very human and fundamental awareness of their circumstances. In victory lay freedom, in capture awaited torture, in defeat stalked death. Moreover, after the initial spasm of revolt, the actual number of slaves who took part in the fighting was not that high. The largest of the rebel armies never contained more than 18,000 men (Murray 1977). As in every revolutionary era, the struggle was carried on by relatively few of those afflicted by the tyranny. The European forces did suffer from fever, but ultimately they were defeated by men—not marauding hordes but relatively small, well-disciplined, and highly motivated rebel armies led by men of some military genius.

If the historians have clouded the character of the struggle, they have also inaccurately idealized the revolutionary leaders— Toussaint L'Ouverture, Henri Christophe, and Jean-Jacques Dessalines, in particular—by disguising their ambitions in lofty libertarian visions that these individuals most certainly did not share. The primary interest of the French, in the immediate wake of the uprising, was the maintenance of an agrarian economy devoted to the production of export crops. How this goal was accomplished was of little concern. Once they realized that the restoration of slavery was not possible—before Napoleon attempted to storm the island by force—the French ministers devised an alternative system whereby freed slaves would be forged into a new form of indentured labor as sharecroppers. The plantations would remain essentially intact. Lacking the military presence to enforce this scheme, the French turned to the leaders of the revolutionary armies and found willing collaborators, including Toussaint L'Ouverture, who became a major figure in the restoration of French authority on the island. The French, however, made a critical error in assuming that this coopted leadership would submit to the whims of Paris. On the contrary, the black leaders did what they had always planned to do. They secured for themselves positions at the top of a new social order.

Toussaint L'Ouverture had no intention of overseeing the dismantling of the colonial plantations. In the abstract he was committed to the freedom of his people, but in practice he believed that the only way to maintain the country's prosperity and the free status of its citizens was through agricultural production. One of the most persistent myths about the Haitian revolution is the belief that the original plantations, having been destroyed in the initial uprising, never regained their former prosperity—the tacit assumption being that, in the wake of the revolt, the blacks who took over were incapable of governing. This is historically untrue. Within eighteen months of attaining power, Toussaint L'Ouverture had restored agricultural production to two-thirds of what it had been at the height of the French colony (James 1963; Murray 1977; Leyburn 1941). Had the French bourgeoisie been willing to share power with the revolutionary elite, an export economy might have been maintained for some time.

It was destined to collapse, however, not from the lack of interest or inability of the new elite, nor even because of the chaos unleashed by Leclerc's invasion. Its eventual demise was assured by an expedient policy begun by the French long before the revolt of 1791. The French plantation owners, faced with the difficulty of feeding close to half a million slaves, had granted provisional plots of land on which the slaves could produce their own food (Murray 1977, 1980). Not only were the slaves encouraged to cultivate their plots, but they were allowed to sell their surplus, and as a result a vast internal marketing system developed even before the revolution. In a calculated gesture the plantation owners had inadvertently sown the seeds of an agrarian peasantry. There is another related, lingering myth concerning the revolution that holds that once the slaves were liberated from the plantations it was virtually impossible to entice them back onto the land. In fact, in the wake of the revolt, most of the freed slaves went directly to the land, where they energetically produced the staple foodstuffs that the internal market of the country demanded. Reading popular accounts of the twelve-year revolutionary war, one might assume that the entire population had scavenged for its sustenance. On the contrary, it was eating yams, beans, and plantains grown and sold by a majority of the former slaves, who now cultivated their lands as freedmen. The problem facing the revolutionary elite was not how to get the people back to the land, but how to get them from their own lands back to the plantations (Murray 1977).

An independent peasantry was the last thing the black military leaders wanted. Jean-Jacques Dessalines, for example, maintained until his assassination in 1806 a dream of an export economy based on chain-gang labor. In the northern half of the country Henri Christophe, who used measures every bit as harsh as those of the colonial era, was able for ten years to produce export crops that allowed him to build an opulent palace and support a lavish court. But eventually his people revolted, and his death in 1820 ended the last serious attempt to create a plantation-based economy (Leyburn 1941).

What emerged in the early years of independence was a country internally vigorous but externally quiescent. Production of export crops declined drastically. At the height of the colonial era, over 163 million pounds of sugar had been exported annually; by 1825, total exports measured only 2,000 pounds, and some sugar was actually imported from Cuba (Courlander 1960; Murray 1977; Rotberg 1971). Foreigners considered the economy dead, and again they cited the inability of blacks to organize themselves. In fact, these statistics indicate the unwillingness of a free peasantry to submit to an economic system that depended on their labor to produce export crops that would profit only a small number of the elite. The Haitian economy had not disappeared, it had simply changed. With negligible export earnings, the central government soon went bankrupt. As early as 1820 the then president, Jean-Pierre Boyer, was forced to pay his army with land grants. By thus unleashing the common soldier onto the land, he dealt the final blow to any lingering dreams of reestablishing the plantations. Recognizing that no income was going to accrue from nonexistent export commodities, he began to tax the emerging structures of the peasant economy. In placing a tax on rural marketplaces, for example, Boyer generated revenue, but more significantly from a historical perspective, he legitimized the institution itself. Then, unable to impose taxes or rent on lands that the peasants had already taken as their own, he took the only step that could raise income: he began officially to sell them the land. It was an extraordinary admission on the part of the central government that the peasants were in firm control of the countryside. The former slaves had moved onto the land, and nothing was going to pry them from it. The central government acquiesced and did what it could to generate at least some revenue from a situation totally beyond its control.

Who were these peasants who had so decisively rooted them-

*Ruins of the palace at Sans Souci, the residence of King Henri
Christophe (1806–20)*

*The northern town of Milot viewed from the surviving gates of the
palace at Sans Souci*

selves in the land? Some were perhaps the descendants of the first slaves to arrive with the Spanish as early as 1510 (Herskovits 1975; Courlander and Bastien 1966), but the majority had actually been born in Africa. The growth of the colony had not been steady. On the contrary, following the American Revolution and France's loss of Canada, French merchants concentrated their efforts on Saint Domingue, and between 1775 and the slave uprising in 1791 the colony had expanded as never before. Production of cotton and coffee, for example, increased 50 percent in a mere six years, and to support such growth the slave population had been almost doubled (Rotberg 1971). Whereas four thousand Africans were imported in 1720 and 5,000 in 1753, by the last years of the colony the annual number of imports ranged around 40,000 (Rotberg 1971). In 1739 the total slave population was 117,400. Some fifty years later, on the eve of the revolt, estimates put the number as high as 480,000 (Mintz 1972). In a mere eleven years between 1779 and 1790, no fewer than 313,200 slaves arrived in the colony (Curtin 1969).

Because of the wretched conditions on the plantations, at least 17,000 slaves died each year, while the birth rate remained at an insignificant 1 percent (Fouchard 1981). The death rate was a horrendous 8 percent, and the working-life expectancy was fifteen years (Murray 1977). At one plantation the entire contingent of slaves turned over in a nine-year period, with three-quarters of the replacements coming from newly imported Africans (Debien 1962). Because it was cheaper to import Africans than to raise Creole slaves from birth, prodigious numbers of slaves had to be imported. During the last fourteen years of undisturbed rule, the French imported no fewer than 375,000 Africans (Fouchard 1981). In other words, the germ of the modern Haitian peasantry quite literally sprouted in Africa.

The revolutionary slaves who settled the tortuous recesses of a mountainous island came from many parts of the ancient continent and represented many distinct cultural traditions. According to historiographer Moreau de Saint Mery (1958), perhaps the authoritative colonial source, the old kingdoms of Fula and Mandingo north of Sierra Leone contributed Senegalese, Yoloffes, Foules, Bambaras, Mandingues, Quiambasa, and Sosos. Taken in bondage from the region between Sierra Leone and the Gold Coast were the Bouriquis, Mesurades, and Cangas, while farther east toward the mouth of the Volta River the Ashanti and

Fanti kingdoms provided Arada, Caplaous, Mines, Agouas, So-cos, and Fantins. Still farther east, toward the Slave Coast and the present countries of Benin, Togo, and parts of Nigeria, were found the Cotocolis, Popos, Fidas, and Aradas. Certain inland groups included the Fon, Mahis, Aoussas, Ibos, Nagos, and Mokos; and other groups as well from the valley of the Niger contributed slaves to the Saint Domingue trade. A large but uncertain percentage of the Saint Domingue slaves came from the Congo Basin and present-day Angola, including members of the Mayombes, Mousombes, and Mondongue peoples. In addition, small numbers of slaves came from as far inland as Central and East Africa and from the south and east as far as Mozambique and Madagascar (Laguerre 1973a; Herskovits 1975).

Among the 900,000 or more slaves to land in the colony during its relatively brief period of florescence (Curtin 1969) were artisans and musicians, herbalists, carvers, metalworkers, boat builders, farmers, drum makers, sorcerers, and warriors (Courlander 1960). There were men of royal blood and others who had been born into slavery in Africa (Métraux 1972). They had in common their experience with a heinous economic system that had ripped them away from their material world; critically, they also shared an oral tradition that was unassailable—a rich repository of religious belief, music, dance, folk medicine, agriculture, and patterns of social organization that they carried with them into every remote valley. The evolution of these various traditions, their fusions and transformations, was deeply affected by a blanket of isolation that fell upon the country in the early years of the nineteenth century.

The nation that emerged from the revolutionary era was a pariah in the eyes of the international community. With the exception of Liberia, which was a limp creation of the United States, Haiti ranked as the only independent black republic for a hundred years. (Cuba, by contrast, remained a colony until the end of the nineteenth century, Jamaica and Trinidad until the mid-twentieth century, and thus those places experienced a sustained relationship with their colonizers and underwent all the concomitant processes of acculturation.) In the nineteenth century Haiti's very existence was a constant thorn in the side of an imperialistic age. The country was not even recognized by the United States until 1862, and its diplomatic status before then is best indicated by the comments of South Carolina Senator Rob-

A Haitian woman riding in a tap-tap

A group of rural Haitian men by the roadside

ert Y. Hayne in 1824, twenty years after Haiti became independent. "Our policy with regard to Hayti is plain," he intoned. "We never can acknowledge her independence . . . which the peace and safety of a large portion of our union forbids us even to discuss" (Schmidt 1971, 28).

Indeed, the free government of Haiti *was* a threat to the established order in the Americas. The Haitian government infuriated the European powers by actively supporting revolutionary struggles that vowed to eliminate slavery. Simón Bolívar, for example, was both sheltered there and also funded before he liberated Gran Colombia. In a more symbolic gesture, the government purchased shipments of slaves en route to the United States only to grant them freedom.

Furthermore, Haiti defied international commercial interests by prohibiting foreigners from owning land or property in the country. By no means did this law bring trade to a standstill, but it dramatically modified the nature of that trade. During a century in which European capital moved into virtually all regions of the world, Haiti remained relatively immune. Even the hegemony of the Roman Catholic church was checked. The clergy, which had never had a particularly strong presence in colonial days (Laguerre 1973b; Desmangles 1979), lost virtually all influence after the revolution (Leyburn 1941). In fact, for the first half-century of Haiti's independence, there was an official schism between the country and the Vatican. Roman Catholicism remained the official religion of the emerging political and economic elite, but during the seminal years of the nation, the church had practically no presence in the countryside (Mintz 1972).

Within Haiti, isolation of a different form occurred. Throughout the nineteenth century, as the colonial infrastructure of roads decayed and was not replaced, the physical gap between town and country widened. This, in turn, sharpened an emerging cultural hiatus between two radically different segments of Haitian society: the rural peasants and the urban elite. The former, of course, were former slaves; the latter, in part, were descendants of a special class of free mulattoes that during the colonial era had enjoyed both great wealth and all the rights of French citizens, including the ignoble privilege of owning slaves. During the early years of independence, the obvious differences between these two groups crystallized into a profound separation that went far deeper than mere class lines. They grew to be more like

two different worlds coexisting within a single country (Leyburn
1941).

The urban elite, though proudly Haitian, turned to Europe for
cultural and spiritual inspiration. They spoke French, professed
faith in the Roman Catholic church, and were well educated.
Their women wore the latest Parisian fashions, and their men
naturally formed the chromatic screen through which European
and American commercial interests siphoned off what they could
of the nation's wealth. The young men frequently traveled
abroad, both for higher training and for amusement, invariably
returning to fill all business and professional positions, as well as
government and military offices. There they promulgated the
official laws of the land, all of which were again based on French
precedent and the Napoleonic Code. By all foreign standards, it
was this small circle of friends and extended families—for the
elite never numbered more than 3 percent of the total population
(Simpson 1941)—that controlled much of the political and economic power of the nation.

In the hinterland, however, the former slaves created an utterly
different society, based not on European models but on their own
ancestral traditions. It was not, strictly speaking, an African society. European influences were inevitably felt, and only very
rarely did pure strains of specific African cultures survive or
dominate. What evolved, rather, was a uniquely Haitian amalgam
forged predominantly from African traits culled in turn from
many parts of that continent. Typically, its members thought of
themselves less as descendants of particular tribes or kingdoms
than as *ti guinin*—children of Guinée, of Africa, the ancient
homeland, a place that slowly drifted from history into the realm
of myth. And, in time, what had been the collective memory of an
entire disenfranchised people became the ethos of new generations and the foundation of a distinct and persistent culture.

THE PEASANT SOCIETY

The remarkable persistence of African traits in the lifeways of
the rural peasant has attracted the attention of virtually every
authority on the Haitian society (notably Herskovits 1975; Simpson 1941, 1951; Courlander 1960; Métraux 1972; Deren 1953;
Price-Mars 1928; Denis and Duvalier 1944). Herskovits (1975),

for example, noted the obvious parallels between the religious beliefs and practices that he had studied in Dahomey (Herskovits 1938) with those of Haitian Vodoun. These included: the belief in a single greater god whose essence becomes manifest in a pantheon of spirits; the worship of these spirits through a song and dance ritual climaxing in spirit possession; a conviction that the souls of the dead are powerful and become more so through time; and the concept that the living must serve these dead through propitiatory rites involving gifts of food and animal sacrifice. He also commented that in both traditions acolytes undergo initiation, including an ordeal by fire, during which they learn to speak the sacred language of the cult. In the social sphere the similarities continued; Herskovits noted the primary role of women in a market economy, the existence of cooperative labor groups (the *coumbite* of Haiti, the *dokpwe* of Dahomey) and the widespread practice of polygyny. Settlement patterns were also similar. In both Dahomey and Haiti the smallest unit of domestic life was the household, with numerous houses clustered around the ancestral temple to form a compound dominated by the eldest male of the extended family.

George Simpson (1945, 1951) noted, in addition to these traits, the deference and respect paid to elders, the dominant role of the mother in family life, the pecuniary tradition again dominated by women, the extensive use of folk narrative (tales, riddles, proverbs) in the socialization of children, and similarities in the subsistence base, as well as a number of technological parallels from house construction to hair tying and the decorative arts.

Indeed, so pervasive were these African-derived features in the Haitian peasant society, and so compelling were the historical circumstances that gave rise to this society, that historian C. L. R. James claimed with some confidence that in the wake of the revolution:

> Two thirds of the population of French Saint Domingue had made the Middle Passage. The whites had emigrated or been exterminated. The mulattoes who were the masters had their eyes fixed on Paris. Left to themselves the Haitian peasantry resuscitated to a remarkable degree the lives they had lived in Africa. Their method of cultivation, their family relations and social practices, their drums, songs and music,

The loa cannot be harmed. Here a Vodoun hounsis,
possessed by the spirits, eats fire.

A typical peasant home in rural Haiti

such art as they practiced; and above all their religion which became famous, Voudoun—all this was Africa in the West Indies (James 1963, 394).

This somewhat romantic sentiment was later echoed, for reasons of ideological as well as academic conviction, by the leading members of the Mouvement de la Négritude, who were most anxious to affirm the value of their African heritage (Price-Mars 1928; Roumain 1942b, 1975; Denis and Duvalier 1936, 1944).

The ubiquity of African traits, however, should not obscure the fact that the peasant society is not static, nor are its institutions diachronically stable. On the contrary, perhaps no single trait better characterizes the significant institutions of peasant life than their ability to change (Murray 1977; Laguerre 1973a, 1973b, 1974b; Mintz 1972). This is particularly true of the Vodoun religion, which like any "complex of belief and ritual is a vital, living body of ideas and behaviors, carried in time by its practitioners, and responsive to the changing character of social life" (Mintz 1972, 12).

Indeed, some authorities have questioned the fundamental usefulness of the African paradigm. M. G. Smith notes that it is imperative to "keep the New World social context which is the matrix of the acculturation process clearly distinct from those Old World social forms which are included in the possible heritage whose form and function is under study." He suggests, in fact, that the entire notion of an "African inheritance is ambiguous to the point of inutility, for as a concept it presupposes a uniformity and uniqueness to African cultures which ethnography does not supply" (Smith 1960, 36). For example, spirit possession may be a shared feature between Haiti and certain African groups, yet there are numerous tribes of West Africa that do not share it, just as there are cults outside of Africa that do. Similarly, neither polygyny nor ancestor worship are universal among nor peculiar to African societies.

Sidney Mintz expresses similar concerns and adds that African forms in Haitian peasant culture were not simple transfers, nor were they modified in a clear-cut way. Haitian agriculture is not African agriculture any more than Haitian domestic organization is African organization, or Haitian religion is African religion. Mintz suggests, in fact, that "to ask whether some feature of Afro-american life is or is not 'African' in origin is somehow to beg the question, since this circumvents the complex tribal heterogeneity of African peoples who played a role in the development of New World cultures" (Mintz 1972, 11). Furthermore, of course, a focus on African origins completely ignores the ways in which socialization to plantation life inevitably disrupted the traditional lifeways of the African slaves. Laguerre (1974b), for example, outlines numerous variables that affected the development of specific peasant religious traditions during the colonial era: the location of the plantation; its ethnic composition; the presence or absence in its population of African religious leaders; its proximity to and interactions with communities of runaway slaves; and the local influence, if any, of the Roman Catholic church. Assertions that African traits came over and were absorbed piecemeal into a set matrix explain very little, and they overlook the fact that a particular strength of the Haitian peasant society is that it is by no means static (Murray 1977; Mintz 1972).

What is of great interest and significance is not necessarily showing how "African" Haiti is but rather elucidating the parameters of social and spiritual life as experienced today by the Haitian peasant and, in doing so, highlighting the contrast between his worldview and that of the politically and economically dominant metropolitan society. I am not suggesting by any means that there is no interaction between the two societies or that the peasant is perennially isolated in the hinterland. Contacts among all regions of the country are maintained by an active internal trading and marketing network (Murray and Alvarez 1975). National institutions such as schools, health services, and military outposts are distributed throughout the nation, and, particularly in recent years, missionaries and various international aid organizations have been an increasingly active presence in the countryside. However, interactions occur through a formidable barrier of economic inequity, language and educational differences, and utterly distinct social and behavioral expectations. A few startling statistics may put the extent of these contacts in perspective.

Although a modern highway now traverses the country, as recently as 1969 there were fewer than fifty miles of surfaced highway, two hundred miles of once-paved road, no passenger railways, a mere two thousand functioning telephone lines (few of which worked consistently) and 4,400 telephones, the lowest

*A frenzy of trucks carrying produce and people
to the market in central Haiti*

percentage in the Western Hemisphere. Haiti had fewer radio
receivers than any other country in the hemisphere, a minimal
daily newspaper circulation of six per thousand, and so little
electrical-generating capacity (one-eighth of neighboring Cuba's) that proprietors in small market centers charged their cus-
tomers per outlet or burning light bulb. In 1969 only 2.6 percent
of the dwellings had piped water (as opposed to 12.6 percent in
impoverished Guatemala), and the number of urban habitations
with indoor water-born sanitation was a negligible .01 percent
(Rotberg 1971). Access to foreign goods and services was limited
by a per capita gross national product of about $67 U.S., less
than half that of Bolivia, the next lowest in the hemisphere. In the
early 1970s the Haitian recurrent budget totaled about $25–30
million—roughly the same size as the annual budget of Brandeis
University or that of Lexington, Massachusetts, a community of
approximately 31,000 (Rotberg 1976).

In 1951 Simpson reported a rural illiteracy rate of 90 percent,
roughly the same figure that had been reported in 1900 (Rotberg
1971; Simpson 1951). Even as recently as 1969 Haiti had by far
the lowest level of functional literacy in the hemisphere—an
astonishingly low 7 to 10 percent. Formal education is officially
mandated by the national government, but those children who

find their way to rural schools must endure lessons in French when the only language they understand is Creole. Western medical facilities are available in the cities and to some extent in rural areas, but in a nation of 6,000,000 inhabitants there are even today only some five hundred licensed physicians (Douyon pers. comm.). Fifteen years ago R. I. Rotberg (1971) noted that, of the three hundred physicians in the country, two hundred practiced in the capital city of Port-au-Prince, where their services attracted 84 percent of the country's Western-trained nurses. Simpson (1951) estimated that there were but twenty-eight medical doctors serving the 2,500,000 Haitians living in small towns and rural areas. Although in recent years the population of the capital has increased dramatically, as little as twenty years ago 90 percent of the Haitian people lived in the rural countryside far removed from medical services; urban poor living in the capital were excluded to some extent from modern medical treatment due to the prohibitive costs. Though theoretically these Western medical facilities and services are available to all Haitians, in practice the vast majority of Haitian peasants have little or no access to Western medicine (Rotberg 1971).

By the same token Roman Catholicism, the official state religion, has never had a particularly strong impact on the peasantry. Indeed, during the colonial era the church failed completely in its token attempts to Christianize the Africans (Laguerre 1973b). Although the Code Noir attempted to rationalize the institution of slavery by mandating the evangelization of the slaves, its stipulations were never followed by the planters, whose policy was "to forget the religion that they themselves did not practice" (Laguerre 1973b, 16). In 1753 there were sixty priests of dubious reputation in the entire colony. Many of these were defrocked monks discharged from their European orders who enjoyed a licentious life in concubinage with their own slaves. On the eve of the slave revolt the number of priests had increased only to seventy, and these were theoretically expected to minister to the white colonists and the mulattoes in addition to the 480,000 black slaves. Needless to say, the "Christianisation of the slaves was, in fact, a farce" (Laguerre 1973b, 22).

The situation did not change during the early years of the republic. The official schism between Haiti and the Vatican lasted until a concordat was signed in 1860. Moreover, the quality and quantity of those professed priests who remained in

Haiti continued to be low. In 1814 the northern half of the country, under the control of Henri Christophe, was said to have had but three Catholic priests (Courlander and Bastien 1966). Under Jean-Pierre Boyer's presidency (1818–43) Roman Catholicism became the official state religion, but as of 1840 there were still only seventy priests in the country, and they were "religious renegades who knew just enough of ritual and theology to use the priestly garb as a cover for easy graft" (Leyburn 1941, 123).

To be sure, in the later nineteenth and early twentieth century the Catholic church periodically surfaced as a vocal opponent of the "pagan" Vodoun cults. It was the church that provoked the virulent antisuperstition campaigns of the late 1930s and early 1940s. Pernicious as these campaigns were, they did not succeed in stopping the practice of Vodoun. If anything, they galvanized the adherents of the Vodoun religion and exemplified by their failure just how deeply entrenched the folk religion was in the Haitian countryside. Nor were the campaigns long tolerated by the peasants themselves. The last of them, known as *Opération Nettoyage* (Operation Cleanup), actually received police support in 1941, but despite this government intervention the effort ended unsuccessfully in 1942 when groups of "unruly peasants threatened the political and economic security of Haiti" (Desmangles 1979, 6).

Significantly, during the first sixty years of the nation's existence Roman Catholicism had little impact on the evolution of the Vodoun religious tradition. Although some Catholic iconographic elements and votive objects were adopted by Vodounists, it is patently misleading to describe contemporary Vodoun as a syncretism of African traditions and Catholic ritual. On the contrary, the two religions coexist even today in a juxtaposition that has not fused one with the other (Desmangles 1979). For example, virtually every Vodoun altar features chromolithographs of various Catholic saints. The presence of these potent images, though, is not evidence of the Westernization of Vodoun ritual, but rather indicates the ability of the Vodounist to transform Catholic icons by noting their similarities to African spirits. St. Jacques mounted on his horse, bearing a red standard and carrying his sword, is restructured in the Vodoun mind into Ogoun Ferraille, the blacksmith god whose color is red and who brandishes a saber. Similarly, the Virgin Mary becomes Erzulie, the goddess of love; and St. Patrick, treading upon the snakes and banishing evil, becomes Damballah, the serpent of the sky and the repository of all spiritual knowledge (Thompson 1983). Clearly, although the Catholic church has been present in Haiti since colonial days, its impact on the peasant way of life has been moderate and its mission of evangelism a complete failure (Laguerre 1973b; Nicholls 1970; Courlander and Bastien 1966).

The inability of the Catholic church to make significant inroads into the lifeways of the Haitian peasant is matched to a certain extent by a similar failure on the part of the administrative structures of the central government. The civil government of Haiti, for example, is divided into five departments, and each of these, in turn, is divided into a number of *arrondissements*, with each one headed by a prefect appointed directly by the president. Each prefecture, or *arrondissement*—there are twenty-seven in all—is composed of *communes* led by the equivalent of a mayor, who is assisted by an administrative council that is based in a village. Beyond the edge of the village itself, the land of the *commune* is divided into a number of *sections rurales*.

The military has its own parallel subdivisions of the country, and while these are somewhat different, at the lowest level the two systems come together, making the *section rurale* the basic level of local government. It is within these *sections rurales* that at least 80 percent of the Haitian population lives (Murray 1977; Lahav 1975).

Gerald Murray has pointed out a curious and important paradox in the governing of these *sections rurales*, and it hinges on the role of an official outside the hierarchical organization of either form of national government. The rural section in no way coincides with a community or village but rather describes "an arbitrary administrative lumping of many communities for the purposes of governance" (Murray 1977, 131). The rural peasants themselves identify not with their particular *section rurale* but with their own extended families and neighbors in the *lakou*, the familiar compounds made up of clusters of thatched houses one sees all over the country. In other words, neither institution of the government, the civil or the military, recognizes in any juridical sense the actual communities in which the vast majority of the rural peasants live and die. To reach these people the national authorities depend on one man, the *chef de section*, an appointee from within the *section rurale* who is expected to establish networks of contacts that will place his eyes and ears in every lakou under his jurisdiction. This he does, but in a very special way.

Although the *chef de section* receives his authority from the central government, the basis of his power is not his official status so much as the consensus of the residents of his own section. He does not act alone, but rather heads a large, nonuniformed force of local peasants, who in turn derive their extrastatutory authority not from him but, again, from their own people. The *chef de section* can be helpless without popular support, and historically, efforts of the central government to place outsiders in the position—most notably when the American occupation forces attempted to replace Vodounists with literate Protestants—have always failed (Comhaire 1955). Haitian law provides for the *chef de section* to retain certain assistants, but as Murray indicates, "the particular form the structure of police control will take in a particular region will be largely governed by local traditions and by adaptive adjustments to local social reality on the part of local law enforcement officials, who are themselves intimately familiar with this reality" (Murray 1977, 161). The national government, in order to reach the peasants, must tap into their own traditional networks of social control, in the person of the *chef de section*.

Who is this *chef de section?* Above all he is himself a local peasant (Lahav 1975; Comhaire 1955). Typically he maintains his own fields, is polygynous, and serves the loa. In many instances he is a prominent *houngan* (Vodoun priest). His behavior, personal values, and expectations are not those of a bureaucrat but rather those of a leader in a traditional society. Although technically he receives a salary from the capital (and sometimes the money actually arrives), he depends financially on his own land, and like the African patriarch he considers it his right to recruit unpaid labor for his fields. This service the community members willingly provide, in effect as compensation for the hours he must spend attending to their affairs. It is his task, after all, to investigate conflicts and convene the informal tribunals at which virtually all local disputes are said to be resolved. With their power thus rooted in their own jurisdictions, the *chefs de section* remain relatively unaffected by political upheavals in the capital, and as Murray points out, they retain, sometimes for indefinite periods, virtually unchallenged control of their area. Threats to that power and to their positions, then, come not from

Port-au-Prince but from dissatisfaction among their own people, so it is with them that the loyalties of the *chef de section* lie.

In brief, though the institution of the *chef de section* serves as an interface between the two separate worlds that make up the Haitian reality, the man himself is a member of the traditional society, and the network of contacts he taps is the network within that society. The full significance of the *chef de section* will become apparent in later chapters. In the meantime, it is enough to stress that the administrative structures of the national government do not reach directly into the daily lives of the vast majority of Haitian peasants. Indeed, theirs is a world apart.

If the Haitian peasant does remain relatively unaffected by the Western institutions of education, medical care, religion, and government, how might peasant society be characterized? First, the language is Creole, which is based in part on French vocabulary but which draws on grammatical patterns and verb conjugations that reveal affinities to the languages of West Africa (Courlander and Bastien 1966). Creole is a rich, metaphorical language, and it is spoken in a demonstrative, vibrant manner, with each word truncated to fit the meter of West African speech. Significantly, the vast majority of the rural peasantry do not understand French, the official national language.

Second, the primary orientation of the individual is not to an administrative unit of the civil government (town, state, etc.) but to his extended family consisting of kinsmen related consanguineously or affinely by folk adoption, legal or folk marriage, or ritual act. The solidarity of the living kinsmen encompasses as well the family's particular spirit and the spirits of the dead ancestors; together they form a corporate body of interdependent households, which work together to confront and solve the vicissitudes of life.

Traditionally, a particular family was linked physically to an ancestral piece of land that was worked communally by the kin group. At a strategic location on the familial land would be situated the lakou: a living compound made up of the houses of the nuclear families, the home of the *chef lakou*—the titular patriarch of the family—the Vodoun temple of the ancestral spirits, and the sacred mapou tree (*Ceiba pentandra*). The eldest surviving male served as a "true patriarch to whom all members of the extended family owe obedience and respect" (Simpson 1942). It was the original role of the patriarch to regulate production and ensure the social and spiritual welfare of the kindred; his was the important voice in the worship of the ancestors and the family gods (Herskovits 1975). Above all, he was the guardian of the property titles to the land, the family's most critical resource. As long as the family continued to function there was no question of the sale of any of its land. On the contrary, every effort was made to expand the collective holdings of the group.

In recent years the rapidly increasing population, the extension of land clearances, and the successful parceling of land has provoked significant modifications in the traditional structure. P. Moral (1961) argued that the lakou settlement pattern was in the process of disintegration. This is true to an extent; gradually the family cult practices that typified Vodoun a century ago have given way, and the Vodoun temple has become increasingly a community- rather than a family-based institution (Mintz 1972; Laguerre 1973a). However, Michel Laguerre (1978) has shown that the essential bonds of the extended family persist today in the milieu of both rural and urban poor and that, as a corporate body, it continues to promote both survival and socioeconomic mobility for its members through mutual aid, economic sharing, and social solidarity reinforced by religious sanctions.

The economic base of the rural peasant is the agricultural productivity of the family lands. Land may be worked singly or collectively by coumbite. The coumbite may be a permanent type of organization with a fixed membership or a makeshift group called together to complete a particular task. Like the *ayni* labor group in highland Peru, the Haitian coumbite serves a recreational as well as practical function (Métraux 1971). Members work to the accompaniment of music made with drums and bamboo trumpets, and the day's labor is rewarded with a specially prepared meal and a social dance. Men are responsible for the clearing of new fields, but women share in all other agricultural activities. In addition, the task of transporting and disposing of the produce is left almost entirely in the hands of women, who invariably control the family finances (Simpson 1942; Murray and Alvarez 1975; Legerman 1971).

Education occurs informally as an integral part of a child's enculturation into the family structure, and it is based largely on the oral transmission of songs, proverbs, riddles, and tales that define situations in the social world. By following the moral lessons inherent in the folklore, children learn their roles and

A cluster of houses reminiscent of settlements in parts of West Africa

develop a self-concept. The fundamental lessons of social and moral life are revealed in children's games, in the Bouqui and Ti Malice tales, and in stories about *loup garou*, zombies, and the demonic *baka*. Tales of the phantasmagoric provide supernatural sanctions to such mores as taboos on murder, incest, theft, and the showing of disrespect to elders (Simpson 1942, 1951; Herskovits 1975).

Sexual relations among the Haitian peasantry do not follow European patterns. Simpson (1942) noted that legal church marriage was beyond the economic reach or desire of all but 20 percent of rural Haitians. Instead, marriageable men resort to *plaçage*, a socially if not legally sanctioned relationship that brings with it a recognized set of obligations for both man and woman. Women in such relationships are known as *placées*, but there is a wide assortment of ranks. Moral (1961) distinguished monogamous relationships as *plaçage honnête*, polygamous ones as simple plaçage. The majority of cases fall into the latter group, for 75 percent of rural Haitians practice polygyny (Simpson 1942). A woman who shares a man's house is known as a *femme caille*. A *maman petite* is a woman who has borne a man a child without living in his house. Depending on the nature of the bond, however, she may live in one of his second houses and cultivate a piece of land. A *femme placée* is a mistress who does not share the

*The distribution of goods in rural Haiti is dominated by the women of
the marketplace, like these Marchand women in the central market of
Port-au-Prince.*

same house with her mate, and who has yet to give him any children. Finally, a *bien avec* is a woman with whom a man has frequent but not exclusive sexual contact. Plaçage may be as stable as legal marriage. Moreover, though on an individual basis there is often bitterness and conflict between rivals, Haitian peasant women fully recognize the rights of their men to have more than one mate, and occasionally two or more placées will share the same courtyard.

Vodoun medicine is based on a thoroughly non-Western conception of the etiology of disease. The Vodounist defines health as a coherent state of equilibrium between the physical and spiritual components of the individual. Health is wholeness, which in turn is conceived as something holy, and in this regard Vodounist perceptions are not far removed from beliefs once held by our own society. The words health, whole, and holy have the same etymological root in the Old English word *hal*, meaning sound, healthy, and whole (Weil 1983).

As a result, Vodoun medicine acts on two quite different levels. There is an entire range of relatively minor ailments that are treated symptomatically much as in our society, only with medicinal plants and folk preparations, many of which are pharmacologically active. A basic knowledge of the leaves utilized in such lay treatments is part of the traditional education of virtually every rural Haitian, and though there are respected specialists known as *dokte feuilles*—leaf doctors—their expertise is considered mundane.

Much more serious are the troubles that arise when the harmony of an individual's spiritual components is broken. In this case it is the source of the disorder, not its particular manifestation, that must be treated, and that responsibility falls strictly within the domain of the *houngan*, or Vodoun priest. Because disharmony will affect all aspects of the individual's life, problems brought to the houngan include both psychological and physical ailments, as well as other troubles such as chronic bad luck, marital difficulties, or financial problems (Kiev 1961, 1962). Each case is treated as unique. As a form of treatment, Vodoun medicine does not ignore the existence of pathogens; it simply comments that the pathogens are present in the environment at all times and asks why certain individuals succumb when others do not.

Restoring the patient's health may involve a number of tech-

*Maintaining the sacred equilibrium of the individual—the state of
wholeness and balance that accompanies health—is one of the tasks of
the houngan or Vodoun priest. Here a young girl is treated at the site
of a sacred pilgrimage.*

niques. First, through divination, the houngan must determine whether the illness or problem has a natural or supernatural origin (Kiev 1961, 1962; Métraux 1953; Snow 1974). Natural diseases may be seen as the just retribution of the greater God, or more often, as in the case of chronic degenerative diseases, as the result of natural forces beyond anyone's control. Treatment under these circumstances depends on the particular condition, and the houngan would be the first to encourage a client to go to the public hospital in cases, for example, of a traumatic injury such as a bone fracture. Supernatural illnesses, however, are caused by malevolent spiritual forces, often sorcery, and they can be treated only by the houngan or *mambo*, the Vodoun priestess. On the material level such conditions, once diagnosed, may be treated by herbal baths and massage, physical isolation of the patient in the *hounfour* or temple, administration of medicinal plant potions, and, perhaps most important, by a sacrifice so that the patient may return to the earth a gift of life's vital energy.

But it is intervention on the spiritual level that ultimately determines the patient's fate (Métraux 1953), and for this the houngan is but a servant of the spirits, the *loa*. The spirit is called into the head of either the houngan or an assistant; and like an oracle the physical body of man dispenses the knowledge of the gods.

All of these themes—indigenous concepts of health and healing, the relationship between the sexes, the value of collective labor, communal land holdings, the authority of the patriarch, the dominant role of women in the market economy, the sacred setting of the temple and lakou, the solidarity of the extended family—are clues to a complex social world. Yet alone they cannot begin to give a sense of the cohesion of the peasant society. Roger Bastide, after having spent time among the Afro-Brazilian groups in the northeast of that country, noted that "a civilization gains its veritable aspect only if one embraces it through its mystical world view, which is more than just its expression or justification but, in fact, its very foundation" (Bastide 1960, 1). This statement may not be universally true, but it does apply to the society of the Haitian peasant. For in this country of survivors and spirits, the living and the dead, it is religion that provides the essential bond. Vodoun is not an isolated cult; it is a complex mystical worldview, a system of beliefs concerning the relation-

The sacrifice of a chicken during a Vodoun service

ship between man, nature, and the supernatural forces of the
universe (Deren 1953). It fuses the unknown to the known,
creates order out of chaos, renders the mysterious intelligible.
Vodoun cannot be abstracted from the day-to-day lives of the
believers. In Haiti, as in Africa, there is no separation between
the sacred and the secular, between the holy and the profane,
between the material and the spiritual (Mbiti 1969). Every
dance, every song, every action is but a particle of the whole, each
gesture a prayer for the survival of the entire community.[1]

The pillar of this community is the houngan. Unlike the Roman Catholic priest, the houngan does not control access to the
spirit realm. Vodoun is a quintessentially democratic faith. Each
believer not only has direct contact with the spirits, he or she
actually receives them into his or her body. As the Haitians say,
the Catholic goes to church to speak about God, the Vodounist

1. Indeed, the roots of Vodoun go deep into the peasant society. G. F. Murray, a
cultural materialist, went to Haiti in 1971 to study the evolution of peasant land
tenure, committed to avoiding the "siren singsong of voodoo" that he felt had
seduced so many students of Haitian society. Instead, after twenty-one months
of fieldwork, he emerged convinced that in rural Haiti "voodoo emerges as the
latent regulatory device sustaining a critical flow of land and functions thus as a
mainspring mechanism in the resource circulating strategies which this population has evolved under the impact of population pressure" (Murray 1977, iii).

dances in the hounfour and becomes God. Nevertheless, the
houngan's role is vital. As a spiritual leader of the community he
is called upon to understand and interpret a complex body of
belief. But Vodoun not only embodies a set of spiritual concepts,
it prescribes a way of life, a philosophy and code of ethics that
regulate social behavior. As surely as one refers to a Christian or
Buddhist society, one may speak of a Vodoun society, and within
that world one finds completeness: art and music, education
based on the oral transmission of songs and folklore, a complex
system of medicine, and a system of justice based on indigenous
principles of conduct and morality. The houngan, as de facto
leader of this society, is at once psychologist, physician, diviner,
musician, and spiritual healer. Particularly with the transformation of the traditional lakou (Moral 1961), the Vodoun temple has
emerged as the focal point of village and community solidarity
(Mintz 1972; Laguerre 1973a). For the *hounsis*, or initiates of the
temple, the hounfour has become "sanctuary, clubhouse, dance
hall, hospital, theatre, chemist's shop, music hall, court and
council chamber in one" (Jahn 1961, 54). As the moral and
religious leader of that community, it is the houngan who must
skillfully balance the supernatural forces of the universe and at
the same time ensure the physical and economic well-being of
his initiates on the mundane level of earthly existence.

Vodoun itself is not an animistic religion. The believers do not
endow natural objects with souls; they serve the loa, the spirits,
which by definition are the multiple expressions of God. There is
Agwe, the spiritual sovereign of the sea; and there is Ogoun, the
spirit of fire and the metallurgical elements. But there is also
Erzulie, the goddess of love; Ghede, the spirit of the dead;
Legba, the spirit of communication between all spheres. Vodounists, in fact, honor hundreds of loa because they so sincerely
recognize all life, all material objects, and even abstract processes
as the sacred expressions of God. Though God (*Bon Dieu*) is the
supreme force at the apex of the pantheon, He is distant, and it is
with the loa that the Haitian interacts on a daily basis (Deren
1953; Maximilien 1982; Rigaud 1946, 1953; Simpson 1980;
Courlander 1960).

If properly served, the loa will reward the hounsis with success
and good fortune. But there are other, less benign forces with
which the Vodounist must contend. Even the most devout acolytes must at times confront the evil intentions of personal ene-

A Vodoun temple or hounfour

Exterior wall of a hounfour (detail)

*The interior of a Vodoun hounfour. Note the battery of drummers and
the characteristic cornmeal ve-ve encircling the poteau mitan*

Inside a Vodoun hounfour, women prepare for a service for the loa

A Vodoun service for the loa

mies and sorcerers and in turn must resort to the same malevolent magical forces to seek their own revenge should they, in fact,
become the target of sorcery. Indeed, as in much of West Africa,
magic and sorcery are an integral aspect of the peasant's worldview, and he or she lives constantly exposed to the threat of
charms, sorcery, and spells. By no means does this imply that
peasants live in perpetual terror of witchcraft or that they approach the supernatural realm with trepidation and fear. For
one thing, suspicions and accusations arise in specific restricted
and intelligible situations; moreover, there are recognized procedures to counteract the threats (Lewis 1977; Douglas 1972).
Indeed, the Vodounist moves in and out of the supernatural
realm with such ease and frequency that his or her initial reaction
upon suspecting the hand of the sorcerer may be anger as much
as fear, and the first inclination is to do something about it.
Manipulation of the occult forces lies within the providence of
the sorcerer, the *bokor*, and it is to him that the aggrieved peasant
must turn.

To do his work the bokor has available a veritable arsenal of
spells, powders, and supernatural entities to draw upon (Simpson 1940). The *baka* take the form of animals and are malevolent
agents dispatched by the bokor to "manger moun"—literally to
eat people, yet idiomatically it is an expression, both in Haiti and

in parts of West Africa, for sending a fatal illness or bringing about an accidental death (Herskovits 1975). Perpetrators of evil may choose to make Faustian compacts, *engagements*, with the *djab*, the devil, a "manlike being that is superhuman, ferocious and terrible" (Courlander 1960, 96). Bokor may transform themselves into *loup garou*, or werewolves, which in turn may disguise themselves by transmuting into other objects or beings (Simpson 1942). Other maleficent entities include the *lutin*, the spirit of a dead person who feels mistreated and ignored and who returns to haunt his or her ungrateful descendants (Courlander 1960). Perhaps the most potent dark act of the bokor is the *l'envoi morts* or *expédition*, the sending of the dead (Métraux 1972). Those who become the victims of dead spirits grow thin, weaken, spit blood, and invariably die unless the condition is diagnosed in time and the healer succeeds in breaking the death spirit's hold on the victim. It is the casting of an *expédition*, as will be seen later, that is a critical aspect in the creation of the Haitian zombie. Finally, there is *wanga*, "the magical weapon par excellence," a term "applied to any object or combination of objects which has received, as a result of magic procedure, a property that is harmful to one or more people" (Métraux 1972, 285). Two features give the wanga its particular usefulness. An object that has been properly *rangé*, or "arranged," by the bokor is dangerous even to the touch, and furthermore its power will affect only the specific individual marked by the sorcerer's spell. Poisonous powders are by definition potent wanga, and that is why, in folk belief, the mere touch of certain substances may prove lethal.

It is an axiom of Vodoun magic that for every force that harms, there is a cure; for every wanga, there is a *garde*. If the wanga represents the antisocial, the carrier of dark magic, then the garde, *arrêt*, and *drogue* represent the passive, socially desirable aspects of magic. The garde may consist of a small bag of mysterious ingredients, or it may be a spiritual tattoo inscribed into the individual's skin. Whereas the garde is specific, protecting the individual, the arrêt may protect an entire household or compound of houses. Yet another protective charm is the *pouin*, the product of ritual magic within the Vodoun temple itself. Pouin are often invisible, "consisting of magical forces unleashed into space by the houngan" (Courlander 1960, 99). The power of the pouin is far-reaching, protecting the individual not only from malevolent forces but from the everyday turns of fortune.

The actuating force between good and evil magic is the loa, the spirits, but the charms themselves fall within the providence of man: and here we come face-to-face with the ambiguous position of the houngan and the bokor. Indeed, the distinction between the former, as a benevolent priest and healer, and the latter, as a malevolent sorcerer, soon falls apart. The houngan, after all, must know and understand evil in order to combat it, just as the bokor must understand good in order to subvert it. What distinguishes the houngan is not his knowledge per se but how, when, and under what circumstances he chooses to use it. He may, in fact, be obliged to enter the realm of darkness to seek revenge for an innocent victim or to punish the perpetrator of evil. Indeed, the same individual may be both a houngan and a bokor, and which side he walks on will depend on the specific task at hand.[2]

Just as it is not very useful to distinguish bokor from houngan in some absolute sense, it is misleading to separate—as some apologists have attempted to do—the religious aspects of Vodoun from its obvious magical components. Public ceremonies for the loa always include elements of sympathetic magic, just as virtually every magical practice derives part of its ritual from traditional religion and depends on the invocation of the loa. No magic act is of value unless it is backed up by the endorsement of the spirits. Magical preparations gain their strength through the blessing of *Maître-Carrefour*, the Master of the Crossroads, and numerous potions and powders include ingredients collected specifically from a crossroads. Indeed, much of the work of the sorcerer is done, if not in the sanctity of his temple, then at the sacred crossroads or at the foot of the cross of Baron Samedi in the graveyard. Even the most powerful bokor cannot kill a man

2. Just as man himself has an ambivalent potential for good or evil, so do objects. According to numerous informants, the most dangerous and poisonous substance is a simple lime, properly prepared by the bokor. If a bokor cuts a lime transversely while it is still on the tree, the half that remains on the limb overnight becomes the most virulent of poisons, more deadly even "than the three drops of liquid that issue from a dead person's mouth." The other half, taken into the temple, becomes its equally potent antidote. The lesson is clear. The lime that is left on the tree remains in the realm of nature—uncivilized, threatening, poisonous. The other half, taken into the abode of the religious sanctuary, is tamed and humanized, and thus becomes profoundly curative.

unless the victim has been first marked and the deed sanctioned by Baron.

In Haiti, then, magic and religion are two parts of a whole, just as the houngan and bokor represent opposite poles of the same existence. Like the sorcerer of West Africa, the bokor may be despised by upstanding members of the society, yet at a more profound level his presence is tolerated because it is critical to the balance of social and spiritual life. The bokor and all his apparently maleficent activities are accepted because they are somehow essential. The sorcerer's dark magic is a potent force to be dealt with, but to a great extent it has been institutionalized as a critical component of the worldview. To ask why there is sorcery in Haiti is to ask why there is evil in the world, and the answer, if there is one, is the same as that provided by all the great religions: evil is the mirror of good, the necessary complement that completes the whole of creation. The Haitians, as we shall see, as much as any other people, are conscious of this sacred balance. In fact, maintaining the balance is the very goal of Vodoun.

The important point, though, is not to measure the "amount of magic" in Vodoun but to recognize that the Vodounist believes in the power of magic, accepts the existence of sorcery, and acknowledges the potency of the spirits. Critically, the inevitable cognitive steps that the society takes—and must take—to protect those beliefs from falsification give rise to a closed circular system of thought wherein no event has a life of its own. In this characteristic Haitian Vodounists do share a significant trait with their African forebears, and the power of their convictions is equally strong. "The fundamental point is that the African [or Haitian peasant] is born into a society which believes in witchcraft and therefore the very texture of his thinking, from childhood on, is woven of magical and mystical ideas. More important still, since magic and witchcraft are lived far more than they are reasoned about, his daily actions are conditioned by these beliefs, till at every turn he is confronted by the threat of witchcraft and meets it with divination and magic. The weight of tradition, the actions and behavior of his elders, the support which chiefs give to the system, all impress on the African the truth of the system, and since he cannot measure it against any other system, he is continually caught in the web of its making" (Gluckman 1944, 61–71).

For individual members of such a society, "there is no incentive to agnosticism. All their beliefs hang together, and were an (individual) to give up faith in witch doctorhood he would have to surrender equally his faith in witchcraft and oracles. In this web of belief every strand depends on every other strand and a (person) cannot get out of its meshes because this is the only world he knows. The web is not an external structure in which he is enclosed. It is the texture of his thought, and he cannot think that his thought is wrong" (Evans-Pritchard 1937, 194).

Similarly, the rural Haitians who serve the loa share a set of religious and magical beliefs and practices, and this collective worldview possesses a certain objectivity and reality that dominates the psychological or physical experience of any one individual. Because the religious tenets permeate the entire peasant society, they in a sense become obligatory, not because of coercion but because for the individual member of that society there exists no other way. He or she "accepts what everybody gives assent to, because he has no choice, any more than of what language he speaks. Even were he a skeptic, he could express his doubts only in terms of the beliefs held by all around" (Evans-Pritchard 1965, 55). In other words, a world of few alternatives makes for an absolute acceptance of established tenets of belief, and those beliefs, in turn, have an absolute and exclusive validity. Within these confines the believer can maneuver with some intellectual ingenuity, but beyond the limits of the beliefs there is only chaos. Within such a system of belief there are no accidents, and no event has a life of its own. It was within such a system of thought that the phenomenon of the Haitian zombie arose.

CHAPTER TWO

THE HAITIAN ZOMBIE

THE ZOMBIE IN POPULAR CULTURE
AND HAITIAN FOLKLORE

The subject of the Haitian zombie is one that has fascinated—indeed titillated—foreign observers for decades. The common image, of course, is one of a corpse in tattered rags, trailing remnants of necrotic flesh as it rises from the cemetery in a state of trance-like animation, entirely subservient and beholden to the nefarious authority of some unknown master. This macabre figure has entered Western popular culture and even academic parlance in an unusual variety of forms. An individual who feels particularly listless and apathetic, for example, may refer to himself or herself as "feeling like a zombie." Such a sensation might result from indulgence the evening before in one too many zombies—an iced cocktail notorious for its alcohol content. Had this person been drinking in a bar whose jukebox was fifteen years out-of-date, she or he might well have listened to one of the many hit records of a well-known English rock-and-roll group of the sixties. Their name?—The Zombies. Of course, a smart person would have stayed home and read a book—*Zombies Gone Wild* (*Les zombies en furie*, Pierre 1978)—or perhaps taken in a play, *The Zombie* (Kelley 1983). The choice of late-night movies on television would be almost limitless: *White Zombies* (1933), *King of the Zombies* (1941), *I Walked with a Zombi* (1943), *Zombies on Broadway* (1945), *Valley of the Zombies* (1946), and even *Zombies of the Stratosphere* (1953).

The academic literature also shows an odd fascination with the topic, as is evident in the casual and gratuitous use of the word itself. Witness, for example, two papers in descriptive linguistics: "Zombies and Other Problems: Theory and Method in Research on Bilingualism" (Johnson 1974) and "Interpretative Semantics Meets the Zombies: A Discussion of the Controversy about Deep Structure" (Katz 1973). Or, in a journal of social psychiatry, the paper entitled simply "Zombi," in which the term is coopted to define a "man who as a child has neither experienced nor been trained in the three ingredients of emotional life: attention, love, and affection" (Bierer 1976). Finally, the word appears in the philosophical literature in a series of articles that again have nothing to do with the correct etymological meaning of the term (Locke 1976; Kirk 1974, 1977).

The proper derivation of the word *zombie* has in fact been the source of some academic debate and confusion. Elsie Clews Parsons (1928) suggested, in the fashion of the period, a French origin in the word *ombres*, shadows, and hence *z'omb'e* and *zombie*. She also mentioned a link to the West Indian term for ghost, *jumbie* or *juppy/duppy*. Maya Deren (1953) refers to the term as part of her evidence for the continuity of indigenous Arawak Indian cultural traits in the predominantly African society of rural Haiti. She notes that the indigenous beliefs concerning the *zemis*, the souls of the dead, are precisely those relating to the zombies—a suggestion that I will deal with at a later time.

Most authorities, however, indicate an African origin for the word. In his *Philologie creole*, Jules Faine (1937) wrote that the word came from the Bonda language—the word *zumbi*—and was probably transmitted to Haiti by Portuguese slave traders. Among the Mitsogho of Gabon the cadaver of the deceased is called *ndzumbi* (Dieterlen 1973). Wyatt MacGaffey (pers. comm.) suggests that the word comes from the Kongo *nzambi*, meaning more or less "spirit of a dead person." This is the derivation I accept for two reasons, both of which will be explained in detail in a later discussion. First, the concept is consistent with the cosmological meaning of the term as conceived by the Haitians themselves, and second, the contribution of the Kongo heritage is now recognized as equal to that of Dahomey in the evolution of the Haitian amalgam.

For all peoples, death is the first teacher, the first pain, the edge beyond which life as we know it ends and wonder begins. Death's essence is the severance from the mortal body of some elusive life-giving principle, and how a culture comes to understand or at least tolerate this inexorable separation to a great extent defines its mystical worldview. In Haiti, the zombie sits on the cusp of death, and the beliefs that mediate the phenomenon are rooted in the very heart of the peasant's being. The existence of zombies is but a confirmation of a fundamental conviction that the dead wield power in the world of the living. On one level, this conviction is reflected in certain customs: a machete dipped in the remains of a cadaver to strengthen the steel, or the placement of black clothes on cemetery tombs to provide the dead with evidence that their period of mourning, with its incumbent costs, has been adequately observed. At a more profound level, as we shall see, the dialogue between the living and the dead in many ways forms the axis about which much of the practice of the Vodoun religion revolves.

The permeability of the frontier between life and death—indeed, between the material and the immaterial—provides an important backdrop for appreciating the magical beliefs evident in all the popular tales of zombies. The following tales, two of which were recorded as the "eyewitness" accounts of an eminent mambo, or Vodoun priestess, and the other taken from the literature, are typical.

GONAÏVES

This girl was standing watching a RaRa band pass by. She was the daughter of a cousin of mine and that night she fell ill, vomited blood and died. She was buried. After that her father went out to discover who had killed his daughter. When he did, he, in turn, killed the daughter of the murderer. This happened months later.

Then one day a friend and I were going to a funeral. When we got to the lakou there was all kinds of commotion and the police had started to arrive. It turned out that the one who had just died was none other than the first girl who had supposedly died five months before. The people said she died because a great light came upon her. The *chef de section* signed a police deposition saying a thunderbolt had hit her. But it couldn't have been for she wasn't burnt and at the time she had a child on her lap that went unharmed. No, it wasn't a thunderbolt, it was an *expédition*, a death spirit.

ARTIBONITE VALLEY, ENVIRONS OF GONAÏVES

I had sewn the hem of the funerary dress of a dead woman. People told me later she was to be raised so I asked to

attend. The bokor agreed and told me to bring a gallon of
clairin. He stood with a rope in hand between two graves
with his legs spread over a third. He called out her name
and clapped and then from the side of the cemetery the girl
appeared. I recognized her. I had sewn her dress, and she
still wore it. I knew that she had died. That bokor wanted to
make a *pwin* [magical force] out of her.

JACMEL

A young man named Mammés was working as a stevedore
on the docks of Jacmel when one evening at a cockfight he
lost 200 gourdes. Unable to pay the debt with his meagre
salary, nor able to sell off a part of his family land, he
contacted an aged houngan who lived alone. Mammés remained there a week, after which the money he owed was
dispatched to his debtors.

Three years later the houngan brought an emaciated,
unkempt creature to the farm of a friend, Vermineux, who
lived close to the Dominican border. This creature was all
that was left of Mammés. The unfortunate stevedore had
sold his soul to the houngan for a period of four years and
during that week at his place the houngan had "succeeded
in performing the same magic operation his own father had
boasted of performing years before"—he had created a
zombi without venturing into the mysterious domain of
death. He had taken a living man's soul.

The new zombi Mammés, like a docile terrified beast
crouched upon the ground cowering against the mud wall of
the hut.

"Are you thirsty?" demanded the master.

The zombi with fixed, sightless-appearing eyes inclined
his head.

"Drink!" ordered Vermineux.

Mammés drank mechanically.

From that time on, the frightened zombi with the drawn
greyish face bereft of memory worked as a slave for Vermineux. The gay laughing Mammés of former days now wore
a corpse-like face with set features and clenched teeth.

One day, many months later a woman of fifty, inexpress-
ibly ugly, toothless and covered by running sores came by
the farm. Foul as she appeared, this woman represented to

the zombi the sole being who could satisfy his overwhelming desire. He came to her house and took her to bed. The old woman understandably was delighted to have finally found love and much was her dismay when one morning Mammés woke up and demanded with utmost disgust to know the identity of the haggard woman who shared his bed. He rushed out into the road, complaining to everyone that a toothless woman claimed to be his wife.

Far away in a thatched hut, the aged houngan had finally died and Mammés had recovered his soul (Taft 1938).

These three accounts contain many of the basic elements of zombie folklore. One notes, for example, that the Haitian peasant recognizes two types of zombies. One is a spirit, a part of the Vodoun soul which has been sold to or been captured by a bokor and which, if released, will be "doomed to wander the earth until its destined time arrives to return to God" (Herskovits 1975). These spirit zombies, once captured, however, are usually carefully stored in jars that they may later be transmuted magically into insects, animals, or humans in order to accomplish the particular work of the bokor (Davis 1985). The other type of zombie is the more familiar living dead: innocent victims raised in a comatose trance from their graves by malevolent sorcerers, led away under cover of night to distant farms or villages where they must toil indefinitely as slaves. These are known as *zombi jardin* (Dewisme 1957) or *zombi corps cadavre* (Davis 1983a, 1983b, 1985). According to folk belief, these sad individuals may be recognized by their docile natures, their glassy, empty eyes, the nasal twang to their voices (not unlike that of the Guede spirits of the dead), and by the evident absence of will, memory, and emotion (Simpson 1945). They are said to dwell in the continuous present, where the past is dead and the future consists of fear and impossible desires. Their existence lies solely in the "misty zone which divides life from death" (Métraux 1972).

A zombie may, however, return to the world of the living by regaining, through one means or another, that part of the human soul that has been bartered away, stolen, or somehow captured by the malevolent sorcerer; often this takes place upon the master's death. A more dramatic metamorphosis, described graphically in innumerable tales, occurs if a zombie is inadvertently fed salt, whereupon his or her apathy is said to explode into rage, and subservience gives way to a murderous disposition, the first victim of which is invariably the master.

Most important, perhaps, these zombie tales reveal that, according to local belief, it takes a magical process to create either type of zombie, and this can occur in a wide variety of ways. Of course, as with so many folktales, these tales are internally inconsistent—for example, one portrays a desireless zombie as craving sexual relations—and often humorous, while at the same time they impart some social or moral lesson.

OTHER TALES, OTHER POSSIBILITIES: REPORTS OF THE POISON

A belief that the spirits of the dead may affect the well-being of the living is by no means restricted to Haiti; on the contrary, it is difficult to name a single culture where there is not some tension between the living and the dead. Our own ghost stories show that our society is no exception. What does appear to be unique to Haiti is the widespread conviction that the *zombi corps cadavres* exist, and that actual people, known or rumored to be known, have undergone this ordeal (Bourguignon 1959; Simpson 1941; Métraux 1972). The strength and calm assurance with which this conviction is held by the Haitian people has drawn heated attention to a large collection of a different type of zombie story: the oft-cited accounts of individuals, declared dead, who later turn up in varying degrees of health in the world of the living. In many cases these accounts have been presented as the literal truth, and the result has been a polemic that has continued for almost a hundred years. Do zombies actually exist? On one side have been ranked the intellectuals, scholars, and government officials who have dogmatically—and perhaps understandably—consigned the phenomenon to fable (Bourgignon 1959; Laroche 1976; Mars 1945, 1947; Métraux 1972; Herskovits 1975; Leyburn 1941; Courlander 1960), and on the other educated individuals—foreign and Haitian physicians and psychiatrists, missionaries, writers, and reporters—who claim that at least some of the accounts are legitimate (Hurston 1981; Dewisme 1957;

Douyon 1980; Diederich 1983; Kline pers. comm.; Lehmann pers. comm.). The following are typical examples of these reports:

PORT-AU-PRINCE

A man from the working class fell ill with a high intermittent fever that the doctors were unable to bring down. He belonged to the congregation of a foreign mission and during the course of a visit from the priest, the man passed away. The priest at the request of the wife and the doctor who had declared the patient dead assisted in dressing the corpse in the proper funerary clothes. The next day the priest conducted the service and watched the coffin being buried.

Several days later an official in Jacmel saw a man dressed in funerary garb tied to a tree whimpering. Later he was identified by the wife, doctor and priest. The man himself never recovered and spent his days in a catatonic stupor. Eventually at the behest of President Nord Alexis he was placed in the care of the guardians of a government farm near Gonaïves (Bonsal 1912).

CAP HAÏTIEN

In 1898 a young Cap Haïtien boy got into trouble with a girl and refused to accept responsibility for her pregnancy. When the girl's family approached his, they were offered no settlement. Two weeks later the boy died suddenly and was buried. Some months later the mother was wandering through the city when she saw some labourers loading ox carts with bags of coffee. In one of their faces she recognized her son. He saw but did not recognize her. She ran for help but by the time she returned the foreman was able to deny ever having seen the youth in question. She never saw her son again (Hurston 1981).

PORT-AU-PRINCE

The daughter of a former minister was buried with much pomp in the capital. Five years later a rumour of her existence having reached a priest through the confessional, what was believed to be the same girl was discovered in a rural village. She was unkempt and demented and had borne three children. The coffin was dug up and in it was found her wedding dress—for though she was only eight at the time, it was the custom to bury young girls in their nuptial garments. But the autopsy proved the remains to be those of a man, with his legs cut off and laid alongside the body (Franck 1920).

PORT-AU-PRINCE

A white missionary conducted the funeral rites of a young man who had collapsed at a dance. He saw the coffin sealed and placed in the ground. Several weeks later another missionary reported having seen the youth in jail. The priest didn't believe his colleague and rushed to the jail only to find the man in question alone in a dismal cell (Hurston 1981).

PORT-AU-PRINCE

The day of the funeral of a young man passed and the mother remained so stricken some friends and relatives remained with her at her home. Late that night the sister of the deceased heard subdued chanting, followed by the sounds of percussion growing louder as they seemed to approach the house. Suddenly she heard the voice of her brother calling out. She woke the rest of the family and together they saw the brother being led away by an entire procession (Hurston 1981).

VALLEY OF MARBIAL

A girl engaged to a young man rejected the advances of a powerful houngan who turned aside muttering vague threats. Several days later the girl took ill and died in the hospital at Jacmel. Her body was taken to Marbial for burial. The coffin, as it happened, was too short and her neck had to be bent that the body might fit in. During the wake someone accidentally dropped a lit cigarette on the foot of the deceased causing a small burn. Two months later rumours passed that the girl had been seen alive in the company of the houngan. No one believed it until months later with the advent of the anti-superstition campaign the houngan grew nervous, repented and set his zombies free. The girl was returned home, where she was recognized by all not only because of her physical appearance but also because of her lame neck and the scar she bore on her foot. She never recovered her sanity (Métraux 1972).

Marie M., the daughter of a prominent family, died October 1909. Five years passed. One day, a group of her former schoolmates were out on a walk with one of the Sisters that ran the school. As they passed a house, one of the girls screamed and swore she saw Marie. Others backed her up. The rumours spread through the high school of the capital and finally obliged the reluctant father to obtain a warrant to enter the house in question. By then the place had been abandoned. Suspicion fell on the sullen father. There was a public outcry for the grave of the child to be opened. Finally it was done. A skeleton was in the coffin but it was too long for the box. What's more, the clothes worn by the girl at her burial were not on the skeleton but rather lay beside it in a neat pile.

It was later discovered according to the newspaper reports of the time that the houngan holding the girl had died and that his wife had turned the child zombie over to an officer of the church. She had been held in that house while plans were laid to get her out of the country in order to prevent embarrassment to the family and the government. Some time later, dressed in a nun's habit, she was smuggled out of the country (Hurston 1981).

This notorious case was later remembered in the memoirs of an American physician:

Marie M. was buried because she was supposed to be dead. She was taken from the ground by a follower of the Voodoo and taken from her state of apparent death three days after her burial. She's alive today and lives abroad. I was among the doctors who treated her during her illness. This case is not unique in our files (Holly in Dewisme 1957).

So profound is the belief that an individual may be raised from the coffin that, in the countryside, relatives often take it upon themselves to ensure that their dead are both truly dead and of little value to the bokor. The limbs or head of the cadaver may be cut off, a blade driven through the heart or a bullet lodged in the temple. Because, according to magical beliefs, a corpse may only be raised if it answers the call of the bokor, the lips of the dead are sometimes sewn up with brass wire. Alternatively, a large pile of sesame seeds or an eyeless needle may be placed beside the body so that the intended victim will be too busy counting or attempting to thread the needle to hear the bokor's call (Métraux 1972; Deren 1953; Herskovits 1975). The reputed efficacy of such preventative practices is described in the following account from the northern town of Port du Paix:

> A young girl fell suddenly ill and death soon followed. Yet from the start things were not the way they should have been. The body stayed warm. The concerned family pursued the mother saying that the death was unnatural and that some further use was planned for the body. So they encouraged her to have the child poisoned before it was buried. The day after the burial the mother went to the tomb and found it open, with the dead body of her child lying on the ground outside the coffin. By local account the bokor had been frustrated in his attempts to make a zombie of the young girl (Hurston 1981).

On the surface, to be sure, there was little reason to believe any of these cases. They were largely unsubstantiated and undocumented and, in many instances, based on hearsay, which in turn reflected the inclination of so many Haitians to mix the possible and the improbable with the truly phantasmagoric. Elsie Clews Parsons (1928), in her discussion of the frequently cited instances of cannibalism, revealed only too clearly the dangers of accepting casual reports as the literal truth. She noted rightly that a bokor who has a zombie, in this case a *zombi astral*, or zombie of the spirit (Davis 1983a, 1985), may transform him into a stone or any kind of animal. Emically, then, such a creature would be considered a person, and thus its flesh, sold in the market, would quite properly be said to be human flesh. This belief, she explained, was the sole basis to the various reports of cannibalism that figured in popular literature and even judicial records in Haiti.

Moreover, despite the rich body of anecdotal lore about zombies, and the frequently cited cases, no physician until recently had examined a certifiable zombie. There was, for example, the notorious case of Felicia Felix-Mentor. On the morning of 24 October 1936, in the village of Ennery in north-central Haiti, the entire population was aroused by the appearance of an old, naked woman whose eyelashes had fallen out and whose face was bound in a ragged cloth. Hysteria swept the village, and in time a member of the Mentor family who lived outside Ennery noticed that the woman bore a resemblance to a sister who had died and been buried in 1907. Moreover, the mysterious woman was lame; the sister had also been lame as a result of a fracture of her left leg.

The case drew national and to some extent international attention (Hurston 1981). The woman was taken to a government hospital and one by one a number of relatives were called upon to verify her identity. Many did, and for a while the case was heralded as the first legitimate instance of zombification. However, the arguments in favor of this conclusion soon fell apart. X-ray examination showed that her leg had never been broken; her lameness was due to nutritional deficiencies and it soon went away when she was placed on a proper diet. She also gained weight and began to menstruate. Felicia Felix-Mentor had been twenty-seven at the time of her death almost thirty years before. The age of this unknown woman, once she had partially regained her physical health, was estimated to be about forty. The attendant physician's diagnosis was schizophrenia and syphilis (Mars 1945, 1947; Simpson 1941).

The case of Felicia Felix-Mentor was highly significant, for it had been critical to the argument of a young American anthropologist, Zora Neale Hurston, who was perhaps the most vocal proponent of the idea that zombies actually existed (Hurston 1981). Hurston became the object of scathing remarks. Alfred Métraux (1972) dismissed her as "very superstitious," while Louis Mars noted: "This American writer stated specifically that she came back from Haiti with no doubt in regard to popular belief in the zombie pseudo-science. Miss Hurston herself, unfortunately, did not go beyond the mass hysteria to verify her information" (Mars 1945, 39). Mars was quite right in exposing the Mentor case as fraudulent. At the same time, he himself was guilty of ignoring the central tenet of Hurston's argument.

Zora Neale Hurston did believe that zombies were created, but not by magic. After she had visited Felicia Felix-Mentor in a hospital near Gonaïves in north-central Haiti, she and the attendant physician "discussed at great length the theories of how zombies came to be. It was concluded that it is not a case of awakening the dead, but rather a matter of the semblance of death brought on by some drug known to a few. Some secret probably brought from Africa and handed down generation to generation. The men know the effect of the drug and the anti-dote. It is evident that it destroys that part of the brain which governs speech and will-power. The victim can move and act but cannot formulate thought" (Hurston 1981, 206).

Although Hurston alone gave credence to this hypothesis, previous and subsequent investigators certainly knew of the re-puted poison. James Leyburn refers to "those who believe that certain bocors [*sic*] know how to administer a subtle poison to intended victims which will cause suspended animation and give the appearance of death. Men in the prime of life suddenly sicken and die for no apparent reason. Once these pseudo-corpses are safely buried, the sinister person who arranged the death will hasten to the graveyard and dig up the body; giving the proper antidote to the poison, he restores the body to activity but the mind only to semiconsciousness" (Leyburn 1941, 163–64). According to Métraux, "it is generally believed that hungan [*sic*] know the secret of certain drugs which can induce such a pro-found state of lethargy as to be indistinguishable from death" (Métraux 1972, 281). Harold Courlander adds: "The victim is not really dead but has succumbed to a virulent poison which numbs all the senses and stops bodily function but does not truly kill. Upon disinterment, the victim is given an antidote which restores most physical processes but leaves the mind in an inert state, without will or the power to resist" (Courlander 1960, 101). George Simpson, in his study of Haitian magic, notes that there can be no doubt as to the sincerity of the peasants' beliefs concerning zombies, and that virtually all the peasants he met claimed to have themselves gone through, or to have known someone personally who had gone through, such an ordeal. Among possible explanations for the phenomenon he lists drugs, hypnosis, and poison (Simpson 1941, 401).

In the popular literature we learn: "That there are Haitian Obeah [Vodoun] practitioners who have so remarkable a knowl-edge of vegetable poisons that they destroy their enemies or those of their clients without being detected seems to be gener-ally admitted. Some of these poisons are said to be so subtle that the victims live for years, dying slowly as from a wasting disease, or going insane, deaf, blind or dumb with the civilized medical profession helpless to revive them. Men of undoubted judgment and integrity, some of them American, claim to have positive proof of such cases" (Franck 1920, 164). Edna Taft even offered a name for this reputed poison:

> Zombies are the living dead; that is, persons who are supposed to have died, been buried, then raised from the dead. . . . As a matter of fact, they have never really died at all; they were merely in a cataleptic trance during their period of interment. These false zombies are the victims of unscrupulous sorcerers who produce the semblance of death by administering to the unfortunates the leaf of *tuer-lever* (kill-raise up) plant. Thus the wicked wizard is able to bring about an artificial death. The victim in a state of suspended animation is duly buried. As people are buried the same day they die, the victim does not have to be kept in a cataleptic trance for many hours. The "corpse" is restored to life, but the brain remains dulled. It is said that the zombies are given regular doses of a certain narcotic to maintain them in a state of apathy (Taft 1938, 257).

Similar reports of a reputed zombie poison and antidote have, in fact, appeared not infrequently in the Haitian literature going well back into the last century. Georges Sylvain suggested:

> On assure que des personnes, plongées en léthargie à l'aide d'un narcotique puissant, et tenues pour mortes d'autant plus aisément qu'elles présentaient toutes les apparences de la mort auraient été ensevelies dans cet état. Longtemps après, des voyageurs les auraient aperçues par hasard dans des champs écartés, au service de quelque houngan ou de quelque mamaloi en renom. Mal réveillées de leur terrible sommeil, elles n'avaient pu rentrer dans la complète possesion de leurs facultés et se trouvaient réduites pars leurs empoisonneurs à la condition de la brute (Sylvain 1901).[1]

———

1. One is assured that people, plunged into lethargy with the aid of a powerful narcotic, and readily taken as dead as they present all the appearances of death, would be sequestered in that condition. Long after, travelers would come upon them by chance, in the fields, working in the service of some houngan or mambo. Startled from their terrible sleep, they nevertheless never regain their mental faculties and find themselves reduced to beasts by their poisoners.

Newspaper articles from the late nineteenth century are explicit and poignant. On 18 June 1887, *L'Oeil* reported the proceedings of a court case held two weeks before on 3 June: "The dead child was carried to the house of this officer, who had it placed in the presence of Pierrine (the mambo), and who pressed her to restore it to life. Pierrine gathered some herbs in the neighbourhood, and made with them a curious beverage which she administered to the child who immediately recovered consciousness. This act produced great emotion among the population." Elsewhere in the same edition the newspaper gave a long account of the trial of two women and one man accused of administering to children a poison that did not kill them, but rather placed them in a deathlike sleep.

Spenser St. John, at one time British consul to Haiti, offers the following accounts which, true or not, nevertheless provide evidence for the widely held convictions concerning this reputed poison:

> The police found a grave disturbed, and near it an open coffin, and lying at its side the body of a lady who had been buried on the previous day. Many arrests were made but the affair was hushed up. It was currently reported (that a spurned mistress of the woman's faithful husband) had applied to the Mamaloi for aid. She received a sleeping potion which she contrived to have given to the lady during her first confinement, and she was hurriedly buried to be restored to consciousness in the graveyard at dead of night (St. John 1884, 236).

Elsewhere St. John reports a story told to him by the previous French ambassador, the Marquis de Forbin Janson, who wrote on 2 August 1860: "Two days after my arrival at Port-au-Prince a woman sent to sleep by means of a narcotic and buried the same evening in the cemetery of the town was disinterred during the night. She still breathed" (St. John 1884, 237). This same incident is reported elsewhere by the Spanish ambassador:

> In July of 1860 there was committed in Port-au-Prince a horrible, almost indescribable crime. A young woman died suddenly and was buried on the following day. At night several individuals of both sexes went to the cemetery, dug up the coffin and opened it. What they actually did is not

known but what is positive is that the unburied began to shriek and shout for help. . . . Already it was too late. [When the soldiers found the grave moments later] they found her dead from a stroke of the dagger (St. John 1884, 237–38).

Finally, there is this account from St. John:

> Of the truth of the following instance of a child being placed under the influence of narcotics in order that, by a pretended burial its disappearance might not draw attention, I have the testimony of ocular witnesses. A foreign lady with whom I was personally acquainted hearing that a child living near her house was ill, went down to see it; she found it lying in a stupified state in its mother's lap. Her suspicions were immediately aroused and she sharply questioned the mother as to what had been done to the child. Her answers were so unsatisfactory yet so mournful that my friend determined to keep a watch on the case. She called in the evening and was told that the child was dead. She insisted on seeing the corpse and found that though the heart was still and the pulse had ceased to beat the child did not look dead and remarked this to the by-standers, but they answered in a chorus "Yes, she is dead." She told the mother that she was not satisfied and that she would return in the morning with her husband and that in the meantime the body must not be buried. Next day she and her husband walked down to the house and asked to see the body. The mother replied that the neighbours having insisted, she allowed them to bury her child and pointed to the grave. The French gentleman called to some of his labourers and had the grave opened; there they found the coffin but the child's body was absent. . . . The child must have been drugged (St. John 1884, 240–41).

The leading citizens of Port-au-Prince took the existence of this reputed poison somewhat seriously. In an editorial in the newspaper *Le Peuple*, dated 23 January 1886, then editor J. J. Audain noted:

> We think that the authorities would do well to have a doctor, or even many of them, to be present when they show what they [the houngan] can do, see them take the life from a body, then put it in a state of lethargy for thirty or forty

hours, then go to the cemetery at night and restore to consciousness the apparent dead. These are things that should be seen, learnt, proved and studied.

These people must positively understand the properties of a thousand and one plants which could be used pharmaceutically, and from which might be drawn their virtues, and by studying them make some useful discoveries. For if there are noxious qualities in certain plants, there must also be good ones—perhaps antidotes.

Finally, the poison and its purported antidote are specifically referred to in graphic terms in the old Code Pénal, Article 249 of which reads: "Est aussi qualifié attentat à la vie d'une personne, l'emploi qui sera fait contra elle de substances qui, sans donner la mort, produissent un éffet léthargique plus ou moins prolongé, de quelque manière que ces substances aient été administrées, quelles qu'en aient été les suite. Si par suite de cet état léthargique la personne a été inhumée, l'attentat sera qualifié assassinat" (Leyburn 1941, 164). This fascinating passage translates: "Also to be considered as attempted murder the use that may be made against any person of substances which, without causing actual death, produce a more or less prolonged lethargic coma. If after the administering of such substances the person has been buried the act shall be considered murder no matter what result follows."

Whereas the anthropologists remained equivocal, it appears that the Haitian government itself recognized the existence of the poison with some assurance. At the least the judicial system wasn't about to take any chances.

Although it now seems remarkable that reports of the poison were not investigated, there are in fact good historical reasons for the oversight. The rumors first appeared during a period when both foreign and Haitian social scientists trained in the traditions of cultural relativism and objective analysis were most anxious to promote the legitimacy of peasant institutions. These intellectuals were repelled by the sensational publications of an earlier decade that, in their minds, had both slanderously misrepresented the Haitian peasantry and rationalized the American occupation of 1915–34 (Bastien 1966).

The most notorious of these publications was a book, *The*

Magic Island, written by an American adventurer, William Seabrook. In it the author presents as fact the reputed use of nine zombies in the fields of the Haitian-American Sugar Company (HASCO). The story in brief is as follows:

One morning a certain Ti Joseph of Colombier appeared with a ragged band of docile men and women. It was a good year for sugar and the company needed cane cutters, and so the zombies went to work immediately with Ti Joseph pocketing their wages.

One day while Ti Joseph was away on business, his wife impulsively decided to take the zombies to see the procession at Croix de Bouquet. She fed them their breakfast of unsalted plaintains and led them into town.

The zombies paid little attention to the procession and the wife taking pity on them offered a small handful of sweets to each one. Little did she know the confections contained salted peanuts. The zombies woke with a dreadful cry and turned immediately back to the mountains. They reached their old settlement at Morne au Diable where they were recognized by their grieving families. But the zombies ignored their families and instead walked directly to the village cemetery, where in turn each dug up his grave, struggling to reenter the earth. The dismayed family members made a collection and bought a wanga to place a curse on Ti Joseph. Lest the spell be ineffective, they also hired a man to cut off his head (Seabrook 1929, 93–103).

On the surface this account was not unlike many zombie tales commonly heard in the Haitian countryside, but what made it potent was the context in which it was presented. For its time, Seabrook's was not a bad travel book, and in many ways the author was remarkably sympathetic to the peasants and the Vodoun religion. This sympathy, of course, only made it that much worse when he presented the story of Ti Joseph not as folklore but as fact. Seabrook went on to describe his own encounter with three reputed zombies, for which there was not a shred of evidence. *The Magic Island* created a furor among the Haitian intellectual elite, but it was not the only such publication.

Indeed, for some time American and foreign correspondents had indulged their readers' perverse infatuation with what had become known as the Black Republic, serving it up garnished with every conceivable figment of their imaginations. To Americans in particular, Haiti was like having a little bit of Africa next door—something dark and forboding, sensual and terribly naughty. These other popular books of the day, with such charming titles as *Cannibal Cousins* and *Black Baghdad*, cast the entire nation as a caricature, an impoverished land of throbbing drums, ruled by pretentious buffoons and populated by swamp doctors, licentious women, and children bred for the cauldron (Craige 1933, 1934; Loederer 1935; Wirkus and Dudley 1931). Most of these travelogues would have been soon forgotten had it not been for the peculiar and by no means accidental timing of their publication. Until the first of this genre appeared in 1884—Spenser St. John's *The Black Republic*, with its infamous account of a cannibalistic "Congo Bean Stew"—most books that dealt with Vodoun had simply emphasized its role in the slave uprising (MacKenzie 1971; Baskett 1971; Brown 1971; Franklin 1970). But these new and sensational books, packed with references to cult objects such as voodoo dolls that didn't even exist, served a specific political purpose. It was no coincidence that many of them appeared during the years of the American occupation (1915–34), or that every marine above the rank of sergeant seemed to land a publishing contract. There were many of these books, and each one conveyed an important message to the American public: any country where such abominations took place could find its salvation only through military occupation.

The Haitian intellectuals—in particular Louis Mars, Jean Price-Mars, Lorimer Denis, and young François Duvalier—were repelled by these publications. Referring, no doubt, to Seabrook and the others, Jules Faine wrote: "Such legends, circumstantially garbed and presented as actual facts by certain unscrupulous authors have served as the theme of books which have made a great commotion in foreign countries. Taking advantage of the credulity of a public avid for exotic matters, for mysteries, for the supernatural, these writers have gained in certain circles the greatest success of publicity" (Faine 1937, 303). The subject of zombies, which had figured so prominently in these sensational books, simply did not interest the intellectual elite. Indeed, it may fairly be said that for many years the sensitive subject was deemed unworthy of serious discussion. Individuals would respond to purported appearances of zombies on a case-by-case basis (Mars 1945, 1947), but no sustained, calm, and systematic study was undertaken that might lay to rest once and for all the troubling and embarrassing suggestions that zombies might be real. Louis Mars expressed the dominant intellectual sentiment of the time. Cases of zombification, he wrote, "merely rekindle the dying embers of archaic superstitious beliefs that were deeply rooted in the traditional culture of a people. [The] extension of psychiatry to the study of the collective behaviour of man may yet reveal the basic principles underlying the social problems of our time. Certainly social psychiatry stands a good chance of exploding the Zombi-psychology of the untutored Haitian peasant" (Mars 1945, 40).

Foreign investigators clearly shared these sentiments. James Leyburn mentions with evident conviction the reputed existence of a zombie poison, but then he concludes rather lamely: "In a mental atmosphere of credulity, coincidence often makes magic seem to work. The Haitian needs an explanation for his ills, for he lacks doctors, lawyers, insurance; the explanation of magic may be incorrect but it is the only one he has" (Leyburn 1941, 164–65). Incredibly, report after report noted the remarkable herbal and pharmacological skills as evidence of the sophisticated knowledge of the houngan (Herskovits 1975; Métraux 1972, 1953; Courlander 1960), and yet no one bothered to look for this widely rumored zombie poison.

To be sure, the case for the poison was suspect on several grounds. First, many of the reports appeared in the same publications that had garnered such a dubious reputation (St. John 1884). Second, many informants insisted that the actual raising of the zombie depended solely on the magical power of the bokor (Herskovits 1975; Leyburn 1941; Métraux 1972). This emic-etic confusion was not helped by suggestions that the poison came from a leaf, one side of which produced the toxin and the other the antidote (Taft 1938). What's more, despite the rich body of anecdotal lore about zombies, no physician had yet examined a genuine case (Mars 1945, 1947). Finally—and perhaps most important at a time when the field of ethnopharmacology was relatively young—no sample of the elusive poison had been obtained for scientific analysis. Zora Neale Hurston did not help her case by concluding: "The knowledge of the plants and the formulae are secret. They are usually kept in certain families, and nothing will induce the guardians of these ancient mysteries to divulge them" (Hurston 1981, 216).

Since Hurston, the few anthropologists to consider zombies have rejected the poison hypothesis out of hand. Erika Bourguignon, for example, in her functional analysis of zombies as folklore, suggests that the idea of a poison allows Haitians "to hold onto a magical belief yet give it the appearance of scientific respectability" (Bourguignon 1959, 40). Maximilien Laroche (1976) makes no mention of the poison but rather sees the figure of the zombie in purely symbolic terms as the "incarnation of fate." René Dépestre (1971) views zombies as a Haitian myth, which he simplistically interprets in Marxist terms: "It is not by chance that there exists in Haiti the myth of the zombi, that is, of the living dead, the man whose mind and soul have been stolen and who has been left only the ability to work. According to the myth, it was forbidden to put salt in the zombi's food since this could revitalize his spiritual energies. *The history of colonisation is the process of man's general zombification.* It is also the quest for a revitalising salt capable of restoring to man the use of his imagination and his culture" (Dépestre 1971, 20; emphasis mine).

RECENT CASES

Recently, however, scientific interest in zombies and the poison was rekindled by the appearance of three reputed zombies, one of whom may be the first potentially verifiable case. The first is a woman, Natagette Joseph, aged about sixty, who was reputedly killed over a land dispute in 1966. In 1979 she was recognized wandering about her home village by the police officer who thirteen years before, in the absence of a doctor, had pronounced her dead. The second case was a younger woman named Francina Illeus but called "Ti Femme," who was pronounced dead at the age of thirty on 23 February 1976. Before her death she had suffered digestive problems and had been taken to the Saint Michel de l'Atalaye Hospital. Several days after her release she died at home, her death was verified by a local magistrate, and a death certificate was prepared.

In April 1979 peasants from the Baptist mission at Passereine noticed Francina wandering around the market in Ennery, recognized her as a zombie, and reported her presence to the American in charge of the mission, Jay Ausherman. Ausherman traveled to Ennery and found an emaciated woman squatting in

Francina Illeus ("Ti Femme")

The house where Francina Illeus was pronounced dead

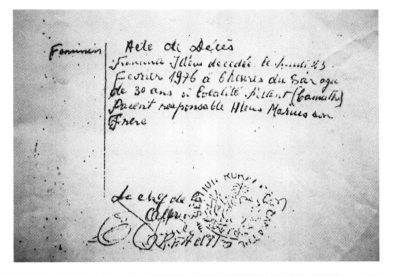

Death certificate of Francina Illeus

the market with her hands crossed like kindling before her face. Three years before, witnesses claimed, she had been pronounced dead after a short illness. The judge at Ennery, uncertain of what to do with someone who was legally dead, willingly granted custody to Ausherman, who in turn passed Francina over to Lamarque Douyon, a psychiatrist and physician and at the time the director of the Centre de Psychiatrie et Neurologie Mars-Kline in Port-au-Prince. Douyon diagnosed her as mute, malnourished, and negativistic (Douyon 1980). He also investigated her case in some detail and found, among other curious features, that Francina's mother had recognized her by a childhood scar she bore on her temple, and that, according to her family, a jealous husband had been responsible for her fate. The grave was excavated and found to be full of rocks.

The Francina Illeus case was not the first to be carefully examined by Douyon. In collaboration with Heinz Lehmann of McGill University and Nathan Kline, director of the Rockland State Research Institute in New York, Douyon had been systematically investigating all reported instances of zombification since 1961. Kline, himself a pioneer in the field of psychopharmacology, had been working intermittently in Haiti for over thirty years; the psychiatric institute in Port-au-Prince, in fact, bears his name.

Douyon's interest in the zombie phenomenon dated to a series of experiments he conducted in the late 1950s while completing his psychiatric residency at McGill University in Montreal, Canada. That period had been the heyday of early psychopharmacological research. Having discovered that certain mental disorders could be successfully treated with drugs, psychiatrists were actively experimenting with a number of potent psychotropic substances on human subjects under controlled circumstances. What Douyon observed during some of these experiments reminded him of accounts of zombies he had heard as a child; he recalled as well the prevalent belief among many Haitians that zombies were created by a poison that brought on a semblance of death from which the victim would eventually recover. By the time he returned to Haiti in 1961 to take up his position as director of the psychiatric institute, he was convinced that such a poison existed. His search for the reputed poison, however, had been in vain, as had his efforts to identify a legitimate case of zombification.

The cases of Natagette Joseph and Francina Illeus, although curious, were still no more substantial than many others that had periodically surfaced in the Haitian literature. However, the next case that Douyon discovered was another matter altogether, for the reputed victim had happened to die at an American-directed philanthropic institution that keeps precise and accurate records.

In the spring of 1962 a Haitian peasant, aged about forty, approached the emergency entrance of the Albert Schweitzer Hospital at Deschapelles in the Artibonite Valley in west-central Haiti. He was admitted under the name of Clairvius Narcisse at 9:45 P.M. on 30 April complaining of fever, body aches, and general malaise; he had also begun to spit blood. His condition deteriorated rapidly, and at 1:15 P.M. on 2 May he was pronounced dead by two attending physicians, one of them an American. His sister, Angelina Narcisse, was present at his bedside and immediately notified the family. Shortly after Narcisse's demise an elder sister, Marie Claire, arrived and identified the body, affixing her thumbprint to the official death certificate. The body was placed in cold storage for twenty hours, then taken for burial. At 10:00 A.M. on 3 May 1962, Clairvius Narcisse was buried in a small cemetery north of his village of L'Estere, and

*Lamarque Douyon, former director of the Centre de Psychiatrie et
Neurologie Mars-Kline in Port-au-Prince. The portraits behind him
are those of François Duvalier and Nathan Kline.*

ten days later a heavy concrete memorial slab was placed over the grave by the family.

Eighteen years later, in 1980, a man walked into the L'Estere marketplace and approached Angelina Narcisse. He introduced himself by a boyhood nickname of the deceased brother, a name that only intimate family members knew and that had not been used since the siblings were children. The man claimed to be Clairvius and stated that he had been made a zombie by his brother because of a land dispute. In Haiti, the official Napoleonic Code states that land must be divided among male offspring. According to Narcisse, he had refused to sell off his part of the inheritance, and his brother had in a fit of anger contracted out his zombification. Immediately following Clairvius's resurrection from the grave he was beaten and bound, then led away by a team of men to the north of the country, where for two years he worked as a slave with other zombies. Eventually the zombie master was killed and the zombies, freed from whatever force kept them bound to him, dispersed. Narcisse spent the next sixteen years wandering about the country, fearful of the vengeful brother. It was only upon hearing of his brother's death that he dared return to his village (Douyon 1980; Diederich 1983; Pradel and Casgha 1983).

The Narcisse case generated considerable publicity within Haiti and drew the attention of the BBC, which arrived in 1981 to film a short documentary based on his story. Douyon, meanwhile, had considered various ways to test the truth of Narcisse's claim. Exhuming the grave would have proved little. If the man was an imposter, he or conspirators could well have removed the bones. On the other hand, had Narcisse actually been taken from the grave as a zombie, those responsible might have substituted another body which by then would be impossible to identify (given the absence of dental records and the lack of facilities in Haiti). Instead, working directly with family members, Douyon designed a series of questions concerning Narcisse's childhood—questions that not even a close boyhood friend could have answered. These the man claiming to be Narcisse answered correctly. Over two hundred residents of L'Estere were certain that Narcisse had returned to the living. Moreover, there was no apparent social or economic incentive that would have led Narcisse or his family to perpetrate a fraud. By the time the BBC arrived, Douyon as well as Kline and Lehmann, who had them-

Clairvius Narcisse by his grave

selves studied the case, were convinced. To close the circle, the BBC took a copy of the death certificate to Scotland Yard and forensic specialists there verified that the fingerprints belonged to the sister, Marie Claire (Douyon 1980; Kline pers. comm.; Lehmann pers. comm.; Hulse, BBC, pers. comm.).

Douyon also took note of Clairvius Narcisse's medical dossier at the time of his death at the Schweitzer Hospital. His symptoms included pulmonary edema leading to acute respiratory difficulties, rapid loss of weight, hypothermia, uremia, and hypertension (Douyon 1980, pers. comm; Pradel and Casgha 1983). To this list I eventually added cyanosis and paresthesia, for both Narcisse and his sisters mentioned that his skin had turned blue and that he felt tingling sensations all over his body (Davis 1983a, 1983b, 1985).

Later, following one of my many interviews with Narcisse, I added the following preliminary comments:

> When representatives of two completely different realities meet, words like normal become relative. I was in no position to judge if Clairvius Narcisse had been permanently affected by his ordeal. Physically he appeared fit. He spoke slowly but clearly. When questioned about his experience he repeated basically the same account that I had heard from Nathan Kline. But he added certain extraordinary details. Before he died he said that his skin had come on fire, with the feeling of insects crawling beneath it. A scar he bore on his right cheek just to the edge of his mouth had been caused by a nail driven through the coffin. Quite incredibly he recalled remaining conscious throughout his ordeal, and although completely immobilised he had heard his sister weeping by his deathbed. He remembered his doctor pronouncing him dead. Both at and after his burial his overall sensation was that of floating above the grave. This was his soul, he claimed, ready to travel on a journey that would be curtailed by the arrival of the bokor and his assistants. He could not remember how long he had been in the grave by the time they arrived. He suggested three days. They called his name and the ground opened. He heard drums, a pounding, a vibration and then the bokor singing. He could barely see. They grabbed him, and began to beat him with a sisal whip. They tied him with a rope and

wrapped his body in black cloth. Bound and gagged he was
led away on foot by two men. For half the night they walked
north until their party was met by another which took custody of Narcisse. Travelling by day and hiding out by night,
Narcisse was passed from one team to the next until he
reached the sugar plantation that would be his home for two
years (Davis 1985, 65).

The evidence surrounding the personal history of Clairvius
Narcisse by no means constituted absolute proof that he had
been a zombie. His case, however, was by far the most provocative yet to enter the Haitian medical and ethnographic literature
(Douyon 1980; Davis 1983a, 1983b, 1983c, 1985; Diederich
1983). In addition to the regular features—Narcisse's personal
testimony as well as that of family and villagers—Douyon had
obtained both the official certificates of death and the medical
dossier that provided a complete description of his symptoms at
the time of his demise. Moreover, the reputed zombie's medical
and psychiatric history and his present condition had been thoroughly studied by Haiti's leading psychiatrist who, together with
two of the most respected of his North American colleagues, had
concluded that the case was legitimate (Douyon 1980; Kline
pers. comm.; Lehmann pers. comm.; Hulse, BBC, 1981).

One of the notable features of the Narcisse case was the
suggestion that he had been made a zombie by a bokor who had
used a drug—a folk preparation, it was suggested—that was
sprinkled across the threshold of the intended victim's doorway
and absorbed through the skin of the feet (Douyon 1980). No
pharmacologically active sample of the reputed poison had been
obtained, nor had the ingredients been identified.

Theoretically, at least, it was completely conceivable that a
drug might exist which, if administered in proper dosage and in
some tenable manner, would lower the metabolic state of the
victim to such a level that he might be considered dead. In fact,
however, the victim would remain alive and an antidote, properly
administered, could then restore him at the appropriate time.
The medical potential of such a drug could be considerable,
particularly in the field of anesthesiology.

Nevertheless, from a strictly medical point of view the plausibility of the Narcisse case was predicated not only upon the
existence of such a folk preparation, but on two other assump-

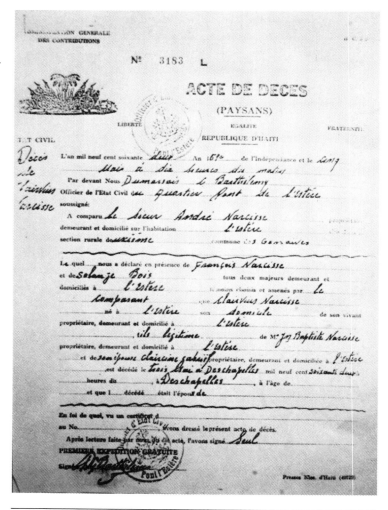

Death certificate of Clairvius Narcisse

tions. First, Narcisse or any other chosen victim would have to be able to survive at least six, and perhaps ten to twelve hours in a sealed coffin beneath the ground. And second, the state of apparent death induced by the drug would have had to be so profound as to fool the two highly trained physicians who had pronounced the victim dead. As it turns out, I did not have to delve far into the medical literature to discover that, under the proper circumstances, both these conditions could be readily met.

CHAPTER THREE

THE PROBLEM OF DEATH

A satisfactory means of diagnosing death has both obsessed and eluded man since earliest times. The Romans had so many difficulties that they officially fixed the interval between death and burial at eight days. The natural histories of Pliny the Elder tell of the consul Acilius, reputedly dead, who was placed on a pyre but awoke as the flames gathered around him. He was not saved. Similarly, Lucius was burned alive by mistake. Tuberus was more fortunate and was removed from the pyre at the last possible moment (MacKay 1880). There are similar reports in Plato's *Dialogues* and Plutarch's *Lives* (Watson 1974). The Renaissance Italian poet Petrarch lay in Ferrara in a state of trance for twenty hours and was about to be buried when a sudden change in temperature caused him to awaken (Kastenbaum and Aisenberg 1972). Abbé Prèvot, author of *Manon Lescaut*, is said to have been killed by a village physician who found his unconscious but living body in the forest and began an impromptu autopsy (MacKay 1880). G. E. MacKay also describes the case of Luigi Vittori, a carabineer in the pope's service, who was certified dead from asthma in a Rome hospital only to be discovered alive by another physician who held a lit candle beneath the victim's nose. Mistakes in the diagnosis of death were not limited to inexperienced doctors. Vesalius, the founder of modern anatomy and personal physician to both Charles V and Phillip II of Spain, carried out an autopsy on a man reputedly dead only to find the heart still beating. He was charged formally with homicide and taken before the tribunal of the Inquisition. Only the direct intervention of the king saved his life (Mant 1968).

Reports of misdiagnosed death occurred frequently throughout European history, climaxing in the late eighteenth and the nineteenth centuries. In 1742 a Paris physician, John Bruhier, documented fifty-two alleged examples of premature burial and seventy-two mistaken diagnoses of death (Bruhier-d'Ablaincourt

1742). A century later Fontenelle (1834) recorded forty-six cases of premature burial or misdiagnosis; Carré (1845) reported forty-six instances in which individuals who were pronounced dead recovered before their interment (Fontenelle and Carré cited in Mant 1968). A. K. Mant cites an extraordinary case in which conception occurred while the mother was reputedly dead. According to a report from a Professor Louis, whom Mant identifies as the "doyen of French medical jurisprudence," a monk stopped at the house where a young girl was laid out for burial and offered to spend the night in the room where the coffin was placed. He stripped the body and had intercourse with it. The following morning he had left; the girl was resuscitated as she was about to be interred, and nine months later this supposed virgin gave birth to a child (Mant 1968, 16).

In the late nineteenth century an epidemic of premature burials colored the popular press and confounded medical authorities. A typical report appeared in the *London Echo* in March 1896. Nicephorus Glycas, the Greek Orthodox metropolitan of Lesbos, was pronounced dead in his eightieth year. According to the traditions of his church, he was immediately garbed in his episcopal vestments and placed on a throne, where his body was exposed day and night to the faithful and guarded constantly by priests. On the second night the old man suddenly awoke and stared with amazement and horror at the parade of mourners at his feet. His priests, according to the report, were no less startled to realize that their leader had not been dead but had merely fallen into a deathlike trance. The impassioned *Echo* correspondent questioned what might have happened had the metropolitan been a layman and concluded that he would have been buried alive. A second popular account was that of a Reverend Schwartz, an Oriental missionary who was reportedly aroused from apparent death by his favorite hymn. The congregation celebrating his last rites was stunned to hear a voice from the coffin joining in on the refrain (MacKay 1880; Watson 1974).

Though today both of these cases may appear preposterous, at the time they were not only seriously discussed but also believed, and they helped fuel a hysterical fear of premature burial that swept late Victorian Europe. In 1905 an English physician and member of the Royal College of Surgeons edited a volume in which were documented 219 narrow escapes from premature burial, as well as 149 cases in which the body was actually interred while still alive. Also noted were 10 instances in which autopsies were erroneously performed on the living and 2 cases in which consciousness returned to a "corpse" during the process of embalming (Hadwen 1905). In France, meanwhile, S. Icard documented in detail a dozen cases of misdiagnosis; in one instance the revival occurred in the midst of funeral ceremonies and in the presence of several physicians who independently reported the case (Icard 1897, cited in Dewisme 1957).

Many prominent citizens of the era were not about to take any chances. Hans Christian Anderson constantly carried a note in his pocket that contained instructions on what should be done with his body in the event of his death. English novelist Wilkie Collins placed a similar precautionary note by his bedside table each night. So did Fyodor Dostoyevski, who urged that his burial be delayed five days lest his apparent death be but a trance. Certain leading members of the British aristocracy took more drastic measures, which, incidentally, were remarkably similar to certain Haitian practices that the nobles' countrymen would no doubt have condemned. The Vodounist, as we have seen, fearing that a family member will be raised as a zombie, has been reported to drive a blade through the heart of the dead. Fearing premature burial, noted antiquary Francis Douce requested in his will that his surgeon, Sir Anthony Carlisle, be permitted to sever the head from his body. So did a certain Harriet Martineau. A well-known actress of the era, Ada Cavendish, left instructions in her will that her jugular be sliced. Lady Burton, widow of the famous African explorer and writer, Sir Richard Burton, provided that her heart be pierced with a needle. Bishop Berkeley, Daniel O'Connell, and Lord Lytton had similar fears and ordered that their burials be delayed, and that one or more of their veins be opened so that their blood would drain and thus assure that they were really dead (Hadwen 1905; Kastenbaum and Aisenberg 1972).

By the turn of this century, fear of premature burial had grown into an overriding public concern (Hartmann 1895; Fletcher 1895). The subject was discussed in all the learned medical journals (See 1880; Anon. 1884; Anon. 1898), and in England it generated parliamentary inquiries that led to the Burial Act of 1900, which among its many statutes specified the length of time that had to transpire between the pronouncement of death and actual interment (Hadwen 1905). On the continent, prizes were offered for the discovery of a conclusive sign of death. In France in 1890 a certain Dr. Maze was awarded the prestigious Prix Dusgate and twenty-five hundred francs simply for asserting that the only reliable sign of death was putrefaction (Mant 1968). The earnest scientific interest in establishing the difference between real and apparent death is evident in an academic textbook on the subject published in 1890, the bibliography of which lists no fewer than 418 citations (Gannal 1890).

Just how serious a threat premature burial was in the late nineteenth century is uncertain. Even at the time many insisted that the reports were greatly exaggerated (Hadwen 1905). But even the most strident of critics did not question whether premature burial occurred, but rather how often and under what circumstances. William See, a professor of medicine, wrote a strong critique of some of the more sensational articles of the day, but he qualified his words by concluding: "The only motive in preparing this paper has been not to contradict the fact that premature burials may have taken place, but to place renewed confidence in the ability of the ordinary general practitioner to recognize the distinction between a state of trance and a state of death, and to induce a disregard of the idle stories of ignorant and superstitious persons upon premature burials" (See 1880, 520). Elsewhere he added: "That the trance state has been mistaken for death, and that premature burials have taken place seems to be fully recognized in the system of morgues and dead-houses in various parts of Europe where bodies are so placed that the slightest movements will be brought to the notice of attendants" (See 1880, 527). Perhaps he was referring to an enormous Gothic building in Munich where the dead lay in long rows, all connected by cords leading to bells in the central office of the guardian (Watson 1974; Hadwen 1905).

Guesses at the numbers of individuals prematurely buried were made by a number of scholars. LeGuern speculated that some sixteen hundred people annually, or two per every one thousand deaths, were prematurely buried in France. Goubert, somewhat more reasonable, suggested a figure of one per thousand. The author of a study in the United States actually disinterred a hundred graves and concluded that one in fifty cadavers showed signs of having been prematurely buried (LeGuern and Goubert cited in Dewisme 1957). In 1899 Count Karnice-Karnicki, a Russian nobleman and chamberlain to the czar, proposed to estimate the number of premature burials that had occurred since the dawn of the Christian era. Using an arbitrary figure of one per thirty thousand deaths, he concluded, rather sensationally, that some four million unfortunate souls had undergone this ordeal. Whether all these figures represented anything more than the authors' fears is difficult to say, but the very fact that the computations were seriously attempted is as important as their conclusions.

Perhaps nothing symbolizes the tenor of the times better than the enormous popularity of another of Count Karnice-Karnicki's contributions: his invention of a most extraordinary apparatus designed to prevent premature burial once and for all. Introduced just before the turn of the century, it was a simple contraption, efficient and inexpensive enough to be well within reach of rich and poor alike. For the truly destitute, the invention was available for rent. It consisted of a hermetically sealed box and a long tube that would be fixed into an aperture in the coffin as soon as it was lowered into the ground. On the chest of the dead person was placed a large glass ball attached to a spring linked to the sealed box. With the slightest movement of the glass ball, as would occur if breathing began, the spring would be released, causing the lid of the box to fly open and admit both light and air to the buried coffin. At the same time, the spring initiated a mechanical chain reaction worthy of Rube Goldberg. A flag sprang four feet above the box, a bell began to ring and continued for thirty minutes and an electric lamp was ignited. The long tube was envisioned not only as a means of admitting oxygen, but also as a megaphone to amplify the presumably weak voice of the almost-dead. Not a hundred years ago this peculiar apparatus was heralded as a technological breakthrough. Many thousands of Frenchmen left specific instructions in their wills that it was to be placed on their tombs. In the United States the device was so popular that societies were formed to promote its subsidized use (Hadwen 1905).

At the root of what now can only be termed hysterical concerns lay the quite legitimate problem of diagnosing death. Of course, the fundamental signs of death have always been known, and they have not changed. Briefly, they are cessation of respiration and heartbeat, changes in the eye, insensibility to electrical stimuli, rigor mortis, pallor, hypostasis, and relaxation of the sphincters (Mant 1968). The problem has always been that no one of these signs is foolproof, and once that fact is recognized and admitted, a floodgate of possibilities opens. One can begin with respiration.

Traditionally, breathing was checked by means of a feather placed beneath the nose, or by placing a mirror below the nostrils, but from the earliest medical writings on death, both methods have been exposed as unreliable (Watson 1974; Mant 1968). For one thing, breathing may be carried on by such gentle or intermittent movements of the diaphragm as to be imperceptible. Also, the absence of respiration may represent merely suspension of the activity, not the cessation. B. K. Anand showed that a yogi could consciously reduce his oxygen consumption to levels that would prove lethal to an ordinary person (Anand et al. 1961). Then there is the famous case of a Colonel Townsend which, in the late nineteenth century, was widely quoted not only in the press but also in academic textbooks of medical jurisprudence (Hadwen 1905; Kastenbaum and Aisenberg 1972; Herbert 1961). According to reports of a panel of physicians called upon to witness the event, this British officer willingly reduced his heart rate, stopped his breathing, and entered a self-induced trance or, as some described it, a state of suspended animation. Heartbeat ceased, respiration stopped, and the entire body assumed the icy chill and rigidity of death. The color drained from Colonel Townsend's face; his eyes became glazed and fixed. After he had been comatose for thirty minutes, the physicians actually certified him dead and prepared to go home. As they did so, Townsend began to recover slowly, and by the next day he was well enough to repeat his feat.

A second traditional sign of clinical death is the cessation of pulse. This, again, is complicated by data from India suggesting that individuals practicing certain conscious techniques have been able to gain control over normally unconscious processes. A French cardiologist working in India found several individuals who could stop their hearts on demand (Wallace and Benson 1972). Watson reports observing a fakir monitored by an electrocardiograph deliberately stop his heart for twelve minutes. His explanation: "A stimulus to the vagus nerve which carries instructions from the hindbrain to the heart seemed to be produced by what yogis call the *valsalva* technique, which involves building up increased pressure on the chest by inhaling deeply and bending sharply forward" (Watson 1974, 40). These reports are difficult to assess, but they do suggest that the body is able to survive objective conditions that would normally be considered lethal. Moreover, these conditions could be approximated with deep narcosis. Any drug that induces severe hypotension could result in an unreadable pulse.

Abnormally low body temperatures are often a good indication of death, but here again there are important exceptions. Sudden death from lightning or internal injuries, for example, may not result in any temperature change for many hours, whereas asthma attacks quickly bring on deathlike temperatures in the living (Watson 1974). The body temperatures of those who die from cholera, tetanus, and smallpox actually go up, and in virtually all bodies the initially low temperature rapidly goes back to normal due to the heat generated during decomposition. At the other extreme, some people have been pulled out of frozen lakes or snowbanks and recovered from body temperatures registered as low as 17°C. During hypothermic surgery, the body temperature of the patient is regularly lowered to 16°C (Mant 1968; Watson 1974). Deep narcosis may also generate a profound drop in body temperature, a fact well known to modern pharmacologists—and not lost on Shakespeare. "No warmth or breath shall testify thou liv'st" were Friar Laurence's words to Juliet as he gave her the potion.

At clinical death there are changes that occur in the eye, but once again these also take place under certain conditions in the living. The eyelids, for example, become equally tractable after death or during deep sleep, poisonings, asphyxia, and drunkenness. Shining a light into the eye is of little immediate use because the muscles of the iris continue to contract for several hours following death. The pallor of death results when the blood stands still and gravity causes the red blood cells to settle, leaving behind a clear serum that shows through the skin as a pale color. Unfortunately, the serum is visible only in light-skinned individuals. The blood does begin to clot at death, but small amounts of the chemical that prevents clotting in life are produced even after death. Hence even hours after death, the blood may still be fluid (Watson 1974; Mant 1968; Kastenbaum and Aisenberg 1972).

Another classic symptom of death is rigor mortis caused by the stiffening of the muscle fibers, which in turn is due to the coagulation of muscle protein that occurs shortly after death. The process begins in the small intestines and then moves to the heart, the diaphragm and the muscles of the face, showing up in the eyelids about an hour after death. It progresses to the jaw and after twelve hours is apparent in all the long muscles of the body. After thirty to thirty-six hours the muscles relax again. The process can, however, be delayed by stress or fright, which leave high levels of adrenalin in the blood (Watson 1974). As a symptom of death, rigor mortis is relatively useless in the case of Clairvius Narcisse. No physicians examined him after he was pronounced dead, and no one did at the time of his burial (Douyon 1980, pers. comm., Hulse pers. comm., Diederich 1983, Pradel and Casgha 1983).

There are only three broad possible causes of death: asphyxia, or respiratory failure (through paralysis or strangulation); circulatory failure (shock, hemorrhage, heart disease); and coma or nervous failure (brain injury, poisons, drugs) (Mant 1968; Watson 1974). In not one of these are there characteristic external symptoms that on their own can be taken as a sure sign of death. Moreover, the cessation of bodily functions, or clinical death, may occur some time before the breakdown of the cells producing those functions. Under normal circumstances, a person is as dead today as he would have been five centuries ago if his heart ceases to beat for five minutes. But when a person is subjected to an abnormal environment or is placed into an abnormal state as a result of drugs or disease, exceptions to any of the accepted criteria of death may occur. In fact, there are only two certain indicators of absolute death. One is by no means infallible and involves a brain scan and cardiogram, procedures requiring expensive machinery and trained technicians. The other—and the only one that is certain—is putrefaction (Mant 1968). When bacteria and fungi begin to proliferate in the intestines, they produce a discoloration on the stomach, gray patches that gradually turn to green and produce a foul smell. That process requires time—more time than passed between Narcisse's reputed demise and his burial the next morning.

It is precisely to avoid the smell of death that Haitians, in their tropical climate, hastily bury their dead. Dewisme cites a case in which a man fell ill and was pronounced dead. Torrential rains prevented the arrival of important relatives, thereby delaying the wake and subsequent burial for more than a day. When after twenty-four hours there were no visible signs of putrefaction, certain family members grew suspicious and the funeral was temporarily postponed. In the middle of the second night the man came back to life. Later it was discovered that he had offended a bokor and his life had been threatened (Dewisme 1957, 133).

The physicians who examined Clairvius Narcisse were no strangers to death. The Schweitzer Hospital caters to the most destitute and seriously ill in Haiti. Procedures that might have shown Narcisse to be alive were, for reasons of practical necessity, not implemented. The foregoing discussion is not intended to imply that the physicians employed by the Schweitzer Hospital misdiagnose death with any frequency. What that discussion does suggest is that a cursory examination of the vital signs of a patient immobilized by a powerful sedative drug could fail to detect evidence of life. If this occurred, it was not the first such case. Physicians working under considerably less difficult conditions have made the same error. On 11 December 1963, thirty-five-year-old Elsie Waring collapsed at home in London and was taken to Willesden General Hospital, where three doctors certified her dead on arrival. Ten hours later she gasped and began to breathe again while being lifted into her coffin at the Kilburn Public Mortuary. The story was reported the following morning by the *Daily Telegraph* and caused some concern among public health officials (Mant 1968; Watson 1974). On 3 November 1967, a severely injured American soldier, apparently dead, was taken to a hospital, and efforts to resuscitate him were abandoned after forty-five minutes. His body was sent to the mortuary, where the embalmer noticed that he was still alive. Eventually, the soldier recovered and was flown back to the United States where he lives today (Mant 1968).

A. K. Mant (1968) describes his own experiences during the London blitz when he was called upon to examine a pile of air-raid victims previously certified dead. He discovered three individuals living. Taylor's *Medical Jurisprudence* records a recent instance of an elderly woman brought to a hospital and examined by a physician who, finding her cold and without a pulse, pronounced her dead. It was only later, as she lay naked on the mortuary table, that it was noticed that she was still breathing (Simpson 1965). Watson (1974) cites a postmortem operation at the New York mortuary that was interrupted just as the first incision was made when it became evident that the patient was still alive. This occurred in 1964.

The Clairvius Narcisse case, of course, is based upon the assumption that a sedative drug of some sort may bring on a state of apparent death. J. Hamburger (1966) reported two cases of complete recovery after an EEG (electroencephalogram) failed to detect any electrical potential in the patients' brains for several hours. Death had been diagnosed, but it turned out that both patients suffered from severe barbiturate poisoning. K. Simpson describes the case of a seventy-eight-year-old woman who was found apparently dead and with an empty container of sleeping pills by her bedside. Her body was taken to the public morgue, where six hours later a police officer attempting to identify the corpse discovered that she was breathing (cited in Mant 1968). Finally, on 28 February 1970 the *Times* of London reported an extraordinary case in which a team of English physicians experimenting with a portable cardiograph at the Sheffield Mortuary detected signs of life in a young woman previously certified dead from a drug overdose (Watson 1974).

Dramatic as they are, these examples only suggest that a severely drugged person *could* be misdiagnosed as dead. But the Narcisse case also assumes that such an individual would be able to survive up to ten hours in a sealed coffin. His ability to do so would depend directly on his level of metabolic activity. In a series of papers published in the *Indian Journal of Medical Research*, a team of physicians proved that certain Indian fakirs can consciously reduce their metabolic function and voluntarily decrease their consumption of oxygen (Anand and Chhina 1960; Anand et al. 1961). A yogi who claimed to have lived for a month in a sealed underground pit was placed in an airtight box $(6' \times 4' \times 4')$ where he remained for ten hours. Stewart Wolf (1967) refers to a yogi who stayed in a sealed coffin underwater for several hours. Deep narcosis induced by a folk preparation could well achieve the same results as these cases.

It is important to note that in the instances described above, as in a case of an individual being buried alive, damage due to oxygen deprivation would be progressive. If certain brain cells are completely without oxygen for even a few seconds, they die and can never recover their functions, for there is no regeneration of brain tissue. The more primitive parts of the brain—those that control vital functions—can endure greater abuse. Under certain conditions an individual might lose personality or the part of the brain that deals with thought and voluntary movement and yet survive as a vegetable because the vital centers are intact (Mant 1968). This condition fits folk descriptions of the zombies—bodies without character, without will.

Any drug that induced a hypothermic state would also greatly reduce oxygen needs. At the low body temperatures reached during hypothermic surgery, circulation and respiration cease to function and the patient must be maintained by a heart-lung machine. Oxygen requirements to the brain are greatly reduced; following surgery, when the body is rewarmed, the vital functions start to operate spontaneously and normal faculties are restored. By traditional definitions the patient has been dead; but in fact he or she has merely been in a state of induced hibernation or suspended animation (Mant 1968). Finally, it should be noted that no two individuals would necessarily respond to the reputed drug in the same fashion. Depending on the dose, the physiological strength and condition of the victim, and the time between administration of the drug and disinterment, there might be a variety of results. Although undoubtedly many would die, either from the toxicity of the drug or from suffocation in the coffin, it is at least theoretically possible that some would survive either in a damaged condition, as with Francina Illeus, or in full control of their faculties, as in the case of Clairvius Narcisse.

THE IDENTITY OF THE POISON: PREVIOUS REPORTS AND AN INITIAL HYPOTHESIS

Clearly the elusive poison so frequently mentioned in the popular and ethnographic literature held the key to both the Narcisse case and the zombie mystery in general. Without it, one was obliged to consider the phenomenon as fable, the Narcisse case itself a fraud. If such a poison could be found, however, it would offer far more than just a pharmacological means by which individuals could be made to appear dead. It would suggest, for example, the existence of a network of men and women who actually created the poison and decided how, when, and to whom it should be administered; these issues would undoubtedly involve explanations rooted in the very structure and beliefs of the

Haitian peasant society. The discovery of such a poison promised to open up ethnographic vistas of considerable significance. It is against the backdrop of this potential that the few known efforts to identify the poison stand in stark relief.

C. H. Dewisme turned to Jamaican literature for clues. He found in the journals of three adventurers independent reports on a practice of the Obeah priests that sounded suspiciously like the reputed use of the zombie poison in Haiti (Gardner 1873; Long 1774; Lewis 1843). The Obeah priest who wanted to display his power to his followers was said to prepare an infusion of rum and the macerated leaves of a plant known as the Branched Calalue, *Solanum nigrum* L. (Ayensu 1978), which is identified in the same passage as both a solanum and a member of the Cucurbitaceae native to Guyana (Dewisme 1957, 126). The recipient of this preparation was spun around by the priest until the potion took effect, whereupon he or she would collapse to the ground unconscious. For several hours the victim would lie without pulse or heartbeat, until the juice of another herb was squeezed between the lips. A paste of other unknown herbs was dabbed onto the eyes and tips of the fingers, and in time the victim would recover completely.

Another unidentified plant of considerable interest is mentioned in the account of African travelers F. G. Carnochan and H. C. Adamson. They saw the powder of the root of the kinoliola plant given to a man who subsequently danced about the village with a weighted object hanging from a thorn driven through his tongue. Carnochan himself tried a pinch of the powder and described his reactions: "I lost all power to move. I could not think. I could not feel. My imagination left me. I experienced no hallucinations or dreams. I had no desire to sleep. I had none of the mental or physical reactions generally associated with narcotics. For two hours I sat on a stool and stared into a mirror. Then, in what seemed like moments later I felt perfectly normal" (Carnochan and Adamson 1938). Unfortunately, the travelers made no attempt to identify this remarkable plant.

Dewisme (1957) reports that a houngan in Haiti, just before he died, gave the name of the plant used in the zombie poison to a priest who claimed it was a species of cactus. Unfortunately, the priest himself died without revealing the precise identification of this purported ingredient. With complete botanical naiveté, Edna Taft (1938) suggested that the poison named *tuer-lever* was based on a narcotic, possibly coca (*Erythroxylum coca* Lam.). Zora Neale Hurston (1981), for her part, concluded that the plant ingredients would never be known, a supposition apparently confirmed by the efforts of Nathan Kline (pers. comm.), who for over thirty years attempted intermittently and unsuccessfully to obtain the formula of the preparation and antidote.

In formulating an initial hypothesis I considered a number of factors. Every report dealing with the means of administering the drug suggested that it was sprinkled across the doorway of the intended victim's house (Kline pers. comm.; Douyon 1980, pers. comm.). This seemed unlikely. Although in East Africa certain tribes surreptitiously administer poisons by coating spiny fruits and placing them along footpaths (Dalziel 1948; Sofowora 1982), without at least this type of mechanical aid it was difficult to imagine any substance, however toxic, passing through the callused feet of the peasant. It was also unclear how the sorcerer, by merely placing the poison on the ground trod upon by many people, would ensure that only the intended victim suffered. Nevertheless, all reports coming out of Haiti were adamant on the method of administration. If they were correct, then the principal chemical constituents had to be topically active. From descriptions of the wandering zombies, it appeared likely that the drug induced a prolonged psychotic state, while the initial dose had to be capable of causing a deathlike stupor. Because in all likelihood the poison and its reputed antidote were organically derived, their source had to be a plant or animal currently found in Haiti. Finally, whatever these substances might prove to be, they had to be extraordinarily potent.

Lamarque Douyon offered the first plausible candidate when he suggested that the poison was based on a species of datura, which he misnamed as "datura methel" (Douyon 1980, 21). Douyon based his opinion on two observations (Douyon pers. comm.). First, another species found in Haiti—*Datura stramonium*—had the provocative vernacular name of *concombre zombi* —the zombie's cucumber (Brutus and Pierre-Noel 1960). Second, while working in the laboratory of Ewen Cameron at the Allen Institute in Montreal, Douyon had tested a number of plants associated with zombie folklore, and he found that subcutaneous and intraperitoneal administrations to mice of a solution based on datura (species unidentified) brought on a catatonic state that lasted three hours (Douyon 1980, pers. comm.). This result, though suggestive, was by no means definitive because any number of plant extracts, injected into mice in sufficient concentration and quantity, might cause the same condition. Moreover, no documented zombie preparation and its ingredients had been obtained. A crude sample of a reputed zombie poison, which was sent to the Rockland State Research Institute for analysis, proved to be completely inert (Kline pers. comm.). In fact, the only clues that implicated datura were its common name and the extraordinary psychoactive properties of the plant itself. At the onset of the investigation, these unique properties appeared to be suggestive enough.

At least three species of datura are native to or have been naturalized in Haiti—*Datura metel* L., *D. innoxia* Miller, and *D. stramonium* L. (Moscoso 1943)—and all are violently psychoactive. They owe their pharmacological activity to the presence of four tropane alkaloids—hyoscine (scopolamine), hyoscyamine, atropine, and nor-hyoscine—which block neurotransmission in the parasympathetic nervous system (Schultes and Hofmann 1980). The result of ingesting these compounds is an anticholinergic syndrome characterized by fever, delirium, hallucinations, agitation, and persistent memory disturbances leading to complete amnesia (McHenry and Hall 1978). The early clinical symptoms, after the ingestion of as few as nine leaves of the plant, are agitation, paranoia, disorientation, toxic delirium, and functional psychosis. A large dose may result in a complete inability to move followed by coma, convulsions, and death (Hall et al. 1978). In even moderate doses, datura brings on a burning thirst, sensations of the skin being on fire, and mad, delirious flights of the imagination that may quite literally lead to visions of hellfire. A common secondary cause of death among those under its influence is drowning—the result of individuals' stumbling into deep water in a futile attempt to slake their thirst. Indeed, it is for good reasons that datura has been called the drug of choice of "poisoners, criminals and black magicians" (Weil 1980, 160).

That the plant is capable of inducing stupor is suggested by the name itself, which is derived from the *dhatureas*, bands of thieves in ancient India who used it to drug their intended victims (Fluckiger and Hanbury 1879; Safford 1920). A similar use of the plant has been recorded elsewhere in India (Lewin 1931; Folkard 1884) and also in Nepal (Hooker 1855), Peru (Schleiffer 1973), Java (Schleiffer 1979), Tanzania, Indo-China (Watt and

Breyer-Brandwijk 1962), and Malaysia (Burkhill 1935). In the sixteenth century the Portuguese explorer Christoval Acosta found that Hindu prostitutes were so adept at using the seeds of the plant that they gave it in doses corresponding to the number of hours they wished their poor victims to remain unconscious (Taylor 1965). A later traveler to the Indies, Johann Albert de Mandelslo, noted in the mid-seventeenth century that women, closely watched by their husbands yet tormented by their passion for the novel Europeans, drugged their mates with datura and then "prosecuted their delights," even in the presence of their husbands, "who sat utterly stupefied with their eyes wide open" (Schleiffer 1979, 158).

In the New World, Padre Bernabe Cobo also recorded the use of datura to knock out an unsuspecting victim: "Not long ago, it happened in the kingdom of Peru that a man whom I knew was walking with a companion who, having plans to rob my friend, gave him chamaico (probably *D. innoxia*) drink. This caused the man to lose his mind and to become so enraged that, naked save for his shirt, he started to throw himself into the river. He was seized like a mad man and restrained. For two days, he remained in this condition without regaining consciousness" (Schleiffer 1973, 117). In both the New and the Old worlds, species of datura or one of its close relatives in the nightshade family (Solanaceae) have long been employed as adjuncts in religious ceremonies involving human sacrifice. In India, preparations of *Datura metel* were used by the Thugs (worshipers of Kali, the goddess of fertility and death) to stupefy sacrificial victims (Hansen 1978). Similarly, the pre-Columbian Chibcha in the highlands of northwestern South America administered a species of *Brugmansia* to wives and slaves of dead kings, before burying them alive with their deceased masters (Lockwood 1979).

Datura is also topically active. Sorcerers among the Yaqui Indians of northern Mexico anoint their genitals, legs, and feet with a salve based on crushed datura leaves and thus experience the sensation of flight (Castaneda 1972). Richard Evans Schultes (pers. comm.) has suggested that the Yaqui may have acquired this practice from the Spaniards, for throughout medieval Europe, witches commonly rubbed their bodies with hallucinogenic ointments made from belladonna (*Atropa belladonna*), mandrake (*Mandragora officinarum*), henbane (*Hyoscyamus niger*), and datura

(*Datura metel, D. stramonium*). In fact, much of the behavior associated with the witches is as readily attributable to these drugs as to any spiritual communion with demons. A particularly efficient means of self-administering the drug, for women, is through the moist tissue of the vagina; the witch's broomstick or staff was considered a most effective applicator. Our own popular image of the haggard woman on a broomstick comes from the medieval belief that the witches rode their staffs each midnight to the sabbat, the orgiastic assembly of demons and sorcerers. In fact, it now appears that their journey was not through space, but across the hallucinatory landscape of their own minds (Harner 1973; Hansen 1978).

The initial pharmacological evidence in the search for the zombie potion was provocative. Datura was topically active and, in relatively modest dosages, induced hallucinations and delusions, followed by confusion, disorientation, and amnesia. Excessive doses resulted in stupor and death. In at least one instance the solanaceous alkaloids appeared to have caused a permanent condition of schizophrenia (Knab n.d.[b]).

There was another, intuitive reason to implicate datura in the zombie phenomenon. Among many traditional peoples, life is conceptually divided into stages beginning with birth and progressing through initiation, marriage, and finally death. The transition from one stage to the next is often marked by important ritualistic activity. The account of Narcisse's reputed resurrection from the grave was a kind of passage rite itself—a perverse inversion of the natural processes of life and death. Perhaps more than any other drug, datura is associated with such transitional moments of passage, of initiation and death. The Luiseña Indians of southern California, for example, felt that all youths had to undergo datura narcosis during their puberty rites in order to become men (Dubois 1908). The Algonquin of northeastern North America also employed datura, calling it *wysoccan*. At puberty, adolescent males were confined in special longhouses and for two or three weeks ate nothing but the drug. During the course of their extended intoxication the youths forgot what it was to be a boy and learned what it meant to be a man (Schleiffer 1973). In South America the Jivaro, or Axuaro, give a potion called *maikua* to young boys when, at the age of six, they must seek their soul. If a boy is fortunate, his soul will appear to him in the form of a large pair of creatures, often animals such as jaguars or anaconda. Later the soul will enter his body (Karsten 1935; Harner 1973).

Many Amerindian peoples closely associate datura with death. In parts of highland Peru a close relative, *Brugmansia sanguinea*, is called *huaca*—the Quechua name for grave—because of the belief that those intoxicated with the plant are able to divine the location of the tombs of their ancestors (Lockwood 1979). The Zuni of the American Southwest chew datura during rain ceremonies, often placing the powdered roots in their eyes as they beseech the spirits of the dead to intercede with the gods for rain (Stevenson 1915). Perhaps more than any other clue, it was this connection between datura and the forces of death and darkness that offered the first indication of the makeup of the zombie poison.

Attention naturally focused on *Datura stramonium*, the species known in Haiti as the zombie's cucumber. The origin of this species is uncertain, with some botanists claiming an American origin (Schultes and Hofmann 1980) and others suggesting that the plant was native to Asia but became widely dispersed throughout Europe and Africa long before the time of Columbus (DeCandolle 1885; Safford 1920). Part of the confusion is due to the pantropical distribution of the genus, as well as some early errors in nomenclature and taxonomy (Safford 1920; Emboden 1972). The exact botanical origins of the species are not of great concern here; without doubt *Datura stramonium* was widely dispersed throughout Africa by the colonial era, and the people there, already familiar with such native species as *D. metel*, had recognized the pharmacological properties that both plants shared. The Hausa of Nigeria used the seeds to heighten the intoxicating effect of ritual beverages. The drug was given to Fulani youths to excite them in the Sharo contest, the ordeal of manhood (Dalziel 1948). Tribal leaders in Tongo administered a drink of its leaves and the root of the potent fish poison *Lonchocarpus capassa* to disputants who appeared before them for a settlement. Datura has been used as an ordeal poison in Zimbabwe (Watt and Breyer-Brandwijk 1962) and implicated in criminal poisonings in Zanzibar, South Africa, and Kenya (Verdcourt and Trump 1969). In many parts of West Africa the use of *Datura stramonium* in criminal poisonings still takes a unique form: women breed beetles, feed them on datura leaves and, in turn, use the feces to kill unfaithful lovers (Watt and Breyer-Brandwijk 1962).

The origins of the Haitians suggested at least the possibility that the poison, as well as the reputed antidote, would be found in Africa. Given the evidence that implicated *concombre zombi*, it was of some significance that the recognized medical antidote for datura poisoning is derived from a West African plant. The substance is physostigmine, a drug first isolated from the Calabar bean (*Physostigma venenosum* Balf.), a climbing liana that grows in swampy coastal areas of West Africa from Sierra Leone south and east as far as the Cameroons (Goodman and Gilman 1970). It is especially well known on the Calabar coast near the Gulf of Guinea at the mouth of the Niger River, precisely the region from which many of the forefathers of the Haitian people embarked as slaves for the plantations of the New World.

The eighteenth-century French plantation owners of Saint Domingue chose their slaves with some care. The carnage on the plantations was horrendous, and as the planters found it cheaper to bring in adult Africans than to raise slaves from birth, they had to import prodigious numbers. In a mere twelve years between 1779 and 1790, for example, the slave ships that plied the coast of Africa from Sierra Leone to Mozambique unloaded 313,200 slaves in Saint Domingue (James 1963; Curtin 1969). Although these unfortunate individuals came from virtually every corner of the continent, the plantation owners clearly had certain preferences. The Senegalese were valued for their superior morality and taciturn character—an ironic assessment for a slaver to make—whereas the people from Sierra Leone and the Ivory and Gold coasts were considered a stubborn group likely to revolt and desert (Simmons 1956b). The Ibos, from the southern Slave Coast of what is now Nigeria, worked well but were prone to suicide. The people of the Congo and Angola were highly regarded, and large numbers of them were imported. But it was the peoples bought along the Slave Coast who were preferred above all others, and much of the European slave trade concentrated there. Such was the scale of the trade that in the kingdom of Dahomey it became a national industry, and the economy of the entire country was based on annual expeditions against neighboring peoples (Herskovits 1938, 1975; Métraux 1972). Many of the captured victims—Nagos, Mahis, and Aradas of the western Yoruba among others—were taken down the Niger, and there they fell into the hands of a notorious and opportunistic tribe of traders, the Efik of Old Calabar (Forde 1956).

Originally fishermen, the Efik were ideally situated near the estuary of the Niger River to take advantage of the bitter competition for slaves. The prevailing winds and currents forced all ships returning to Europe or the Americas from the Ivory and Gold coasts to pass eastward toward the Slave Coast and close to the shores of Efik lands (Holmstedt 1972). As avaricious middlemen who were soon equipped with European arms, the Efik came to control the entire trade with the hinterland; their name, in fact, is derived from an Ibibio-Efik word meaning "oppress," a name they received from those neighboring tribes on the lower Calabar and Cross rivers whom the Efik prevented from establishing direct contact with the Europeans. They demanded lines of credit and were regularly entrusted with trade items—salt, cotton cloth, iron, brass, and copper—valued in the thousands of pounds sterling. In addition to exchanging goods for slaves, the Europeans had to pay a duty for the privilege of trading with the Efik chiefs. Though some of the slave ships anchored off the coast for up to a year, no European was ever permitted to touch shore; they could only wait, sometimes for months, to pick up their cargo (Forde 1956; Simmons 1956a; Jones 1956).

Each major Efik settlement was ruled outwardly by an *obong* or chief, who enforced laws, mediated in disputes, and led the armed forces in times of war. Besides this secular authority, however, there was a second and perhaps more powerful social and political force, a secret society called the Egbo or Leopard Society. The Egbo was a male, hierarchical association consisting of several ranks, each of which had a distinctive costume. Although the Egbo Society and the secular authority were institutionally separate, in practice powerful individuals of the tribe sat in council for both groups. Fear of the clandestine and mysterious Egbo was often exploited by members of the secret society themselves, and the obong, the secular chief, invariably ranked high in the society (Holmstedt 1972; Forde 1956; Simmons 1956a).

Under a secret council of community elders that constituted the supreme judicial authority, the Leopard Society promulgated and enforced laws, judged important cases, recovered debts, and protected the property of its members (Jones 1956). It enforced its laws with a broad range of sanctions: it could impose fines;

prevent an individual from trading; impound property; and arrest, detain, or incarcerate offenders. Serious cases resulted in execution of the offender, either by decapitation or by fatal mutilation, in which the victim was tied to a tree and his lower jaw was sliced off.

The tribunal of the secret society determined guilt or innocence by a most singular form of judgment. The accused was made to drink a toxic potion made from eight seeds of the Calabar bean, ground and mixed in water. In such a dosage, physostigmine acts as a powerful sedative of the spinal cord; it causes progressively ascending paralysis from the feet to the waist and eventual collapse of all muscular control, leading to death by asphyxiation (Robb 1957). The defendant, after swallowing the poison, was made to stand still before a judicial gathering until the effects of the poison became noticeable. Then he was ordered to walk toward a line drawn on the ground ten feet away. If the accused was lucky enough to vomit and regurgitate the poison, he was judged innocent and allowed to depart unharmed. If he did not vomit, yet managed to reach the line, he was also deemed innocent and was quickly given a concoction of excrement mixed with water that had been used to wash the external genitalia of a female (Simmons 1956a). Most often, however, given the toxicity of the Calabar bean, the accused died a ghastly death. The body was wracked with horrible convulsions, mucus flowed from the nose, the mouth shook horribly. If a person died from the ordeal, the executioner gouged out his eyes and cast the naked body into the forest (Simmons 1956b).

At any one time during the later years of the slave trade, the Efik lands were crowded with newly acquired slaves, most of them thoroughly demoralized and with nothing to look forward to but a life of toil in a foreign land. To keep order and discipline, the Efik depended on the agents and the executioners of the Egbo Society (Jones 1956). During the weeks and sometimes months that the slaves were awaiting shipment to the Americas, they must have heard of the gruesome ordeal of the Calabar bean, and many may have undergone the judgment themselves.

Here was a viable hypothesis. Datura was a violently psychoactive plant, well known and widely used in Africa as a stuporific poison by at least some of the peoples that were exported to Haiti. The Calabar bean that yields the recognized medical antidote for datura poisoning came from the same region, and knowledge of its toxicity would almost certainly have passed across the Atlantic. African species of datura (*Datura metel*) were apparently common throughout contemporary Haiti. The Calabar bean, though unreported from Haiti (Moscoso 1943), has a hard outer seed coat and could easily have survived the transoceanic passage; like datura, it could later have been accidentally or deliberately sown in the fertile soils of Saint Domingue. The pharmacological properties of both plants would be well known. Adapted to fit new needs, or perhaps conserved as adjuncts to ancient magical practices, they provided the material basis upon which the contemporary belief in zombies was founded.

This hypothesis was mere conjecture, but it provided a skeletal framework upon which other data could be placed as a solution to the zombie mystery took form. The hypothesis was simple, and it fit the limited data available before my first fieldwork period in Haiti. In the end it proved wrong, yet its formulation had uncovered an ethnographic connection that eventually provided a key to the entire zombie phenomenon: the secret societies of West Africa—their political and judicial functions as well as their extraordinary knowledge and use of toxic plants and animals.

CHAPTER FOUR

THE POISON

Between April 1982 and July 1984 I documented eight complete preparations of the zombie poison at four widely separated localities in rural Haiti: the environs of Saint Marc (3); the environs of Gonaïves (2); the Valley of Léogane (2); and the coastal village of Petite Rivière de Nippes (1). In addition, I verified the principal ingredients in the poison during oral interviews at three other sites: Archaie, L'Estere, and Petite Rivière de l'Artibonite. The process by which I obtained these data, as well as complete biographical notes on my principal informants, has been detailed elsewhere (Davis 1985). In this chapter, therefore, I will simply describe in some detail the preparation of the poison and discuss the ingredients themselves.

MAKING THE POISON

Preparation—Petite Rivière de Nippes

To the Vodounist, the creation of a zombie is essentially a magical act (Davis 1983a, 1983b, 1983c, 1985) and thus, before the preparation of each poison, the participants must seek spiritual and material protection. This may be a simple matter of the houngan rubbing a magic solution on each individual, but it can also involve rather elaborate ritualistic cleansings as well as the preparation of protective magic potions. At the small fishing community of Petite Rivière de Nippes, this initial stage of the elaboration of the poison was particularly complex, as the following excerpt from my journal indicates:

> The houngan began by dipping a small pre-Columbian axehead, known to the Vodounist as a *pierre tonnere* (see below) into a strong ammonia based solution, and then rubbing vigorously all the participants. He sprinkled a small

sample of the poison in a protected corner of the hut, and
then handed me a robust rooster and a jar of water, instructing me to pour a portion of the water down the bird's throat.
Moments later he took the rooster, placed it on top of the
poison and covered it with a hemp sack.

With the constant accompaniment of the sacred asson, or
rattle, and the songs and chants of the secret society, the
houngan sanctified my protection bottle. I named my intended victim and he whispered it to the bottle. The *president* of the secret society meanwhile inverted a bottle of rum
causing it to bubble in a peculiar fashion, a certain sign that
the poison would successfully complete my work. A match
placed into the bottle exploded into flames that momentarily
illuminated the entire enclosed temple.

His assistant ground up pieces of an unidentified wood,
cadavre gaté, and mixed the dust with bits of dried human
cadaver and the shavings of a human tibia. The president
pulled four feathers from the rooster's wing and instructed
me to tie them in the shape of a cross as I asked them to
bless my proposed work. At that point Madame Jacques (my
associate) accompanied the houngan's assistant as he took
the rooster to the sea in order to bathe its left foot. Upon
their return to the temple, the president threw sulphur powder into a flame as he released the rooster to wander about
the room. Placing seven drops of clairin and seven drops of
rum into a bottle, the president began to mix the actual
protection, adding sugar, basil leaves (*Ocimum basilicum* L.),
ground human bones, cadavre gaté and corn (*Zea mays* L.).
Then he rasped a human skull and added further bits of
dried human flesh provided by the guardian of the cemetery.
He then handed me three poisonous powders and gunpowder, instructing me to knead the powders into the wax before braiding the candles.

To administer the poison, it was critical, for both my own
safety and the success of the work that I follow his instructions precisely. On the night of the deed I was to light the
braided candle and hold it before the evening star and wait
until the sky darkened. To cast the death spirit I would first
have to beseech the star, saying:

By the power of Saint Star,
Walk, Find,
Sleep without eating.

Then, having saluted a complex sequence of stars, I was to place the burning candle in one of two holes dug beneath my victim's door. Next I was to drink from my protection bottle to imbibe the power of the cemetery. To "set the trap" I had merely to sprinkle the powder over the buried candle, staying carefully upwind while I whispered the name of my intended victim. Once the fated individual stepped over the buried candle, death would be imminent. As a final precaution, I was warned to sleep with the cross of feathers beneath my pillow. Each time I handled the poison I was to drink from my protection bottle.

By this time the president of the society was possessed by Ogoun, the spirit of fire and the metallurgical elements, and I was told that for complete protection I would have to be bathed with the rooster. The energy of the bird would thus pass to me, and by the end of the bath the rooster would be dead. As I stripped for the bath, I was instructed to drink from the protection bottle. Then the president with wide strokes of the rooster washed my entire body with an aromatic herbal solution. Indeed, by the end of the bath the rooster lay on the ground, flaccid and quite dead (Davis 1983b).

Only after this elaborate protective ritual was it safe to make the poison. There were four ingredients: a mixture of four samples of colored talc; gunpowder; a mixture of talc and the dust ground from the dried gall bladders of a mule and a man; and the ground skin of a frog. These were pounded in a mortar and sifted to yield a fine powder. A second proffered preparation consisted entirely of the skins of the *crapaud blanc*—the white toad, a common hyla tree frog (*Osteopilus dominicensis* Tschudi). Small glands beneath this toad's skin secrete a compound that, while irritating, is hardly toxic. Indeed, it was immediately apparent that none of the ingredients in either of these reputed poison preparations would be pharmacologically active.

The houngan insisted, however, that both preparations were "explosive," and that they would leave "your enemy but one ark, the earth that shall take him." My associate, Madame Jacques, was the cousin of both the houngan and president and herself a queen of the local secret society. She cautioned that "there are dozens of powders. They walk in different ways. Some kill slowly, some give pain, others are silent. These [the ones collected at Petite Rivière de Nippes] they 'carbonize,' but it is the magic that makes you the master." With other preparations, she claimed, it was easier. They could be placed in food. Or the skin might be pricked with a thorn. Sometimes the poison makers place ground glass in the mortar. "It is all a matter of power. If you want to learn the powders, you best walk at night."

Preparation—Saint Marc

At Saint Marc, the ingredients of the poison, with one notable exception, were gathered in a casual, even desultory fashion, without any overt signs of ritual. The bokor went down to the beach at dawn, as the fishermen hauled in their nets, so that he might salvage three or four small puffer fish that would normally be discarded. I recognized two types: the *crapaud du mer*, or sea toad (*Sphoeroides testudineus* L., *Sphoeroides spengleri* Bloch), and the *poisson fufu*, or fufu fish (*Diodon hystrix* L., *Diodon holacanthus* L.). When possible, the bokor obtained from the fishermen a specimen of a polychaete worm (*Hermodice carunculata* Pallas) which he called a sea snake, but a number of times he substituted a nonvenomous terrestrial snake of any sort. Meanwhile a village youth was dispatched to capture a specimen of the large *buga* toad (*Bufo marinus* L.) as well as several lizards (*Ameiva chrysolaema* Cope and *Leiocephalus schreibersi* Gravenhorst) and tarantulas known as *crabe araignée* (Theraphosidae).

In the afternoon the toad and sea snake were placed in a sealed container, to be left there overnight before they were killed the next morning. The bokor believed that the snake enraged the toad, increasing the power of its poison. This makes sense, for *Bufo marinus* has large parotoid glands on its back that secrete some two dozen potent chemicals, and its production increases when the toad is threatened or irritated. In the morning the bokor's assistants killed the animals and placed them in the sun to dry. At dusk the two plant ingredients were collected. Both were members of the Leguminosae, and in each instance both the legume and its seeds were required. One was *Albizia lebbeck* L., known in Haiti as *tcha-tcha* and planted throughout the coun-

Bokor gathering fish for the folk toxin

try as a shade tree. The other was *pois gratter*, the itching pea, *Mucuna pruriens* (L.) DC., a weedy climbing liana whose fruit-pods are covered with vicious urticating hairs.

The final ingredient—and the one the bokor considers the most potent—is the crushed and ground remains of a human cadaver. Fresh material is considered the most deadly, and the graveyards are raided with considerable stealth in the early hours after midnight. A coffin is disinterred, placed in a burlap sack, and carried back to the hounfour, where it is once again buried in the courtyard. There it must remain for forty-eight hours before the poison may be made. I have fully described elsewhere this aspect of the gathering of the ingredients (Davis 1985).

The poison itself was prepared in an isolated scrubland some distance from any human settlement. First, the bokor placed a thunderstone—a *pierre tonnere*—in an enamel dish and covered it with a magic potion. Thunderstones are sacred to the Vodounist, forged as they are by Sobo and Shango, the spirits of thunder and lightning. The spirit hurls a lightning bolt to the earth, striking a rock outcropping and casting the stone to the valley floor. There it must lie for a year and a day before the houngan may touch it. Despite their divine origins, thunderstones are not uncommon in Haiti; Westerners think of them as pre-Columbian ax heads and attribute their origins to the Arawak Indians.

The bokor struck a match to the dish and the potion exploded into flame. Dipping his right hand into it, he set his own skin on fire with the alcohol and then passed the flame to each of us, slapping the joints of our arms and rubbing our skin vigorously. He then tied satin scarves around our faces to ensure that we did not inhale the dust of the poison. As a final protective measure, he coated our exposed skin with an oily aromatic emulsion.

Earlier in the day his assistant had dug up the cadaver in the courtyard and, with great caution, his hand dripping with oil, the bokor had lifted pieces of the child's skull and brain into a glass jar. Now, with equal concern, he placed these fragments, along with the carcasses of the lizards, sea snake, and tarantulas, on a grill, roasting them to an oily consistency before transferring them to a mortar. The bones of the child stayed on the grill until they had burned almost to charcoal. Then they, too, were placed into the mortar. Another assistant had meanwhile taken a metal grater and begun to grind the tip of a human tibia and a skull, collecting the shavings in a small tin cup. A small handful of the

The bokor's assistant gathering human remains

The poison makers showing off their paraphernalia

seeds of *Albizia lebbeck*, eight fruits of *Mucuna pruriens*, and several shards of broken glass were also placed in the mortar. The dried fish were then placed carefully on the grill and left only long enough to ensure that they were completely dried, whereupon they, too, were added to the other ingredients in the mortar. The assistant then ground all the contents of the mortar to a coarse consistency and sifted them. He pounded the residue a number of times, until the bulk of the raw ingredients had collected as a fine brown powder at the base of a calabash. The final product was placed into jars to be carried back to the hounfour, where it would be buried inside the coffin in the lap of the dead child for forty-eight hours.

The bokor claimed that the poison could be administered in two ways. As Douyon (1980) had suggested, it might be spread in the form of a cross on the threshold of the victim's doorway. But one might also place it inside the victim's shoes, down his back, or inside a wound. This was an important indication that the powder might be applied directly to the intended victim.

Preparation—Valley of Léogane

The bokor of Léogane prepared two poisons. The more toxic, by his account, was made solely from human remains. It consisted

Disinterring the coffin in anticipation of making the poison

*Human remains, believed by Vodounists to be the
critical ingredient in the preparation*

Drying the preparation

The prepared poison is buried, along with the corpse, in the bokor's
courtyard for two days.

of a ground legbone, forearm, and skull mixed with dried and
pulverized parts of a cadaver. It was used as Douyon had indicated. Having rubbed his or her hands with a protective lotion—
a mixture of lemons, ammonia, and clairin—the user sprinkled
the powder in the form of a cross on the ground while naming the
intended victim. The recipient then needed only to walk over
that cross to be seized with violent convulsions. If the powder was
placed in the victim's food, it caused an immediate reaction.

The second preparation was a mixture of centipedes (Spiro-
bolida, Polydesmida), tarantulas (Theraphosidae), and lizards
including *miti verde* (*Anolis coelestinus* Cope) and *mabouya* (*Epicrates striatus* Fischer). In place of the buga toad, the bokor added
two locally recognized forms of the common tree frog (*Osteopilus
dominicencis* Tsudi). These were known as the *crapaud blanc*—the
white toad—and the *crapaud brun*—the brown toad. In addition—acknowledged as the most essential animal ingredient—
were two species of puffer fish, one named *bilan* (*Diodon holacanthus*) and the other the *crapaud du mer* (*Sphoeroides testudineus*).

Both poisons prepared at Léogane consisted only of animal
constituents. As had been the case with the three preparations
obtained at Saint Marc, the puffer fish and sea toads were sun-
dried, carefully heated, and placed in a mortar. Fresh specimens
of the two local varieties of tarantulas and the three nonvenomous lizards were roasted with the two tree frogs, the *crapaud brun*
and *crapaud blanc*. The bokor at Léogane especially emphasized
the toxicity of the human remains and included both ground
human bones and dried pieces of human cadaver in the preparation. The final product was a sifted powder, somewhat coarser
than the Saint Marc products. Of note at Léogane were the
extraordinary precautions taken by the poison makers themselves; they rubbed all surfaces of their bodies with oil emulsion,
placed cotton plugs in their nostrils, and wrapped hemp sacks
around their entire bodies. Both men wore large protective hats.

According to the bokor the onset of the poison was characterized by a feeling as of ants crawling beneath the skin, precisely
the way Narcisse had described his first sensations. The bokor
also indicated the importance of correct dosage. He mentioned
that the animal poison was most effective if it was ingested by the
victim, and he cautioned that the two preparations should never
be mixed.

Grating human bones

Poison maker. Note the protective garb and cotton nose plugs.

Preparation—Gonaïves

The poison maker at Gonaïves distinguished three stages or degrees to the preparation, which altogether took a week to complete. During the first a snake and the buga toad (*Bufo marinus*) were buried in a jar until they "died of rage." Then approximately twenty grams of ground centipedes and two whole tarantulas were mixed with four plant products: thirty seeds of *tcha-tcha*; forty seeds of *consigne* (*Trichilia hirta* L.), a tree in the mahogany family (Meliaceae); and four handfuls each of the dried leaves of *pomme cajou* (*Anacardium occidentale* L.) and *bresillet* (*Comocladia glabra* Spreng.). These last two plants are members of the Anacardiaceae, the poison ivy family, and both—but particularly *bresillet*—can cause severe and dangerous dermatitis.

Once these ingredients were ground to a powder, the bokor placed them in a jar and left them below ground for two days. Then, at the second degree, he added two botanically unidentified plants known locally as *tremblador* and *desmembres*. For the third and final degree, he mixed in four other plants capable of causing severe topical irritations. Two were members of the stinging nettle family (Urticaceae), *maman guepes* (*Urera baccifera* [L.] Gaud.) and *mashasha* (*Dalechampia scandens* L.), and the other two were *calmador* (*Dieffenbachia sequine* [Jacq.] Schott.) and *bwa pine* (*Zanthoxylum martinicense* [Lam.] DC.).

At the third degree the bokor also added a number of animals. He ground two species of tarantulas with the skins of the white tree frog (*Osteopilus dominicencis*). Other ingredients included the buga toad and not one but four species of puffer fish (*Sphoeroides testudineus*, *S. spengleri*, *Diodon hystrix*, and *D. holacanthus*). Thus, in common with the poisons prepared at Saint Marc, that of Gonaïves included the toad, the puffers, the sea toad, and the seeds of *Albizia lebbeck*. The bokor at Gonaïves also prepared a second poison, which contained only the principal animal ingredients. This was similar to the Léogane formula in that it contained the white tree frog and the two species of puffers, *D. hystrix* and *S. testudineus*.

My informant at Gonaïves provided several critical pieces of information that I verified during subsequent interviews. First, he named four additional preparations used to create zombies—*tombe levé*, *retiré bon ange*, *tué*, and *levé*—and though he refused to describe the specific formulas, he did comment that one killed immediately, another made the skin rot, and a third caused the victim to waste away slowly. All four of these preparations, however, had one ingredient in common—the *crapaud du mer* (*Sphoeroides testudineus*), the most toxic of the puffer fish found in Haitian waters. He also mentioned that the best powders were made during the hot months of the summer and were then stored and distributed throughout the year. At the same time, he cautioned that some of these were excessively "explosive," that they killed "too completely." There were, he insisted, two quite different means of administering these preparations. If one merely wanted to capture the soul of the victim, one could put the powder upon the ground. But if one wanted a *zombi cadavre* to work, one had to blow the powder on the victim and rub it into his skin. As he put it: "The powder is the support of the magic. Only the truly great work magic alone. Small people pretend, but watch and you'll see the hand of powder."

Finally, and of great interest, he noted that as a zombie is taken from the ground, it is force-fed a paste made up of three constituents: sweet potato, cane syrup, and *concombre zombi* (*Datura stramonium*). A second dose of this hallucinogenic paste is given to the victim the morning after the resurrection, when it reaches

The final product—a dried powder

its place of confinement. The full significance of this information will become apparent later.

THE INGREDIENTS OF THE POISON

Although each geographical region of Haiti has a unique poison formula, botanical and zoological analyses of the voucher specimens indicate that the principal ingredients are the same at three of the four localities and in seven of the eight sample preparations. These include one or more species of puffer fish (*Diodon hystrix, D. holacanthus, Sphoeroides testudineus, S. spengleri*), the large buga toad (*Bufo marinus*), the hyla tree frog (*Osteopilus domincencis*), ground human remains (*Homo sapiens*), and several plants—some of which have well-known, pharmacologically active constituents, and some of which are capable of severely irritating the victim's skin.

Analysis of the raw ethnobiological data, particularly in reference to the Narcisse case, raised three immediate questions. Did any of the ingredients contain pharmacologically active compounds that might cause a dramatic and pronounced reduction in metabolic rate? If so, was the strength and concentration of the compounds sufficient to be effective in the doses used by the various bokor? And finally, were the preparations topically active, or did they have to be ingested? All three questions were tempered by an important consideration: very often, in folk preparations, different chemicals in relatively small concentrations effectively potentiate each other, producing powerful synergistic effects—a biochemical version of the whole being greater than the sum of the parts. Therefore, my primary concern was to demonstrate whether any of the plant or animal ingredients contained interesting chemical compounds.

Plants

Albizia lebbeck L., Leguminosae (*tcha-tcha*)

Frequently the difference between a medicine, a poison, and a narcotic is merely a matter of dosage, and this seems to be the case with members of the genus *Albizia* of the Leguminosae. In mild doses, for example, the Masai women of Kenya use the bark of *Albizia anthelmintica* A. Brogn. as a sexual stimulant (Hedberg et al. 1983). In higher concentrations the rootbark serves as a highly effective febrifuge, purgative, and anthelmintic, particularly for tapeworm (Githens 1949; Hedberg et al. 1983). The seedpods are antiprotozoal, and the bark kills roundworms (*Ascaris lumbricoides*) and exoparasites (Watt and Breyer-Brandwijk 1962; Oliver-Bever 1983). Excessive dosages may lead to death (Hedberg et al. 1983).

Other species of *Albizia* are employed throughout Africa for a number of medicinal purposes. The Zulus use an infusion of the bark and root of *A. adianthifolia* W. F. Wight to treat scabies, and in Liberia the same plant treats snakebite and internal parasites (Watt and Breyer-Brandwijk 1962). Throughout tropical Africa an infusion of the bark of *A. glaberrima* (Schumach and Thom) Benth. is drunk to cure bilharzia. Tannins present in the bark of many species have astringent properties that are effectively exploited to relieve diarrhea and dysentery (Githens 1949). Other unrelated conditions commonly treated with species of *Albizia* include epilepsy, cystitis, syphilis, leprosy, gonorrhea, rheumatism, and nervous complaints; the plant has also been used as a contraceptive (Watt and Breyer-Brandwijk 1962; Githens 1949; Hedberg et al. 1983; Oliver-Beyer 1983).

The various species of *Albizia* owe their pharmacological activity to a large and diverse group of glucosides known as saponins. In excessive dosages the saponins are quite toxic, but generally they are not absorbed by the intestines, and to be effective they must must enter the bloodstream directly. In East Africa various tribes take advantage of this property by grinding the roots of *Albizia versicolor* Welw. ex Oliv. as an arrow poison (Watt and Breyer-Brandwijk 1962). Several species of *Albizia*, including *A. chinensis* Merr. and *A. procera* Benth., have been employed as fish poisons. Ichthyotoxins work in two ways. Some act internally following topical absorption to weaken the fish's heart or muscles. Those based on saponins act on the gills to interfere with respiration; the fish, in effect, suffocate and float to the surface, where they are easily gathered (Githens 1949).

That the Haitian bokor may have been aware of the pharmacological action of these compounds and therefore applied the poison topically was not inconceivable, especially when the symptoms of the poison are considered. In large dosages, saponins induce vomiting and nausea accompanied by excessive secretions in the respiratory passages. In simpler terms, the victim drowns in his or her own fluids. The interim result is pulmonary edema, a condition suffered by Clairvius Narcisse at the time of his death (Githens 1949; Douyon pers comm. 1980; Pradel and Casgha 1983).

Interestingly, many species of *Albizia*, including *A. lebbeck*, contain a special class of saponins known as sapotoxins that are absorbed by the intestines and may therefore be administered orally. Sapotoxins interfere with cellular respiration throughout the body, causing death by weakening all vital functions. Once again these quite specific pharmacological properties were recognized by the West Africans. The Efik traders of Old Calabar used the bark of *Albizia zygia* MacBride in a potion known as *ibok usiak owo*. This was a truth serum, a "medicine for mentioning people," and was administered orally as an ordeal poison (Sofowora 1982; Forde 1956).

Trichilia hirta L., Meliaceae (*consigne*)
In Cuba the leaves of this tree are used as a tonic and are given in infusions for anemia, asthma, bronchitis, and pneumonia. For use in rituals, it is considered one of the most powerful magic trees by the acolytes of the Cuban Yoruba-Bakongo cults. In West Africa the bark of *T. zenkeri* is used to treat gonorrhea and skin lesions, as is the bark of *T. prieureana* A. Juss. (Ayensu 1978; Githens 1949). In South Africa the tannins present in the bark of *T. emetica* are effective in the treatment of dysentery. The Ronga, Zulus, and Xhosa use the bark and leaves of *T. roka* Chiov. as an enema and also to treat dysentery; the powder is blown into the inflamed anus of the inverted patient. The plant may be similarly administered as a purgative enema, which also induces vomiting and sweating. In excessive dosages, the powder may prove fatal (Watt and Breyer-Brandwijk 1962).

Mucuna pruriens DC., Leguminosae (*pois gratter*)
The seeds of this climbing liana contain psychoactive compounds that cause pronounced behavioral changes marked by hallucinations (Schultes and Hofmann 1980). Chemical analysis has revealed the presence of tannins, viscous fixed oil, acid resin, toxic dihydroxyphenylalanine, and alkaloids including mucunine, mucunadine, prurieninine, and prurienidine (Ayensu 1981; Wong 1976). In Colombia the plant has been used medicinally to treat internal parasites and cholera (Garcia Barriga

1974). A related species, *Mucuna flagellipes*, is known to contain toxins similar to physostigmine, the active principle in the Calabar bean, and in central Africa the plant is used as an arrow poison (Githens 1949).
It is, however, less the pharmacological constituents than the mechanical properties of the trichomes that densely cover the fruit that have attracted such attention to this plant. The active itching agent is a proteolytic enzyme, mucunain. The trichomes also contain several histamine-releasing substances, one of which is similar to a histamine liberator present in snake and bee venoms (Watt and Breyer-Brandwijk 1962). These surface hairs are truly vicious, producing erythema, burning, itching, blistering, and stomatitis; for those with the courage to drink an infusion, these properties prove just as noxious to internal parasites, and the plant has been frequently reported as a very effective vermifuge (Watt and Breyer-Brandwijk 1962). The severity of exposure to the surface of an entire fruit may be judged by the fact that a single trichome beneath the skin is enough to produce itching in man.

Urera baccifera (L.) Gaud., Urticaceae (*maman guepes*)
Dalechampia scandens L., Urticaceae (*mashasha*)
Both of these plants are members of the stinging nettle family, and like *pois gratter*, both have ferocious stinging hairs. It has been known for some time that nettle stings are caused by the percutaneous injection of a fluid produced at the base of the hair. Contact with the hair results in the breaking off of the tip and the injection of the fluid. The result is reddening accompanied by marked itching, swelling, and an intense burning sensation. It was long assumed that the chemical responsible for the action was formic acid, but the actual active principles have now been identified—they are acetylcholine, histamine, and 5-hydroxytryptamine (Watt and Breyer-Brandwijk 1962).
It comes as no surprise that plants with such dramatic characteristics should have attracted the attention of man. But, as with most such plants, the indications for their use are not well defined, and they are employed for many unrelated conditions including gout, rheumatism, paralysis, dysentery, eczema, bronchial catarrh, internal hemorrhages, edema, hemorrhoids, jaundice, and urinary problems. The way the plant is administered in many instances suggests that it is the mechanical rather than

pharmacological activity that is desired. Flagellation with fresh nettles has been a treatment for chronic diseases since ancient times (Watt and Breyer-Brandwijk 1962).

Dieffenbachia sequine, Araceae (*calmador*)

Calmador is the common dumbcane of Jamaica. In its tissues are calcium oxalate needles that act like small pieces of glass. The English name derives from the nineteenth-century practice of forcing recalcitrant slaves to eat the leaves; the needles, by irritating the larynx, cause local swelling, making breathing difficult and speaking impossible. In Afro-Cuban culture (Yoruba-Bakongo), the entire plant is used as a charm and is said to turn virility into impotence. A woman need only pass the charm over the body of her lover to condemn him to impotence for the rest of his life (Cabrera n.d.). Use of an infusion as a contraceptive has been reported from Dominica, Cuba, Puerto Rico, and Guadeloupe (Ayensu 1981).

Zanthoxylum martinicense (L.) DC., Rutaceae (*bwa pine*)

This tree has been reported as a narcotic (Ayensu 1981), and chemical analysis has yielded resins, tannins, alkaloids, and glycosides (Asprey and Thornton 1953, 1954, 1955a, 1955b). Cubans make a decoction of the leaves and bark for use as a general tonic and to treat syphilis and rheumatism, or as a cure for alcoholism. Toothaches are relieved by chewing the bark (Cabrera n.d.). In Jamaica, an infusion of the bark treats syphilis, and the astringent juice of the young roots is used for colic and gastrointestinal problems and as an antispasmodic (Ayensu 1981).

In Africa, both European settlers and the Zulus use the bark of a related plant, *Fagara capensis* Thumb, as a widely heralded snakebite cure. After the wound is lanced, powdered bark is applied topically and ingested as an infusion. The bark of another species, *Fagara macrophylla* Engl., is said to be narcotic and is used as an arrow and fish poison. In addition, decoctions of as many as a dozen different species of *Fagara* are employed by diverse tribes as general tonics and blood purifiers (Watt and Breyer-Brandwijk 1962).

Anacardium occidentale L., Anacardiaceae (*pomme cajou*)
The resins of this and many plants in the poison ivy family
contain a number of active principles including cardol, anacardic
acid (hydroxycarbolic acid), anacardol, and cardanol. Topical
exposure to any part of the plant can cause serious and even
dangerous inflammation of the skin, the severity of which depends both on the species and on the idiosyncratic reaction of the
person exposed. Responses vary from a mild rash around the
mouth, suffered by certain people after eating mangoes (*Mangi-
fera indica* L.), to swelling, rubefaction, blistering, and even acute
dermatitis. Although raw cashews (*Anacardium occidentale* L.) are
commonly sold, particularly in natural food stores, they are actually poisonous and have been known to kill horses (Watt and
Breyer-Brandwijk 1962). But if they are roasted until all the
pericarp oil has been exuded, they are quite safe.

Anacardium occidentale is a multipurpose plant. In India and
tropical America the tree is a source of a dyestuff and tannin.
The oil has been used to preserve fishnets in the Andaman
Islands, as a medicine and wood preservative in India, and as an
insecticide in a number of regions. In Tanzania, the plant has
been deliberately used during scarification rituals. Medicinally,
the root has been reported as a purgative, the fruit as a diuretic,
the bark as a febrifuge, and the young shoots and leaves as an
infusion to treat coughs. Both the fruit and seed are edible if
properly prepared, and in parts of South Africa an intoxicating
beverage is made from the fruit (Hill 1952; Watt and Breyer-
Brandwijk 1962).

The plant also has a number of industrial applications. It
yields a gum which is a mixture of true gum and bassorin and
which, being only partially soluble in water, produces a mucilage
with good adhesive properties that is used in bookbinding.
Cashew nut shell liquid is the raw material employed in the
manufacture of the resins and plastics used in brake linings and
insulating materials. Because of the fluid's electrical properties, it
is of some value in the insulation of airplane ignition systems.
The toxic principles are present in all these industrial products,
and many of them cause irritation to those who handle them. In
Europe, for example, dockworkers unloading vanilla beans are
subject to a condition known as the vanilla itch, which is due to
an extract of *Anacardium occidentale* painted onto the beans to give

them a brown, shiny appearance (Watt and Breyer-Brandwijk 1962).

Comocladia glabra Spreng., Anacardiaceae (*bresillet*) Plants of the genus *Comocladia* are among the most dangerous of the Anacardiaceae. In Cuba adherents of the Yoruba-Bakongo cult have this to say about a related species, *Comocladia dentata* Jacq.:

> The only thing to do with this shrub is *ika*, harm. Its touch, its shadow and its exhalations are all evil. There is no more diabolical plant in the *monte*; nothing better to kill, destroy, demolish and finish off something. Evil comes naturally to it and no one dares touch it. The slightest contact with this bush will cause swelling and sometimes a fever. The area around where it grows is also pernicious.
>
> It is used in many curses to cause an enemy to swell. Most important, it is used to *falaina*, provoke tragedies, ruin a household, sow discord within a family or turn friends into enemies.
>
> A traditional formula for this *mpolo*: mix powdered *guao* [*Comocladia dentata*] with pulverized cat's claw, *pica-pica* [probably Urticaceae] and the skull bones of a cat or a dog, hot pepper, guinea pepper and pepper from a drug store, a hairy spider, a *macao* [hermit crab], alum, quicksilver, salt, charcoal and soil from a cemetery (Cabrera n.d.).

In Haiti, species of *Comocladia* are equally noxious and similarly detested. Local attempts to eradicate *Comocladia glabra* trees have been frustrated by the fact that the smoke given off when the branches are burned is extremely dangerous and, in Vodoun belief, has been imbued with numerous nefarious powers. The only use for the plant besides poisonous preparations is for scarification; young men will sometimes use the resin to tattoo the names of their girlfriends on their skin.

While collecting voucher specimens of this plant, I was inadvertently exposed to the resin on both my abdomen and chest and was bedridden for several days with severe inflammation and dermatitis. The itching was so extreme as to provoke self-inflicted wounds. The Vodoun treatment consisted of immobility combined with the application of a caustic mudpack made from the ashes of certain plants mixed with aloe juice (*Aloe vera* L.).

This treatment served as an effective counterirritant: the pain resulting from the application of the alkali was so severe that all thoughts of scratching vanished, giving the exposed skin an opportunity to heal.

Summary

The plants used in the various preparations that I witnessed include some with known pharmacologically active constituents (*Albizia lebbeck, Mucuna pruriens, Trichilia hirta*) and others that are capable of irritating the skin of the victim, either by means of urticating hairs (*Urera baccifera, Dalechampia scandens, Mucuna pruriens*) or toxic resins (*Anacardium occidentale, Comocladia glabra*), or mechanically with needles of calcium oxalate (*Dieffenbachia sequine*) or with spines (*Zanthoxylum martinicense*). The addition of these irritants may be related to the method of applying the poison. Any one of the poison variations is said to be particularly effective if applied to an open wound. In one of the Saint Marc preparations ground glass was added to the mortar. One of my informants suggested pricking the victim's skin with a thorn before applying the toxic powder. Several of the plants induce such acute irritation that the victim, in scratching himself or herself, may cause open wounds. Subsequent laboratory experiments suggested that the poison, though it was topically active, was even more effective where the skin had been broken (Davis 1983a). According to a number of informants, the poison may be applied more than once to the victim, and it is possible that self-inflicted wounds increase susceptibility to later doses.

In reference to the application of the reputed poison, Zora Neale Hurston notes:

There is swift punishment for the adept [member of the secret society] who talks. When suspicion of being garrulous falls upon a member, he or she is thoroughly investigated, but with the utmost secrecy without the suspect knowing that he is suspect. But he is followed and watched until he is either accounted innocent or found guilty. If he is found guilty, the executioners are sent to wait for him. By hook or crook he is gotten into a boat and carried out beyond aid and interference from the shore. After being told the why of the thing, if indeed that is necessary, his hands are seized by one man and held behind him, while another grips his head under his arm. A violent blow with a rock behind the ear stuns him and at the same time serves to abrade the skin. A deadly and quick-acting poison is then rubbed into the wound (Hurston 1981, 230–31).

Animals

Miscellaneous ingredients

The human remains added to the preparation are burned almost to charcoal and probably are chemically inert. The lizards used (*Ameiva chrysolaema, Leiocephalus schreibersi, Anolis coelestinus, Anolis cybotes* Cope, and *Epicrates striatus*) are not known to be toxic. *Ameiva dorsalis*, a related species from Dominica, is said by natives to make the hair fall out and the skin turn green. Skinned and gutted, this lizard can be eaten, but a Dominican folktale cautions, "if the ground lizard were good to eat, it would not be so common." A species in the related genus *Cnemiedophotus*, the Florida bluetail, causes loss of balance in domestic cats. The polychaete worm used at Saint Marc (*Hermodice carunculata*) has setae that inflict a "paralyzing effect" (Mullin 1923) and may be venomous (Halstead 1978). However, all these ingredients are thoroughly burned before they are added to the potion and are unlikely to have any pharmacological effect.

The skin of the tree frog, *Osteopilus dominicensis* (*crapaud brun, crapaud blanc*), is covered with irritating glandular secretions (Lynn 1958), and a related species, *Osteopilus septentrionalis* Dumeril and Bibron, has caused temporary blindness in Cuba (Williams pers. comm.). However, in none of the preparations is the frog used in sufficient quantity to cause significant biological activity. The same may be said of most of the other ingredients, including the tarantulas and the centipedes. In fact, only two of the documented animal ingredients could result in a toxic preparation that actually offered a material basis for zombification. One is the large terrestrial toad, *Bufo marinus*, and the second is one or more species of the toxic puffer fish, *Sphoeroides testudineus, S. spengleri, Diodon hystrix*, and *Diodon holacanthus*.

Bufo marinus L. (*buga*)

The poisonous toad *Bufo marinus* is native to the New World, where it is a common denizen of low swampy habitats ranging from Florida west along the Gulf Coast to Mexico, then south to

The animal ingredients. Note Bufo marinus *L.*, Diodon hystrix *L.*, *and* Sphoeroides testudineus *L.*

Panama and northern South America. In post-Columbian times, it dispersed rapidly throughout the Antilles and south along the Pacific coast of South America, as well as inland into the Amazon basin (Zug 1979). The large parotoid glands on the back of the toad have been described as "veritable chemical factories" (Kennedy 1982, 284); they produce and secrete at least twenty-six compounds, all of which are biologically active. Some of these—the phenylethylamine bases and derivatives such as the catecholamines dopamine, epinephrine, and norepinephrine, as well as a number of indole derivates such as serotonin—are benign and occur naturally in human tissues. Acting as neurotransmitters, they are the chemical messengers between the synapses which connect individual neurons. These indole derivatives and catecholamines are found in many species and are not toxic in animals.

However, the venom glands secrete other compounds of considerably greater interest, including bufotenin, a purported hallucinogenic agent (Fabing and Hawkins 1956), and two extremely toxic cardioactive steroids, bufogenin and bufotoxin. These compounds are found in the skin or glands of a number of toads, including the common European species *Bufo vulgaris* (Wieland and Alles 1922), and it is their unique toxic properties

Bokor's assistant with a dried specimen of Bufo marinus

Bufo marinus, *the common marine toad, showing the prominent
parotoid glands (*photo by Dennis Cornejo*)*

that have earned the animal a notorious place in the repertoire of
poisoners and black magicians throughout the world.

As early as Roman times Juvenal (60–128 A.D.) described
women using toads (presumably *Bufo vulgaris*) to kill unsuspecting husbands (Chen and Jensen 1929). The toxicity of the venom
provided the basis upon which the *Talmud* differentiated between
frogs and toads, classifying the latter with all animals that were
poisonous to the touch—a belief that persists to this day in
Western societies (Abel and Macht 1911). At the beginning of
the fourteenth century, Bishop Guichard of Troyes was accused
of poisoning the wife of Philippe le Bel with a preparation of
scorpions, toads, and spiders (Chen and Jensen 1929). In that
same period, English sorcerers noted erroneously that toads derived their venom from the earth by eating mushrooms—hence
the name toadstool—and they commonly prepared potions using
toads that had macerated in menstrual blood for a month or more
(Chen and Jensen 1929). It is to these "menstrums" that Shakespeare referred in *Macbeth*:

> "Toad, that under cold stone,
> Days and nights hast thirty-one
> Swelter'd venom sleeping got,
> Boil thou first i' the charmed pot."

Medieval witchcraft boasted a complete collection of such recipes. One from the court astrologer and alchemist for Frederick
II reads: "Five toads are shut up in a vessel and made to drink the
juices of various herbs with vinegar as the first step in the preparation of a marvelous elixir for the purposes of transformation"
(Kennedy 1982).

Soldiers in the Middle Ages believed that a discreet way of
killing an enemy was to rub his skin or wounds with the secretions of *Bufo vulgaris*. *Bufo marinus* reached Europe very soon
after the voyages of Columbus, and poisoners quickly discovered
that when the toad was placed in boiling olive oil, the secretions
of the glands could easily be skimmed off the surface (Holmstedt
pers. comm.). In early sixteenth-century Italy, poisoners devised
sophisticated processes for extracting toad toxins into a salt,
which could then be sprinkled on the intended victim's food
(Lewin 1920). In fact, so highly regarded was the toxicity of toad
venom that at the beginning of the eighteenth century it was
actually added to explosive shells and mixed with the saltpeter

used in making gunpowder (Chen and Jensen 1929; Chilton et al. 1979). Presumably, the commanders believed that if the cannon did not kill their enemies, the toad toxins would.

Not surprisingly, European physicians incorporated toad venom into their *materia medica* at a very early point. Dried and powdered toad warranted a prominent place as a treatment for dropsy, fever, and a number of other ailments in numerous important pharmacopoeia, including *Thesaurus Pharmakologicus*, written by Johannes Schroder and published in Leyden in 1672, *Pharmacologia*, by Samuel Dale (London 1692), and *The London Dispensatory*, by William Salmon, published in 1702. Michael Etmuller (1644–1683), professor of medicine at Leipzig, noted of the toads that "living toads aroused to the point of fury are venomous, but found dead they are entirely devoid of poison. Transfixed alive in the month of July, dried, powdered and administered in doses of twelve grains on alternate days, they furnish an excellent cure for dropsy. Others administer this remedy in burning fevers at its height. Powdered toad is also an effective remedy against incontinence of urine, and is said to be efficacious because of its anodyne character while its volatile, penetrating salt acts as a diuretic" (Abel and Macht 1911). Toads remained a prominent therapeutic agent throughout the eighteenth century, appearing in *Pharmacopeia Universalis* by R. James (London 1747) and *The English Dispensatory* by John Quincy (London 1749). As late as 1833, powdered toad was mentioned in an important medical compilation, *Pharmacologia*, written by J. A. Paris.

As in so many things, the Chinese were far ahead of their Western colleagues in their knowledge of the properties of toad venom. For centuries they had been forming the toxic secretions into smooth disks which they named *Ch'an Su*, or "toad venom" in Mandarin. According to the *Pentsao Kang Mu*, a famous herbal written at the end of the sixteenth century, this venom was used to treat toothache, canker sores, inflammations of the sinus, and bleeding of the gums. Taken orally, it was said to break up the common cold (Chen and Jensen 1929).

From this list of rather mundane afflictions, it is difficult to appreciate that the Chinese were dealing with an extremely toxic preparation. Although early medical reports are uncertain as to the species of toad used (Tu et al. 1923; Penget et al. 1921; Chen and Jensen 1929), analysis of Ch'an Su revealed the presence of

both bufogenin and bufotoxin (probably from *Bufo vulgaris*). Separate studies suggested that Ch'an Su was fifty to a hundred
times more potent than digitalis, a powerful cardiotonic based on
the common European foxglove (*Digitalis purpurea*), which had
been used as a heart stimulant in Britain since the tenth century
(Chen and Jensen 1929). In one experiment a cat was injected
with as little as 0.020 grams of crude toad venom; its blood
pressure tripled almost immediately and it collapsed following
massive heart failure (Abel and Macht 1911). If a human were to
respond in the same way, it would mean that as little as half a
gram of dried venom, injected intravenously, would do similar
damage to a 150-pound man. If the venom were applied topically, the result would be at least a rapid increase in blood pressure. It was possibly significant that one of Clairvius Narcisse's
prominent symptoms at the time of his death was hypertension.

The toxic properties of toads and frogs had certainly not been
overlooked by the natives of the Americas. Lacerdo de Filho
reported in 1878 that indigenous groups in the Amazon made an
arrow poison from the toad *Bufo agua* (Abel and Macht 1911).
The Choco Indians of western Colombia learned to milk poisonous frogs by placing them in bamboo tubes suspended over open
flames. The heat caused the creature to exude a yellow liquid
which dripped into a small ceramic vessel, where it coagulated
into the proper consistency of poison. According to an early and
perhaps exaggerated report (Pagenstecher 1906, cited in Abel
and Macht 1911), these preparations were extremely potent; a
deer struck by an arrow that had been dipped in the poison
survived only two to four minutes, a jaguar perhaps ten.

The action of the toad-based arrow poisons is of particular
interest. D-tubocurarine, the principal constituent of the toxic
lianas of the Amazon (*Chondrodendron* sp., *Curarea* sp.), acts as a
muscle relaxant, causing death by asphyxiation. The skin of *Bufo
marinus*, on the other hand, contains chemical substances resembling the active principles of the strongest African vegetable
arrow poisons (Flier et al. 1980). These latter are derived from
a number of plants (*Strophanthus kombe, S. gratus, Acokanthera
venenata* G. Don), and they act in quite a different way. The
active compound is ouabain, a powerful heart stimulant. In moderate dosages, ouabain is used today to treat emergency heart
failure; in excessive doses, it makes the heart pump wildly until it
collapses (Robb 1957).

Given the toxicity of these compounds, it is perhaps difficult to appreciate a controversy that has developed in the anthropological literature in recent years over whether *Bufo marinus* was used as a hallucinogen by New World Indians—in particular by the advanced civilization of the lowland Maya (Dobkin de Rios 1974; Kennedy 1982; Furst 1972). Although the hypothesis initially seems untenable from an ethnobiological point of view, it is worth exploring, for it now appears that a solution may be at hand, and the explanation is one of startling simplicity.

The argument in favor of the toad as hallucinogen has rested until now on several lines of evidence. First, throughout Central America the toad was a prominent symbol, particularly in Mayan iconography (Furst 1972). Numerous Mayan artifacts that have been discovered, including small ceramic serving bowls, have obvious representations of the toad and especially graphic portrayals of its distinctive parotoid glands (Furst 1974; Kennedy 1982; Dobkin de Rios 1974). Second, at one post-Classic Mayan site on Cozumel Island, Mexico, an archaeologist found that virtually all amphibian remains were *Bufo marinus* (Hamblin 1979). This report complemented an earlier, similar discovery at San Lorenzo, Mexico, that led one prominent archaeologist to suggest that the Olmec civilization used the toad as a narcotic (Coe 1971). Third, one of the substances secreted by the toad is bufotenin, a compound that is found in a hallucinogenic snuff made today by South American Indians from the seeds of a tree, *Anadenanthera peregrina* [L.] Spegazzini. This member of the Leguminosae is common in the upper Orinoco Valley of Venezuela and elsewhere in South America (Schultes and Hofmann 1980). One report from Western medical literature has suggested that pure bufotenin, injected intravenously into human subjects, induces hallucinations (Fabing and Hawkins 1956). Fourth, the proponents of the hallucinogen hypothesis all cite an unpublished report of the contemporary use of *Bufo marinus* in a hallucinogenic preparation in Veracruz, Mexico (Knab n.d., cited in Furst 1974; Kennedy 1982).

On the face of it, however, this cumulative evidence is fairly inconclusive. Whether or not Mayan iconography represents the toad *Bufo marinus*, the werejaguar, or any other symbol is for the archaeologists to decide; it is specious at best to argue that if the motifs do represent *Bufo marinus*, one may conclude, ipso facto, that the Maya used the toad as a hallucinogen. Symbols, in particular ritual symbols, incorporate a wide range of meanings. Moreover, they are not necessarily diachronically stable. Allison Kennedy (1982) herself points out the remarkable fecundity of the toad. One could speculate with equal assurance that the toad motifs relate to fertility, to water or rain, or even, given the life cycle of the creature, to some notion of sacred metamorphosis and renewal.

By the same token, it is not always possible to draw a direct relationship between a decorative motif applied to ceramic wares and a purported use of the depicted object itself. N. M. Hellmuth, in an amusing comment, has noted that today, in the central market in Guatemala City, native women sell a great variety of modern toad-shaped artifacts. Does this imply, he asks rhetorically, that "these little old ladies secretly imbibe mind-expanding doses of toad-juice cocktails under their counters?" (Hellmuth 1974, 156). Certain investigators (Schultes 1979; Schultes and Hofmann 1980; Sharon 1978) have noted correlations in the provocative shapes and decorations of archaeological artifacts, but they have made such pronouncements only when their conclusions are supported by contemporary documentation as well as extensive ethnohistorical records of the use of the hallucinogen in the particular region. It is a different and purely speculative exercise to draw conclusions in the complete absence of corroborative ethnographic and/or historical evidence (Dobkin de Rios 1974; Kennedy 1982).

The paucity of such evidence presents yet another apparent flaw in the argument. It seems likely that, if the use of *Bufo marinus* as a hallucinogen was an important enough element of a state religion to warrant iconographic representation, there would be some record of it in the early chronicles. Dobkin de Rios (1974) speculates that the notable absence of ethnohistorical documentation is due to the fact that use of the drugs by the general population was suppressed by the Mayan hierarchy and, in turn, concealed from the Spanish. Yet it was precisely this "diabolical" use of hallucinogens, along with other indigenous religious practices, that the Spanish so zealously ferreted out and described in detail in their writings—if only as a way of rationalizing their own nefarious actions. It comes as no surprise to find extensive accounts of the use of ololoiuqui (*Rivea corymbosa*); teonanacatl (*Psilocybe* sp., *Panaeolus* sp., *Conocybe* sp.); peyote (*Lophora williamsii*); San Pedro-achuma (*Trichocereus*

pachanoî); cohoba-vilca (*Anadenanthera peregrina*); tlapatl-cha-
maico (*Datura* sp.) (Schleiffer 1973).

Moreover, although it is true that the Spanish tried to suppress
the use of psychotropic drugs in Mesoamerica, they mostly succeeded in driving these practices underground. In the case of
virtually all the known hallucinogens, it has been possible to
demonstrate the continuity and subsequent modifications of the
pre-Columbian practices into colonial times; in most instances,
extensive ethnographic evidence exists documenting their contemporary use (Schultes and Hofmann 1980; Sharon 1978;
Furst 1972; Davis 1983d). What, one is forced to ask, happened
to *Bufo marinus*?

At least one ethnohistoric source does mention the use of a
toad in a ritual preparation. Peter Furst notes that the "17th
century English friar, Thomas Gage, described the Potoman
Maya practice of steeping venomous toads in fermented beverages used for ritual intoxication, to give them extra potency"
(Furst 1974, 154). The original source, however, is somewhat
less precise. It speaks of a *chicha* consisting of water, honey or
sugar cane, tobacco leaves, various roots "which they knew to be
strong in action," and a live toad. This mixture was placed in a
sealed container "till all that they have put in be thoroughly
steeped, the toad consumed, and the drink well strengthened"
(Thompson 1970, 120). It appears from the original syntax that
the potency of the preparation was believed to be enhanced as
much from the month it spent fermenting as from the addition of
an unidentified toad.

Interpretations of ethnographic data have been equally imprecise. Furst (1974) cites a paper by Robert Carneiro (1970) which
suggests that the Amahuaca Indians of Peru introduce frog or
toad venom into self-inflicted skin burns to bring about a trance
state. Yet neither Carneiro nor Furst identify the animal in question. They use the terms toad and frog interchangeably and take
no account of the existence of numerous genera of toxic amphibians completely unrelated to and morphologically dissimilar to
Bufo marinus.

Those who suggest that the toad was used as a hallucinogen
also draw attention to the distribution of *Bufo marinus* remains at
a number of archaeological sites (Hamblin 1979; Coe 1971).
Michael Coe noted in discussing his osteological remains at San
Lorenzo: "These toads are a puzzle, as they cannot be skinned

without an extremely dangerous poison getting into the meat. We are now looking into the possibility that the Olmecs used them for an hallucinogenic substance called bufotenine [*sic*], which is one of the active ingredients" (Coe 1971, 74). As it turns out, a survey of the archaeological literature shows that a significant quantity of *Bufo marinus* remains have been found in middens throughout Central America, leading other archaeologists to believe that pre-Columbian Indians used the toad, not as a hallucinogen, but as food, after carefully cutting away the skin and parotoid glands (Cooke 1979, 1981). In spite of Coe's cautionary words, Richard Cooke (1979) himself butchered and cooked several specimens, which he was pleased to note tasted rather pleasantly like smoked chicken. Based on the temporal and spatial distribution of the *Bufo marinus* remains, he proposed that the toad was not used as a drug, but as a survival food, a suggestion partially corroborated by the fact that it is today employed for precisely that purpose by the Campa Indians of the lower Apurimac River in Peru (Weiss pers. comm.).

A central fallacy of the hallucinogen hypothesis has been the fact that no one has been able to demonstrate how this reputed toad preparation could have been consumed safely. It is true that the glands secrete bufotenin, a known constituent of South American hallucinogenic snuffs (Schultes and Hofmann 1980). Bufotenin is the methylated derivative of serotenin or 5-hydroxytryptamine. Unlike its parent compound, it is mildly lipid soluble and so is weakly capable of crossing the blood-brain barrier. Thus it might well have psychotropic properties.

However, also present in the toad venom are the extremely potent cardioactive steroids bufotoxin and bufogenin (Chilton et al. 1979; Chen and Jensen 1929). It is almost certain that ingesting a straight maceration of the parotoid glands would cause cardiac failure long before the recipient would get a chance to enjoy the putative hallucinogenic properties of bufotenin (Alger 1974). It seems unlikely that the Maya would have been interested in poisoning vast numbers of their priesthood, who presumably would have been the ones taking the drug. Only if some process had been developed that selectively neutralized the toxic constituents could *Bufo marinus* have been made into much of a hallucinogen. Folk healers have often demonstrated a sophisticated biological knowledge, as is evident in their ability to enhance certain hallucinogenic potions by the careful use of various admixtures (Schultes and Hofmann 1980). However, the knowledge of chemistry and differential solubilities required to eliminate both bufotoxin and bufogenin in an orally ingested preparation would represent, on the face of it, a formidable achievement.

Such a process was not altogether inconceivable. Kennedy (1982) elaborately discusses her suggestion that the Maya used ducks as bioprocessors of the toxin; the idea was that the toad toxins were somehow metabolized, leaving the psychotropic components in the flesh of the bird, which could then be safely consumed. She went as far as demonstrating that ducks could safely eat the toads, but she failed to take the obvious next step of butchering the birds and bioassaying their meat.

A more promising attempt was made by Timothy Knab, who searched the backcountry of Mexico for evidence of a contemporary *curandero* who might have preserved the ancient knowledge. It is Knab's unpublished account that is heralded by Kennedy. "Knab," she writes, "has penetrated the arcana of several curanderos in the Veracruz area and details a recipe for the preparation of *Bufo marinus* parotoid glands which eliminates the most toxic compounds" (Kennedy 1982, 285). Furst mentions the "taped interview by Timothy Knab with a curandero from Veracruz describing precisely how a 'brujo' treats the venom extracted from Bufo to eliminate or neutralize its more dangerous toxic effects when preparing his magic potion" (Furst 1974, 154). It is to Knab's credit that he is somewhat more modest in reporting his own discovery.

After considerable effort, Knab finally located an old curandero in the mountains of southern Veracruz who claimed to know the formula of a preparation that had not actually been used by his people in fifty years. The old man ground the glands of ten toads into a thick paste, to which he added lime water and the ashes of certain plants. The mixture was boiled all night, or until it no longer smelt foul, and then was added to corn beer and filtered through palm fiber. The liquid was mixed into corn meal and then placed in the sun for several days to ferment. Finally the mixture was heated to evaporate the remaining liquid, and the resulting hardened dough was stored until the time came to rehydrate it to prepare the final potion.

Although Knab had persuaded the curandero to prepare the potion, under absolutely no circumstances would the recalcitrant old man actually sample it. Only very reluctanctly did he consent to give a dose to Knab. From what happened, it appears that he knew something the anthropologist did not. Knab's intoxication was marked by sensations of fire and heat, convulsive muscle spasms, a pounding headache, and delirium. He writes of his experience:

> The drink starts to take effect within a half hour; profuse sweating is noted along with a sudden increase in heart beat. The heart beat becomes continuously harder and stronger. A pronounced chill sets in with twitching of the facial and eye muscles. A pounding headache and delirium shortly follow the onset of twitching. During this delirium, the individual is unable to walk, sit up or move about, as he lies in a specially excavated depression in front of the fire. This state usually lasts from three to five hours and wears off slowly. (Knab n.d.)

Knab reports no hallucinations, and from his subjective description of the intoxication it appears that he merely suffered the initial symptoms of a severe poisoning (Knab pers. comm.). He never did find out whether or not the preparation actually neutralized any of the toxic compounds, for the preparation was never analyzed.

Yet another unresolved issue in the controversy is the pharmacological activity of the purported hallucinogenic agent itself, bufotenin. Virtually every report that characterizes bufotenin as a psychotomimetic dates to a single experiment completed by a medical doctor, Howard Fabing, in the 1950s. Fabing obtained permission to inject bufotenin intravenously into a number of inmates at the Ohio State Penitentiary. The recipient of the mildest dose complained of a prickling sensation in his face, nausea, and slight difficulty in breathing. With a higher dosage these symptoms became more pronounced and the subject's face and lips became purplish. The final dose caused mild hallucinations and delirium, and the skin turned "the colour of an eggplant," indicating that the drug was preventing oxygen from getting to the blood. The hallucinations were ephemeral. Three minutes after injection, the subject vomited, and at that time, "he saw red spots passing before his eyes and red-purple spots on the floor. Within two minutes, these visual phenomena were gone, but they were replaced by a yellow haze, as if he were looking through a yellow lens filter" (Fabing and Hawkins 1956, 887).

That is the extent of the hallucinations experienced by any of the recipients of the bufotenin injections.

W. J. Turner and S. Merlis (1959) attempted but failed to replicate these results. They noted that upon muscular injection of bufotenin, the recipient "suddenly developed an extremely rapid heart rate; no pulse could be obtained; no blood pressure measured . . . onset of auricular fibrillation . . . extreme cyanosis developed." Massive resuscitative procedures were immediately implemented and fortunately the pulse eventually returned to normal (Chilton et al. 1979). After the failure of this and other experiments the investigators concluded that "we must reject bufotenin as capable of producing the acute phase of cohoba (*Anadenanthera perigrina*) intoxication" (Chilton et al. 1979, 64).

On the basis of this and other reports, Schultes himself concluded, "it seems probable that 5-OH-DMT (bufotenin) does not contribute to the psychotomimetic activity of the snuffs" (Schultes and Hofmann 1980, 90). In other words, even assuming that a folk preparation could eliminate the toxic constituents in the toad venom, it became questionable whether bufotenin alone would be hallucinogenic. This issue was never resolved by a full range of experiments, including different techniques of administering the drug, but the doubts cast on the psychoactive properties of bufotenin led many to conclude that *Bufo marinus* could not have been used as a ritual narcotic, let alone as the basis of a state religion.

Crosscutting this negative evidence, however, and perhaps beginning to resolve the matter once and for all is the important recent discovery by Andrew Weil (pers. comm.) of a group of individuals in New Mexico who apparently have been using the toad as a ritual hallucinogen for several years. Their means of administration is simple and direct. They milk the parotoid glands by hand, taking some care to avoid contact between the secretions and their mucous membranes. They then smoke the toad venom and, according to preliminary reports, the psychoactive effects are unmistakable while the noxious side effects one might expect from the associated compounds in the secretions are negligible. If true, this discovery suggests that the cardioactive steroids bufogenin and bufotoxin may be denatured by smoking, while the potential of the active constituent, presumably bufotenin, is fully realized. The form of administration is consistent with the known pharmacological properties of other tryptamines. In general, these compounds may be smoked or absorbed as snuffs; ingested orally they are in most instances inactive. The full significance of Weil's discovery will be determined by a battery of field and laboratory experiments. For the moment, however, he has provided the only firsthand, concrete evidence of the psychoactive properties of this remarkable amphibian.

Hallucinogen or not, the crude exudate of the parotoid glands of *Bufo marinus* is certainly toxic, and its pharmacological activity is well documented. It is this activity, not the purported psychotropic principles, that is of interest in the zombie investigation. The toad venom would have a direct effect as a cardiovascular stimulant, and the biological activity of the other constituents would cause both cyanosis (bluing of the skin) and paresthesia (tingling sensations). Both of these latter conditions, in addition to severe hypertension, were prominent symptoms of Clairvius Narcisse at the time of his death.

Marine Fish

Although each of the documented preparations has a unique formula, there is, in addition to the human remains, one consistent animal ingredient: one or more species in two genera of marine fish: the *poisson fufu* (*Diodon hystrix* L.), the *bilan* (*Diodon holacanthus* L.), and the sea toad or *crapaud du mer* (*Sphoeroides testudineus* L. and *S. spengleri* Bloch). In English, we know these as the porcupine fish and the puffer or blowfish because of their ability to swallow large amounts of water when threatened, thus assuming a globular shape and making it more difficult for predators to swallow them (Halstead 1978; Fuhrman 1967). One would hardly think such a passive defensive mechanism necessary. These species all belong to a large pantropical order of fish, the Tetraodontiformes, many of which have tetrodotoxin in their skin, liver, ovaries, testicles, and intestines. This deadly neurotoxin is one of the most poisonous nonprotein substances known (Kao 1966; Mosher et al. 1964; Fuhrman 1967; Woodward 1964). Laboratory studies measuring the relative concentrations necessary to achieve axonal blockage have shown that tetrodotoxin is approximately 160,000 times more effective than cocaine (Mosher et al. 1964; Kao 1966). As a toxin, it is reportedly 60 times more potent than D-tubocuraine and strychnine and 1,000 times stronger than sodium cyanide (Mosher et al. 1964). Extrapolating from experiments with mice, and accepting for the sake of comparison the physiologically absurd equation of mice and men, as little as 0.5 milligrams of the pure toxin would be sufficient to kill a 70-kilogram adult man (Mosher et al. 1964; Woodward 1964). A single lethal dose of tetrodotoxin could rest on the head of a pin (Vietmeyer 1984).

The toxicity of the viscera and skin of the fish is equally impressive. Tokushi Fukuda and Iwao Tani (1941) reported that the oral ingestion of twenty grams of the skin of *Sphoeroides vermicularis* (*Fugu vermicularis vermicularis* Temminck and Schlegel) or *Sphoeroides pardalis* (*Fugu pardalis* Temminck and Schlegel) would prove lethal. There is in the liver and ovaries of *Sphoeroides rubripes* (*Fugu rubripes rubripes* Temminck and Schlegel) enough toxin to kill eleven and twelve people respectively; the liver of *Sphoeroides porphyreus* (*Fugu vermicularis porphyreus* Temminck and Schlegel) could kill as many as thirty-two adults.

Tetrodotoxin is an extremely complex molecule. The first tentative attempts to elucidate its structural formula were made in the late nineteenth century by Takahashi, the first chair of pharmacology in the Imperial University in Tokyo. He initiated chemical work and concurrently studied the distribution of the toxin within various species of fish, the relative toxicity of different organs, and the comparative impact of the poison on different laboratory animals. In 1894, Y. Tahara announced the isolation from the eggs of the puffer fish of a "pure" extract, which he called tetrodotoxin (Kao 1966). This extract, though it is now known to have been only 0.2 percent pure, was the basis of a series of subsequent experiments conducted in the early years of this century (Hashimoto 1979). Research on the toxin did not advance appreciably until after World War II, at which time, aided by chromatography, two independent teams of Japanese researchers were able to isolate a pure crystalline toxin (Yokoo 1950; Tsuda and Kawamura 1952). The actual structure of the toxin—$C_{11}H_{17}N_3O_3$—remained unknown until 1964 when it was announced at a conference at Kyoto by four independent teams of organic chemists, including R. B. Woodward's group from Harvard (Woodward 1964).

Physiologically, tetrodotoxin interferes with the normal functioning of nerves and muscles, eventually causing complete neuromuscular paralysis. These biological effects result from the toxin's very specific mode of action. Under normal circum-

A bokor with dried specimens of Diodon hystrix

stances, nerve impulses in the body are relayed from the spinal cord along the axons to a particular neuromuscular junction. The essential conditions for this process are differences in the concentration of sodium and potassium ions inside and outside the axon and an axon membrane capable of undergoing rapid temporary changes in permeability to these ions. When the nerve is stimulated, an action potential is generated and moves up and down the axon like a wave. Many drugs impede this process by making the axon membrane equally permeable to both sodium and potassium, thus preventing the maintenance of an electrical potential. The unique heterocyclic structure of tetrodotoxin, however, prevents the generation of the action potential by specifically blocking the sodium channels alone, while having absolutely no effect on the flow of potassium (Ritchie 1975; Kao 1983; Narahashi et al. 1964). It is this particular and unique feature that has made tetrodotoxin such an important neurobiological tool for the study of nerve function (Kao and Walker 1982). Its selective impact on excitable membrane also provides the underlying mechanism by which tetrodotoxin causes complete neuromuscular paralysis.

Tetrodotoxin's role in human history reaches back literally to the dawn of civilization. The Egyptians knew of the poison almost five thousand years ago (Halstead 1958); a figure of a puffer fish appears on the tomb of Ti, one of the pharoahs of the fifth dynasty (2500 B.C.) (Gaillard 1923). It has been suggested that the deadly Red Sea puffer was perhaps the reason for the biblical injunction against eating scaleless fish that appears in Deuteronomy (Vietmeyer 1984).

In the East there is, in fact, a continuous history that reflects an increasingly sophisticated knowledge of the biology and toxicology of the puffer fish. In China, the toxicity of the fish is acknowledged in the *Pentsao Chin*, the first of the great pharmacopoeia supposedly written during the reign of the legendary Emperor Shun Nung (2838–2698 B.C.). This famous herbal, which contemporary scholars believe was actually written during the first or second century B.C., lists 365 drugs in three categories based on their toxicity—superior, medium, and inferior. Puffer fish eggs were placed in the second group among the drugs believed to be tonic yet known to be lethal in excessive doses (Kao 1966). Another early Chinese source—a volume of natural history entitled *Sankaikyo*, written about the time of Christ—also notes the toxicity of these fish (Hashimoto 1979). By the time of the Han Dynasty (202 B.C.–220 A.D.), it was recognized that the toxin was concentrated in the liver of certain species (Mosher et al. 1964); four hundred years later, during the Sui Dynasty, a treatise by Chan Yanfang, *Studies on the Origins of Diseases*, contains an accurate account of the toxicity of the liver, eggs, and ovaries (Mosher et al. 1964). The last of the great herbals, the *Pentsao Kang Mu*, written by Li Shih-Chen in 1596, recognizes that toxin levels vary in different species, and that within any one species they may fluctuate seasonally. Shih-Chen also offers a succinct but vivid description of the results of eating the liver and eggs: "In the mouth they rot the tongue, if swallowed they rot the gut," a condition that "no remedy can relieve." This is but one of the herbal's many injunctions warning of the dangers of these fish.

Yet the *Pentsao Kang Mu* also reveals an extraordinary development that had taken place in Mandarin society. Despite the obvious risks, by 1596 the fish had become something of a culinary delicacy. Several recipes describe in great detail methods of preparing and cooking the fish that are said to eliminate some of the toxin and render the fish edible. One account suggests soaking the roe overnight in water (tetrodotoxin is water

soluble); another heralds the delight of eating "salted eggs and
marinated testes." Just how much range of error these methods
allowed is uncertain. The herbal also records a folk saying that
remains popular to this day in China and Japan: "To throw away
life, eat blowfish" (Kao 1966; Hashimoto 1979; Mosher et al.
1964; Vietmeyer 1984).

The subtleties of safely preparing puffer fish were quite unknown to the first European explorers to reach the Orient, and
as a result they have left some of the most vivid accounts of
the capabilities of these toxins. On 8 September 1774, during
his second circumnavigational voyage, Captain James Cook anchored his flagship, the H.M.S. *Resolution*, offshore from the
newly discovered island of New Caledonia. That afternoon the
ship's clerk obtained a fish from the local inhabitants. The expedition's naturalists, J. R. Forster and his son Georg, recognized
the specimen as a new species, and they made drawings and a
description of it before dinner. The elder Forster noted that the
fish "was of the genus, by Linnaeus, named Tetrodon, of which
several species are reckoned poisonous. We hinted this circumstance to Captain Cook, especially as the ugly shape, and large
head of the fish were greatly in its disfavour, but he told us he had
eaten this identical sort of fish on the coast of New Holland,
during his first voyage, without the least bad consequence" (Forster 1777, 403–24).

Cook ignored the warning of his naturalist and ordered the
fish prepared for his supper. Then, in the unassuming way of a
captain of the Royal Navy, he invited Forster and his son to eat
with him. Fortunately, as Cook later confided to his journal:

the operation of describeing [*sic*] and drawing took up so
much time till it was too late so that only the Liver and Roe
was dressed of which the two Mr Forsters and myself did
but just taste. About three to four o'clock in the morning we
were seized with most extraordinary weakness in all our
limbs attended with numbness of sensation like that caused
by exposing one's hands and feet to a fire after having been
pinched much by frost. I had almost lost the sense of feeling
nor could I distinguish between light and heavy objects, a
quart pot full of water and a feather was the same in my
hand. We each took a vomit and after that a sweat which
gave great relief. In the morning one of the pigs which had

eaten the entrails was found dead. In the morning when the natives came aboard and saw the fish hanging up they immediately gave us to understand it was by no means to eat, expressing the utmost abhorrence of it and yet no one was observed to do this when it was sold or even after it was bought (Beaglehole 1961, 534–35).

Captain Cook and his naturalists were lucky. Two sailors on the Dutch brig *Postilion*, which rounded the Cape of Good Hope some seventy years later, fared less well. This account is offered by the ship's surgeon, a Dr. Julius Hellmuth, who reached the sailors not ten minutes after they had eaten the fried liver of a species identified as *Diodon oscellatus*. The boatswain's mate lay between decks and could not raise himself without the greatest exertion; his face was somewhat flushed, his eyes glistening, and his pupils rather contracted. His mouth was open and, as the muscles of the pharynx were drawn together by cramp, the saliva flowed from it. The lips were tumid and somewhat blue, the forehead covered with perspiration, the pulse quick, small, and intermittent. The patient was extremely uneasy and in great distress but was still conscious. The state of the patient quickly assumed a paralytic form: his eyes became fixed in one direction; his breathing became difficult and was accompanied by dilation of the nostrils; his face became pale and was covered with cold perspiration; his lips were livid; his consciousness and pulse failed; his rattling respiration finally ceased. The patient died scarcely seventeen minutes after partaking of the liver of the fish (Richardson 1893, 216; Richardson 1861).

The other sailor, the purser's steward, suffered the same symptoms, except that he vomited several times, which made him feel momentarily relieved. The surgeon expressed some hope for this victim until "a single convulsive movement of the arms ensued, whereupon the pulse disappeared and the livid tongue was protruded from between the lips" (Richardson 1893, 216). His death occurred about one minute after that of his shipmate.

While Cook and the rest of the Europeans were having their difficulties on the high seas, the Japanese had adopted the Chinese passion for the puffer fish and carried its preparation to the level of art. Indeed, such was its popularity that throughout the Edo era (1603–1868) references to the fish appear frequently in literature, particularly in senryu and haiku poetry (Hashimoto

1979). The ardor with which the Japanese consumed their *fugu* fish bewildered early European observers. Engelbert Kaempfer, a physician attached to the Dutch embassy in Nagasaki near the turn of the eighteenth century, wrote of a certain fish, *Furube*:

> The Dutch call him Blazer, which signifys [*sic*] Blower, because he can blow and swell himself up into the form of a round Ball. He is rank'd among the poisonous Fish, and if eat whole is said unavoidably to occasion death. . . . This the Japanese reckon a very delicate fish, and they are fond of it, but the Head, Guts, Bones and all the garbage must be thrown away, and the Flesh carefully wash'd and clean'd before it is fit to eat. And yet many People die of it, for want, as they say, of thoroughly washing and cleaning it. People that by some long and tedious sickness are grown weary of their lives, or are otherwise under miserable circumstances, frequently chuse [*sic*] this poisonous Fish, instead of a knife or halter, to make away with themselves (Kaempfer 1906, 134–35).

Kaempfer also observed that the fish was so dangerous and yet so popular that the emperor had been obliged to issue a special decree forbidding his soldiers to eat it. Indeed, during the Japanese invasion of Korea in 1590, numerous soldiers died around Shimonoseki from eating toxic fish (Hashimoto 1979). Curiously, though Kaempfer seems to have watched many people eat and enjoy the puffer ("The Japanese won't deprive themselves of a dish so delicate in their opinion," he writes elsewhere), he concludes this passage by writing: "The poison of this sort is absolutely mortal, no washing nor cleaning will take it off. It is therefore never asked for, but by those who intend to make away with themselves" (Kaempfer 1906, 134–35). This Dutchman, like countless generations of Western visitors who came after him, missed the point of the puffer experience completely. As the Japanese explain in verse, "Those who eat *fugu* are stupid. But those who don't eat *fugu* are also stupid" (Vietmeyer 1984).

Today the Japanese passion for puffers is something of a national institution. In Tokyo alone, puffers are sold by over 1,800 fishdealers (Halstead 1978). Virtually all the best restaurants offer it, and to retain some semblance of control the government actually licenses the specially trained chefs who alone are permitted to prepare it. An individual seeking certification must have at least two years experience in handling the fish and must pass a rigorous practical and written examination; as of 1972, some 5,000 certified fugu chefs were employed in Tokyo (Hashimoto 1979). When a cook sells or serves fugu, he is obliged to remove all the toxic organs, wash the flesh thoroughly, and deposit the discarded viscera in a specially locked container. Generally the meat is eaten as sashimi. Thus sliced raw from the nontoxic back muscles, the flesh is relatively safe (Fuhrman 1967). Not infrequently, however, improperly prepared fugu has been dangerously tainted by the toxic constituents, and in one instance poisonous samples of frozen puffers, misbranded as angler fish, were exported to Europe, causing several severe poisonings in Italy (Pocchiari 1977). The testes of the fugu are also relatively safe, except that they are sometimes confused with the deadly ovaries by even the most experienced chefs. Yet many connoisseurs prefer a dish known as *chiri*—partially cooked fillets taken from a kettle containing toxic livers, skins, and intestines. Lovers of *chiri* are invariably among those killed each year (Fukuda 1937; Fukuda and Tani 1937a, 1937b, 1941).

The Japanese prefer, and pay premium prices—as much as $25.00 per pound—for, four species of puffers: *Fugu rubripes rubripes* Temminck and Schlegel, *Fugu pardalis* Temminck and Schlegel, *Fugu vermicularis vermicularis* Temminck and Schlegel, and *Fugu vermicularis porphyreus* Temminck and Schlegel. All of these species are commonly known to be violently poisonous. Why would anyone play Russian roulette with such a creature, especially as the waters surrounding Japan teem with literally hundreds of kinds of delicious and nutritious fish? The answer, of course, is that fugu is one of the few substances that walks the line between food and drug. For the Japanese, consuming fugu is the ultimate aesthetic experience. The refined task of the fugu chef is not to eliminate the toxin, it is to reduce its concentration while assuring that the guest still enjoys the exhilarating physiological aftereffects. These include a mild numbing or tingling of the tongue and lips, sensations of warmth, a flushing of the skin, and a general feeling of euphoria (Halstead 1978). As in the case of so many stimulants, there are those who can't get enough of a good thing. Though it is expressly prohibited by law, certain chefs prepare for zealous clients a special dish of the particularly toxic livers. The organ is boiled and mashed and boiled again and again until much of the water-soluble toxin is removed.

Unfortunately, many of these chefs succumb to their own cook- *153*

ing. It was such a dish that caused the controversial death in
1975 of Mitsugora Bando VIII, one of Japan's most talented
Kabuki actors—an artist who had been declared a living national *The Poison*

treasure by the Japanese government (Vietmeyer 1984). Apparently Bando, like all those who eat the cooked puffer livers, was
among those who in the words of one fugu specialist enjoy "living
dangerously" (Fukuda 1951).

The number of deaths from ingestion of puffer fish vary within
Japan from year to year. Fukuda and Tani (1937) recorded 909
deaths between 1927 and 1937. Severe survival conditions during and shortly after World War II resulted in the death of some
400 Japanese troops (Lalone et al. 1963), while in one year, 1947,
there were 470 civilian deaths (Halstead 1978). From 1949 to
1951, 389 cases were reported, with a mortality rate of 51 percent (Lalone et al. 1963). Between 1956 and 1958 there were
715 poisonings, of which 420 or 59 percent proved fatal (Mosher
et al. 1964). Fuhrman (1967) reported 90 deaths out of 176 cases
in 1957. Five hundred intoxications were reported in 1958–59,
of which 294 proved fatal. Kao (1966), perhaps the best single
authority on puffer fish poisoning, estimates that since 1886
there have been approximately 100 fatalities each year. Although
inconsistency in the diagnosis and reporting of minor cases
makes it difficult to ascertain the absolute annual number of fugu
poisonings, of those serious enough to be reported approximately
60 percent prove lethal (Mosher et al. 1964; Halstead 1978; Kao
1966).

Because of its popularity as a food and the relatively high
incidence of accidental poisonings, the fugu fish has generated
an enormous medical and biomedical literature. Exploring that
literature for clinical descriptions and case histories, one is immediately struck by the parallels to the zombie phenomenon. In
describing his experience, Clairvius Narcisse recalled remaining
conscious at all times, and although he was completely immobilized, he could hear his sister's weeping as he was pronounced
dead. Both at and after his burial, his overall sensation was one of
floating above the grave. He remembered as well that his earliest
sign of discomfort before entering the hospital was difficulty in
breathing. His sister remembered that his lips had turned blue or
cyanotic. Although Narcisse did not know how long he had
remained in the grave before the zombie makers came to release

him, other informants insist that a zombie may be raised up to seventy-two hours after the burial. The onset of the poison itself was described by several houngan as the feeling of "insects crawling beneath the skin." Another houngan offered a poison that would cause the skin to peel off the victim. Popular accounts of zombies claim that even female zombies speak with deep husky voices, and that all zombies are glassy-eyed. Several houngan suggested that the belly of the victim swells after he or she has been poisoned.

At the time of his death in the Schweitzer Hospital, Narcisse suffered digestive troubles with vomiting, pronounced respiratory difficulties, pulmonary edema, uremia, hypothermia, and rapid loss of weight. Although he was diagnosed as suffering from chronic hypertension, at one point his blood pressure was an impossibly low 26/15 (Pradel and Casgha 1983; Douyon 1980; Douyon pers. comm.; Kline pers. comm.). These symptoms are quite specific and certainly peculiar.

Now compare Narcisse's constellation of symptoms with the following specific description of the effects of tetrodotoxin:

> The onset and types of symptoms in puffer poisoning vary greatly depending on the person and the amount of poison ingested. However: symptoms of *malaise*, pallor, dizziness, *paresthesias* of the lips and tongue and ataxi develop. *The paresthesias which the victim usually describes as a tingling or prickling sensation* may subsequently involve the fingers and toes, then spread to other portions of the extremities and gradually develop into severe numbness. In some cases the numbness may involve the entire body, in which instances the patients have stated that *it felt as though their bodies were floating.* Hypersalivation, profuse sweating, extreme weakness, headache, *subnormal temperatures, decreased blood pressure*, and a *rapid weak pulse* usually appear early. Gastrointestinal symptoms of *nausea, vomiting*, diarrhea and *epigastric pain* are sometimes present. Apparently the pupils are constricted during the initial stage and later become dilated. As the disease progresses, the *eyes become fixed* and the pupillary and corneal reflexes are lost. . . . Shortly after the development of paresthesias, *respiratory distress* becomes very pronounced and . . . the *lips, extremities and body become intensely cyanotic.* Muscular twitching becomes progressively worse

and finally terminates in *extensive paralysis*. The first areas to become paralyzed are usually the throat and larynx, resulting in *aphonia, dysphagia* and complete *aphagia. The muscles of the extremities become completely paralyzed and the patient is unable to move.* As the end approaches the *eyes of the victim become glassy. The victim may become comatose but in most cases retains consciousness, and the mental faculties remain acute until shortly before death* (Halstead 1978, 456; emphasis mine).

Other documented and pronounced symptoms of tetrodotoxin poisoning include pulmonary edema (Larsen 1925; Benson 1956); cyanosis (Tahara 1896; Richardson 1893; Larsen 1942; Bonde 1948; Fukuda and Tani 1937a, 1937b, 1941; Kao 1966); dilation of the pupils (Tahara 1896; Bonde 1948). Hypothermia has been observed in clinical studies (Akashi 1880; Ishihara 1918; Bonde 1948; Noniyama 1942; Yano 1937) and induced in the laboratory (Borison et al. 1963; Clark and Coldwell 1973; Clark and Lipton 1974). Paresthesia and numbness of the extremities, together with respiratory distress, are in almost all instances the first noticeable symptoms (Mosher et al. 1964; Larsen 1942). Nausea and vomiting are also ubiquitous symptoms reported by virtually every authority; H. S. Mosher (1964, 1106) notes that tetrodotoxin is "probably the most potent known emetic." Y. Tahara (1896) reported that patients sometimes develop distended bellies. B. W. Halstead reports that skin blisters may appear by the third day after exposure to the toxin; by the ninth day the skin begins to peel off (Halstead 1978, 457, fig. 1). One patient admitted to Queen's Hospital in Honolulu complained that he felt "numb from neck to toes with a feeling of ants crawling over him and biting him" (Larsen 1942, 417).

This list is not exhaustive. In all, Clairvius Narcisse shared twenty-one or virtually all the prominent symptoms of tetrodotoxin poisoning (Davis 1983a, 1983b, 1983c, 1985). Of these, perhaps none is more incredible than his assertion that he had been conscious the entire time, that he had been able to hear himself pronounced dead, hear his sister begin to weep, sense the sheet being pulled up over his face (Douyon 1980; Pradel and Casgha 1983; Narcisse pers. comm.). Yet innumerable clinical studies from the medical literature indicate that, during the state of profound paralysis that invariably results from a severe intoxication, consciousness is retained and most mental faculties remain normal (Leber 1927; Bagnis et al. 1970; Fukuda and Tani 1937a, 1941; Akashi 1880; Torda et al. 1973; Halstead 1958; Tahara 1896; Bonde 1948; Benson 1956). One physician notes:

> If the patient tried to take anything in his hand or to stand up, he feels that his limbs are powerless. The patient remains conscious. If he goes to sleep after eating, he finds that he is suffering from poisoning when he awakes and cannot move or speak. In serious cases, the patient may die while asleep. After some time, the motor nervous system is completely paralyzed and it becomes impossible to move any part of the body. The eyes do not respond and the mouth stays closed, making speech impossible. The pulse and respiration slow down. The body temperature drops. Asphyxia occurs as a result of all this and, sometimes, the patient even dies. The patient's comprehension is not impaired even in serious cases. When asked about his experiences, he can describe everything in detail after recovery (Akashi 1880, 19–23).

A recent case from Australia is even more dramatic. A boy of fourteen was camping with his parents and two brothers on the coast, and they caught twenty small puffer fish which they boiled in seawater and ate. One fish, different in appearance from all the others and later identified as *Amblyrhynchotes richei*, was eaten by the young boy. As the meal was being prepared, the mother fed one fish to an injured crow, a family pet, and shortly after it was seen staggering about in the grass where it fell over dead. The family ate their meal, and as the weather was closing in, they broke camp and prepared to return home. By the time their gear was stowed, the young boy was complaining of a numbness in the tongue, a feeling of swelling in the lips, and a general sensation of lightness. Minutes later he vomited. He later wrote to his physician: "I couldn't be bothered with anything. . . . My father tried to give me milk but I couldn't swallow and I was cold, very cold. I was losing air fast. It was painful and slow. I thought of panic but I became quite paralysed and then unconscious" (Torda et al. 1973, 600). On arrival at the hospital he was diagnosed as "unreactive. Had flaccid paralysis and is areflexic. Pupils fixed and dilated." Yet the patient himself recalled clearly his trip in the ambulance: "I could hear them talking but I couldn't move or

anything. I was completely conscious . . . and I really heard them.
They were laughing and chattering and they even played with the
hooter" (Torda et al. 1973, 600). Twelve hours after eating the
fish, the boy was still completely paralyzed but quite conscious:

> I heard nurses later on and they were trying to talk to me,
> specially one who said good morning and good night. I
> could also hear surgeons talking mumble jumble. . . . I tried
> to move and talk but that was impossible. I felt them spray-
> ing stuff on me which turned from hot to cold around my
> legs and body. They usually told me what they were going to
> do. . . . It was terrible because they opened my eyelids every
> now and then and I found out I could see but just couldn't
> open my lids (Torda et al. 1973, 600).

The patient remained paralyzed until 6:00 A.M. the following
morning when a slight movement was noticed in his eyelid. Four
hours later he could move his limbs feebly and was able to
breathe on his own. The following day he could eat normally and
was able to get out of bed. The day after that he was discharged
from the hospital, completely recovered (Torda et al. 1973, 600–
601).

On Christmas Eve, 1977, a forty-year-old resident of Kyoto
was admitted to a hospital after being poisoned by fugu. The
patient soon stopped breathing and all symptoms were consistent
with brain death. Physicians immediately initiated artificial respiration and other appropriate treatments. These did not help,
but twenty-four hours later the patient spontaneously began to
breathe again. He eventually recovered completely and later remembered having heard his family weeping over his body. The
physicians had given him up as dead, but his senses were un-
impaired. He wanted desperately to let his family know that he
was alive, but he was unable to do so. "That," he later told
medical investigators, "was really hell on earth." This case was
reported on 2 February 1978 in the *New Tide Weekly*.

The difficulty of diagnosing the death of victims of fugu poisoning is demonstrated by several other case histories. A Japanese peddler shared a dish of chiri with several mates and later
suffered all the classic symptoms of puffer poisoning. Unable to
walk, he was carried to the hospital, where his symptoms were
complete peripheral paralysis, dilated pupils, difficulty in breathing, cyanosis, hypothermia, and apparent unconsciousness. The

physician gave up, certain that the man was dead, but the individual recovered, and not fourteen hours after he had eaten the poisonous food he walked out of the hospital (Fukuda and Tani 1937b). In another case, a Korean miner and his son ate the ovaries of a species of *Sphoeroides*, and within an hour they were taken to the hospital. The father retained "clear consciousness" until he died; his son suffered complete immobility for about two hours but recovered naturally without treatment (Fukuda and Tani 1937a).

Fukuda and Tani (1941) cite another instance of a physician who returned home after confirming the death of his patient, only to be summoned back by the family of the deceased because the body temperature of the corpse had returned to normal. Investigators speculated that the patient's heart had continued to beat even after the cessation of breathing and thus maintained the peripheral circulation of blood. This possibility is apparently affirmed by an earlier case in which the attending physician had been able to hear the heart beating even after respiration had ceased and the patient appeared to have died (Fukuda and Tani 1937b). Benson (1956), however, reports the opposite possibility: an American woman suffered circulatory collapse following the ingestion of *Sphoeroides testudineus*. Hospital attendants were unable to detect a pulse, even though she maintained rapid, shallow breathing. Unable to speak, but evidently conscious, she died within an hour after exposure to the toxin.

These accounts illustrate one of the most eerie characteristics of puffer poisoning. Tetrodotoxin induces a state of profound paralysis, during which the border between life and death is not at all clear, even to trained physicians. T. A. Torda and his colleagues note that "totally paralysed patients, with dilated, unreactive pupils, can retain consciousness. This must make the puffer fish poisoning a terrifying experience. Sensible use of guarded communications with the patient is probably more important than sedation, even with patients who appear to be totally unresponsive" (Torda et al. 1973, 601). The physician's dilemma is further complicated by the fact that "the bodies of persons who die of fugu poisoning show no sign of decay and should not be buried because it is very difficult to distinguish between asphyxia and true death" (Akashi 1880, 19–23). The significance of these observations in regard to the Narcisse case and the zombie phenomenon in general need hardly be expressed. It is quite clear

that tetrodotoxin is capable of inducing a physical state that
might actually allow an individual to be buried alive.

In Japan, apparently, it has already happened. As long ago as
1880, the Japanese physician Akashi reported the following incidents:

> A dozen gamblers voraciously consumed fugu at Nakashi-
> mamachi of Okayama in Bizen. Three of them suffered
> from poisoning; two eventually died. One of these being a
> native of the town was buried immediately. The other was
> from a distant district . . . under the jurisdiction of the
> Shogun. Therefore the body was kept in storage and
> watched by a guard until a government official could exam-
> ine it. Seven or eight days later the man became conscious
> and finally recovered completely. When asked about his
> experience, he was able to recall everything and stated that
> he feared that he too would be buried alive when he heard
> that the other person had been buried (Akashi 1880, 19–
> 23).

What happened to the unfortunate individual who was buried is
not explained. The second case was equally dramatic: "A man
from Yamaguchi in Boshy suffered from fugu poisoning at
Osaka. It was thought that he was dead and the body was sent to a
crematorium at Sennichi. As the body was being removed from
the cart, the man recovered and walked back home. As in the
case previously cited, he too remembered everything" (Akashi
1880, 19–23).

These cases are by no means unique. In fact, such incidents
are apparently frequent enough that, in some parts of Japan, a
person declared dead from eating puffer fish must by local law
and custom be allowed to lie alongside his or her coffin for three
days before burial (Larsen 1925). A recent case was brought to
my attention by C. Y. Kao, perhaps the world's best authority on
the pharmacology of tetrodotoxin. In July 1983 a Japanese man,
poisoned by toxic fugu, recovered after he was nailed into his
coffin (Kao pers. comm.).

These reports cast the zombie investigation in a totally different light. Suddenly it appeared not only possible but likely that,
given the proper conditions, the poisons prepared by the various
bokor could induce a state of apparent death. Now a dozen more
specific questions could be examined. Did the species used in

the various potions contain the critical toxin? If so, could they have survived the preparation, or would the tetrodotoxin have been denatured by the heat of the charcoal grill? What about the application of the toxin? How could the bokor make certain that the victim would not die from the poison? Once again, many of these questions could be answered from the literature.

Tetrodotoxication is caused principally by the members of four families of the Tetraodontiformes: the Tetraodontidae, the puffers; the Diodontidae, the porcupine fishes; the Canthigasteridae, the sharp-nosed puffers; and the Molidae, the molas or ocean sunfishes (Halstead 1978; Shipp 1974). Both the Molidae and Canthigasteridae have but a single species known to be toxic, and of the two, only *Mola mola* L. is found in Haitian waters. Diodontidae contains two genera with poisonous species, *Chilomycterus* and *Diodon*. Only *Chilomycterus atinga* L., *C. schoepi*, and possibly *C. antennatus* Cuvier are both toxic and found in the Caribbean. *Diodon hystrix* and *D. holacanthus*, two species found in the zombie poisons, have a pantropical distribution, and both are known to be toxic (Bouder et al. 1962; Halstead 1978; Kao 1966). It was a species of *Diodon* caught off the Cape of Good Hope that was responsible for the poisoning of the two Dutch sailors from the *Postilion* (Richardson 1861; Richardson 1893).

By far the most significant family of toxic puffers is the Tetraodontidae, which includes the important genera *Arothron*, *Lagocephalus*, *Fugu*, and *Sphoeroides*, and some thirty-eight species known to be poisonous (Halstead 1978). Most of these are native to the Indo-Pacific. Both *Lagocephalus laevigatus laevigatus* L. and *L. lagocephalus* L., however, are found in tropical waters of the Atlantic. So are both *Sphoeroides spengleri* Bloch and *S. testudineus* L., the two other fish that regularly appear in the zombie preparations. Members of the genus *Sphoeroides* are closely related to the Japanese fugu fish and are known to be especially virulent (Halstead 1978). The liver of a specimen of *S. testudineus* was responsible for the death of an elderly woman in Florida in the mid-1950s (Benson 1956). Tetrodotoxin has been found in both species of puffer used by the Haitian bokors. In addition, there are two other morphologically similar species, *Sphoeroides annulatus* Jenyns and *S. maculatus* Bloch and Schneider, which are found in Haitian waters; both are known to be toxic (Goe and Halstead 1953; Lalone et al. 1963; Larson et al. 1960; Kao 1966). The Haitian bokor did not distinguish between *S. spen-*

gleri and *S. testudineus*, referring to both by the vernacular name
crapaud du mer—the sea toad—and so it may be possible that
these other superficially similar species may also be used in the
zombie preparations. At any rate, there can be no doubt that the
species used by the Haitian bokor are toxic.

Other issues relevant to the zombie mystery were clarified by
a remarkable account handed down by the Mexican historian
Francisco Javier Clavigero. In 1706, while seaching for a new
mission site in Baja, California, four Spanish soldiers came upon
a campfire where indigenous fishermen had left a roasted piece
of the liver of a *botete* (identified as *Sphoeroides lobatus*). Despite
the warnings of their guides, the soldiers divided the meat. One
of them ate a small piece, another chewed his portion without
swallowing, and the third only touched it. The first man died
within thirty minutes, the second shortly thereafter, and the third
remained unconscious until the next day, when he recovered
(Clavigero 1937). This story makes two critical points. That the
soldiers were poisoned by roasted meat demonstrates the important fact that heat—frying, boiling, baking, or stewing—does not
denature tetrodotoxin. B. W. Halstead and N. C. Bunker (1953)
found that the poison was not affected by the commercial canning process, which included placing open cans of fish in a steam
exhaust at 100°C for ten minutes; the cans were then sealed and
placed in a steam retort under a pressure of 12.5 pounds per
square inch at 116°C for seventy-five minutes. Neither step
deactivated the tetrodotoxin. T. Fukuda (1937) reported that
poisonous material could be placed in boiling water for an hour
without losing its toxicity. Finally, J. Benson (1956), as we have
seen, presented the case of an elderly woman who died after
having eaten the fried liver of *Sphoeroides testudineus*.

The fate of the three soldiers in Clavigero's account also
illustrates the fact that, although tetrodotoxin is one of the most
poisonous substances found in nature, like any drug its effects
depend on dosage and the method of administration. Having
studied over a hundred cases of tetrodotoxication, the Japanese
investigators Fukuda and Tani (1937a, 1937b, 1941) distinguished four degrees of poisoning. The first two are characterized by progressive numbing sensations and the loss of motor
control. The third degree includes paralysis of the entire body,
difficulty in breathing, cyanosis, and low blood pressure—all
suffered while the victim retains clear consciousness. In the final

A. Sphoeroides dorsalis *Longley*

B. Sphoeroides spengleri *Bloch*

C. Sphoeroides testudineus *L.*

D. Sphoeroides maculatus *Bloch and Schneider*

Species of the genus Sphoeroides *known to be toxic and found in the
coastal marine waters of Haiti (*photos courtesy of Robert Shipp*)*

E. Sphoeroides nephalus *Goode and Bean*

F. Sphoeroides parvum *Shipp and Yerger*

G. Sphoeroides pachigaster *Müller and Troschel*

degree, death comes quickly as a result of respiratory failure; the blood pressure takes a precipitous fall, and the heart generally continues to pulsate for a while after the cessation of breathing (Fukuda and Tani 1941). Tetrodotoxin is topically active, and some of the first-degree symptoms have shown up in individuals who merely handle the toxic organs (Boyé 1911; Phisalix 1922). If the poison is ingested, the onset of the third degree may be very rapid. The sailors on the *Postilion* died within seventeen minutes of eating the toxic fish (Richardson 1861). Larsen (1942) documents a fatality that occurred four minutes after the appearance of the first symptoms. On the other hand, Tahara (1896) described a case in which severe intoxication did not occur until almost twelve hours after exposure. In another clinical example, the patient died fourteen hours after eating the ovary of a puffer (Fukuda and Tani 1937a). Generally, the first symptoms occur within an hour, and most deaths occur between three and eight hours after ingestion of the toxin (Fukuda and Tani 1937a, 1937b, 1941; Bonde 1948; Benson 1956; Mosher et al. 1964; Kao 1966).

The Haitian bokor recognize the potency of their preparations and acknowledge, at least implicitly, the importance of proper application and correct dosage. Although they believe that the creation of the zombie is a magical act, and that the poisons always kill, they note that certain combinations of the powders are "too explosive" or that they "kill too completely." Each poison preparation must be carefully "weighed," a notion that has both spiritual and practical connotations. One houngan suggested, it will be recalled, that he had three zombie poisons, all of which contained the sea toad (*Sphoeroides testudineus*); one poison killed immediately, another caused the victim to waste away, whereas the third caused the victim's skin to peel away before death. Furthermore, it is perhaps of some significance that the poison supposedly is never put into the victim's food; rather, it is applied repeatedly to the skin or placed in open wounds. There are three possibilities here. Though it was repeatedly denied by each bokor, it may be that the poison *is* on certain occasions put into the victim's food. On the other hand, given the toxicity of the fish, the bokor might in fact recognize that, ingested orally, the preparation would simply kill the victim outright. Finally, it is possible that quite the opposite is the case. If the preparation were weak rather than excessively potent, it would be much more efficient to administer the toxin directly into the bloodstream. Tetrodotoxin is forty to fifty times as toxic when administered parenterally as when it is ingested (Mosher et al. 1964). A complete understanding of the action of the zombie preparation will have to await the outcome of laboratory studies.

One final point is critical. In Japan, those who are poisoned by tetrodotoxin generally reach a crisis after no more than six hours (Fukuda and Tani 1941). If the victim survives that period, he or she may expect a full recovery, at least from the effects of tetrodotoxin. This makes it at least theoretically possible for a poison victim to appear dead, be hastily buried, and then recover in the coffin.

The implications of these conclusions were impressive. Here was a possible material basis for the entire zombie phenomenon—a folk poison containing known toxins fully capable of pharmacologically inducing a state of apparent death. The peculiar symptoms described by Clairvius Narcisse closely matched the quite particular symptoms of tetrodotoxin poisoning and suggested that he had been exposed to poison. If this did not prove that he had been a zombie, it did, at least, substantiate his case. And there was one more especially haunting fact. Every indication pointed to the possibility that Narcisse had remained conscious the entire time. Totally paralyzed, he may have been a passive observer of his own funeral.

CHAPTER FIVE

THE "ANTIDOTE"

Each zombie powder has a locally recognized "antidote" (*contre poudre*), which for the well-being of all concerned must be prepared on the same day and before the poison itself is made. It will be recalled that all the poisons described in the last chapter were prepared some distance from human habitation, and that, although the houngan's presence assured the safety of participants, he himself did not touch any of the ingredients or take part directly in the process. The zombie poison was made by an associate who is neither an apprentice nor assistant, but rather is perceived as the physical support of the houngan (Davis 1985). The reputed antidote, on the other hand, is prepared within the hounfour itself, inside the *bagi*, the inner sanctum of the temple, and it is the houngan who gathers the ingredients, concocts the preparation, and directs the activity. In one case, the jars containing the finished zombie poison are placed inside the coffin that has been dug up in the graveyard and reburied in the court of the hounfour; the liquid antidote is poured into a rum bottle, which is placed upright over the grave, its base buried in the earth, its mouth pointing to the sky.

Unlike the poison, the ingredients and composition of the various antidotes are completely inconsistent from one region to the next. For example, the antidote prepared at Saint Marc consisted of over thirty ingredients. The houngan began by placing in a mortar several handfuls of the dried or fresh leaves of six plants: aloe (*Aloe vera* L.); guaiac (*Guaiacum officinale* L.); *cedre* (*Cedrela odorata* L.); bois chandelle (*Amyris maritima* Jacq.); and *cadavre gaté* (cf. *Capparis* sp.). This plant material was ground with a quarter-ounce of rock salt, then added to an enamel basin containing ten crushed mothballs, a cup of seawater, several ounces of clairin or cane alcohol, a bottle of perfume, and a quarter-litre of a solution purchased from the local apothecary and known as *magic noire*, "black magic." Additional ingredients included ground human bones, shavings from a mule's tibia and

Gathering leaves for the "antidote"

a dog's skull, various colored and magically named talc powders, ground match heads, and sulphur powder. It was a straightforward procedure devoid of ritual or danger. The end product was a green liquid with a strong ammonia scent.

At Gonaïves, on the other hand, the antidote contained a handful of bayahond leaves (*Prosopsis julliflora* (Sw.) DC.), three handfuls of avé leaves (*Petiveria alliacea* L.), a litre of clairin and ammonia, and three magically prepared lemons. The antidote prepared in the Valley of Léogane consisted solely of ammonia, clairin, and various aromatic solutions purchased at the local apothecary. Finally the representative antidote at Petite Rivière de Nippes included clairin, rum, sugar, basil leaves (*Ocimum basilicum* L.), ground human bones, *cadavre gaté* (cf. *Capparis* sp.), and corn (*Zea mays* L.). Integral to this last preparation was the ritual paraphernalia—a candle composed of wax into which magic powders had been kneaded, a cross of feathers plucked from the sacrificed rooster—that promised to guard the individual from the power of his own poison. In this sense, the antidote was believed not only to neutralize the effects of the poison on the actual victim, but also to protect the poisoner. This same preparation could also be used for protection during other phases of the process of creating the zombie. It was, for example, rubbed on the skin before lifting the coffin of the dead child from the ground when the human bones were obtained for the poison.

The houngan supervising the preparation of the contre poudre *in the inner sanctum of the hounfour*

The final preparation ready to be bottled

Similarly it promised to protect the bokor and his assistants when they went to the cemetery to raise the zombie. It was this potion which, like a smelling salt, was said to be passed beneath the nose of the comatose victim.

Most of the plants used in the fabrication of the various reputed antidotes are well-known medicinal plants both in Haiti and elsewhere. These are discussed in turn below.

Aloe vera L., Liliaceae (aloes)

Species of the African genus *Aloe* contain anthraquinone cathartic principles and have been used commonly as potent laxatives in many regions. The Zulu steep the crushed leaves of *Aloe macracantha* Bak. in water and administer the preparation as an enema to clean out the intestines following ritual purgatives (Watt and Breyer-Brandwijk 1962). The fresh leaves of *Aloe vera* L. are used as a purgative in Haiti (Brutus and Pierre-Noel 1960) and in the Bahamas (Eldridge 1975). Similar use has been made of both *A. ferox* Mill. and *A. davyana* Schonl. (Watt and Breyer-Brandwijk 1962).

Extracts from the leaves and roots of various species of *Aloe* are employed in both the Americas and the Old World to treat skin conditions. In Haiti the juice from the leaves of *A. vera* is applied to burns, boils, ulcers, topical sores, and to relieve the itching of dermatitis, eczema, psoriasis, and inflammation (Brutus and Pierre-Noel 1960). Throughout the Antilles the juice of *A. vera* has been reported as an efficacious treatment of sunburn, and its therapeutic properties have found a place in modern medicine in the treatment of X-ray burns (Eldridge 1975). Species of *Aloe* are commonly used to treat sunburn in Africa, and in many regions the leaf juice, diluted in water, is employed as a body wash and general tonic. The Zulu apply a decoction of the leaf of *A. ferox* Mill. to venereal sores. Throughout Africa, species of *Aloe* are also employed to aid in the healing of wounds. The Kone of Sekukuniland use the leaf of *A. burgersfortensis* Reynolds for this purpose. The Tswana and Kwena incise snakebite wounds and dress them with a pulp of *A. davyana*, whereas the Xhosa simply cut open the leaf of *A. saponaria* Haw. and apply it directly to any surface wound (Watt and Breyer-Brandwijk 1962).

Both in the Antilles and in South Africa, decoctions of aloe leaves are administered to women just before they give birth in order to assist the delivery (Eldridge 1975; Watt and Breyer-

Brandwijk 1962). Elsewhere, species of aloe have been used as abortifacients, fish poisons, anthelmintics, insecticides, vermifuges, rodent repellents, and antisyphilitics, as well as in the treatment of gonorrhea and ophthalmia. Several species, including *A. candelabrum* Berger and especially *A. marlothii* Berger, are universal ingredients in African snuffs. The nectar of the flower of *A. ferox* has also been reported as a narcotic (Watt and Breyer-Brandwijk 1962). In Haiti, *Aloe vera* is said to treat madness and drive off evil spirits (Huxley 1966).

Guaiacum officinale L., Zygophyllaceae (guaiac, *gaiac franc*)
Throughout the Antilles *lignum vitae* is an important medicinal plant. The wood and bark contain saponins, as well as an aromatic resin known as *gum guaiacum*. Haitians use the resin as a rub to fortify their teeth and gums, and they also dissolve it in alcohol and drink it as a treatment for gout and arthritis. They mix the roots with a number of other plants in a decoction which is both diuretic and purportedly a treatment for venereal disease. A tea made from the bark is taken for rheumatism and to relieve pain (Brutus and Pierre-Noel 1960).
    Similar uses of the plant have been reported elsewhere in the Antilles. Jamaicans dissolve the resin in gin for use as a painkiller. A decoction made from the bark and wood treats venereal disease, gout, rheumatism, and intermittent fevers and is also used as a cathartic in Jamaica, the Bahamas, Trinidad, and Tobago. The resin soaked in rum is a gargle for sore throat and reportedly relieves pain if applied topically to cuts and bruises. The flower is employed as a laxative and the boiled leaves are abortifacient (Ayensu 1981).

Cedrela odorata L., Meliaceae (*cedre*)
This plant is the basis of one of the oldest colonial folk remedies in Haiti. The wood is grated and infused in white wine for eight days and then taken orally twice a day for the relief of malarial fever. The leaves, roots, and bark are steeped in clairin for a month and taken for rheumatism. A topical rub made from the aromatic leaves serves as a general body tonic and as a means of realigning the various components of the Vodoun soul (Brutus and Pierre-Noel 1960). In Jamaica the leaves and twigs are used in baths to treat fever and pain. The seeds reportedly make an effective vermifuge and the rootbark a febrifuge. Analysis has

shown that 3 percent of the wood is composed of an aromatic oil (Ayensu 1981).

Capparis cynophyllophora L., Capparidaceae
(*bois ca-ca*, "shit tree")
Capparis sp., Capparidaceae (*cadavre gaté*, "spoiled corpse")

As the vernacular names suggest, both of these plants smell foul. Haitians use the roots of *C. cynophyllophora* in an infusion to treat edema and make the leaves into magical charms. Some uses of these charms are to protect the newborn, drive away the *loup garou* (werewolves), clear haunted houses, cure madness, and capture the love of a desirable mate (Huxley 1966). The Vodoun houngan recognize the unidentified wood *cadavre gaté* as one of the most important healing plants, and shavings of the wood are used in numerous folk remedies and as protective charms.

Related species of the genus *Capparis* are among the most important magico-medicinal plants in Africa. In Tanzania *Capparis tomentosa* Lam. has been reported as a purgative, whereas the Zulu chew the leaf as a treatment against snakebite and to cure madness. The Zulu also rub the powdered, burned roots into scarifications incised into their skin as a remedy for headache, and they prepare an infusion for the relief of stomach problems; they also use the roots to treat hepatitis and malaria. The Lobedu of Zimbabwe smoke the bark to relieve chest pains. Elsewhere in Africa the plant has been reported as a counterirritant, expectorant, and diuretic, and as a treatment for leprosy, ophthalmia, and wounds (Watt and Breyer-Brandwijk 1962).

The plant is generally believed to possess magical powers. The Zulu use it as a charm against misfortune. The smoke of the burned bark is said by the Lobedu to ward off storms. The Venda rub the root shavings into a paste, which is placed on the end of a stick and pointed to the heavens when rain becomes excessive and threatens to inundate the fields. After a Vendu woman has given birth to twins she and her husband must be ceremonially cleansed. A tunnel is dug into an anthill and leaves of *C. tomentosa* mixed in water are poured into the hole. The couple then creep in. They drink some of the same infusion and spill the remainder across the threshold of the tunnel. The opening is closed in. A small hut is built at the opposite end of the tunnel and a fire is laid, over which a decoction of *C. tomentosa* leaves is prepared. The parents crawl out of the anthill, step over the

boiling decoction, leave by the opposite door of the hut, and go
home without looking back (Watt and Breyer-Brandwijk 1962).

Capparis citrifolia Lam. is another equally important magical
plant in parts of Africa. The Xhosa administer an emetic made
from its root to alleviate the suffering of the bewitched. They use
the same plant as a war charm, believing that it renders the
warrior invisible. Small branches of the tree are thrust into the
thatch over the doorway of huts to ward off lightning. During the
Xhosa circumcision ritual, a small piece of meat cooked over the
embers of *C. citrifolia* and wrapped in the covering of the thorny
twig of the same plant is thrown to each initiate in turn. The boy
must catch the offering in midair and thus harness the plant's
power to gain strength and courage in the lifelong battle against
evil (Watt and Breyer-Brandwijk 1962).

Petiveria alliacea L., Phytolaccaceae (*avé*)

This weedy shrub contains mustard oils that account for its foul
smell (Ayensu 1981). In Haiti an infusion of the leaves is employed as an enema to treat intestinal parasites. A bath in which
the leaves have been steeped is said to induce sweating and serve
as a febrifuge (Brutus and Pierre-Noel 1960). It has also been
reported as an antispasmodic and is believed to drive away insect
pests such as roaches and bedbugs. It is a love charm and, in
addition, it offers protection against the nefarious aims of the
loup garou (Huxley 1966). Other peoples in the Antilles use the
plant to treat venereal disease, influenza, malaria, jaundice, cystitis, skin eruptions, and arthritis. It is a counterirritant for visceral
pain, an abortifacient, and many believe that it is also an aphro-
disiac (Ayensu 1981).

Prosopsis juliflora (Sw.) DC., Leguminosae (bayahond)

Haitians use the resin exuded by the trunk of this tree to guard
against colds and influenza. They suck crude pieces of the resin
to relieve the pain of sore throat and grind the fresh root into an
infusion which they use to treat diarrhea (Brutus and Pierre-
Noel 1960).

Ocimum basilicum L., Labiatae (basilic)

This aromatic herb is said in Haiti to aid digestion and relieve
stomach pain. It is a major ingredient in the aromatic "sweet"
baths that are believed by the Vodounist to restore an individual's

spiritual equilibrium (Brutus and Pierre-Noel 1960). The leaves also reportedly treat bronchitis, rheumatism, colic, headaches, and pains of the eye. In the sphere of magic, the plant is believed to bring good luck, attract clients into business establishments, dominate spirits, and ward off the forces of evil, particularly the maleficent *loup garou*, the werewolf (Huxley 1966).

Ingredients: Summary and Discussion

All the various preparations have two features in common: aromatic ingredients, which along with the inorganic constituents—ammonia, mothballs, perfume, pharmaceutical potions—give the antidotes strong, pungent odors; and magico-religious associations, both from Haitian and from African cultures, which the Vodounists believe imbue the potions with magical strength and potency. The composition of the various antidotes, however, is inconsistent from locality to locality and, unlike the poison itself, is comparatively uninteresting from a chemical point of view.

In each case the initial treatment of the victim involves the topical application of the antidote as a vigorous massage. In no instance, however, is this procedure intended to revive the victim from the dead; on the contrary, the potion is believed merely to prevent him or her from succumbing to the poison, and although it may be administered as a protective measure to those making the poison, it is mainly applied to those who know that they have been exposed to the poison but have yet to die. The antidote is effective only during the two or three weeks immediately following exposure to the poison. After that time the houngan or mambo must resort to the standard Vodoun curing ceremony that is used to exorcise any death spirit.

For the treatment, the victim is dressed in the clothing of the dead, has his or her jaw bound, and cotton placed in the nostrils. The feet and hands are tied together and he or she is placed in a narrow trough dug into the ground of the hounfour. The mambo covers the entire body with a white sheet. A *pierre tonnere* and the skulls of a human and a dog are placed on top of the sheet, and the sucker of a banana tree (*Musa paradisiaca* L.) is placed alongside the victim's body. Seven candles cradled in orange peels surround the "grave," and calabashes rest by the victim's head and on the abdomen and feet. These three offerings represent the sacred concepts of the crossroads, the cemetery, and Grans

Bwa, the spirit of the forest. The mambo straddles the grave and invokes Guede, the spirit of the dead. She then takes a live chicken and passes it slowly over the body of the victim, then breaks each of the bird's limbs to extract the death spirit from the corresponding limbs of the patient. The sacrifice of the chicken is complete when the mambo bites off its head so that the victim may partake of the sacrificial blood and be bathed by the antidote. A ritual water jar is then broken over the grave, and the contents of the calabashes, along with the water and the hot wax and oil from the lamps, are rubbed into his or her skin. Finally, as the victim lies in the ground seven handfuls of earth taken from the crossroads, the cemetery, and the forest are flung into the grave. The mambo's sharp cry orders him or her from the ground. As her assistants hurriedly push the loose dirt into the grave, two men tear the victim from the grave. The victim leaps up and the spirit is believed to flee into the banana plant. After a ritual bath with the blood of the sacrificed chicken and a restful night in the sanctity of the temple, the victim is well.

Considering the composition of the various "antidotes" and the way they are administered, it appears that the ingredients are probably either chemically inert or else are used in insufficient quantities to result in any pharmacological activity. In short, the recognized antidotes appear to be merely symbolic supports for what is essentially a magico-religious healing ceremony. A pharmacologically active antidote may, in fact, exist in Haiti, but it is certainly not among the ingredients and preparations concocted by the houngan with whom I worked. Nor did they deny this. They believe that the true antidote is the power of their own magic.

There is no known medical antidote to tetrodotoxin, and therefore treatment of poisoning cases is, of necessity, largely symptomatic (Kao 1966; Halstead 1978). Laxatives and emetics are useful in removing as much of the tainted material from the body, and as rapidly, as possible. Taizo Akashi (1880) mentions the use of two plants, *taisei* (*Isatis oblongata* DC.) and *shosei* (*Crataegus cuneata* Sieb. and Zucc.), in folk preparations that also include common grasses and human feces. Yoshizumi Tahara (1896) employed numerous emetics, including camphor, nux vomica, castor oil, and senna leaves. Among all clinically studied emetics, apomorphine has been found to be the most effective and useful (Fukuda and Tani 1937a). Unfortunately, the value of emetics and purgatives is somewhat questionable as the first symptoms may show up several hours after ingestion of the fish, by which time the tetrodotoxin has been absorbed into the body. S. Kimura (1927) recommended the ingestion of large amounts of bicarbonate of soda, a possibly efficacious remedy as tetrodotoxin is highly pH sensitive and is readily denatured by alkali (Kao 1966).

The single most important therapeutic measure is artificial respiration (Halstead 1978). T. A. Torda and his colleagues concluded that treatment should be aimed at: (1) maintenance of airway and ventilation; (2) maintenance of adequate circulation and renal function; and (3) treatment of cardiac dysrhythmias (Torda et al. 1973). In brief, even the modern physician can do little except allow the toxin to run its course, meanwhile doing whatever is possible to maintain the vital physiological functions. It is significant, however, in regard to the zombie problem, that those who do survive tetrodotoxication generally suffer little or no permanent damage. One lives or one dies, and there appears to be no middle ground.

There is, however, in the process of creating the Haitian zombie, a very curious feature which may prove to be merely coincidental, but which may turn out to be significant. According to numerous informants the zombie, as it is taken from the grave and again on the following day, is fed a paste that contains significant quantities of *Datura stramonium*, the plant known in Haiti as the *concombre zombi*, or the zombie's cucumber. As previously discussed, this plant is violently psychoactive, and it owes its pharmacological activity to a series of tropane alkaloids including scopolamine and atropine. The biogenesis of tetrodotoxin within the puffer fish is not yet understood, but it is of some significance to the zombie phenomenon, particularly in regard to the purported use of *Datura stramonium*. Tetrodotoxin is a most peculiar compound, and it does not appear to be readily accessible via the known biogenic pathways from acetate, mevalonate, or the amino acids (Woodward 1964; Kim et al. 1975). Generally, such a specialized and structurally unique substance appears only once in the course of evolution and, as a result, is found only in closely related organisms that are derived presumably from a common ancestor. For many years, tetrodotoxin appeared to be restricted to a single order of marine fish, the Tetraodontiformes.

Then, surprisingly, it turned up in the California newt *Taricha*
torosa (Mosher et al. 1964). Subsequent research has identified it
in ten other species in four genera of the one family Salamandri-
dae (Kao 1966); a goby fish (*Gobius criniger*) found in the sea
off the shore of Taiwan (Noguchi and Hashimoto 1973); atelopid
frogs (*Atelopus varius, A. chiriquiensis*) from Costa Rica (Kim et
al. 1975); and the blue-ringed octopus (*Hapalochlaena maculosa*)
from the Great Barrier Reef of Australia (Sheumack et al. 1978).
Such an erratic distribution has been described both as an "evo-
lutionary mystery" (Fuhrman 1967, 67) and as a "coincidental
genetic development" (Kim et al. 1975, 152), but it has also
suggested to some authorities that the toxin originates in the food
chain, either as a toxin or in the form of a nontoxic chemical
constituent that is later metabolized into a toxic product (Halstead 1978).

Within the puffer fish themselves, there is considerable variability in toxin levels among natural populations. Toxin levels
differ not only according to sex, seasonality, and geographical
location, but also among the individual fish within a single population. K. Tsuda, for example, found that even during the season
of greatest toxicity only about 50 percent of the tested specimens
from a single site were toxic. Halstead and Schall (1955) observed a similar trend from among the poisonous puffers they
captured in a single spot off the Galapagos Islands. Two specimens of the same puffer species (*Arothron meleagris*) captured
about the same time of year, one from the Hawaiian Islands, the
other from the Phoenix Islands, differed in toxicity; the one from
Hawaii was innocuous while the other was violently poisonous
(Halstead 1951). A puffer fish from Brazil, *Tetrodon psittacus*, now
known as *Colomesus psittacus* (Bloch and Schneider) Corrotucho
(Shipp 1974), is reportedly poisonous only in June and July
(Gonsalves 1907). Among Japanese species of the fish, toxicity
begins to increase in December and reaches a peak in May or
June (Tani 1940). The Caribbean species, including *Sphoeroides
testudineus*, are most toxic in July—precisely the month when
the most potent zombie preparations are said to be made (Kao
pers. comm.). *Sphoeroides maculatus* is toxic only between May
and June (Robinson and Schwartz 1968). In general, the fish's
toxicity is correlated with the reproductive cycle and is higher in
females, but the remarkable variability in toxin levels even among
separate populations of the same species has prompted sugges-

tions that concentration or presence of the toxins may be correlated with food habits (Halstead 1978). Bo Holmstedt (pers. comm.) notes that puffer fish grown in culture do not develop tetrodotoxin. Bruce Halstead reports experiments in which nontoxic species which were fed poisonous puffer meat became toxic within a fortnight. It is possible that puffer fish, in addition to synthesizing tetrodotoxin endogenously, may serve as transvectors of either tetrodotoxin or ciguatoxin (Halstead 1978; Habekost et al. 1955).

Ciguatoxin is an ichthyosarcotoxin of uncertain origins that contaminates a wide variety of phyllogenetically distinct fish (Halstead 1978). Its toxicological action appears to be related to its direct effects on excitable membranes, and the clinical symptoms of severe poisoning include "paresthesia with prickling about the lips, tongue and nose together with a tingling sensation in the extremities . . . a state of malaise . . . nausea . . . digestive distress . . . gastrointestinal, cardiovascular and nervous pain . . . with death resulting from respiratory paralysis" (Dufra et al. 1976, 61).

In Australia the Aborigines know of a very strange plant, actually a tree, that they call *ngmoo*. They carve holes in its trunk and fill them with water, and within a day they have a beverage that produces a mild stupor (Schleiffer 1979). The branches and leaves, when placed in standing water, effectively stun eels, forcing them to the surface where they can be killed. Knowledge of the remarkable properties of this plant found its way north to New Caledonia. There the native inhabitants discovered that the leaves could be used as an effective antidote to mild ciguatera poisoning, an observation that modern science has confirmed (Dufra et al. 1976; Jacques 1945; Barrau 1957). The plant is *Duboisia myoporoides* R.Br. and, like certain other members of the Solanaceae, it contains a number of potent tropane alkaloids, including atropine and scopolamine (Dufra et al. 1976). As I mentioned above, there is no known medical antidote for tetrodotoxin, but laboratory experiments have suggested that, as in the case of *Duboisia myoporoides* and ciguatera, atropine does relieve certain symptoms (Benson 1956; Torda et al. 1973; Golin and Larson 1969).

Datura stramonium, like its relative from New Caledonia, contains atropine and scopolamine. Could this plant, so provocatively named *concombre zombi*, be serving as an effective but un recognized counteragent to the zombie poison? The timing of administration suggests not. It is nevertheless curious that a plant known to contain compounds reputed to relieve certain symptoms of tetrodotoxication should be administered following the resuscitation of the victim. Counteragent or not, a strong and timely dose of *Datura stramonium* would undoubtedly be instrumental in inducing and maintaining the zombie state. For if tetrodotoxin provides the physiological template upon which cultural beliefs and fears work, datura amplifies those mental processes a thousand times. Alone, its intoxication has been characterized as an induced state of psychotic delirium marked by disorientation, acute confusion, and complete amnesia (Weil pers. comm.). Administered to an individual who has already suffered the effects of tetrodotoxin, who has already passed through the ground, and who may have actually remained conscious the entire time, the devastating psychological effects would be staggering. It is in the course of that datura intoxication that the zombie is baptized with a new name and led away to be socialized into a new existence.

Before abandoning the issue of reputed antidotes for a consideration of the cultural beliefs and psychological forces that mediate the zombie phenomenon, some mention should be made of the widespread contention that salt immediately returns the zombie to the realm of the living. This belief has been referred to by a number of authorities (Parsons 1928; Leyburn 1941; Kerboull 1977; Mars 1945, 1947; Bourguignon 1959). Alfred Métraux notes that "if imprudently they are given a plate containing even a grain of salt the fog that cloaks their minds instantly clears away and they become conscious of their terrible servitude" (Métraux 1972, 283). Jules Faine adds, "nourished on food from which salt is rigorously excluded, they are thought to be able to regain their natural senses and all their mental faculties if they taste the least grain of this substance" (Faine 1937, 303). Similar convictions have been described in numerous popular books, and it will be recalled that a bar of candy containing salted peanuts was said to have released the fury of the zombies in Seabrook's notorious account in *The Magic Island* (Seabrook 1929; Taft 1938; Franck 1920; Hurston 1981; Loederer 1935).

There is, on the face of it, no pharmacological basis to this widely held belief. The quantities of salt in question are so small that the issue must be interpreted for its symbolic value. It is of note, for example, that according to Vodoun belief an unbaptized child may be taken by the devil, incarnated in the form of Baron Samedi, the spirit of the dead, and that to release the infant from his grasp, a small taste of salt must be placed upon the child's tongue (Dewisme 1957).

It is, nevertheless, remarkable that this belief in the therapeutic value of salt should be so widely held. Tetrodotoxin prevents the generation of action potentials by blocking the voltage-sensitive sodium channels of the excitable membrane of nerve and muscle (Kao 1983; Ritchie 1975; Narahashi et al. 1964). R. J. Down (1969) mentions the possibility, based on his laboratory research, that an increased concentration of sodium ions (Na +) might offer some protection against tetrodotoxication. In discussing the pharmacological basis of zombification in reference to one of my early articles on the phenomenon (1983a), Raymond Prince concluded that "the salt restriction belief could have some basis in neurochemistry" (Prince 1985, 190). I disagree, as any adminstration of salt to the purported zombies would occur long after the effects of their initial exposure to the zombie poison and to tetrodotoxin would have run their course. It is, however, a curious coincidence "that it is salt, or rather a reversible block of the sodium conductance by tetrodotoxin, which, *cum grano salis*, may be the chief aetiological factor of zombification" (Anon. 1984, 1220–21).

CHAPTER SIX

EVERYTHING IS POISON,

NOTHING IS POISON:

THE EMIC VIEW

The lengthy discussion in the previous chapters of the ingredients of the zombie powder and the purported antidotes must not obscure the fact that the constituents themselves explain very little about the zombie phenomenon. All that the formula of the powder suggests is a means by which an individual might, under rare circumstances, be made to appear dead. The same thing has occurred in Japan, however infrequently, but those who succumbed to toxic fugu preparations did not become zombies; they were merely poison victims. Any psychoactive drug—remembering that the difference between a hallucinogen, a medicine, and a poison is often a matter merely of dosage—has within it a completely ambivalent potential. Pharmacologically, it induces a certain condition, but that condition is only raw material to be worked upon by particular cultural or psychological forces and expectations—what medical experts call the "set and setting" of any drug experience. Set, in these terms, is the individual's expectations of what the drug will do to him or her; setting is the environment—both physical and, in this case, social—in which the drug is taken (Weil 1972). In the northwest rain forests of Oregon, for example, there are a number of native species of hallucinogenic fungi. Collectors who deliberately seek out and eat these mushrooms usually experience a pleasant intoxication. Those who inadvertently consume them while foraging for benign edible mushrooms invariably end up in the poison unit of the nearest hospital. The mushroom itself, however, has not changed.

I do not mean to suggest that the zombie powder might be a pleasant hallucinogen. But, like the fungi, its potential is latent. The Japanese victim lying conscious but paralyzed while his family mourns his death may, upon recovery, rationalize his terrifying experience within the expectations of his society. Everyone understands what fugu poisoning can be like. In the phantasmagoric cultural landscape of Haitian peasant society, Clairvius Narcisse doubtless had his own expectations that he may have carried with him literally into and out of the grave. Until we understand these expectations, we cannot claim to know anything about the zombie phenomenon.

At this point, it is worth reiterating that the Vodoun worldview, like any other, including our own, is moved by a fundamental quest for unity—a struggle to create order out of perceived disorder, integrity in the face of diversity, consistency in the face of anomaly. This vital urge to render coherent and intelligible models of the universe lies at the root of all religion, philosophy, and, of course, science. What distinguishes scientific thinking from that of traditional and, as it often turns out, nonliterate cultures is the tendency of the latter to seek the most direct means to achieve total understanding of the world. The Vodounist spins a web of belief that is all-inclusive, that generates an illusion of total comprehension. No matter how an outsider might view it, for the individual member of that society the illusion holds, not because of coercive force, but simply because for him or her there is no other way. Within the parameters of ritual behavior and mystical belief, of course, there is a vast realm available for intellectual speculation and experimentation. As E. E. Evans-Pritchard so precisely wrote: "Within the limits set by their patterns, they show great intelligence, but it cannot operate beyond these limits. Or, to put it another way: they reason excellently within the idiom of their beliefs, but they cannot reason outside, or against their beliefs, because they have no other idiom in which to express their thoughts" (Evans-Pritchard 1937, 338).

A first step toward assessing and understanding the Haitian zombie is the elucidation of the categories and rules maintained and endorsed by the Vodounists themselves. Vodoun, of course, is an eclectic tradition with some local variation, but, allowing for this, the basic thrust of any emic analysis must be consistent with the tenets of local belief. The accuracy of one's observations is measured by their ability to generate statements and conclusions with which the native would concur, and indeed it is the Vodoun believer who is the ultimate judge. A second level of analysis, however, lifts the observer to the position of judge and obliges him or her not simply to understand how the informants see their world, but also to generate scientifically useful explanations to account for social and cultural phenomena. At this etic level of analysis, "the observer is free to use alien categories and rules derived from the data language of science. Frequently etic operations involve the measurement and juxtaposition of activities and events that native informants may find inappropriate or meaningless" (Harris 1979, 32). The importance of understanding the emic perspective of the society under study cannot be overstressed, but to confuse this with an etic interpretation is "an invitation to ethnological disaster" (Marano 1982, 385). It is fair to say that most studies of the Haitian zombie and the application of the purported poisons and antidotes have made precisely this mistake (Hurston 1981; Douyon 1980; Kerboull 1973).

This chapter explores three issues. First, it outlines the emic notion of zombification, emphasizing that, in Vodounist belief, the creation of a zombie is essentially a magical act involving the manipulation and eventual dominance of various components of the victim's spiritual and physical being. Second, it examines the role of the folk powder in the process and describes the circumstances under which such a preparation could be implicated in the actual creation of a physical zombie. I argue that, to the Vodounist, a zombie of the spirit (*zombi astral, zombi ti bon ange*) and a zombie of the flesh (*zombi corps cadavre*) are equally real entities, but that for the latter to exist, one must seek an etic, or in this case pharmacological, explanation. The third issue involves an exploration of the literature on psychogenic or "voodoo death" and illness. Extending the model of set and setting as it has been applied to the study of hallucinogenic drugs, I present evidence suggesting that the potential victim of zombification in fact suffers a form of voodoo death in which psychosocial factors contribute to his expectations, and those in turn mediate both the potency of the sorcerer's spell and the pharmacological efficacy of the zombie powder.

Passage of   A zombie sits on the very cusp of death, at the intersection
Darkness   between the natural and supernatural realms, and the concepts
that circumscribe the phenomenon rest at the very base of the
Vodounist's cosmological worldview. It is with that worldview that
any exposition of the emic interpretation of zombification must
begin. For the Haitian Vodounist, the demarcation between the
material and the spiritual levels of being is a fine one indeed.
Through spirit possession, for example, the Vodoun acolyte
walks in and out of the supernatural world with an ease, frequency, and impunity that have consistently astonished ethnographic and medical observers (Deren 1953; Mars 1977; Lowenthal 1978; Wittkower 1964; Kiev 1962; Bourguignon 1976;
Zuesse 1985).[1] In Vodounist thought, the immediacy with which
the believer interacts with the spirits is but a consequence of the
remarkable dialogue that exists between humans and the loa.
The spirits are powerful and, if offended, can do great harm, but
they are also predictable and, if propitiated, will gratefully provide all the benefits of health, fertility, and prosperity. But just as
man must honor the spirits, so the loa are dependent on man, for
the human body is their receptacle. Usually they arrive during a
religious ceremony, ascending up the axis of the *poteau mitan*,
called forth by the rhythm of the drums or the vibration of a bell.
Once mounted, the possessed person loses all consciousness and

---

1. Early medical authorities viewed spirit possession as a form of pathology
(Dorsainvil 1975), whereas anthropologists have indicated that it is a completely
normal phenomenon that occurs when and where appropriate, usually within
the context of religious worship (Lowenthal 1978; Bourguignon 1976). They
have accurately characterized it as involving some kind of separation, transformation, and reintegration of the diverse aspects of the human psyche (Kiev
1962; Zuesse 1985; Deren 1953). Others have noted that spirit possession is a
culturally learned and reinforced response that has a therapeutic value as a
spiritual catharsis (Bourguignon 1976; Lowenthal 1978). But some central and
disturbing questions remain. How is it, for example, that a Vodounist who is
possessed experiences total amnesia, yet still manifests the predictable and often
complex behavior of the particular loa (Deren 1953)? And what psychological
mechanism can explain the fact that in certain documented instances, possessed
individuals have been able to expose themselves to fire without being physically
harmed (Wittkower 1964; Kiev 1962; Jahn 1961)?

A Vodoun acolyte or hounsis possessed by the loa

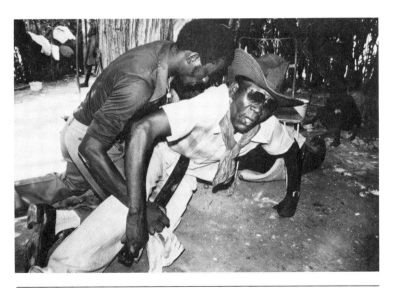

A houngan possessed by Ogoun

sense of self; he or she becomes the spirit, taking on its persona and powers. That, of course, is why the body of the possessed cannot be harmed.

But the human form is by no means just an empty vessel for the gods. Rather, it is the critical and single locus where a number of sacred forces may converge, and within the overall Vodoun quest for unity it is the fulcrum upon which harmony and balance may be finally achieved. The players in this drama are the basic components of man: the *z'étoile*, the *gros bon ange*, the *ti bon ange*, the *n'âme*, and the *corps cadavre*. The latter is the body itself, the flesh and the blood. The *n'âme* is the spirit of the flesh that allows each cell of the body to function. It is the residual presence of the n'âme, for example, that gives form to the corpse long after the clinical death of the body. The n'âme is a gift from God, which upon the death of the *corps cadavre* begins to pass slowly into the organisms of the soil; the gradual decomposition of the corpse is the result of this slow transferral of energy, a process that takes eighteen months to complete. Because of this, no coffin may be disturbed until it has been in the ground for that period of time.

The *z'étoile* is the one spiritual component that resides not in the body but in the sky. It is the individual's star of destiny, and it is viewed as a calabash that carries one's hope and all the many ordered events for the next life of the soul, a blueprint that will be a function of the course of the previous lifetime. If the shooting star is bright, so shall be the future of the individual.

The two aspects of the Vodoun soul, the *ti bon ange* and the *gros bon ange*, are best explained with a metaphor commonly used by the Haitians themselves. Sometimes when one stands in the late afternoon light the body casts a double shadow, a dark core and then a lighter penumbra, faint like the halo that sometimes surrounds the full moon. This ephemeral fringe is the *ti bon ange*, the "little good angel," while the image at the center is the *gros bon ange*, the "big good angel." The latter is the life force that all sentient beings share; it enters the individual at conception and functions only to keep the body alive. At clinical death, it returns immediately to God and once again becomes part of the great reservoir of energy that supports all life. But if the *gros bon ange* is undifferentiated energy, the *ti bon ange* is that part of the soul directly associated with the individual. As the *gros bon ange* provides each person with the power to act, it is the *ti bon ange* that

molds the individual sentiments within each act. It is one's aura,
and the source of all personality, character, and willpower.[2]

As the essence of one's individuality, the *ti bon ange* is the
logical target of sorcery, and its peril is compounded by the ease
and frequency with which it dissociates from the body. It is the *ti
bon ange*, for example, that travels during sleep to experience
dreams. Similarly, the brief sensation of emptiness that immediately follows a sudden scare is due to its temporary flight. And,
predictably, it is the *ti bon ange* that is displaced during possession
when the believer takes on the persona of the loa. At the same
time, because it is the *ti bon ange* that experiences life, it represents a precious accumulation of knowledge that must not be
squandered or lost. If and only if it is protected from sorcery and
permitted to complete its proper cycle, the *ti bon ange* may be
salvaged upon the death of the individual and its legacy preserved. Only in this way can the wisdom of past lives be
marshaled to serve the pressing needs of the living. Much ritual
effort, therefore, is expended to secure its safe and effortless
metamorphosis. During initiation, for example, the *ti bon ange*
may be extracted from the body and housed in a *canari*, a clay jar
that is placed in the inner sanctum of the hounfour. In this way
the *ti bon ange* continues to animate the living body while remaining directly within the protective custody of the houngan. Yet
even with these precautions there are no guarantees. Though it is

---

2. My findings are at odds in certain ways with those of Deren (1953) and
Métraux (1946), but the most important difference is actually one of semantics.
What I refer to as the *ti bon ange*, for example, other investigators have called the
gros bon ange; the actual functions of the two aspects of the Vodoun soul are
consistent. Métraux himself suggested that research into the nature of the
Vodoun soul is made "difficult by the wide range of beliefs and theories found
among Haitian Vodu worshippers according to their intellectual sophistication,
their religious background and contacts with the modern world" (Métraux 1946,
84). Métraux's interpretation was formed largely by interviews with a single
informant at the Bureau of Ethnology in Port-au-Prince. He notes that many of
her statements were contradicted outright by the one houngan he also interviewed. Métraux based his conclusions on his "impression that [his informant's]
candid statements reflected more closely the general beliefs of the Haitian
peasantry" (Métraux 1946, 85). The important point, though, is that Vodounists
share a conception of two aspects of the soul, one of which is the raw energy of
life, the other a more precise component that marks each individual with his or
her particular personality and persona.

difficult to kill one whose *ti bon ange* has been placed in a canari, if the magic used against the individual is strong enough, the resulting misery may be so great that the victim will ask the houngan to release the soul and end his or her ordeal. And even if the individual does survive life, he or she is still at risk in death, for with the demise of the *corps cadavre*, the houngan must break the canari so that the the the *ti bon ange* may return to hover about the body for seven days. Then, because the Vodounist does not believe in a physical resurrection of the body, the soul must be definitively separated from the flesh. This takes place during the *Dessounin*, which is the major death ritual. Throughout the period between death and Dessounin the *ti bon ange* is extremely vulnerable, and only when it is liberated from the flesh to descend below the dark abysmal waters is it relatively safe.

The *ti bon ange* remains below in the world of *Les Invisibles* for one day and one year and then, in one of the most important of Vodoun ceremonies—the *Wété Mo Nan Dlo* ("return the dead from the water")—it is reclaimed by the living and given new form. In place of the body that has decayed, the soul, now regarded as an *ésprit*, is deposited in another clay jar called a *govi*. The Haitians do not view this reclamation of the dead as an isolated sentimental act; on the contrary, it is considered as fundamental and inescapable as birth itself. One emerges from the womb an animal, the spiritual birth at initiation makes one human, but it is the final reemergence that marks one's birth as divine essence. The spirits in the govi are fed and clothed and then returned to the forest to dwell in trees and grottos, where they wait to be reborn. After the last of sixteen incarnations, the ésprit goes to Damballah Wedo, where it becomes undifferentiated as part of the *djo*, the cosmic breath that envelops the universe.

This lengthy passage of the *ti bon ange* corresponds to the metamorphosis of the individual into pure spiritual energy. With the successive passing of generations, the individual identified with the ésprit in the govi is transformed from the ancestor of a particular lineage into the generalized ancestor of all mankind. Yet even this pure spiritual energy must be made to serve, and for it to function it must become manifest. Thus, from the ancestral pool emerge archetypes, and these are the loa. It is, of course, possession, the return of the spirits to the bodies of men and women, that completes the sacred cycle—from man to ancestor,

ancestor to cosmic principle, principle to personage, and personage returning to displace the identity of man. Hence, while the
Vodounist serves his gods, he also gives birth to them, and this is
something that is never forgotten; as much as the spirit is the
source of the flesh, so the flesh gives rise to the spirit. Instead of
opposition between the two, there is mutual dependence. Thus
the regular arrival of the divine is not considered miraculous, but
inevitable.

Within this cosmic exchange, perhaps an individual's most
critical contribution is the preservation of his or her own equilibrium, for without it the receptacle of the gods is placed in danger.
The ideal form of humanity, therefore, is one of coherence,
wherein all the sacred components of the individual find their
proper place. The maintenance or restoration of this balance is
the duty of the houngan, and it accounts for his unique role as
healer. In our secular society, life and death are defined in strictly
clinical terms by physicians, with the fate of the spirit being
relegated to the domain of religious specialists who, significantly,
have nothing to say about the physical well-being of the living. In
Vodoun society, the physician is also the priest, for the condition
of the spirit is as important as—and in fact, determines—the
physical state of the body. Good or bad health results not from
the presence or absence of pathogens but from the proper or
improper balance of the individual. Sickness is disruption, im-
balance, and the manifestation of malevolent forces in the flesh.
Health is a state of harmony, and for the Vodounist it is something holy, like a perfect service for the gods.

Inevitably, however, there are times when the forces arrayed
against the individual are simply too powerful. If disharmony at
the core of man results in sickness, the irrevocable separation of
the spiritual components will bring death. But death, like life,
stretches far beyond the temporal limits of the body. Life begins
not at physical conception but at an earlier moment when God
first decides that a person should exist. Death is not defined just
by the passing of the flesh; rather, it is the moment when all the
spiritual components find their proper destination. Thus the
Vodoun adept, believing in the immortality of the spirit, fears
death not for its finality but because it is a critical and dangerous
passage during which the five vital components of man dissoci-
ate, leaving the *ti bon ange*, in particular, vulnerable to capture by
sorcery. It is the loss of the *ti bon ange*, that part of the soul that

manifests willpower, personality, and individual identity, which breaks the equilibrium of an individual and leaves in his or her wake the zombie.

To create a zombie, then, the bokor must capture the *ti bon ange* of the intended victim, and this magical act may be accomplished in a variety of ways. There is only one hitch. As in the case of illness and disease, death may be one of two kinds, unnatural and natural, with the latter being defined as a call from God (*mort bon dieu*) and thus beyond the influence of man. By Vodoun definition, only someone who dies an unnatural death can be made into a zombie, for only in such a circumstance will he or she be vulnerable to sorcery. At times, in fact, it may be in the bokor's interests to cause the unnatural death, and there are countless ways of doing so. Causing an unnatural death does not create a zombie; it just makes the victim immediately susceptible. But the distinction between natural and unnatural deaths is critical, because it provides the bokor with an obvious out should he fail, and an essential element of any witchcraft belief is its inherent ability to explain away failures while emphatically recording successes (Evans-Pritchard 1937).

How the bokor goes about capturing the *ti bon ange* of the intended victim depends on the circumstances of the case. A particularly powerful sorcerer, for example, might through his spells gain control of the *ti bon ange* of a sailor who dies at sea or of a Haitian who is killed in a foreign land. Alternatively, the bokor might capture the *ti bon ange* of the living and thereby indirectly cause the unnatural death when the individual, left without intelligence or will, slowly perishes. One way of thus capturing the *ti bon ange* is the *l'envoi morts*, the *expédition*, the sending of the death spirit. (That is why the ritual treatment for an individual who fears that he or she is to be made a zombie is the same as that employed to exorcise any death spirit, described in chapter 5.) Another means of stealing the *ti bon ange* is to spread toxic powders, in the form of a cross, on the threshold of the victim's doorway. The magical skill of the bokor who has "arranged" (*rangé*) those powders guarantees, as in the case of any wanga, that only the intended victim will suffer. Preliminary—and erroneous—medical reports suggesting that the zombie preparation was absorbed through the feet as the victim walked over a cross of the powder were simply literal interpretations of this magical belief and practice. Control of the *ti bon ange* can also be gained by capturing it immediately following the death of the *corps cadavre*, during the seven days that the soul hovers around the corpse. Finally, a bokor might directly cause the unnatural death by the use of toxic powders.

Hence the sorcerer may or may not be responsible for the unnatural death of the victim, and the *ti bon ange* may be captured by magic before or after the death of the *corps cadavre*. Whatever the circumstances, however, the capture of the *ti bon ange* effects a split in the spiritual components of the victim and creates not one but two complementary kinds of zombies. The spirit zombie, or the zombie for the *ti bon ange* alone, is carefully stored in a jar and later may be magically transmuted into insects, animals, or humans to accomplish the particular work of the bokor. The remaining components—the n'âme, the *gros bon ange*, and the z'étoile—together form the *zombi cadavre*, the zombie of the flesh.

The creation of a *zombi cadavre* in the graveyard requires a particularly sophisticated knowledge of magic. Above all, the bokor must prevent the transformations of the various spiritual components that would normally occur at the death of the body. First, the *ti bon ange*—which, if not already in the possession of the bokor, may float above the body like a phosphorescent shadow—must be captured and prevented from reentering the victim. One way to prevent the reentry is to beat the victim violently, as in the case of Clairvius Narcisse. Second, the *gros bon ange* must be prevented from returning to its source in the vast pool of cosmic energy. Third, the n'âme must be retained to keep the flesh from decaying. The *zombi cadavre* that has its *gros bon ange* and n'âme can function; however, separated from the *ti bon ange* the body is but an empty vessel, subject to the direction of the bokor or whoever maintains control of the *zombi ti bon ange*. It is this notion of alien, malevolent forces taking control of the individual that is so terrifying to the Vodounist. In Haiti, the fear is not of being *harmed* by zombies as much as *becoming* one. The *zombi cadavre* is a body without a complete soul, matter without morality.

Emically, it is not a powder that creates a zombie; it is the magical force of the bokor as it is employed during two only indirectly related events—the prerequisite unnatural death and the ceremony of resurrection at the grave. This does not mean that the bokor do not recognize the pharmacological properties of their preparations. They most assuredly do. Some comment, for example, that the powders, if improperly prepared, will "kill too completely." Others observe that "only the truly great work magic alone. For all their talk, watch the hands of the little ones, you'll always see the powders." One informant suggested that the most potent preparations are made during the hot summer months, precisely the spawning season of the puffers and therefore the time when the female fish would be most toxic. Yet another prominent houngan insisted that if you actually wanted someone to rise from the earth "you couldn't fool with a little powder on the ground, you had to get it into the skin."

Yet critically, to recognize the toxic properties of the preparations is not necessarily to assign a functional and linear causality to those properties. On the contrary, the bokor insist that the actual deed of capturing the *ti bon ange* and raising the dead may be accomplished only by those possessing a particularly sophisticated knowledge of magic. In fact, it was due to this conviction that many of my informants felt so comfortable discussing and preparing the zombie powder with and for a foreigner. Most emphatically, the formula of the folk preparation was not a dark secret. Why should it be? Alone, the preparation at best might kill somebody; only knowledge of the appropriate magic could make that individual rise again. Besides, without the possession of the victim's *ti bon ange*—again something acquired by magic—one could never hope to control the zombie, an intolerable situation which to the Vodounist would be unthinkable. Moreover, because of their notion of the etiology of zombification, Vodounists accept the existence of the physical zombie (*zombi cadavre*) and the zombie of the spirit (*zombi ti bon ange, zombi astral*) with equal assurance, and—again because of the magical beliefs—it is conceptually inconceivable for one to exist without the other. A poisonous preparation alone, no matter what its pharmacological properties, by emic definition could not produce either type of zombie. The distinction that the scientific observer would perhaps instinctively make between the validity and importance of the physical zombie and that of the spirit zombie is not made by the Vodounist. To a believer, the two types of zombie are equally real, although their functions are different, and in fact the *zombi astral* has perhaps the greater value. This point is illustrated by an amusing anecdote from my fieldwork. Once, when asked to bring me a zombie, a bokor returned several days later with a small clay jar. When my contact reprimanded him for not bringing a zombie of the flesh, the bokor was taken aback, and then with complete sincerity he asked how on earth I would get a zombie of the flesh through the U.S. Customs. He also reminded me that the spirit zombie would be of more use, because I as master would be able to transmute it into various creatures that would have a wider range of applications than a mere working slave.

Of course, even though the bokor might view the zombie powder as only a support for his magic, the pharmacological properties of that preparation are of central interest if the existence of physical zombies is to be scientifically accepted. In formulating an etic explanation of zombification, it is imperative to separate what is known from what is only surmised as being probable or possible. We know that tetrodotoxin is an ingredient in folk preparations said to be used to cause the prerequisite unnatural death in the process of zombification. We know from the Japanese biomedical literature that tetrodotoxin poisoning can cause a person to appear dead, even though that person subsequently revives. And we know that, like the occasional Japanese victim of fugu (tetrodotoxin) poisoning who appears to be dead but is not, there are documented cases of death, burial, and subsequent revival of Haitians who have been subjected to the zombie preparations. The causal hypothesis is obvious. The alternative hypothesis is that the presence of tetrodotoxin in the zombie powder and the effect of apparent death during the initial stages of zombification are coincidental.

The latter hypothesis is supported, on first examination, by one important peculiarity of the poison. Tetrodotoxin is very sensitive to pH, and two samples of the zombie preparation contain enough calcified materials that, if the powders were put into a nonbuffered solvent (water, for example), the resulting solution would have a basicity that would denature the tetrodotoxin. This fact would falsify the hypothesis linking the toxin to the zombie phenomenon were it not for three considerations. First, laboratory tests have revealed the presence of tetrodotoxin (Rivier pers. comm.).[3] Second, given the diversity of formulas— some of which contain large amounts of calcified material, others very little; some of which contain toxic plants, toads, frogs, polychaete worms, tarantulas, and snakes, others only the toad, fish, and a few shavings of a human skull—it is reasonable to expect a wide range of pH values, and to judge the plausibility of the entire phenomenon by the proportion of ingredients in two samples would be premature. Of greater import is the consistency with which the fish that are known to be toxic appear in the various preparations.

Third, the powder is never put into a solution; it is not administered orally or made into a salve or cream for topical administration. All my informants insisted on this point, and their assertions are backed by other ethnographic reports (Hurston 1981). The powder is always applied in a specific way—directly into the blood through abraded skin—and the application is carefully mediated by various additions to the preparation such as ground glass and toxic plants that irritate and inflame the skin. Dry powders do not have interacting hydrogen ions, and in this sense they do not have a pH. Blood is a well-buffered solution. If a powder containing tetrodotoxin is put into direct contact with

3. Samples of the zombie preparation were analyzed by Takeshi Yasumoto at Tohoku University, Sendai, Japan; Michael Lazdunski at the University of Nice, France; and Laurent Rivier at the University of Lausanne, Switzerland. Three distinct analytical techniques provided "unequivocal evidence that tetrodotoxin is present in sample D" (Rivier 1987, pers. comm.). Other results were negative, though Rivier notes that all tests were complicated by the fact that tetrodotoxin is stable in neutral or mild acidic solutions but breaks down in basic solutions. The amount of tetrodotoxin in sample D is low and clearly insufficient to account, in itself, for the pharmacological activities proposed here. This observation has been a source of concern and controversy among certain individuals (Yasumoto and Kao 1986). It is my contention, however, that given the universally acknowledged and significant variability of the toxin in natural populations of the fish, and given the fact that the folk powders are not prepared under modern laboratory conditions, it would be premature to judge the viability of the hypothesis strictly on the basis of the analysis of these particular samples. Critically, absence of evidence is not evidence of absence. Of greater interest is the empirical observation that the bokor recognize the toxicity of these fish and include them in the powders, and that at certain times of the year these fish contain a toxin known to have induced apparent death.

blood, molecules of the toxin enter the circulatory system without being exposed to the pH that would have resulted if that powder had first been dissolved in a solution. These facts lead one to appreciate more fully what at first appears to be a cumbersome method of administering the poison.

One other important observation about the formulas of the various preparations concerns the synergistic role of the various admixtures, which may chemically potentiate the critical ingredients in ways not yet understood. For example, most laboratory studies concerning the *in vivo* effects of tetrodotoxin involve microgram/kilogram amounts of the drug, administered intravenously (IV) or intraperitoneally (IP). Given alone, very little if any tetrodotoxin crosses the blood-brain barrier. However, W. G. Clark and his colleagues, B. A. Coldwell and J. M. Lipton, found that if tetrodotoxin is administered directly into cerebrospinal fluid, nanogram amounts have more dramatic effects than do microgram amounts administered IV or IP (Clark and Coldwell 1973; Clark and Lipton 1974). It may be that some of the zombie powder's other ingredients enable increased transport across the blood-brain barrier, and that therefore the effective dose of tetrodotoxin can be reduced by three orders of magnitude. Such a synergistic effect—a biochemical version of the whole being greater than the sum of the parts—is an important feature of many psychoactive folk preparations (Schultes and Hofmann 1980).

The causal hypothesis linking the presence of tetrodotoxin in the zombie powder with the effects of zombification suggests that the bokor may choose to cause the prerequisite unnatural death by means of a powder that he believes will kill the victim slowly, discreetly, and efficiently. That powder contains tetrodotoxin, which dramatically lowers the metabolic rate of the victim almost to the point of death. Pronounced dead by attending physicians and considered materially dead by family members and perhaps by the bokor himself, the victim is, in fact, buried alive. Given the complexities inherent in the process, the physical resurrection of a zombie is likely to be an exceedingly rare event, much as the sporadic reports in the popular and ethnographic literature would suggest. Because of the acknowledged variability of toxin levels in natural populations of the puffer fish—as well as the diversity of formulas concocted by the bokor—dosage is bound to be imprecise. One sample preparation may prove inert, while another may be lethal. Even in cases where the correct dose is achieved and the state of apparent death attained, the victim might still suffocate in the coffin.

Yet all of these complications are tempered by one overriding consideration. A bokor's failed attempts are not counted—only his successes become apparent. In other words, if a bokor attempts to raise a physical zombie but fails, the failure is readily rationalized by the belief system. Should the victim actually succumb to the toxin or to asphyxia in the coffin, the death might be considered a natural call from God, and thus beyond the control of the sorcerer. On the other hand, the failure of the powder to have any effect could be attributed to the preventive intervention of a houngan. Significantly, the bokor can keep trying and experimenting with his preparation until the dosage has the desired effect. If he administers an overdose, actually killing the victim, who is the wiser? No one questions the absence of resurrection. It is only when a bokor succeeds that his machinations become apparent—only when he causes others to believe that he has killed and then revived the victim. His failures go unnoticed. Even if the bokor had only one success in dozens of attempts, his success in bringing back the dead once every few years would support the powerful reputation earned by the zombie phenomenon. Indeed, there is no suggestion of an assembly-line production of zombies in Haiti. On the contrary, it is almost certainly an infrequent and highly unusual occurrence. However, the phenomenon's potency as a social sanction depends not on how often it occurs but rather on the fact that it can and apparently has occurred.

The widespread belief in physical zombies is based, therefore, on those rare instances in which the victim receives the correct dose of a toxic preparation, revives in the coffin, and is taken from the grave by the bokor. The victim, affected by the drug and traumatized by the set and setting of the total experience, is reportedly bound and led before a cross to be baptized with a new name. After the baptism, or sometimes the next day, he or she is made to eat a paste containing a strong dose of a potent psychoactive drug—*Datura stramonium*, the *concombre zombi* or zombie's cucumber—which induces a state of disorientation and amnesia. During the course of that intoxication, the zombie is socialized into a new existence.

In distinguishing the emic view of zombification from possible pharmacological explanations, we have only begun the inquiry. It is one thing to outline the nature of a belief system, but quite another to understand how that belief system affects the individual believer. It is well known, for example, that no psychoactive drug produces a uniform effect in different individuals, or even in the same individual at different times. What the individual perceives from the particular experience will depend not on the drug alone but also on other factors: the mood and setting of the experience; his or her physical and mental state, as well as that of any companions; and his or her expectations, which in turn are based on a rich repository of folk tradition and belief. The drug itself will induce a powerful but neutral stimulation of the imagination; it will create a template, as it were, upon which the user's own cultural beliefs and psychological condition may be amplified a thousand times. Therefore, as important as the pharmacology of a particular substance is the set of expectations that the individual brings to the experience.

An emic analysis of the zombie phenomenon should make it clear that the Haitian peasant believes that zombies do exist, fears becoming one, and recognizes that the machinations of the sorcerer, if not detected and neutralized, can indeed lead him or her to such a fate. An individual thus cursed would presumably respond with a mixture of fear and rage, which if not relieved by the successful intervention of a houngan could readily turn to despair. To what extent could that psychological condition influence physical well-being and mediate the effect of the sorcerer's spell and perhaps the pharmacological efficacy of the zombie powder? Possible answers to this question are suggested in the voluminous medical and anthropological literature on psychogenic illness and/or death.

It has long been recognized that, just as an individual's illness may have a psychosomatic basis, it is possible for a closed society to generate physical ailments and conditions that have meaning only within the mental belief structure of its members (Eisenbruch 1983). The word psychosomatic, of course, does not mean "fake"; it is derived from the Greek roots *psycho* and *somatos*, meaning mind/body, and just as psychosomatic medical symptoms have an objective reality, so do culture-bound psychological syndromes. Examples of these last would include anxiety states, such as *koro* in Southeast Asia or *susto* in Latin America; hysterical disorders, including the Japanese *latha*; phobic states of oppression by the evil eye in Mediterranean and Islamic cultures; depressive reactions such as the *windigo* psychosis found among the northern Cree and Ojibway; dissociative states including *Hsieh-ping*, the Chinese double sickness; and *amok*, the acute homicidal form of mania found among the Malays (Kiev 1972). By the same token, sorcery by curse or hex is fully capable of generating an incapacitating anxiety which, if not relieved, can manifest physical symptoms (Farmer and Falkowski 1985; Cappannari et al. 1975; Golden 1977; Gomez and Carazos 1981; Mathis 1964).

Reports of death or illness by suggestion abound in the early ethnographic literature and in the journals of numerous missionaries and explorers (Warner 1941; Mauss 1926). As early as 1587, for example, Soares de Souza claimed to have seen Tupinambas who had been sentenced by a "medicine man" die of fright (Cannon 1942). A. G. Leonard (1906) described a Hausa warrior in West Africa who slowly died because he believed himself bewitched. Perhaps the most dramatic accounts come from Australia. Aborigine sorcerers reputedly carry bones extracted from the flesh of giant lizards, and when these slivers are pointed at a person while a death spell is recited, the individual invariably sickens and, according to medical reports, sometimes dies. One physician noted that the victim of the curse

> stands aghast, with his eyes staring at the treacherous pointer, and with his hands lifted as though to ward off the lethal medium which he imagines is pouring into his body. His cheeks blanch and his eyes become glassy and the expression on his face becomes horribly distorted. . . . He attempts to shriek but usually the sound chokes in his throat, and all that one might see is froth at his mouth. His body begins to tremble . . . he sways backward and falls to the ground . . . writhing as if in mortal agony. After awhile he becomes very composed and crawls to his (shelter). From

this time onwards he sickens and frets, refusing to eat and keeping aloof from the daily affairs of the tribe (Basedow 1925, cited in Cannon 1942, 172).

At this point only the *nangarri*, or tribal healer, can save the curse victim by initiating a complex ritual. But should the *nangarri* refuse to cooperate, the victim might, in fact, die.

Similar reports of death by sorcery come from Australia, South America, and Africa, as well as New Zealand, certain regions of the South Pacific, and Haiti (Cannon 1942; Mauss 1926). Anthropologists refer to the phenomenon as "voodoo death," and its basic pattern is cross-culturally consistent. An individual breaks a social or spiritual code, violates a taboo, or for one reason or another believes himself or herself a victim of sorcery. Conditioned since childhood to expect disaster under such circumstances, he or she then acts out what amounts to a self-fulfilling prophecy. Often the death knell is sounded by a hex or, as in Australia, a simple gesture rife with meaning. Sorcerers may use particular props as media of transmission: African "witchdoctors" have knucklebones, and European witches use carved wooden dolls. Alternatively, the transmission may be direct; in Islamic societies the harbinger of death need only squint the evil eye.

Understandably, the legitimacy of many reports of voodoo death, particularly those from the early literature, has been questioned. Often the accounts were based on hearsay, and among those in which the death was actually documented the possibility of poisoning was not ruled out by forensic examination (Clune 1973). Other cases can doubtless be explained by organic illness or the unnoticed intervention of kin or vindictive societal members (Barber 1961). H. D. Eastwell (1982), for example, has suggested that voodoo death among the Aborigines is a purely social phenomenon, in which the victim is deprived of vital nutritional requirements by a kindred that already considers him or her dead (Cawte 1983; Glascock 1983). He notes that the victim of voodoo death is not an unfortunate but benign presence, but rather one who, by definition having crossed into the realm of the spirits, has become an actual threat that must be removed. In the case of the Australian Aborigines, this is precisely what occurs. Weakened by the long ordeal, the victim of sorcery receives no relief even from close relatives. On the contrary, these former supporters actually take away food and water, on the theory that a dead person has no need for either and with the motive, as Eastwell was told, "if real close up finish, take water away so spirit goes" (Eastwell 1982, 14). In the deserts of Australia, where the daytime temperatures average over one hundred degrees Fahrenheit in the shade, death by dehydration may occur in about twenty-four to forty-eight hours (Cawte 1983).

This evidence from Australia, of course, does not disprove the existence of death by suggestion; on the contrary, it explains one mechanism by which such a death may occur (Lester 1972). Unfortunately, not all cases of voodoo death are so easily explained as these examples from Australia, where because of a harsh climate a relatively simple act by the kin eliminates the victim's life supports. More usual in cases of voodoo death, but again more enigmatic, are the instances when the victim dies despite succor from his or her family. Although some ethnologists remain skeptical (Barber 1961; Lewis 1977), many ethnographic fieldworkers have consistently maintained that, at least in their particular regions, the accounts had some credibility (Levi-Bruhl, cited in Cannon 1942). After reviewing many reports of voodoo death, Marcel Mauss encouraged all anthropologists to consider the problem of death by suggestion and come up with possible explanations (Mauss 1926).

It was physician W. B. Cannon, one of the great physiologists of the first half of the twentieth century and an individual with impeccable scientific credentials, who offered the first telling argument that voodoo death might actually exist (Cannon 1942). No scientist, of course, would suggest that there is a direct causal relationship between, say, the physical act of pointing a hexed doll and the death of an individual. Clearly it had to be the victim's mind that mediated the sorcerer's curse and the fatal outcome. Cannon recognized the element of suggestibility, implicating fear and rage as powerful human emotions deeply rooted in biology, and he cited William James to draw attention to the potentially devastating psychological impact of complete ostracism from one's peers and family. More important, he offered the first suggestion of a physiological mechanism that might allow voodoo death to occur. Cannon noted similarities between the recorded cases of psychogenic death, prompted by a sorcerer's curse, and a number of peculiar cases that he and others had

witnessed on the battlefields of Europe during World War I. In
the nightmare of despair and death on the western front, certain
traumatized but unwounded soldiers inexplicably died of shock,
a medical disorder normally brought about by a critical drop in
blood pressure due to excessive bleeding. Cannon speculated
that individuals terrified by a magic spell suffered, like the soldiers, from an overstimulation of the sympathetic-adrenal system, which in turn produced vasoconstriction and damage to the
capillary endothelium of the visceral blood vessels, resulting in
loss of blood volume and pressure, and ultimately fatal shock.
Fear, in other words, could initiate actual physiological changes
that quite literally lead to death (Cannon 1942).

C. P. Richter expanded the scope of Cannon's study by noting
the occurrence of what he termed "sudden and unexplained
death" in Western societies, citing examples of individuals who
died upon sudden immersion in water or at the sight of blood.
He interpreted Cannon's physiological explanation as a state
of shock caused by continuous production of adrenalin, which
overstimulated the heart and led to death by cardiac systole.
However, Richter's subsequent laboratory studies with rats under stress indicated that death had occurred due to a slowing
down of the heart, not an overstimulation. Autopsies revealed
large hearts distended with blood, and he concluded that the
laboratory animals had suffered a vagus death due to overstimulation of the parasympathetic nervous system (Richter 1957).
Anthropologist T. X. Barber (1961) criticized the conclusions of
both Cannon and Richter as premature and questioned whether
there were any reported cases of voodoo death that were not
based on hearsay.

In the last ten years, the subject of voodoo death has resur-
faced in anthropological literature after a considerable hiatus,
and both the etiology of the phenomenon and its very existence
continue to be a matter of debate. The view of the skeptics
echoes that of Barber and is best summarized by Gilbert Lewis,
who asks: "Is it really the case that healthy people have died in a
day, or three days, because they know they were the victims of
sorcery? Who has seen this happen with his own eyes? Is there no
explanation but sorcery?" (Lewis 1977, 111). F. J. Clune (1973),
in a short communication to the *American Anthropologist* unsup-
ported by documentation, claimed that reputed cases of voodoo
death were actually poisonings. H. D. Eastwell (1982), A. P.

Glascock (1983), and John Cawte (1983) suggested that dehydration was the causal mechanism, but this, as pointed out above, was merely one explanation; it was emphatically not a repudiation of the phenomenon of voodoo death itself. B. W. Lex, who believes that voodoo death does occur, augmented the earlier physiological explanations of Cannon and Richter with information about neurophysiological research on sensitization, or tuning of the autonomic nervous system. Death by suggestion, she concluded, "is accomplished by the practitioner's manipulation of the autonomic nervous system through the victim's cognitive apprehension of the meaning of witchcraft" (Lex 1974, 822). David Lester (1972), who also accepts the idea of voodoo death, emphasized the psychological component in the potential victim's mindset: a sense of helplessness and hopelessness reinforced by social process that, if unrelieved, may lead to death—perhaps, he suggested, by making the individual vulnerable to pathogenic disease.

Yet of all the recent ethnological studies, only Lester's mentions the fact that contemporary clinical studies leave little doubt that psychological and emotional factors may precipitate sudden death in Western society (Gomez 1982; Engel 1976). Anthropologists interested in the phenomenon of voodoo death in traditional societies would do well to examine our own medical literature. G. L. Engel (1968, 1971), for example, has documented 170 cases of sudden death mediated by psychological factors and has enumerated the life settings in which they occurred. In a related study W. A. Greene investigated 26 instances of sudden death that took place in an industrial population of 44,000. In at least 50 percent of these cases—all of them men—there were identifiable psychological and social factors associated with the time of sudden death. The majority had been severely depressed for a period ranging from a week to several months, and the sudden deaths occurred in settings of acute excitation engendered by circumstances which had precipitated reactions of anxiety or anger. The findings suggested that a "combination of depressive and arousal psychological states or abrupt transition from one state to another may produce disharmonious responses in the hormonal and autonomic nervous systems, as well as central nervous system mediated behavior, which are conducive to sudden death" (Greene et al. 1972, 725). The infrequent but certain occurrence of psychogenic death in Western settings is perhaps best indicated by the outpouring of corroborative letters received by the *British Medical Journal* in 1965, following its publication of one case study of a woman who had died, possibly of fright, after going through routine surgery (Elkington et al. 1965; Barker 1965; Fry 1965; Nixon 1965; Young 1965; Hunter 1965).

The actual lethal mechanism to account for instances of psychogenic death remains a matter of debate. Efrain Gomez (1982) lists three conditions that may contribute to a sudden cardiac arrest. The first is an electrical instability of the myocardium, often due to ischemic heart disease. The second is the presence of a strong psychological disturbance such as depression or a sense of entrapment without possible escape, and the third is an emotional catalyst such as fear, anger, or despair. Other authorities have suggested that sudden death results from the cessation of either cardiac or respiratory functions, leading to cerebral anoxia (Davis and Wright 1980). Still others have noted that strong emotions of stress and fear may trigger impulses from the brain, which in turn affect the functioning of the heart through the mediation of the autonomic nervous system (Vaisrub 1959; Wolf 1967). Environmental stress, both psychological and social, can lower the threshold for ventricular fibrillation or provoke potentially malignant ventricular arrhythmias, either of which could lead to sudden cardiac arrest (Lown et al. 1977; Lown et al. 1980). A break in the synchronized and rhythmic contractions of the heart can cause it to abruptly cease beating, bringing about irreversible brain damage (Gomez 1982). Whatever the actual mechanism, there is no doubt that psychological and neuro-physiological factors can provoke life-threatening heart attacks, even in the absence of organic heart disease (Lown et al. 1976; Schwartz and Walsh 1971).

If we accept that psychological factors can precipitate physiological crises among individuals in Western societies, then there is no reason not to expect the same thing to occur among traditional peoples. As Lester comments: "Sudden and unexplained deaths are common in medically sophisticated countries, and sudden and unexplained deaths are probably common in primitive societies also" (Lester 1972, 389). Indeed, a number of medical authorities have made an explicit comparison between curse-mediated voodoo death and psychogenic death as witnessed in modern hospitals. R. J. W. Burrell (1963) cites fifty cases of psychogenic death among South African Bantu who had been cursed. Efrain Gomez and Ninsa Carazos (1981) document the sudden death of one of their patients following a "maldicion" or hex uttered by his mother; postmortem examination, including complete toxicological studies, ruled out the possibility of poison or organic disease. J. L. Mathis presents a case in which a previously healthy adult male developed severe and ultimately fatal asthma following his mother's threatening prophecy. The physicians studying the case believed that the mother's death curse was the "triggering mechanism for the asthmatic attacks," and they concluded that "fatal psychosomatic conditions can be modifications of the more primitive and direct 'voodoo death'" (Mathis 1964, 104).

G. W. Milton (1973) questioned whether the self-willed death, witnessed in modern hospitals, of someone who suffers from a fatal disease is fundamentally different from the psychogenic death suffered by the recipient of a sorcerer's curse. For example, the diagnosis of terminal cancer by an authoritative medical expert, in the unfamiliar setting of the modern hospital, might adversely affect the course of the illness. As in the case of a sorcerer's curse which can be removed through the intervention of a more powerful healing spell, so the intervention of a higher medical authority, who contradicts the diagnosis of his junior colleague, might result in a demonstrable recovery by the patient (Gomez 1982). By the same token, within the closed belief system of a society that accepts the reality of sorcery, the sorcerer's curse can and does have physiological manifestations. As Barbara Lex suggests: "The extreme fright experienced by the individual who has thus been singled out [by sorcery] can be as fatal as a dose of poison" (Lex 1974, 822).

It is clear that the term *voodoo death*, which has been canonized by the anthropological literature despite its inaccurate and pejorative connotations, should be superceded by the concept of psychogenic death, for the phenomenon appears to occur among many, if not all, human societies. But even the latter term is misleading, because the negative effects of psychological suggestion are not necessarily death—they may result in acute or chronic illness (Gomez 1982; Lachman 1982–83). S. J. Lachman explicitly notes that, just as voodoo death corresponds to formulations of psychosomatic death, so voodoo illness is a form of psychosomatic illness. Cases in which the patient's physical condition has been affected by psychosocial stress, which is caused in turn by the patient's attribution of his or her ailment to hexing or sorcery, appear with some regularity in the medical literature (Golden 1977; Cappannari et al. 1975; Tingling 1967; Wintrob 1973; Snow 1974). Raymond Prince has noted that a curse victim's feelings of panic can precipitate nonlethal psychotic and neurotic disorders as well as loss of appetite, insomnia, nightmares, and hallucinations (cited in Kiev 1972)—conditions which in turn leave the victim vulnerable to the power of suggestion (Lester 1972). Psychosomatic or psychophysiological disorders instigated by emotional stimuli may include ulcerative lesions of the stomach or the duodenum, dilation of the heart, cerebral hemorrhage, arterial aneurysm, neurodermatitis, or functional disorders such as anginal syndrome, hyperhydrosis, thyrotoxicosis, and cardiovascular hypertension (Lachman 1982–83).

Interestingly, Gomez (1982) has emphasized that psychogenic illness and/or death is a psychological process that may occur over a matter of days, weeks, or even months. Although the precise mechanisms remain uncertain, the essential explanation makes intuitive sense: if faith can heal, fear can maim or kill. Physicians have backed up with statistical studies something that most people take for granted—that the likelihood of becoming ill or even dying depends, to some extent at least, on one's state of mind. Feelings of depression, hopelessness, or despair somehow create a vulnerable state (Pattison 1974; Rahe et al. 1971; Rahe et al. 1973). Loneliness would hardly seem to be a fatal affliction, yet a disproportionate number of spouses die in the first year after the death of their mates (Parkes et al. 1969; Rees and Lutkins 1967). Psychologists have labeled this the "giving up/ given up" complex and have suggested that, when an individual responds thus to a particular life situation, disease and/or death may intervene (Engel 1968, 1971).

The "giving up/given up" complex provides a useful conceptual framework for considering psychogenic death or illness within the closed belief system of a society that recognizes the reality of sorcery (Lester 1972). According to this model, the victim of the sorcerer's curse or spell becomes caught in a vicious cycle of belief that indirectly, through the mediation of his or her own emotional response, provokes pronounced physiological changes. The psychological process is easy to imagine. The victim has shared an uncompromised belief, engendered since childhood, that illness or death will befall anyone who transgresses the societal code of behavior; and his or her acceptance of the supernatural power behind the instigator of the curse is equally fixed and unshakeable. He or she is doomed to die by a malevolent curse in which everyone involved deeply believes. The victim becomes despondent, anxious, and fearful—feelings that are both recognized and expected by other members of the society who not only believe in sorcery but have a vested interest in maintaining that belief, just as the system itself has its own inherent need for validation. Belief in the power and efficacy of the curse are therefore both sanctioned and encouraged by the group. Family members or neighbors may, in fact, join the victim in wondering how long he or she can expect to survive or in speculating who has caused the curse. Indeed, some might offer preventive magic to counteract the sorcery. But if the victim's condition continues to deteriorate a strange thing happens. A consensus is reached among all concerned that the end is near, and the victim's friends and family retreat as from the smell of death. They return, but only to wail and chant over the body of a person whom they consider already dead. Physically the victim still lives; psychologically he or she is dying; socially he or she is already dead. Anyone who doubts the plausibility of such a process occurring in traditional societies need only spend some time in a modern hospital ward for terminally ill cancer patients.

From the foregoing discussion, it appears that the anthropological phenomenon of voodoo illness or death may be incorporated into the established framework of psychosomatic theory, which maintains that the psychological and biological components of the individual are but two parts of a whole. Strong emotional stimuli, though their sources might differ from culture to culture, may provoke physiological arousal patterns common to all people. The mechanisms that activate the chain of mind, brain, autonomic system, and cardiopulmonary system have yet to be completely identified. Given the clinical evidence, however, it would be querulous to doubt the existence of psychogenic illness and death in both modern and traditional societies. Clearly, the phenomenon occurs, and the process involves a number of complementary factors. In traditional societies, fear of sorcery can initiate physiological changes, particularly if the individual in question is already physically predisposed to those

changes, whether genetically or due to an acquired biological
weakness (Lachman 1982–83). Certainly, fear makes the victim psychologically vulnerable, and this in turn affects physical
health. Neurophysiologists still do not fully understand the process, though the response of family and society must influence
the victim's psychological and physical well-being. Although a
universal mechanism to account for psychogenic illness and
death has not been identified, the basic assumption is clear. As
one researcher has put it, the brain has the power to kill or maim
the body that bears it (Watson 1974).

If his case is believed, the metamorphosis of Clairvius Narcisse from human to zombie represents a very special instance of
psychogenic death. A sorcerer's spell initiated a long process that
exploited the victim's greatest fears, mobilized the reinforcing
beliefs of the community, and finally led to apparent death. According to Vodoun belief, Narcisse really did die, and what was
taken from the ground was no longer a human being. I once
asked a houngan if a zombie could ever be made whole. He
replied in the affirmative, indicating that the *ti bon ange* could be
magically returned. On the other hand, he suggested: "Who is
going to ask a *zombi savanne* [former zombie] to dance?" The
point is, of course, that a zombie is socially dead, and it becomes
dead in a very specific way. Like many sorcerers around the
world, the bokor responsible for Narcisse's fate had a prop—in
this case an ingenious preparation that amplified the victim's
worst fears many times over. In the end, however, even accepting
the causal connection with the toxin, it was not a powder that
made Narcisse a zombie—it was his own mind.

Consider for a moment what he went through. As a Haitian
peasant, he had been socialized since childhood to believe in the
reality of the living dead. This conviction had been reinforced
throughout his life both by a complex body of folklore and, more
important, by the direct testimony of friends and family; in Haiti
virtually everyone has a vivid zombie tale to tell. In Narcisse's
belief, a zombie was a being without will, on the very frontier of
the natural world, an entity that could be manifest as either spirit
or body. Zombies do not speak, cannot fend for themselves, do
not even know their names. Their fate is enslavement. Given the
availability of cheap labor, there is no apparent economic incentive to create a force of indentured servants. Instead, because of

the colonial history, the concept of enslavement implies that the peasant fears and the zombie suffers a fate that is literally worse than death—the loss of physical liberty that is slavery, and the sacrifice of personal autonomy implied by the loss of identity. For Narcisse, as for all Haitian peasants, the fear is not of being harmed by zombies, but rather of becoming one. It is to prevent such a horrid fate that the relatives of the dead may reluctantly mutilate the corpse if there is any suspicion of foul play—unless, of course, the family itself was involved in the zombification.

The full circumstances of Narcisse's reputed death in 1962 may never surface. Certain issues, however, have come to light. At the time of his demise, Narcisse was involved in a serious dispute with other members of his family over land. Moreover, Clairvius had done well financially but showed no willingness to share his earnings with his family. Once, according to his sister's testimony, his brother Magrim sought a loan, which Narcisse categorically refused. An intense argument followed, which culminated in Magrim striking Clairvius in the leg with a log, while Clairvius responded by hurling stones. Both of them ended up in jail. According to the other family members and neighbors interviewed between 1982 and 1984, this was but one example of many disputes between Clairvius and his siblings.

Apparently Clairvius did not antagonize just his family. He also compromised innumerable women, scattering children to all corners of the Artibonite Valley. For none of these did he accept responsibility, nor did he build houses for the various mothers. As a result, he approached middle age with few financial burdens and was therefore free to advance further than his more responsible peers. Narcisse had profited at the expense of his community, and in all likelihood—according to the opinion of his eldest sister, Angelina—it was one of the aggrieved members of that community, probably a mistress, who sold him to the bokor. Narcisse himself insists that a brother betrayed him.

Whatever the cause of Clairvius's demise, the family lost no time taking over his fields, which are still worked by his sisters today. Although Clairvius has made a claim for his land in the national courts, his sisters have absolutely no intention of releasing anything to him. As far as they are concerned, Clairvius remains a dead man, a spirit that should never have returned to the village. In fact, the first member of the family to recognize him when he appeared in the L'Estere market in 1980 sent for

Angelina and then told Clairvius to go away. Another sister arrived from the lakou and offered Clairvius money but also ordered him to leave the village. By then a large crowd had gathered, and the police arrived to take him to the protection of the government jail. To say the least, his family's reception was neither sympathetic nor cordial, though none of them expressed doubt that the man was their long-departed brother.

The testimony of his family suggests that their relationship with him was no more amiable in 1962. At that time, not only did Narcisse believe in zombies, but he undoubtedly was aware of how and why they were created. When his world began to close in on him, he was already personally isolated. Within his lakou he had been ostracized because of his antisocial behavior; within his own family he was actively engaged in a dispute with his brother over the right to sell heritable land. Eventually, by his own account, it was his brother who sold him to a bokor. Yet there is something amiss in his testimony. After all, had Narcisse been in the right, and had he been zombified by his adversary without the support of the community, it is difficult to imagine that the brother would have been tolerated in that community for close to twenty years afterward. But in fact the brother was, and even today Narcisse is not.

It is probable that, at the time of his demise, Clairvius Narcisse had support from neither his immediate society nor his kin; his closest relatives may have been his greatest enemies. And because family members were involved, gossip and rumors undoubtedly took their toll, especially when Narcisse began to suffer physical symptoms that he had never before experienced. According to his sister, he was ill for some time, perhaps a year. Then, by his own testimony, he was taken before the basin, where "they prick the skin and call the spirit and the water changes into blood." A cousin also referred to the tribunal that had judged Clairvius; Narcisse himself called those responsible for his fate the "masters of the land, and they do as they please."

Clairvius Narcisse knew for some time that he had been the victim of sorcery. But following his exposure at the basin his symptoms got worse and worse. He consulted houngan, but they did nothing. By then desperate, he entered the alien environment of the Albert Schweitzer Hospital. His condition deteriorated rapidly, and then something even more extraordinary occurred. I have discussed above the devastating impact that social death has on a victim of sorcery. The zombie model takes this one step further. Narcisse was actually pronounced dead in a hospital by Western-trained physicians. Even more incredible, from the known action of the toxin in the poison and from his own testimony, there is reason to believe that he remained conscious much of the time. He may actually have heard himself pronounced dead. He claimed to have been aware of his sister's weeping and to have heard the nurses discussing the case. Like the Japanese victim of tetrodotoxin, he strove desperately to communicate, but the paralytic poison made communication impossible.

Then Narcisse entered another realm. Having caused such a dramatic, virtually complete reduction in metabolic rate, the poison took its victim quite literally to the edge of death. Indeed, it very nearly killed him, as it may have killed many others. His symptoms remained the same, yet at one point there seems to have been a qualitative change. Perhaps not surprisingly, the advanced symptoms of known tetrodotoxin poisoning merge with those of what Western physicians have termed the autoscopic near-death experience (NDE) (Sabom 1982). Recall once again Narcisse's description of what happened after his supposed death. He sensed that his soul was about to take a great journey; and it did travel, he insisted, making great passages over the land, timeless passages, immaterial yet powerfully real. His travels were multidimensional, yet they always returned him to the grave site. His notion of time was lost. His tomb, he maintained, was the only axis of his existence.

Peculiar things happen to people when they die, if we believe the word of those who come back. Those who have been close to death speak of an ineffable dimension where all intuitive sense of time is lost. Like a dreamscape it is timeless, but unlike a dream it is impossibly real, a place of acute awareness wherein the process of death is acknowledged as something positive, calm, even beautiful. Like Clairvius Narcisse, virtually every medical patient who has been to the edge of death experiences a profound separation between the material body and an invisible, nonmaterial aspect, one that often hovers above the body; and in nearly all cases the patient identifies not with the body, but with the spirit. An elderly woman who nearly died of severe complications following surgery in a Chicago hospital wrote her physician, "I was light, airy, and felt transparent" (Sabon 1982, 21). Often, patients distinctly remember floating above their bodies, looking down at their material selves. A cardiac patient noted: "I was going up slowly, like floating. . . . I was looking from up, down . . . they were working the hell out of me" (Sabom 1982, 28). Also typical is the amazement of a construction worker from Georgia following cardiac arrest: "I recognized me lying there. . . . [It was] like looking at a dead worm or something. I didn't have any desire to go back to it" (Sabom 1982, 28).

Sometimes those who endure autoscopic near-death experiences recall conversations between attending physicians and nurses. Often they describe their frustration at not being able to communicate with others physically present at their bedside. "I tried to say something," one patient remembered, "but she [the nurse] didn't say anything. . . . She was like looking at a movie screen that can't talk back and that doesn't register you're there. I was the real one and she was unreal. That's the way I felt" (Sabom 1982, 32). Certain survivors describe an extraordinary ability to "travel" through space and time. "It was just a thought process," one explains. "I felt like I could have thought myself anywhere I wanted to be instantly. I could do what I wanted to . . . it's realer than here, really" (Sabom 1982, 34).

Those who go through a near-death experience and survive share one thing in common: they all retain a distinct awareness that at one point their immaterial aspect returned to its physical body. It was at this moment, many remember, that they regained consciousness. In hospital patients, this often occurs instantaneously, coinciding with a particular resuscitative procedure. A cardiac patient responded to electric shock: "She [the nurse] picked up them shocker things. . . . I seen my body flop like that . . . it seemed like I was up here and it grabbed me and my body, and forced it back, pushed it back" (Sabom 1982, 35). Another experience ended with the sudden arrival of a loved one. The patient explained, "I was up at the ceiling. . . . Then when someone in the family came to the door and called . . . I was instantaneously back in my body" (Sabom 1982, 35).

This sudden return to the body is what Clairvius Narcisse remembers happening. One moment he was floating above his tomb, and the next he heard someone call out. But, if his testimony is to be believed, the voice came not from a loved one but from the bokor, and when he returned to his body it was not in a hospital bed, it was in a coffin. And for Narcisse, the ordeal was only beginning. Completely traumatized by the experience, he was taken from the ground and severely beaten. He was led before the cross of Baron Samedi and baptized with a new name. Then, or perhaps the next morning, he was forced to consume a paste containing a potent dose of *concombre zombi* (*Datura stramonium*), a psychoactive plant that would have induced a state of psychotic delirium marked by confusion, disorientation, and subsequent amnesia. During the course of that intoxication he was led away to an isolated farm, where he began a new existence. There, he was kept in isolation, fed a physically debilitating, salt-free diet, and perhaps made to labor in the tropical heat.

The creation of a zombie is a complex process that mobilizes many, if not all, the elements reported by the ethnological literature on "voodoo" or psychogenic death. First, there exists a matrix of belief deeply rooted in the collective consciousness of the Haitian peasant society, and this belief defines the very texture of an individual's conception of self and of his or her place in the order of the universe. Acceptance of these beliefs (e.g., the power of sorcery) is strong and uncritical, and it is constantly reinforced by the group. The belief system's inherent need for validation and the purpose of zombification itself create a form of social death for the victim, and this in turn has physical ramifications. The sorcerer's spell marshalls a wide range of potent psychological forces that, depending on the idiosyncratic predisposition of the victim, may affect physiological processes. Ostracism from the group produces an increased psychological sensitivity, which in turn heightens awareness of any deterioration in his or her physical well-being. At some point the victim is poisoned by a preparation which, by permitting the retention of consciousness while bringing on the outward signs of death, actually allows the individual to learn that he or she is dead. Taught since childhood to believe in zombies and to fear becoming one, the victim is interred in a coffin, conscious but quite helpless. Once taken from the grave, the zombie's fate is sealed because, within the closed system of belief that is his or her world, there is no other way.

CHAPTER SEVEN

ZOMBIFICATION AS A

SOCIAL PROCESS

The evidence presented up to this point has suggested a means by which both physical and spirit zombies may be created, but it has explained very little about the process of zombification within Haitian traditional society. Remember that, in Vodounist belief, anyone who dies an unnatural death—one caused by the intervention of sorcery—may be claimed as a zombie. Emically, it is not a poison but the performance of a magical rite by a bokor that creates a zombie; zombification is perceived as a strictly magical process that is totally dependent on the special and esoteric powers of the bokor. The bokor creates a zombie by capturing the victim's *ti bon ange*, that component of the Vodoun soul that controls personality, character, and willpower. A zombie appears cataleptic precisely because it has no *ti bon ange*. Separated from the *ti bon ange*, the body is but an empty vessel, subject to the direction of an alien force, the one who maintains control of the *ti bon ange*. It is the notion of external forces taking control of the individual that is so terrifying to the Vodounist.

It is worth repeating that Haitians fear becoming a zombie more than they fear being harmed by one. This fear is pervasive and has given rise to a complex body of belief and folklore that continues to influence behavior (Bourguignon 1959). Both the threat and the fact of zombification confer on the bokor a potent means of social control, if he chooses to use it. Under what circumstances, then, does the bokor invoke this power? Or, put another way, the formula of the poison and the psychological effects of the sorcerer's spell explain how an individual might be made into a zombie, but why is he or she chosen as a victim in the first place?

Many observers, including those who formulated Haiti's national laws, have considered zombification as a random criminal activity—yet another symptom of the conspiracy of fear that was presumed to be the common plight of the peasant (Douyon 1980; Kerboull 1973). But the suggestion that zombification was a haphazard phenomenon dependent on the caprice and greed of an individual bokor was contradicted by a number of observations that I made during the initial stages of my ethnobiological investigation (Davis 1985). During the course of obtaining the various preparations of the zombie powder, I came into direct and prolonged contact with a number of Bizango secret societies, and in certain instances it was clearly the leaders of these societies who controlled access to the formula of the preparation. Moreover, I found strong circumstantial evidence that the two documented victims, Clairvius Narcisse and Francina Illeus, had been exceedingly unpopular in their respective communities. On the basis of interviews conducted among residents of her village as well as family members, it appears that Francina Illeus was a chronic thief, completely untrustworthy in the marketplace; one influential mambo who traded in the region described her as *maloktcho*, a Creole invective that translates poorly as "crude, uncivilized, raw." That same informant went so far as to suggest on record that it was the market women who had secured Illeus's fate as a zombie.

At the time of his demise Clairvius Narcisse, as I have said earlier, was involved in a land dispute with members of his family that resulted in his being ostracized by the community. Interviews with family members and villagers resulted in a number of provocative statements. A cousin, for example, suggested that Narcisse had been summoned before an informal tribunal, where his fate was decided. When I suggested to a prominent houngan that Narcisse had taken his case before the legal authorities in Port-au-Prince, the man derisively questioned how Narcisse expected to find protection in the capital from his own people. Narcisse himself, when I interviewed him alone, mentioned that he had been taken for eight days of judgment by individuals he described as "the masters of the country," people who "do as they please."

A close examination of the case histories of both Clairvius Narcisse and Francina Illeus suggested the possibility that the threat of zombification was not enacted in either a criminal or random way. Because the bokor who prepare and administer the

poison live within the communities wherein the zombies are
created, it is highly unlikely that any bokor who did not have the
support of that community could, with impunity, engage in creating zombies purely for personal gain. The evidence from known
cases indicated that zombification might be a social sanction,
administered by the bokor with the full knowledge and complicity of members of his community. It is a practice designed to
enforce order and conformity, not to disrupt it. In fact, the authority to create a zombie may rest not with an individual bokor,
but with the secret society of which he is a member.

THE HAITIAN SECRET SOCIETIES:
COLONIAL GENESIS IN MARONAGE

Bloated by wealth unlike anything seen since the early days of the
conquest, the colonial planters of Saint Domingue made an
institution of cruelty. Field hands who were caught eating cane
were forced to wear tin muzzles while they worked (Rotberg
1971). Runaways had their hamstrings sliced. Brandings, indis-
criminate floggings, rapes, and killings were a matter of course,
and for the slightest infraction a man was hanged from a nail
driven through his ear (Leyburn 1941; James 1963; Fouchard
1981). Slaves, like cane, were grist for the mill, and the death
toll in some years rose as high as eighteen thousand (Fouchard
1981). The documented excesses of certain owners almost defy
belief. One slave was kept in chains for twenty-five years. A
notorious planter always carried a hammer and nails with him
just so as to be prepared to hang from the trees the severed ears
of those he punished. Other common tortures included spraying
the flesh with boiling cane syrup, sewing the lips together with
brass wire, castration and sexual mutilation of both men and
women, live burial, binding men—their skin glazed with molas-
ses—across the paths of ants, enclosing people in barrels studded with inward-protruding nails, and stuffing the anus with
gunpowder which was then ignited; the latter practice was common enough to give rise to the colloquial expression, "blasting a
black's ass" (Fouchard 1981). So systematic was the abuse of the
slaves that it supported a profession of executioners whose fees
were regulated by law. The fee for burning someone alive, for
example, was set at sixty French pounds. A hanging was only

thirty, and for a mere five pounds one could have a slave branded and his or her ears cut off (Fouchard 1981; Leyburn 1941).

Such savagery was the rule, not the exception, and the fact that first the Indians and then thousands of whites—indentured servants, petty thieves, convicts, or simply urban poor who were kidnapped from the port cities of Europe—had toiled in servitude before them did little to still the rage of the Africans. Forced labor was the foundation of an entire economic system that knew no color boundaries. Like an open sore the plantations grew upon the Caribbean islands, and when the Indians died and the supply of poor whites failed to meet demand, the merchants tapped deeper into Africa, drawing away men and women not because they were black, but because they were cheap, seemingly limitless in number, and better laborers. The European upper class, which thought nothing of hanging a child for petty theft, or of packing indentured workers—white or black—like herring into the festering holds of ships bound for the New World, cared less about the origins of their laborers than the products of their labor. Slavery was not born of racism; rather, racism was the consequence of slavery (Williams 1971). In the first days of colonialism, the color of the workers meant no more to the merchants who traded in them than it did to the kings of Africa who lorded over thousands of their own slaves, and who for suitable profit were more than willing to pass them along. Of course, all this mattered little to the men and women unloaded into bondage in Saint Domingue. For them, the enemy had a face, and there was no doubt as to its color.

Confronted by unrelenting intimidation and torture, the options of the slaves were few. Those who chose to submit and endure did what was necessary to ease their plight: self-inflicted wounds allowed a respite from the brutal labor in the fields; women gave themselves to the overseers, or spared their unborn children by practicing abortion (Fouchard 1981; James 1963). Others sought immediate relief through suicide (Herskovits 1975). But those who could not be broken and whose desire for freedom drove them to take desperate measures fled the plantations under the cover of night and became known as maroons. Some runaway slaves remained close by in hiding, dependent on the collusion of families and friends who remained behind. Others, especially skilled workers who were fluent in Creole, slipped into anonymity in the cities, passing themselves off as freedmen among the faceless crowds in the markets or on the docks. Still others made for the Spanish frontier of Santo Domingo, overland across the savannas and mountains and through the dense forests that still blanketed the island. Like stray cattle, these *Zombification* runaways were but a nuisance to the planters, readily dealt with *as a Social* by professional bounty hunters and their dogs. If recaptured on *Process* the fringes of the plantation, they were simply returned to be flogged and publicly humiliated, and they were made to kneel outside the Roman Catholic church to beg forgiveness for "insubordination to the situation in which God placed him" (Fouchard 1981, 249). Should the runaways be unfortunate enough to be discovered some distance away, or should they resist capture, they were summarily killed—shot and ravaged by the hounds once their identifying brands had been sliced from their skin.

But there was another type of maroon: individuals who, by desire or circumstances, fled the plantations with no expectation of ever returning. These were Africans who in some sense took responsibility for their fate, men and women who sought not just to survive but to fight and to seek revenge for the weight of injustice that had tormented their people (Maniget 1977; Debien 1979). When these slaves left the plantations, taking with them a mule, a knife, a machete, field tools, clothing, or anything of value that they had managed to pilfer, they joined organized bands in remote sanctuaries deep in the hinterland. There they lived in armed camps, sealed off by palisades surrounded by wide ditches, which were fortified at the bottom by pointed sticks (Moreau de Saint-Mery 1979). They planted gardens and to a great extent were self-sufficient, supplementing what they grew with periodic raids on the plantations. If solitary runaways were a mere irritation to the French, these independent maroon retreats were no less than training grounds for guerrilla fighters who threatened the order and stability of the entire colony (Fouchard 1981; Laguerre 1980b; Maniget 1977; Debien 1979).

The French regime responded by waging an incessant campaign of extermination. Specialized military forces known as *marechaussée* were sent on frequent and costly forays into the mountains. Some of these expeditions were moderately successful, returning with captives who were publicly broken at the wheel. Others never came back at all. And not one was able to penetrate or destroy the principal strongholds. The French could not be everywhere, and the maroons were—in the mountains rising behind the plantations of the northern plain at Cap Francis, the Cul-de-Sac near Port-au-Prince, or the rolling valleys near Cayes in the south (Maniget 1977; Fouchard 1981). As a result, by the mid-eighteenth century entire regions were effectively sealed off to whites. One rebellion, which covered a vast mountain block in the south, lasted a hundred years, until the French finally abandoned the zone altogether (Moreau de Saint-Mery 1979). Further north, a maroon community in the Bahoruco Mountains thrived for eighty-five years, until the French imposed a truce under the terms of which the maroons would be permitted to form an independent clan. When the leader of that particular band of rebels arrived to negotiate, it was discovered that he had been a maroon for over forty-five years (Fouchard 1981).

As the French military expeditions collapsed in the mountains, the colonial administration did what it could to destroy the clandestine network that maintained the flow of goods and information between the plantations and the maroons. Fear of the rebels was behind the constant legislation restricting the movements and interactions of the slaves. Blacks were forbidden to go out at night, to visit neighboring plantations, to use boats, or even to talk among themselves without the master's permission (Fouchard 1981). Night searches were frequent, and anyone caught hiding weapons or aiding runaways was brutally and publicly punished. But at a time when slaves outnumbered whites a hundred to one on the plantations, there was really very little the French could do (James 1963; Leyburn 1941). Even if some of the slaves came to fear the wrath and disruption of the maroons as much as they hated the planters' whips, there could be no doubt that the rebel bands fought for freedom, and as a result their legend grew with each successive generation (Maniget 1977; Laguerre 1973a, 1974a, 1974b). With increasing impunity the guerrillas came out of the hills, raiding stores, pillaging plantations, and spreading along with terror the idea of liberty. By 1770, according to a contemporary report, the number of maroons had reached such proportions that "security became nonexistent" and it was unwise for whites to wander alone in the hills (Fouchard 1981, 327).

Just who and how many chose to follow this desperate path is uncertain, but colonial records provide some clues. Between

1764 and 1793, for example, newspaper advertisements alone
indicated some 48,000 cases of maronage (Fouchard 1981).
How many of these runaways ended up in the maroon enclaves is
not known, but the figure does provide a sense of the problem
that faced the French. Significantly, a large percentage of those
who did flee had lived in the colony less than a year, and many
escaped virtually off the docks (Debien 1979). One colonial
document, which covers a single port for a fifteen-day period in
January 1786, lists 43 new slaves who either escaped or were
recaptured. In 1788, out of 10,573 slaves who disembarked over
a ten-month period at Cap Francis, more than 2,000 got away
(Fouchard 1981). Whereas the Creole maroon could slip incon-
spicuously into the bowels of the city, these fresh arrivals from
Africa, ignorant of the ways of the colony, were the ones who
invariably fled to the hills. Therefore, a good many of the recruits
to the maroon communities were the individuals least socialized
into the regime of the whites. Into their new homes, then, they
brought not the burdens of slavery but the ways of their African
homelands.

Behind a veil of secrecy critical to their survival, these maroon
communities developed genuine political, economic, and religious systems of their own (Laguerre 1980b). Their leaders were
culled from what contemporary observers described as a "new
class of slaves" that arrived in the colony throughout the eighteenth century (Moreau de Saint-Mery 1958). These were men
of royal blood, often educated not just in their own traditions but
also by Arab teachers, and endowed by birth with intelligence,
moral vigor, and the call of a militant tradition (Maniget 1977).
Their people were also a chosen lot, mostly young men between
the ages of seventeen and thirty-five, each one the product of a
tortuous selective process. Merely to reach the maroon camps
meant surviving the brutal passage from Africa, enduring the
abuse on the plantations, and then outwitting the hounds of the
bounty hunters, to face willingly a life of daily risk, physical
deprivation, and constant adversity.

Acceptance into the ranks of the maroons was strictly controlled. Only those who came voluntarily were taken, and these
only after making sure that they were not colonial spies. Blacks
captured during raids could be made slaves and, on the slightest
suggestion of betrayal, were put to death (Moreau de Saint-Mery
1958). Newly arrived runaways had first to erase their past,

mutilating their brands with knives or with the juice of toxic plants—*acajou* (*Anacardium occidentale*) or *bresillet* (*Comocladia glabra*)—that caused disfiguring welts. They endured rigorous initiations, during which they learned the secret handshakes and passwords that would distinguish friend from foe during the raids. Publicly they swore allegiance to the community, and they were warned in graphic terms of what would occur should they betray the secrets of the group. Secrecy defined and protected the integrity of these communities, and the obvious models for their internal organization were the secret societies of Africa that at least some of the former slaves must have joined in their youth.

During the colonial era, as they are today, secret societies were a dominant social force throughout much of West Africa, particularly among the coastal rain forest peoples who were taken in bondage to Saint Domingue (Butt-Thompson 1929; Brown 1951; Magid 1972; Ottenberg 1982a, 1971; Forde 1956; Little 1965, 1966; Morton-Williams 1960). The parallels between these groups and the later maroon communities are striking. Membership was conferred through initiation, a lengthy process that exposed the candidate to physical hardships, tests of endurance and pain, following which he or she learned the secret passwords, symbols, language, and handshakes of the society. As in Saint Domingue, it was knowledge of these esoteric signs that defined the group; in virtually every regard the societies were not secret, and in fact their function demanded that their existence be completely known. For these societies were no peripheral feature of West African culture; they lay at its very core and remained, both before and after the colonial era, the principal and militant champions of the traditional way of life (Little 1948). The Poro Society of Sierra Leone, for example, left its mark on almost every facet of Mende life, taking responsibility for tribal education, the regulation of sexual conduct, the supervision of political and economic affairs, and the operation of social services, including recreation and medical care (Little 1965). A key to the strength of the West African secret societies—and particularly applicable to the needs of the Haitian maroons—was the fact that their interests and activities were defined in terms of the community rather than a lineage or clan (Little 1948). Because of this emphasis, they provided the maroon bands with an invaluable model for the consolidation of the diverse cultural backgrounds of the individual slaves.

A vital function of the West African secret societies, as the most important arbiters of culture, was the administration of justice, and, as in the case of the Leopard Society among the Efik of Old Calabar, their tribunals delivered a verdict based on the outcome of the poison ordeal. Judgment by ordeal could cover any and all personal or social crimes and was inevitably invoked in suspected cases of sorcery. Not surprisingly, the secret societies developed a particularly refined knowledge of toxic preparations, learning not only to identify and experiment with different species of plant and animal, but also to control the dosage, the means of administration, and even the psychological set of the potential recipient (Robb 1957; Holmstedt 1972). Indeed, ownership of supposedly supernatural medicines and preparations is one of the fundamental features and sources of authority and power in the West African secret societies (Little 1965).

But the use of toxic preparations was not restricted to the secret societies or, even among them, to the ordeal tribunals. Perhaps as much as any single material trait, the manipulation of poisons was a recurrent thread throughout sub-Saharan African cultures. In certain regions, for example, criminals were executed by pricking their skin with lances dipped in the juice of toxic plants. In parts of West Africa, when a king died his heir had to submit at least twice to poison ordeals to prove his supernatural strength; should he fail and die, the lineage was broken and the throne was declared vacant. Individual sorcerers often used potions, of course, but also, in an extraordinary development, poisons were used systematically by established rulers in vain attempts to purge entire populations of evil. The leaders of the Cazamance and Balantes peoples of West Africa, for example, used a preparation based in part on the bark of a tree known as *tali* (*Erythrophleum guineense* G. Don, of the Leguminosae). Other ingredients included a powder ground from the dried hearts of previous victims and a number of admixtures reminiscent of those used in contemporary Haiti—ground glass, lizards, toads, crushed snakes, and human remains. After having been placed in a vat and allowed to ferment for a year, this toxic preparation was ceremoniously paraded on a day of great festivities and given to every citizen. Each year as many as two thousand people died (Robb 1957). With the advent of the slave trade, however, West African rulers discovered an even better means of purging their societies. According to Moreau de Saint-Mery, certain kings made use of their treaties with the European merchants to get rid of their poisoners by deporting them to Saint Domingue (Moreau de Saint-Mery, cited in Kerboull 1977).

Within the colony the African knowledge and use of toxic preparations posed a constant and very real threat to the social order of the whites. As early as 1738 a royal declaration was published prohibiting their use, but eight years later the problem had grown so serious that a second decree explicitly forbade any slave, on pain of death, from concocting "any remedies in powder or whatever form and to undertake the curing of any malady with the exception of snakebite" (Fouchard 1981, 315). The worst punishments were reserved for slaves accused of being poisoners (James 1963). By 1755 an epidemic of poisoning threatened the entire colony, and the central administration was obliged to mobilize all its resources in an attempt to identify the source. Over a ten-year period on one plantation, a full two-thirds of slave deaths were attributed to poisonings (Fouchard 1981). Notoriously cruel colonist Nicolas le Jeune reported in 1788 that "his father had lost through poisoning four hundred slaves in twenty-five years and fifty-two in just six months and that in less than two years he had lost forty-seven blacks and thirty mules" (cited in Fouchard 1981, 329). One magistrate presiding over a slave trial identified the purpose of the poisonings. Their single motive, he declared, was "revenge for the abuse of the slaves especially of women by masters and overseers" (Fouchard 1981, 329). The political potential of these unknown folk toxins, both as a weapon for the slaves and as a nefarious threat to the planters, was made explicit upon the arrest in 1757 of the maroon leader Medor, who told his captors: "If blacks commit poisonings, the end purpose is to gain freedom. Among those whose only thought is to destroy the colony there is also a secret which the whites know nothing about" (Fouchard 1981, 317).

The most spectacular use of poisons as a weapon in the organized resistance of the maroons was that orchestrated by François Macandal, a Mandingue slave originally from a plantation located near the northern center of Limbé. After he lost an arm in a mill accident in 1740, Macandal was made an animal herder, and his early wanderings in the mountains brought him in touch with the maroon bands. Charismatic and reputedly blessed with apocalyptic visions and dreams, he was seen by the blacks as an emissary of the gods, and he was able over the course of a six-year period to spread an extraordinary clandestine network of agents into every corner of the colony. He mobilized literally hundreds of slaves with one expressed purpose. Once, when asked to interpret one of his dreams, he called for a clay vessel and placed into it three kerchiefs. He pulled out one that was yellow and explained to the crowd that it was the color of the ones who were born on the land. The next one was white, and it was they who now ruled. The third was black, and it was they, he promised, who would eventually rule the island (Fouchard 1981; Rotberg 1976).

Before his betrayal and subsequent execution in 1758, Macandal shook the foundations of the colony. His poisons appeared everywhere—baked into bread, in medicine vials, in kegs of ale lifted directly from the ships and drunk because the water from the wells could no longer be trusted. According to colonial documents, all the guests at a banquet might succumb, sometimes from the wine, sometimes from the food, or even from fresh-picked fruit. The terror of the whites gave way to rage, and frequently innocent slaves were flayed alive. The slightest suspicion of collaboration with the poisoners meant a horrible death. But the enemy could not be seen; only its mark was felt, particularly by the whites but also by any black who showed signs of betraying the agents of Macandal. The colonial administration declared a state of siege and emptied its garrisons to parade the soldiers up and down the streets of the Cap, their guns shouldered and useless against an invisible enemy. The courts condemned anyone they imagined to be guilty, and work gangs were decimated in attempts to secure the names of the leaders of the conspiracy. Chemists and herbalists convened in an attempt to identify the source of the plague, whether plant or animal, some compound taken from the apothecary or some potion brought by the blacks from Africa. Royal proclamations were continually issued prohibiting any slave from working with folk remedies. But nothing the government did could stop the contagion. Before Macandal was finally captured and his network exposed, as many as six thousand were killed (Fouchard 1981).

Macandal's was not the first, and it was certainly not the last maroon revolt to threaten the colony. As early as 1681, before the colony had passed from the Spanish to the French and at a time when there were as many indentured whites working the plantations as there were Africans, with a total colonial population of only six thousand, maronage was already an acknowledged threat. Two years before, in one of the earliest documented revolts, a slave named Padrejean had killed his master, recruited a band of twenty Africans, and embarked on his goal of strangling every white in the land. The revolt failed, but it was the type of incident that drew the attention of the king and led to the Royal Edict of 1685, which, among other injunctions, specified that a captured maroon should have his or her ears cut off and one shoulder branded with a fleur de lys; should the offense be repeated, the hamstrings would be cut and a second brand applied to the other shoulder (Leyburn 1941). The publication of this decree indicated a growing concern among the free whites— a fear that would become hysteria as the population of slaves soared. By the early years of the eighteenth century, seditious plots, mysterious killings, and rumors of impending catastrophe had become a staple of colonial life (Fouchard 1981).

By the last years of French rule it was patently clear that the greed of the entire system had set the colony on a path of self-destruction. Only the potential for massive profits could possibly have numbed the whites to the imminent disaster. As absentee planters scrambled to increase their holdings, the borders of the plantations touched and then, to meet the rising demand for coffee, in particular, rose higher and higher into the mountains, displacing bands of maroons and ironically forcing more and more of them to depend on pillage (Rotberg 1971). The voracious consumption of labor, meanwhile, doubled the population of slaves in a mere fifteen years (Fouchard 1981). How long could the whites possibly have expected to control close to a half-million blacks, the vast majority of them born in Africa and steeped in a military tradition of their own that had spread kingdoms across half a continent (Leyburn 1941)?

It was within the maroon communities that the Vodoun religion took its definitive form and, equally important, it was there that its political and messianic potential became realized. Vodoun became, for the slaves, "a language, a way of expressing and resisting their cultural and religious oppression . . . [and] the focus for the development of political consciousness" (Laguerre 1974a, 28). Increasingly, known maroon leaders frequented the plantations, preaching "the desertion of slave quarters, the hatred of the colonists, the sabotage of plantations, the poisoning of cattle" (Price-Mars 1928, 10). By the end of the eighteenth century Vodoun had emerged as the single most critical unifying factor in the impending struggle of the revolutionary slaves. The primary purpose of the secret meetings of Vodoun acolytes on the plantations was to "create cohesion among the participants in plots against the existing order. . . . Vodoun was the cement which bound the members of the conspiracy and . . . it served as a catalyst when the time for action came" (Bastien 1966, 43).

Like Macandal, the slaves plotted their final revolt with care. As their network spread and desertions swelled the ranks of the maroons, the colony reverberated with the sounds of mutiny. In 1786 a planter from Marmelade reported the frequent secret meetings of two hundred or more slaves, during which a mulatto named Jerome preached independence and distributed protective cabalistic objects to the slaves (Fouchard 1981). The pervasive undercurrent of intrigue that haunted the colony is evident in the following contemporary document, which suggests the possibility that secret societies may have been present well before the slave uprising. "A great deal has been said of slave superstitions and of their secret organisations and the scheming and crimes for which they provide pretext—poisonings, infanticide, etc. . . . Whites were not admitted to these secret meetings and legal documentation was usually held secret or destroyed" (Gressier de la Jalousiere, cited in Fouchard 1981, 337). From these nocturnal assemblies, and within the passion of the Vodoun rituals, the idea of liberty spread. Maroon bands grew larger and more numerous, and the names of their leaders—Hyacinthe, Macaya, Romaine la Prophetesse—spread through the ranks of the slaves. The flash point came in the summer of 1791, and the spark was struck at a Vodoun ceremony attended by delegates from every plantation on the northern plain.

The historic gathering was invoked by the maroon leader Boukman Dutty and was held on a secluded knoll at Bois Caiman near Morne-Rouge on the night of 14 August 1791 (Bastien 1966). An old woman possessed by Ogoun, the god of fire and the metallurgical elements, drew a cutlass and sacrificed a pig. The leaders of the revolt were named—Boukman himself, Jean François, Biassou, and Jeannot—and one by one the hundreds of slaves present swore allegiance. Boukman stood up and, according to the popular reports canonized by the historians, declared: "God who made the sun that shines on us from above, who makes the sea to rage and the thunder roll, this same great God from his hiding place in the clouds, hear me, all of you is looking down upon us. He sees what the whites are doing. The God of the whites asks for crimes; ours desires only blessings. But this God who is so good directs you to vengeance! He will direct our arms, he will help us. Cast aside the image of the God of the whites who thirsts for our tears and pay heed to the voice of liberty speaking to our hearts" (Fouchard 1981, 341).

Two days later the first plantation burned, and then, on the night of 21 August, the slaves from five plantations around Macandal's old territory rose up and moved on the center of Limbé. By morning Acul was in flames, Limbé destroyed, and throughout the next day the uprising rode the sound of the conch trumpets as, one by one, each settlement in the north fell—Plaine du Nord, Dondon, Marmelade, Plaisance. In a single night of indescribable horror, a thousand whites were strangled and two thousand sugar and coffee mills were destroyed. For days dark columns of smoke rose beyond a wall of flames that isolated the entire northern half of the colony. Fire rained from clouds of burning straw torn from the fields and swept up by the fireballs. Ash coated the sea, and the reflection of an entire land aflame reddened the clouds as far away as the Bahamas (James 1963).

After the first weeks of the uprising, as the frenzy of destruction gave way to skirmishes and then to out-and-out battles with the colonial militia, the ranks of the slaves coalesced around certain leaders who in turn drew their inspiration from the gods. In the western province Romaine la Prophetesse marched, to the music of drums and conch shells, behind an entourage of houngan chanting that the weapons of the whites—their cannon and muskets—were bamboo, their gunpowder but dust; his personal guard carried only long cowtails blessed by the spirits and thus capable of deflecting the bullets of the whites (Fouchard 1981). Madiou reported that the guerrilla leader Halaou was similarly protected by talismans and when, at the head of a considerable army, he was received in the capital by the French legation he sat "almost nude, covered with fetishes, holding a cock on his side" (Mennesson-Rigaud 1958, 63). Sorcerers and magicians composed the staff of Biassou, and much of his own tent was devoted to amulets, sacred objects, and devotions. In his camps great fires flared at night as naked women invoked the spirits, singing words only known in "the deserts of Africa" (Madiou, cited in Métraux 1972, 43). Biassou walked in triumph, exalting his people, telling them that if they were fortunate enough to fall in battle, they would rise again from the hearth of Africa to seed their ancient tribes. A contemporary report from Cap Francis suggests that the black women of the capital went out at night singing words unintelligible to the whites. For some time they "had adopted an almost uniform dress, around their bellies wearing kerchiefs in which the colour red dominated. . . . The Voodoo King had just declared war on the colonials [they said] and accompanied by his Queen dressed in a red scarf and agitating the little bells decorating the box containing the snake, they marched to the assault of the colony's cities" (Fouchard 1981, 346).

If Vodoun charged the revolt, the tactics and organization of the rebel bands came directly from the precedent established by the maroons (Maniget 1977). With increasing boldness the rebels ravaged plantations, disrupted communications, and plundered supply trains. Raiding by night, they left in their wake fire, poison, and corpses, before retreating at daybreak into every inaccessible gorge and ravine in the land. There they lived as they always had, protected by palisades and rings of sentinels, and by the potent magic of their sorcerers. A French force of some twenty-four hundred troops, dispatched in early February 1792 to invade and destroy rebel camps, reported "being astonished to see stuck in the ground along the route large perches on which a variety of dead birds had been affixed. . . . On the road at intervals there were cut up birds surrounded by stones, and also a dozen broken eggs surrounded by large circles. What was our surprise to see black males leaning about and more than two hundred women dancing and singing in all security. . . . The Voodoo priestess had not fled . . . she spoke no creole. . . . Both the men and women said that there could be no human power over her. . . . She was of the Voodoo cult" (Malenfant, cited in Fouchard 1981, 344–45). The leader of the French expedition also encountered the cloak of secrecy that continued to protect the rebels as it had the maroons. From a female initiate he learned that "there was a password but she would never give it to me. . . . She gave me the hand recognition sign: it was somewhat similar to that of the Masons. She told me this as a secret,

Zombification as a Social Process

assuring me . . . I would be killed or poisoned if I tried to pene-trate the great mystery of the sect" (Malenfant, cited in Fouchard 1981, 344).

Perhaps unfortunately for the former slaves, they were not alone in their quest for freedom. For some time tension had been growing between the white planters and the enfranchised mulat-toes. The latter, though equal in numbers to the whites and entitled by law to all the privileges of French citizens, were, in fact, treated as a separate class. Social discrimination of the crudest sort had made them resentful, but at the same time their energetic exercise of their right to property had made them exceedingly wealthy and powerful; this was a dangerous combi-nation for the French, especially once the mulattoes came into contact with the rebellious ideas that had grown from the Ameri-can and French revolutions. Even before the slave uprising, a force of mulattoes had demanded full implementation of the accords worked out by the revolutionary assemblies in Paris. Their incipient revolt failed, and the leaders were brutally tor-tured, but it was the first incident in a struggle that would, in time, pit whites against mulattoes, whites against mulattoes allied with blacks, and mulattoes against whites working sometimes with and sometimes against the interests of the black former slaves. The result was a reign of confusion, chaos, and destruc-tion that, after two years, left the French in control of the cities, the blacks firmly entrenched in the countryside, and the mulat-toes still caught in between (Leyburn 1941; James 1963).

In February 1793 the Haitian Revolution was profoundly af-fected by the European war between Republican France and England, which was allied with Spain. To the problems of the colonial administration—already preoccupied by political events in Paris, stunned by the uprising of the slaves, and torn asunder by the power struggle between mulatto and white planters—was now added the threat of an enemy army moving overland from the Spanish colony of Santo Domingo. The maroons predictably aligned themselves with the invaders, and their leaders Biassou and Jean François—Boukman was dead by this time—became officers in the Spanish army, as did Toussaint, a former slave who had not left bondage until some months after the uprising, but who was about to begin his meteoric rise to power.

The French, hard-pressed even before the Spanish invasion, were now forced to negotiate with the maroons, and in the

summer of 1793, under pressure from the rebel leaders, the
colonial administration officially abolished slavery. But the maroons soon recognized the proclamation for what it was: a desperate attempt to defuse the explosive potential of the blacks
while retaining intact the essential structure of the colonial economic order. Biassou and Jean François rejected the French
offer and defiantly remained allied with the Spanish, who had
promised unconditional emancipation. But for reasons that became clear only in the light of subsequent events, Toussaint
shifted his allegiance back to the French. Then, at a time when
he remained unquestionably less powerful than the prominent
maroon leaders, Toussaint and his forces ambushed the camps of
Biassou and Jean François, killing many of their followers and
turning those who survived over to the French authorities.

Toussaint moved quickly to consolidate his position, and by
1797, having defeated two foreign armies as well as a rival mulatto force, this former slave, by now christened Toussaint
L'Ouverture, emerged as the absolute ruler of all of Saint
Domingue. He then set to work to restore, under French rule,
the order and prosperity of the colony. And of what type of
colony, there could be no doubt. The people, though nominally
free, were in fact compelled to work under a system very like
the one they had fought so desperately to overthrow (Murray
1977; James 1963; Fouchard 1981). Toussaint's autocratic de-
crees prohibited movement between plantations and ordered
those without urban trades to the fields, where they labored
under military supervision. True, he eliminated the worst excesses of the colonial brutality, but the essential structure of the
plantation system remained just as the French had intended. As
for the traditional beliefs of the people, Toussaint, as a devout
Roman Catholic, had no interest in what he considered the
pagan beliefs of Africa (Bastien 1966; Rotberg 1976).

If there were any doubts as to the ambitions of the new black
military elite, they were quelled by the events that took place
following the invasion of Leclerc's French army in 1801, the
betrayal of Toussaint by Napoleon, and his ignoble deportation
to France. The French, of course, had never intended to tolerate
black rule in the colony, and even as Toussaint struggled to
rebuild the plantations, plans for his overthrow were laid in Paris.
Napoleon himself clearly identified his real military enemy in the
colony, and he ordered his brother-in-law to concentrate his

efforts, after the deportation of Toussaint, on destroying the remnants of the maroon bands. As predicted in Paris, this was a task that the French commander was able to delegate to local generals who had recently served under Toussaint—in particular to Jean-Jacques Dessalines and Henri Christophe, who by historical record applied themselves and their troops willingly to the slaughter (Fouchard 1981).

Still the maroons resisted, and as the pressure mounted, they received both black freedmen and mulattoes into the final alliance that would wage the war of independence. There were a number of pitched battles, but there is little doubt that the tried and proven tactics of the maroons—raids, fire, poison, ambush—provided the margin of victory. But after the final defeat of the French, the maroons were forgotten as they had been after the wars of Toussaint L'Ouverture. The dictatorial rulers who emerged in the vacuum of independence lost no time in revealing the depths of their dedication to equality or liberty. According to the historian Madiou, Dessalines, when appointed inspector-general of culture in the western provinces, "relentlessly hunted down all the secret societies in which African superstitions were practised" (Madiou, cited in Métraux 1972, 49). Once he became emperor, Dessalines prohibited Vodoun services and ordered all the acolytes shot on sight (Métraux 1972). Like Toussaint before him, Dessalines feared the secrecy of Vodoun and its potential challenge to the state (Rotberg 1976). Christophe—a former slave who had fought by the side of Toussaint, taken part in the deceitful raid on the forces of Biassou and Jean François, and then temporarily joined hands with the French armies of Leclerc—became ruler of the northern half of the country in 1806. He declared himself king and, in the way of kings, he wasted the lives of twenty thousand subjects to build himself an opulent palace and a fortress that would never be needed (Leyburn 1941).

With Christophe's depredations, the betrayal of the maroons appeared to be complete, but in 1820 Christophe fell, and the popular uprising that prompted his suicide in one sense signified the triumph of Vodoun (Bastien 1966). From that time on, "no head of state had the same opportunity, resources and personality or energy to launch a movement of national proportions to stamp out the apparent obstacle to the Europeanization of Haiti" (Bastien 1966, 50). Yet in the early years of the republic, and in the face of a history of betrayal at the hands of the military leaders, the struggle of the maroons continued. In certain parts of the country independent maroon bands persisted until as late as 1860, but on the whole, as the former slaves took to the land and the peasant society was born, the role of the maroons was transformed from one of fighting the French to one of resisting a new threat to their people: an emerging urban and political elite who were distinguished not by the color of their skin but by the plans they harbored for the land and the labor of the peasants. And whereas the war with the French could be won, the new struggle promised to become a permanent feature of peasant life. In the early years of the nineteenth century Vodoun, which had developed as both a religious and a revolutionary ideology (Laguerre 1974a), remained the focus for the development of political consciousness within the emerging peasant society. The leaders of the maroon bands faced with new oppressors found a new and remarkable means of protecting their interests and freedom. Even after the official independence of Haiti in 1804, "cells of maroon communities have continued to exist through the formation of secret societies" (Laguerre 1980b, 149). From being an overt and independent military force, the maroons went underground and became a clandestine institution charged with the political protection of traditional Vodoun society. In this way were conceived the immediate predecessors of today's secret societies.

THE HAITIAN SECRET SOCIETIES: ETHNOGRAPHIC REPORTS

The term "secret society" appears with some frequency in the ethnographic literature on Haiti, but the nature and function of these groups, and indeed their very existence, has been and continues to be a source of considerable controversy. R. B. Hall described in some detail the "Model de Paris," a secret society that he encountered on the remote island of La Gonave. According to his report, this organization served as a cooperative labor group and mutual benefit society that provided social entertainment, afforded physical and spiritual protection for its members, and performed religious and disciplinary functions as well. The Model de Paris was only one of many similar societies on the island, and each one had its own music, songs, dances, insignias, costumes, archives, and ceremonies. The societies, though open to men and women on an equal basis, were hierarchical, with each one ruled by an elaborate array of officers including the presiding *queen, president, président de la confidence, chef de société, division de société, reine drapeau* (flag queen), *sergent d'armes*, and *conseils*, as well as a number of miscellaneous officers of lesser rank. In addition to the agricultural, social, and protective and benevolent functions, the society convened informal tribunals in which the transgressions of individual members were discussed and judged. For serious offenses, "expulsion from the society is the common penalty. It is said by non-members that bodily torture and even death are meted out to those who betray the society or commit serious offenses against it" (Hall 1929, 699). Hall noted that territorial secret societies were ubiquitous on La Gonave and on the adjacent mainland of Haiti, and he explicitly traced their lineage to the secret societies of West Africa. He maintained that, like their African counterparts, the secret societies of La Gonave dominated the social and economic life of the people.

By contrast, other early workers describe the Haitian secret societies as being almost peripheral to the mainstream of village life. M. J. Herskovits believed that there were secret societies in Haiti, but he noted that they were "so feared by Mirebalais folk because of their reputation for working all kinds of evil that it was with some difficulty that even the names of two of them could be learned—the 'Bisago,' whose members appear at night wearing horns and holding candles, and 'Les Cochons Sans Poils'" (Herskovits 1975, 243). The former, he said, were believed to be capable of transmuting themselves into animals in order to perpetrate evil deeds. The societies all "meet in the open country at night and each has a small drum. They are called together by the beating of one rock against another in a manner reminiscent of the Zangbeto Society of Porto Novo, Dahomey" (Herskovits 1975, 244).

Alfred Métraux referred to the secret societies as "bands of sorcerers, criminals of a special kind" (Métraux 1972, 293), and he alluded to their reputed magical skills, noting their ability to change innocent victims into animals which are then slaughtered and consumed. Although he was uncertain whether the societies actually existed, he nevertheless recorded several names —zobop, bizango, galipotes, vlanbindingues, macandal, and voltigeurs—and he observed that the societies gathered at night in clandestine ceremonies during which individual members were identified by means of "passports" and secret passwords. The members were garbed in red robes, and "holding candles in their hands and cracking a whip they march in column like soldiers . . . to some crossroads and there they celebrate a ceremony in honour of Maitre-Carrefour" (Métraux 1972, 294). Erika Bourguignon (1959) mentioned an account of a secret society of demons, the Société Zobo, made up of magical beings—ordinary people by day who transform themselves by night to accomplish evil deeds. Both Métraux and Bourguignon maintained that the secret societies are directly descended from the sorcerer societies of West Africa, but they cautioned that evidence for their presence in contemporary Haiti has yet to be established by firsthand ethnographic observation.

Harold Courlander acknowledged that secret societies were once common in Haiti, but he suggested that the contemporary groups are but a shadow of their former selves, so vitiated that "they have been supplanted by the société, a kind of mutual aid association with both economic and recreational functions" (Courlander 1960, 166). He listed the names of what he considered "true secret societies"—the vinbindingue, cochon rouge, zeaubeaups, cochons gris—but he claimed that they "appear to survive in name rather than in fact" (Courlander 1960, 167).

Kerboull, on the other hand, had no doubt about the existence of nocturnal sects, and he described in some detail a specimen of a secret society passport that came into his possession (Kerboull 1979, 181). Like Métraux, he emphasized the criminal aspect of the secret societies, carefully distinguishing their nefarious practices from what he considered the pure and righteous traditions of Vodoun. "The crimes of these sects," he stated, "if they are not rather the fantasies of sick imaginations . . . have nothing to do with the orthodox familial Vaudou, are isolated and abnormal and can be attributed to sociological monsters" (Kerboull 1973, 121). The presidents of these societies, he added, are generally bokor, and the gatherings are convened at night under the direction of a titular president and queen of the society. Their principal function is to terrorize the peasants (Kerboull 1973). A similar conclusion was reached by Rigaud, who viewed the *secte rouge* as the inversion of the Vodoun religion, a "criminal secte" that drank blood and took pleasure in murder (Rigaud 1953, 249).

Zora Neale Hurston provided a detailed, though highly subjective, description of the activities of the secret societies. Her first marginal encounter occurred late one evening in 1936 in Port-au-Prince when she awoke to the sound of a high staccato drumbeat, highly repetitious and unlike any rhythm she had heard in a hounfour. She woke her housegirl and suggested they investigate, much as they had done many times before. But instead of the eager companion to whom she had grown accustomed, Hurston beheld for the first time a trembling child, unwilling to step beyond the threshold of their doorway. Some weeks later, again at night, Hurston was disturbed by the acrid smell of burning rubber in her yard. When she questioned the man responsible, he apologized profusely but explained that the fire was necessary to drive away those who planned to take his child—the *Cochons Gris*, or Gray Pigs, whom he claimed ate people. Apparently he had already seen them parading by the house, figures draped in red gowns and hoods. Yet a third incident occurred on a sailboat en route to the island of La Gonave, where Hurston encountered a force of militia moving in to suppress a society based in a remote section of the island. No details were provided, just a few words followed by a hush of uneasiness, which Hurston interpreted as fear. Finally, back in the capital, a contact led her to the house of a houngan in the Bel Air slum, and there she saw a temple unlike anything she had known. At the center of the sanctum was an immense black stone attached to a heavy chain, which in turn was held by an iron bar whose two ends were buried in the masonry of the wall. As she stood before the stone, her host handed her a paper, yellow with age and patterned with cabalistic symbols, and a "mot de passage"— password of the secret society known as the *Cochons Gris*.

Following these and other leads over the course of several months, Hurston managed to put together an astonishing portrait of the Haitian secret societies. According to her informants, they met clandestinely at night, called together by a special high-pitched drumbeat; members recognized each other by means of ritualized greetings that they learned during their initiation, and by identification papers—the passports. In a vivid description of a nocturnal gathering, Hurston mentioned a presiding emperor accompanied by a president, ministers, queens, officers, and servants, all involved in a frenzied dance and song ritual that she likened to the "sound and movement of hell boiling over" (Hurston 1981, 225). The entire throng formed a procession and marched through the countryside, saluting the spirits at the crossroads, and picking up additional members before convening in the cemetery to invoke Baron Samedi, the guardian of the graveyard, and to beg him to provide a "goat without horns" for the sacrifice. With the spirit's permission, scouts armed with cords made from the dried entrails of victims combed the land for some traveler foolish enough to be still journeying after dark. If the unfortunate wayfarer was unable to produce a passport indicating his membership in a society, and thus his right to move by night, he was taken to be punished.

Unfortunately it appears, from her writings at least, that Hurston was never able to attend one of these gatherings herself. Perhaps because of this she was unable to get beyond the public face of the societies as perceived and feared by the urban elite. A Haitian physician warned her that direct contact with the societies "will cost you more than you are willing to pay, perhaps things will be required of you that you cannot stand. Many Haitian intellectuals have curiosity but they know if they go to dabble in such matters, they may disappear permanently" (Hurston 1981, 218). Another physician told her:

We have a society that is detestable to all the people of Haiti. It is known as the Cochons Gris, Secte Rouge and the Vinbrindingue and all of these names mean one and the same thing. It is outside of, and has nothing to do with voodoo worship. They are banded together to eat human flesh. These terrible people were kept under control during the French period by the very strictures of slavery. But in the disturbances of the Haitian period, they began their secret meetings and were well organized before they came to public notice. It is generally believed that the society spread widely during the administration of Geffrard (1858–1867). Perhaps it began much earlier, we are not sure. But their evil practices had made them thoroughly hated and feared before the end of this administration. It is not difficult to understand why Haiti has not even yet thoroughly rid herself of these detestable creatures. It is because of their great secrecy of movement on the one hand and the fear they inspire on the other. . . . The cemeteries are the places where they display the most horrible aspects of their inclinations. Someone dies after a short illness, or a sudden indisposition. The night of the burial the Vinbrindingues go to the cemetery, the chain around the tomb is broken and the grave profaned. The coffin is pulled out and the body spirited away (Hurston 1981, 220–21).

Yet who were these secret societies? Hurston never really ventured to say. She concluded simply by emphasizing that they were secret, and that the very lives of their members depended upon the confidence of the group. But she also, rather remarkably, described their primary means of punishment, which is provocatively similar to the reported means of applying the toxic zombie preparation. She writes:

There is swift punishment for the adept who talks. When suspicion of being garrulous falls upon a member, he or she is thoroughly investigated, but with the utmost secrecy without the suspect knowing that he is suspect. But he is followed and watched until he is either accounted innocent or found guilty. If he is found guilty, the executioners are sent to wait upon him. . . . He is gotten into a boat and carried out beyond the aid and interference from the shore. After being told the why of the thing, his hands are seized by one man and held behind him, while another grips the head under his arm. A violent blow with a rock behind the ear stuns him and at the same time serves to abraise the skin. A deadly and quick-acting poison is then rubbed into the wound. There is no antidote for the poison and the victim knows it (Hurston 1981, 231).

It wasn't until almost forty years later that a young Haitian anthropologist, Michel Laguerre, began to answer some of the questions raised by Hurston's fieldwork. In the summer of 1976, Laguerre met a number of peasants who had been members of secret societies, but who had later converted to Protestantism and therefore were willing to talk, provided they were not obliged to reveal secret languages, strict rules, and individual members' names (Laguerre 1980b). There were, according to these informants, secret societies in all parts of the country, and each one maintained control of a specified territory. Names varied from region to region but included zobop, bizango, vlinbindingue, san poel, mandingue, and, most interestingly, macandal. Membership was by initiation and invitation, was open to men and women, and was strictly hierarchical. Laguerre verified the existence of passports, ritual handshakes, secret passwords, banners, flags, and brilliant red and black uniforms as well as a specialized body of spirits, songs, dances, and drumbeats. He also noted the central importance of the cyclical rituals performed to strengthen the solidarity of the group—gatherings that occur only at night, begin with an invocation to the spirits, and end with the members in procession flowing beneath the symbol of the society, the sacred coffin known as the *sekey madoule* (Laguerre 1980b).

But according to Laguerre, the function of the secret societies was unlike anything reported by Hurston and was, in fact, much closer to the political and judicial role alluded to by Hall. The contemporary secret societies constitute a power, if not an institution parallel to the Vodoun temples headed by the houngan (Hurbon 1979; Laguerre 1984). In no way could they be described as criminal organizations (Laguerre 1980b). On the contrary, Laguerre described them as the very conscience of the peasantry, a quasi-political arm of the Vodoun society that is charged, above all, with the protection of the community. Like the secret societies of West Africa, those of Haiti seemed to Laguerre to be the single most important arbiter of culture. Each one was loosely attached to a hounfour whose houngan was a sort of "public relations man between the outside world and the members of the secret society" (Laguerre 1980b, 157). In fact, so ubiquitous were the societies that Laguerre described them as nodes in a vast network that, if and when linked together, would represent a powerful underground government capable of competing head-on with the central regime in Port-au-Prince (Laguerre 1980b). And of the origins of these secret societies, Michel Laguerre had no doubts.

It was his view that the secret societies of Haiti are descended from the sorcerer societies of West Africa, but that they were transformed in the unique circumstances of colonial Haiti. The contemporary secret societies had their genesis in the isolated communities of escaped slaves. After independence, the function of those bands changed from fighting a slave system to protecting their own community interests from outside threats. Today they constitute a force that protects community resources, particularly land, as they define the power boundaries of the village (Laguerre 1980b). Within a single community, access to land by an ever-increasing population is guaranteed by Vodoun-mediated land transfers between community members who are fulfilling ritual obligations (Murray 1977). As religious obligations protect the community from within, so the secret society is hypothesized to guarantee the integrity of the total community land holdings from external threats. As the maroons during the colonial era fought for liberty, the contemporary secret societies, according to Laguerre, "stand strong to keep safe the boundaries of power of their local communities and to keep other groups of people from being a threat to their communities" (Laguerre 1980b, 149).

If Laguerre's analysis was correct, the implications for the zombie investigation were significant. In the ethnographic literature the secret societies frequently had been linked to the creation of zombies. According to Courlander a zombie is "a human being who has died and been resurrected from the graveyard by members of the Zeaubeaup Society, by a wicked sorcerer, or by some other person who has realized the 'power' to perform this act" (Courlander 1960, 101). A police report from 1954 suggests that, in the inaccessible hill country of the Black Mountains, a band of Sans Poils was terrorizing the local population. The local guard eventually arrested their leader who, once incarcerated, "confessed to fourteen victims he had either converted into zombies, or else simply done away with" (Kerboull 1979, 125). Hurston was informed that in "the cemeteries are the places where they [the secret societies] display the most horrible aspects of their inclinations. Someone dies after a short illness. . . . The night of the burial . . . the tomb is broken and the grave profaned. The coffin is pulled out and opened and the body spirited away" (Hurston 1981, 221). Jean Kerboull (1979, 68–70) recorded the claims of a number of peasants who reputedly had observed columns of secret society members exhuming zombies from the cemetery. True or not, these accounts reflect the generally held folk contention that the secret societies have a direct role in the creation of zombies.

Elsewhere one learns that it is the secret society that controls the zombie preparation: "A zobop had been entrusted with the

drugging of a poor fellow to make him into a zombi. The drugging was carried out and the victim, thought by his family to have
died, was buried. On the night after the funeral, the criminal
made his way to the tomb in the company of his followers,
according to the custom. The person responsible for the 'death'
must always be the one to reawaken the victim. He called the
man's name three times. The tomb was opened and they broke
the coffin to resurrect the corpse". (Kerboull 1979, 120). Another account runs: "A heartless man sold his stepchild to a band
of Sans Poils which caused it to fall ill. The child grew worse.
After twenty-four hours of complete prostration, he lay seemingly dead. At about four in the morning, the houngan arrived.
. . . He declared that the child was not dead and that he would
proceed to seek out the zebop who was responsible for making
him so" (Kerboull 1979, 120). Of her discussion with two Haitian physicians concerning the formula of the zombie preparation, Hurston noted: "The two doctors expressed their desire to
gain this secret, but they realised the impossibility of doing so.
These secret societies are secret" (Hurston 1981, 206).

My own preliminary research had revealed that in at least
some instances the zombie powders were controlled and manip-
ulated by the secret societies. A knowledge of poisons and their
complex pharmacological properties could be traced in direct
lineage from the contemporary societies to the maroon bands,
and beyond them to the secret societies of Africa. There was no
doubt that poisons were used in West Africa by judicial bodies to
punish those who broke the codes of the society, and Zora Neale
Hurston had suggested that the same sort of sanction was applied among the secret societies of Haiti. There was every reason
to believe that Clairvius Narcisse and Francina Illeus had received a poison, and that at the time of their "deaths" they were
both pariahs within their respective communities. Narcisse's
transgression was directly related to access to land—precisely the
sort of issue that, according to Laguerre's analysis, would attract
the attention of the secret societies. By his own account, Narcisse
had been taken before a tribunal, judged, and condemned. The
possible link to the tribunals of West Africa was obvious. Moreover, Narcisse had referred to those who judged him as the
"masters of the country" and had implied that he would only
encounter more trouble if he created more problems himself

(Davis 1985). Finally, certain houngan had stated independently and explicitly that the key to the zombie phenomenon would be found in the councils of the secret societies.

If the identification of the zombie preparation revealed a possible material basis for the zombie phenomenon, the work of Michel Laguerre suggested a sociological matrix. It was conceivable that, within the traditional society, zombification was not a random criminal activity but, on the contrary, a social sanction imposed by recognized corporate groups whose responsibility included the protection and policing of that society.

Nonetheless, with the exception of Hall's, none of the reports concerning the structure and function of the secret societies were based on firsthand experience. For all the speculation no one, including Michel Laguerre, had established and maintained direct contact with members of the Bizango societies. All the ethnographic reports were based on hearsay, or at best on the testimony of former members. The dilemma of current students of Haitian society was summarized by Kyle Kristos. "What," he asked, "is the truth concerning the Red Sects? This is almost impossible to discover. . . . There is much evidence to show that secret societies such as the Sect Rouge have existed in Haiti for centuries. However, because of the extreme secrecy regarding their activities it is difficult to know if they still go about their work. Perhaps no one can know the truth about the Sect Rouge until they have some experience of it" (Kristos 1976, 78).

Clearly, in order to assess the hypothesized connection between the secret societies and the zombie phenomenon, it would be necessary to enter into a sustained relationship with one or more of the societies. That became my purpose during the final phase of the zombie investigation.

CHAPTER EIGHT

THE BIZANGO SECRET SOCIETIES.

The following description and analysis of the organization and function of the Bizango secret societies is based on my own participant observation and is heavily dependent on the contacts that I established within these societies. My research strategy was that of the "community study" (Arensberg 1954, 1960, 1961), an anthropological methodology that requires immersion and ongoing involvement in the day-to-day routine of the individuals whose lifeways are the object of the investigation. However, because the principal focus of my study was an ill-defined and clandestine subset of the greater population, the project became essentially a study carried out within a community rather than a study of that community per se. Although the interrelationship between the Bizango societies and the greater community eventually proved to be of great interest, I initially focused largely on the structure and function of the societies themselves. Given that no firsthand descriptive account of the Haitian secret societies had entered the ethnographic literature, and that indeed the very existence of these groups had been subject to question, one of my primary goals was simply to document their activities.

From the start I realized that this research, though by no means exhaustive, would establish a corpus of data that would stand by itself and demand explanation regardless of the fate of whatever theoretical framework was used to analyze these data. Consequently, my major lines of inquiry attempted to outline the overall characteristics of these corporate groups. Were they, in fact, secret societies by anthropological definition? If so, what was the nature of their organization? What was the age, status, and sexual composition of the membership? Was this membership exclusive or inclusive, and what was the process by which an individual became a member? What was the nature and character of the hierarchy? Was the leadership primarily ritualistic or executive, or did it combine both functions? What were the grades, divisions, and titular posts and positions within the society, and how was power divided among the membership?

Other obvious issues included the relationship between different societies, their degree of integration, and the possibility of a national network linking regional societies under a general authority. Were the societies associated with a geographic territory or did they coalesce around a particular charismatic individual? What was the relationship between the Bizango and other institutions of the traditional (e.g., houngan and hounfour) or metropolitan (e.g., Tonton Macoute, *chef de section*, Duvalier regime) society?

What about the function of the societies? Were they magico-religious, ritualistic, and/or sociopolitical in character? What was their range of activities, and how did members and nonmembers interpret the significance and meaning of those activities? Were the societies involved in education, social services, religious initiation, economic affairs, community affairs, or the production and distribution of magical potions? Did they have an effective role in the maintenance of social control and, if so, how did they regulate conduct? If they had a judicial function, with what regularity was that function invoked, and what range of sanctions empowered it? What decision-making process, if any, led to the imposition of sanctions—the consensus of the majority or the direct authority of the executive? Given the fact that secret societies, by definition, act as a subset of the greater society and must be able to respond to the dynamic transformations of that society, was there evidence in Haiti that might suggest diachronic changes in the function and structure of its secret societies? Finally—and of critical importance to this study—was there a possible connection between the Bizango societies and the zombie phenomenon?

These were the issues that I addressed over the two-year period that encompassed the Zombie Project. My interaction with the clandestine societies grew from the first tentative contacts established during my search for the zombie powder to sustained and close working relationships with a number of bokor. These in turn led, in the spring of 1984, to an intense, four-month involvement that culminated in my being invited to become initiated into the societies at the lowest grade. The information presented here was gathered through extensive interviews with the members and the presidents of five Bizango

societies in the environs of the northern center of Saint Marc in
the Artibonite Valley. Additional information was provided by
three Bizango presidents in the town of L'Archaie, one in the
village of Montrouis, and one in the city of Gonaïves. I documented nocturnal ceremonies in all these places, and in Saint
Marc I attended the cyclical rituals of two prominent societies on
a regular basis. For obvious ethical reasons, and in order to
respect and protect the generosity of my informants, much of
what I learned about the inner workings of the Bizango must
remain confidential. My primary purpose here is not to present a
complete study of the Haitian secret societies. It is, rather, to
present an outline of the structure and functions of these groups
only insofar as regards their sociopolitical status and their role in
zombification.

Saint Marc was selected as the principal site for several reasons which will become clear in the following discussion. First,
the region of Saint Marc was one of the traditional centers of
maronage during the colonial era (Fouchard 1981), and the community to this day has a reputation within Haiti as a center of
Bizango secret society activity. Second, the community falls
within the influence of one of my most important informants, a
prominent houngan who at one time was the *chef* of the Tonton
Macoute for the entire Artibonite Valley, a region comprising
fully one-fifth of the country. His active cooperation gave me an
entrance to the societies and assured that I could safely and
effectively gather data among their leadership and members.
Third, during the initial phase of the zombie investigation I had
informally established numerous friendly contacts with members
of the various societies within the region, and this in turn assured
me access to a wide range of groups. Fourth, a personal contact
with the former prefect offered me both protection and an opportunity to assess confidentially the interrelationship between
the traditional societies and a representative of the national government. Finally, because my purpose was not only to document
the structure and function of these societies but also to assess
their possible role in the creation of spirit and/or physical zombies, it was important to work in a region with a strong local
tradition of zombification. Within the immediate territory of
Saint Marc there was recent evidence of a possibly valid instance
of zombification (Douyon 1980); the region was known for the
activities and purported magical prowess of its sorcerers, and

several resident bokor known to me had demonstrated familiarity with the preparation and application of the zombie powder.

Throughout my fieldwork among the Bizango I continued my ethnobiological work with the various folk preparations, for it provided an opportunity to listen to villagers in informal settings describe their experiences with and perceptions of the Bizango. In particular, if the Bizango had a role in the creation of zombies, and if zombification was indeed a form of social sanction, I needed to understand how villagers experienced and coped with conflict situations. These informal interactions allowed me to assess the full range of perceived sanctions. What, I asked, does a child fear if he or she misbehaves, lies, cheats, steals? What happens to a spouse who cheats in socially unacceptable ways; who persistently beats his or her mate; who robs, kills, or neglects familial or religious obligations? These types of questions some- times were and sometimes were not asked or answered directly. They did, however, provide a framework for the formulation of questions that could appropriately be asked of informants, sug- gested the correct wording of those questions, and identified informants with whom I subsequently carried out formal inter- views (Spradley 1970).

The results of my research suggest that the secret societies are a dominant social force that affects many facets of the life and culture of the peasant. But before I enumerate those influences and describe in some detail the organization of the societies, it is important first to examine the overall concept of "secret soci- eties" for beyond a doubt, by any current anthropological defini- tion, the corporate groups currently active in rural Haiti are indeed secret societies.

ON SECRET SOCIETIES

In its broadest definition, a "secret society" is simply a voluntary or, in rare instances, involuntary association whose members possess by virtue of their membership some knowledge of which nonmembers are ignorant (Wedgewood 1930). A more compre- hensive definition was offered by Peter Morton-Williams, who suggested that secret societies have three diacritical features: (1) there must exist a secret, the knowledge of which allows members to claim mystical and hence secular power and privileges in regard to nonmembers; (2) the membership must be selective, with admission being determined by some sort of achievement on the part of the aspiring candidate; and (3) the society has the right to impose sanctions on those who reveal its secrets and procedures to others (Morton-Williams 1960, 362). The hallmark of a secret society, then, is the premium placed on secrecy and the formal ritual designed to protect that secret knowledge.

The nature of this knowledge varies from group to group. In certain instances, it might consist of esoteric spells, potions, or magico-religious formulations; in others, it might be an awareness of the existence and location of sacred objects, the identity of the membership, or the very existence of the society itself (Wedgewood 1930). Significantly, the nature of the information withheld from nonmembers is less important than the fact that it is concealed. Georg Simmel wrote that secrecy lies at the foundations of these societies, for it is "the secret [that] determines the reciprocal relations among those who share it in common" (Wolff 1950, 345). As a result, a secret society almost invariably possesses some symbol—a name, a password, or a ritual—by which its existence as a corporate body is emphasized and by which its members are marked off as a group from all other peoples. Typically, this separation between members and nonmembers is explicitly established through a passage rite marked by initiation, ritualistic instruction, ordeal, oath, and the discovery of the myth, legend, or beliefs that support the secrecy (Webster 1968).

In thinking about these groups, however, contemporary anthropologists have grown understandably wary of the emphasis that has been placed on the element of secrecy because it has resulted in a conceptualization of these groups that is general to the point of inutility. Simmel, for example, defined a secret society simply as a group whose existence is concealed from the public. However, because the secret society must recruit its members from the society at large, it is unreasonable to believe that its existence will never be known. Simmel offered an alternative definition, which suggested that a secret society is a group whose existence may be open but whose goals, rituals, and structures are concealed from the public. This definition is also limited, for there are numerous secret societies that remain "secret" despite the fact that their goals and rituals and structures are known to the public (Daraul 1961). L. F. Mak has noted that although the static aspect of any secret society might be known to the external authorities, it is highly unlikely that the dynamic aspect of the society will be known. He offers a definition of the secret society as "a group whose existence may be open, but whose activities and the identities of its leaders and members remain unknown to the public" (Mak 1981, 8). Nonetheless, all three of these definitions are formulated from the perspective of the external society and ignore the organizational rationale of the groups themselves. An alternative and preferable definition is "a group which has a set of well-defined norms, secret rituals and an oath that are intended subjectively to bind the members to secrecy regarding the group affairs" (Mak 1981, 8).

This last formulation is more useful because it places analytical emphasis not on the concept of secrecy, but on the dynamic processes that maintain the integrity of the secret. To protect a secret permanently, any group of individuals must be highly organized and their behavior normatively patterned. And because the purpose of secrecy is protection, it follows that the first relationship typical of a secret society is a reciprocal confidence among its members. If the secret is, in its essence, a separating or distancing mechanism between the external population and the subordinate group, then within the secret society it is an incentive for cohesion and solidarity.

It is toward the maintenance of that trust and solidarity that many of the activities and institutions of a secret society are consciously or unconsciously directed. The line between members and nonmembers, between the authorized and the unauthorized, must be sharply drawn. Admission into the societies is controlled, and initiation is a comprehensive educational process that results in the complete socialization of the initiate. The initiation rituals include tests of endurance, patience, and fortitude, deliberately inflicted suffering, and disciplines of silence, followed by the gradual revelations of the mysteries of the group (MacKenzie 1967). The ritual culminates with a binding oath tempered by a grave promise of punishment for betrayal. The progressive degrees of initiation into the hierarchical societies mark an increasingly formal separation from the society at large, and the process in general promotes a concomitant intensification of the secret society's internal cohesion.

The solidarity of the group is actively reinforced by the em-

phasis placed on the cyclical rituals. These rituals fortify the
bonds among the members and demonstrate the loyalty and
obedience of the members to the authority of the leadership and
to the purposes of the society as a whole. Indeed, no other trait is
so typical of a secret society as the high "valuation of usages,
formulae and rites, and their peculiar preponderance over the
purposive contents of the group" (Wolff 1950, 358). The ritual
itself is rigorously observed and anxiously guarded as a secret in
its own right. The symbolism of the ritual and the excitement
that it generates provoke "a whole range of vaguely delimited
feelings beyond all particular, rational interests," and in doing so
the "secret society synthesizes those interests into a total claim
upon the individual. By means of the ritual form, the particular
purpose of the secret society is enlarged to the point of being a
closed unit, a whole, both sociological and subjective" (Wolff
1950, 360). The regular performance of the corporate activities,
then, is directed not only toward carrying out the ostensible
function of the society but also toward reaffirming its existence as
an organic whole.

The cohesion of a secret society is further enhanced by the
fact that its interests are defined in terms of the community,
rather than those of a family or residential group. The societies
bring together men and women who would otherwise be opposed
or indifferent to each other, and by regulating their mutual behavior the society serves as a unifying force. Within the secret
societies there is often a fraternal equality among the members,
in sharp contrast to their differences in everyday life. This leveling process is reinforced by the deindividualization that results
from the subordination of a member to the group as a whole.
Typical secret society rituals involve self-imposed anonymity
through the use of masks or ceremonial garb, or simply through
the imposition of ritualistic titles in place of individual names.
But this leveling tendency does not contradict the essentially
despotic character of the secret society. As Simmel notes, in all
kinds of other groups despotism is correlated with the leveling of
the ruled. Indeed, the secret societies are almost invariably rig-
idly hierarchical, with a complex series of ranks and degrees,
often with high-sounding and archaic titles, through which the
member progresses from novice to senior official. Through all
these processes—the consciously constructed ritual formality,
the deindividualization and identification of the member with the

collective, and the hierarchical organization itself—the secret society makes itself into a sort of counterimage of the official world to which it contrasts itself.

Interactions with the external world, however, are both inevitable and in many ways desirable, for if one of the motives in joining the societies is independent power and prestige, then one of the prerogatives of membership is the chance to demonstrate the secrecy publicly. Secret societies symbolically expose themselves to the public with some regularity—by parading and dancing through villages in masks, for example, or by ambushing the uninitiated and terrifying them. The performance of such rituals, of course, flaunts in the public sphere the independence and power of the secret societies; it is by means of these periodic surfacings that a secret society exists and to some extent maintains its authority (Weckman 1970).

These periodic demonstrations of authority are critical, though, for typically secret societies do not exist or come into being in a vacuum, but on the contrary emerge strictly as a counterpoint to the institutions of the external society. Camilla Wedgewood (1930) viewed the development of secret societies as a dynamic process, a "pathological growth." For a community to be healthy, the government, whatever its form, must have the backing of public opinion. When that support ceases but the government remains too strong to be openly opposed, then secret societies may arise and become important to the functioning of the community. Simmel also notes the interrelationship between the genesis of secret societies and the nature and condition of the central authority; he attributes to the secret society the same explicitly political function that Michel Laguerre (1980b, 1984) associates with the Bizango societies in Haiti. "As a general proposition," Simmel writes, "the secret societies emerge everywhere as a correlate of despotism and of police control. It acts as a protection, alike of defence and of offence against the violent pressure of central powers" (Wolff 1950, 472).

To sum up, the diacritical characteristics of a secret society include: (1) the existence of a secret body of knowledge that separates members from nonmembers (passwords, symbolic gestures, esoteric cult knowledge); (2) cyclical rituals that reinforce the solidarity of the collective, often by means of a process of deindividualization which corresponds to the subordination of the member to the rigid hierarchy of the group; (3) the existence

of recognized sanctions known to members and invoked to punish those who transgress the codes of the societies; (4) periodic
public displays, which demonstrate the authority and independence of the group; (5) a dialectical relationship with the institutions of the society at large that allows the secret society to
respond and adapt to diachronic changes in that society.

STRUCTURE OF THE HAITIAN SECRET SOCIETIES

If we accept the above criteria in defining secret societies, there
can be no doubt that such societies exist today throughout Haiti.
Names vary from region to region and include Vlinbinding,
Zobop, Makandal, Mandingue, Cannibal, and a host of other
appellations. Individual societies bear specific titles assigned
them by their founding presidents. Two generic terms for the
societies, known and often employed interchangeably by all Haitians, are Bizango and Sans Poel. A more precise use of these
terms, and one recognized by the society members themselves,
defines Bizango as the religious rite practiced by the society
members, who in turn are referred to as Sans Poel, or literally
"those without skin." The word Bizango may be traced etymo-
logically to the name of one of the groups of slaves brought to
Haiti during the colonial era from the Bissago Islands, an archipelago located off the coast of Kakonda between Sierra Leone
and Cape Verde (Laguerre 1980b).

Membership in the Bizango is voluntary but exclusive. Those
who want to join must be invited to do so by a member, and they
must be willing to undergo an initiation process consisting of the
recruitment, the learning of the esoteric knowledge, and the
rigorous induction ceremony itself. Initiation is limited to adults
and, although there are no explicit economic or class restrictions
on membership, the composition of any one society will generally
reflect the socioeconomic status of its particular locality. As in the
case of virtually all social institutions in Haiti, the Bizango is
open to individuals of both sexes. When I questioned one prominent Bizango leader about the role of women in the societies he
replied, "Women have a function everywhere. What kind of society would not have women?" Another member, similarly que-
ried, responded: "It is women who constitute societies. It's not a
matter of more men or women. But it is a fact that without

women, you cannot have societies." Indeed, an examination of the hierarchy of the Bizango reveals that women play an inordinately powerful role in the societies.

The Bizango societies are strictly hierarchical and consist of at least the following ranks:

empereur	emperor
président définitif	definitive president
président honorific	honorary president
vice président	vice president
président fondateur	founding president = emperor
présidente	president
première la reine	first queen
deuxième la reine	second queen
troisième la reine	third queen
reine dirigeur	directing queen
reine voltige (loup garou)	flying queen (werewolf)
reine drapeau	flag queen
mère la société	mother of the society
général	general
prince	prince
premier ministre	prime minister
conseiller	advisor
avocat	lawyer
secrétaire	secretary
trésorier	treasurer
brigadier générale	brigadier general
superviseur	supervisor
intendant	intendant
surintendant	superintendent
préfet de discipline	prefect of discipline
majeur	major
moniteur	monitor
exécutif	executor
bourreau	executioner
chasseur	hunter
chef détente	guard
sentinel	sentinel-scout
soldat	soldier

This elaborate hierarchy appears to have both a symbolic and an executive function. At one level the preponderance of symbolic titles enhances the personal prestige of a member while simultaneously absorbing him or her as but another subservient and anonymous element of the overall society. This encourages a process of deindividualization which undermines differences in the economic backgrounds of the members and provides a key to the solidarity and cohesion of the group. Yet at another level the hierarchical structure reflects real differences in authority and power. Promotions and demotions within the societies are common, and certain of the ranks have clearly delineated responsibilities. It is the task of the *bourreau*, or executioner, for example, to enforce the collective decisions of the society. The *chasseur*, or hunter, is dispatched to bring culprits before the society for judgment and punishment. The *sentinel* is the scout, positioned at the entrance gate to any Bizango temple, who prevents unwelcome individuals from entering a secret society gathering. The *superviseur* or supervisor is a courier specifically charged with delivering messages from one society to another. At the top of the societal hierarchy is a special group of leaders known as the *Groupe d'État Majeur*. The titular members of this ruling group may vary from society to society, but they generally include four or five individuals including the emperor, the first and sometimes second and third queens, the guard, the president, and occasionally the executioner. Although it is the Groupe d'État Majeur that collectively initiates the executive functions of the society, the undisputed leader of the secret society is the emperor or founding president—a man, or in certain instances a woman (empress), invariably endowed with strong personal magnetism.

To a great extent, the prestige of any society depends on the personal power and authority of its leader. The potential extent of an emperor's authority was indicated by one prominent individual who controls a region in the environs of Saint Marc:

I am here at Fresineau. Everyone knows that Leophin is the master of the area. If another society is formed, they must tell me. I establish my limits. For me, it's from Gros Morne up to Montrouis. That's my quarter. Another society can't leave Archaie to catch someone in my territory unless he comes to me first. He may say, "Tomorrow I have to come to get so and so because he did this and that." Then I'll explain to him, "We'll have a reunion to see if we can give you this fellow." If it's impossible, I'll say so and tell him that this fellow is under my protection and that's it. I can't give him away. I command here so no other society can come.

Although the societies do control specific territories, it is possible, as this passage intimates, for a particularly charismatic individual to start his or her own band. As a result, among the ten or more principal societies in Saint Marc, there is a wide range in size and influence. In one instance an individual who had first been demoted and then expelled from a prominent society for disobedience responded by founding his own band in the environs of his temple.

Not surprisingly, considerable competition exists between the different societies, and there is an extremely elaborate ritual that occurs should two societies meet during their nocturnal forays. At the same time, there is no doubt that the societies are interconnected as a single fraternity. Within the Saint Marc region, for example, the societies gather together periodically, and virtually all the Bizango leaders I contacted named one particular emperor as the undisputed patriarch of the region. In fact, many of the other emperors had first been initiated in this individual's society, the Quartier Générale, and one of them, from respect, named his own society Le Fils de Quartier Générale. Other evidence of the existence of complex ties between the societies is the Bizango passport that is issued to members or nonmembers to give them freedom of movement after dark. In addition, although one may join only one society, the secret passwords and ritual gestures learned at initiation are honored by all societies, and members frequently visit the gatherings of rival societies.

BIZANGO RITUAL: INITIATION

Initiation into the Bizango society involves a series of steps that progressively integrate the prospective member into the group. First, the individual's candidacy must be recommended to the founding president by at least one and often several active members of the society. If judged acceptable, the candidate meets privately with the president and learns formally of the obligations and responsibilities incumbent upon any society member: periodic financial contributions, absolute obedience to the hierarchy, and a commitment to maintain the secrecy upon which the entire society depends. Invitations to the biweekly meetings of the societies may follow, and gradually, over the course of several weeks, the candidate learns the identity of the members, their positions in the hierarchy, the function of each position, and the existence and territorial limits of neighboring societies. At any point during this initial period the discretion and loyalty of the aspiring candidate may be tested. Gradually the candidate becomes privy to the inner secrets of the group, learning not only the magical beliefs that form the philosophical foundation of the society, but also the specific forms of ritual greeting, salutations, and passwords that distinguish member from nonmember and allow the individual to perform his or her societal function.

The lessons of the Bizango are imparted to the initiate in secret within the confines of the bagi, the inner sanctum of the temple, by the founding president, who may or may not become possessed by the mystical force of the society (*pouin*). The prospective member must become familiar with the ritualistic symbols of the society, learning the character of the spirits specifically associated with the Bizango—Erzulie Dantor (the Black Virgin), Ti Jean, Marinette, Baron La Croix, Baron Samedi, etc.—and the significance of the sacred coffin, the *madoule*, the principal icon of the Bizango. Then the initiate must learn the secret passwords and greetings, ritual handshakes, and euphemistic verbal repartee. The cryptic communication between two members of the Bizango may be exceedingly complex; the handshake alone has its own secret language. Each finger, for example, corresponds to a ranking within the hierarchy, and by subtly manipulating the placement of the index finger the society member is able to communicate his or her precise position in that hierarchy.

Central to the Bizango signs and signals of recognition is a notion of opposites. In a ritualistic exchange between two members, for example, heaven becomes the earth, the mouth becomes the anus, front is back, up is down, the eyes are ears, the knee is the elbow, the hand is the foot and the foot the hand. The sky becomes the ground, night is day, the stars rocks and the rocks stars. These inversions are incorporated into phrases of greeting and also into more elaborate tests that consist of set questions and answers. These are proverbial in nature and involve various elements of Bizango ritual; they are surprisingly similar in structure to those used in West Africa among the Poro

Typical altar in the bagi of a Bizango secret society temple

(Dorjahn 1982; Little 1948). The result is a sophisticated means of communication utterly unintelligible to the uninitiate. The following exchanges are typical, with the questions being asked by a society member who is testing the knowledge of the unknown individual:

Q. Who are you?   A. Bête Sereine (animals of the night).
Q. Where are you coming from? A. I come from the hill.
Q. Where are you going?   A. Into the toes.
Q. How many stars are you?   A. Three.
Q. What toe are you?   A. I am the fifth.

In this case, the answers identify the respondent as a member of the Bizango, a soldier of the lowest rank who in his travels is accompanied by three others.

Other ritualized exchanges merely test whether or not an individual is a society member. If, for example, a visitor approaches the ceremonial gathering of a different society, he or she is stopped at the gate by the sentinel, who demands that the intruder take three steps forward and three back. The visitor, if a member of the Bizango, knows to comply by reversing the order and stepping first back three steps and then forward. Next, the sentinel or *chef détente* tests the individual's knowledge of the ritual salutations and handshakes and a specific password. Then an exchange such as the following might occur:

Q. Where do you drink water?   A. In the dew.
Q. If you can't find dew?   A. In the banana tree.
Q. If not there?   A. In the mule's hoof.
Q. If not there?   A. I'll find it in the big pipe (pipe of Baron).

Q. They say the society serves 3 leaves. A. Yes.
Q. What are they?   A. Consigne, zacassi, flamboyant.

Q. Who is your mother?   A. La Veuve (the sacred coffin).

Q. Who is your father?   A. I have no father. I am an animal.

Q. But your father.   A. I don't know. My mother made me

but she told me its
a shooting star and
rumbling thunder
that was my father.

In addition to these stylized forms of address, the initiate must become familiar with the Bizango ritual itself, learning the songs and dances, the ritual procedures, the symbols of the society, and the spiritual beliefs that validate those symbols. Most important, the initiate must learn the functions of the society and the political and spiritual foundations that underlie those functions. When the president finally decides to accept the individual as a permanent member of the society, an induction ceremony is held. The initiate drinks two potions, one sweet, the other bitter, and together these embody one of the fundamental metaphors of the Bizango. Their motto is "sweet as honey, bitter as bile"—sweet because the society is "only good to those who serve it," bitter because, in the words of one president, "when you are asked to serve on the bitter side of the society, you won't know your own mother." Following the ingestion of these two potions (which have no psychoactive properties), the candidate is taken before the entire society to offer his or her gratitude and to promise, on pain of death, not to reveal any of the societal secrets. There follows the ingestion of a third drink and the "hard initiation," a physically grueling affair that tests the initiate's resistance, an ordeal that leaves "the clothes on your back in shreds."

BIZANGO RITUAL: THE NOCTURNAL GATHERINGS

The Séance Ordinaire

Each Bizango society meets weekly or biweekly, in an evening ceremony known as a *séance* or *entrainment*. Because these clandestine gatherings have played a large part in establishing and maintaining the nefarious public image of the Bizango, it is worthwhile to describe them in some detail. The following account was originally lifted from my field notebooks:

> The peristyle was similar to others we had visited, with a single centerpost and three sides of bamboo and thatch running up upon a solid wall of wattle and daub. A tin roof on top of flimsy rafters seemingly supported by the web of

strings displayed what must have been a hundred faces of President Jean-Claude Duvalier and ten times as many small Haitian flags. Three doors in the wall led to the inner sanctum of the temple, and there were two exits—the doorway we had entered through, and an open passage at the other end. The benches were full, but the people continued to arrive—the men stolid and unusually grave, the women determined and everyone wearing fresh clothes: cotton beaten over river rocks, hung out to dry on tree limbs, pressed with ember irons and liberally scented with talcum powder. As at other Vodoun gatherings I had attended, there were more women than men. Many of them had arrived with pots of food that they hastily carried to charcoal cooking fires flickering beyond the far end of the enclosure.

But there were other symbols before us I had never seen: the black skirting around the pedestal of the poteau mitan; and the colour red in the cloth that entwined the centerpost, on the wooden doors that led into the bagi, and in the flags whose significance I finally understood. Red and black—the colours of the Revolution, the white band in the French tricolor ripped away and the blue in the time of François Duvalier becoming black, the colour of the night, with red the symbol of transition, life blood, and rebellion. On the wall hung paintings of the djab—the devil—gargoyle-like with protruding red tongues pierced by red daggers and lightning bolts, and with inscriptions beneath, again in red paint dripping across the whitewash, "The Danger of the Mouth." Figures of other strange spirits—Erzulie Dantor, the Black Virgin, and Baron Samedi, the Guardian of the Cemetery. Arched across one of the entrances to the bagi, again in red but this time etched carefully in Gothic script, was yet another inscription that read "Order and Respect for the Night" (the motto of the Bizango). Finally at the foot of the poteau mitan lay a human skull wearing a wig of melted wax and crowned with a single burning candle.

The drums began, and as we passed back into the tonnelle small groups of dancers swirled before them, challenging each other to greater and greater bursts of effort. The appearance of Jean Baptiste (the president) had a sobering effect, and as he began to sing the dancers drew into a fluid line that undulated around the poteau mitan. Knees

bending slightly and bodies inclined backwards, they answered him with a chorus that praised Legba, the spirit of
the crossroads. Salutations to other familiar loa followed—
Carrefour, Grans Bwa, Aizan, and Sobo. It struck me that
this gathering of the Bizango was like the beginning of any
Vodoun service. Women continued to mingle about, and the
old men on the cane-bottomed chairs passed bottles of
clairin peppered with roots and herbs. An hour went by, and
although the atmosphere became charged with activity no
spirit arrived. Instead, just before eleven o'clock, a cry went
out from the President and was answered by all present.

"Those who belong!"

"Come in!"

"Those who don't belong!"

"Go away!"

"The Sans Poel is taking to the streets! Those who belong come in, those who don't go away! Bête Sereine! Animals of the Night! Change skins!" A man with ropes across
each shoulder like bandoliers came hurriedly across the
tonnelle carrying a sisal whip and took up a position just
outside the exit. The door slammed shut, and the dancers
rushed into the bagi.

"Seven cannon blows!"

From outside came the deep penetrating moan of a conch
trumpet, followed by seven cracks of the sisal whip, the fwet
kash. Moments later the dancers reemerged from the bagi
and, encouraged by steel whistles, took up marshall positions around the poteau mitan. On one side stood the men,
dressed uniformly in red and black, and across from them
the women, clad in long red robes.

With the President standing to one side and all the members in place, a woman in a high plaintive voice sang out a
solemn greeting asking God to salute in turn each officer of
the society. As they were called, one by one men and women
stepped out of rank, stood before the group, and then,
following the slow almost mournful rhythm of the prayer,
moved to form a new line still facing the poteau mitan.
Their titles were mostly unfamiliar: Secrétaire, Trésorier,
Brigadier, Exécutif, Superintendant, Première Reine, Deuxième Reine, Troisième Reine. Suddenly a whistle broke the
tension, eliciting shrill ritual laughter from the ranks. Unac-

companied by the drums, and with the members formally bowing and curtsying in time, the society began to sing:

> I serve good, I serve bad,
> We serve good, we serve bad,
> Wayo-oh!
> When I am troubled, I will call
> the spirit against them.

Then came a song of warning, set off from the last by whistles and the cracking of the whip:

> What we see here,
> I won't talk,
> If we talk,
> We'll swallow our tongue.

The singing continued until three people reemerged unexpectedly from the second door of the temple. One was the Secrétaire, only now he carried a machete and a candle and wore a black hat covered by a sequined havelock. Beside him came a woman, perhaps one of the Queens cloaked in green and red, and following these two a woman in red with a small black coffin balanced on her head. The rest of the society fell in behind her, and singing a haunting hymn of adoration the small procession circled the poteau mitan, eventually coming to rest with the woman laying the coffin gently on a square of red cloth. An order went out commanding the members to form a line, and then the secretary, the President, and one of the women walked ceremoniously to the end of the tonnelle, and pivoting in a disciplined military fashion returned as one rank to the coffin.

President Jean Baptiste, flanked by his two aides and speaking formally in French, officially brought the assembly to order.

"Before God the Father, God the Son and God the Holy Ghost, I declare this Séance open. Secretary, Make your statement!"

Holding his machete in one hand and a worn notebook in the other, the secretary exclaimed, "Gonaïves, 24 March 1984, Séance Ordinaire. By all the power of the Great God Jehovah and the Gods of the Earth, and by the power of the Diabolic, of Maître Sarazin, and by the authority of all the imaginary lines, we declare that the flags are open! And now we have the privilege of passing the mallet to the President for the announcement of the opening of this celebration. Light the candles!"

One by one each member solemnly stepped out of line and in graceful gestures of obeisance paid homage to the coffin, leaving a small offering of money and taking a candle which was passed before the flame burning at the base of the poteau mitan. A line of soft glowing light spread slowly down one side of the tonnelle, and the society members, their heads bowed and their hands clasping the candles to chests, began to sing once more. Three songs, each an eloquent call for solidarity. The first posed a potent question:

> President they say you're solid,
> And in this lakou there is magic.
> When they take the power to go and use it outside,
> When they take the power who will we call?
> When we will be drowning, what branch will
>   we hold onto?
> The day we will be drowning, who will we call?
> What branch will we hold onto?

Then as if to answer this lament, the second song continued:

> Nothing, nothing can affect us,
> Before our President,
> Nothing can hurt us,
> If we are hungry, we are hungry among ourselves,
> If we are naked, we are naked among ourselves.
> Before our President nothing can harm us.

The final song was raised in defiant, raucous voices with the feet of all members stamping the dry earth, raising small clouds of dust:

> I refuse to die for these people,
> This money is for the djab,
> Rather than die for these people,
>   I'd rather the djab eat me,
> This money is for the djab,
> I will not die for these people!

By now the tension in the rank had become palpable, and the President had to slap a machete against the concrete base of the poteau mitan to restore order. At his command a man later identified as the treasurer advanced with one other to count the money, and with an official air they announced, "sixteen medalles—sixteen guordes," a sum of less than five dollars U.S. The President stepped forward reciting a Catholic litany blessing the offering and seeking the protection of God for the actions of the Society. As his final words expired, the drums exploded, breaking open the ranks at long last. Other songs rose in strange rhythms, with one of the four drums played on its side, giving the staccato sound of wood striking hollow wood. The drums ceased as suddenly as they began, and once again attention focused on the President, now standing alone by the poteau mitan, his hands cradling a weeping and terrified baby. His own voice, high and soft with reverence, was soon joined by all the others:

> They throw a trap to catch the fish,
> What a tragedy!
> It is the little one who is caught in the trap.

The baby's mother stood by the President's side, and as the others sang tears came into her eyes and ran in rivulets down her cheeks. With gentle gestures Jean Baptiste led her and the baby around the poteau mitan, and then he lifted the child tenderly above his head to salute the four corners, the four faces of the world. As he turned slowly, the society members beseeched him in song:

> Save this little one,
> Oh! President of the Sans Poel!
> Save the life of the child we are asking,
> Oh! President of the Sans Poel!
> Save the life of this child!
> Yawe! Yawe!

The unbroken circle of the Sans Poel closed around the body of the President, and one by one they lifted the child from his arms and bathed it with a warm potion of herbs. Then, the treatment completed, the drums resounded once

more and the members of the Bizango danced long into the
night (Davis 1985, 226–32).

This particular ceremony, which occurred on the night of 24
March 1984 in Gonaïves, featured many of the consistent
themes that I observed at every séance ordinaire. The initial
phase of the ritual bears the patina of any Vodoun service for the
loa. Then, at a specific moment, the president or occasionally the
secretary demands that the evening's work begin. The tone of the
gathering shifts. The songs, dances, and drumbeats change to
those of the Bizango, and the easy, relaxed mood sharpens as the
conch shell trumpets and the sisal whip issue an ominous warning to those outside the society enclosure not to interfere. To
keep out intruders, the sentinel positions himself outside the
sealed entrance to the temple. Those inside shed their own
clothes to don the ritual red and black garb of the society, and
they emerge from the inner sanctum of the temple transformed.
The Creole expression describing this act is *Wété Po, Meté Po*—to
remove the skin to put on a new skin—and the metaphor is apt.
In leaving their own clothes, the members in effect shed their
personas, and they emerge as anonymous members of the society
who are identified not by name but by their rank and position in
the hierarchy. Indeed, in the first part of the ritual the president
formally introduces each member by rank, and the member in
turn salutes the society.

A central element in the Bizango séance is the "adoration" of
the sacred coffin, the madoule. At some point in every gathering
the coffin, which is normally kept under lock and key in its own
sanctuary, is paraded before the society. In turn each member is
expected to pay his or her respects, a complex and stylized series
of gestures and genuflections that are among the secret knowledge imparted during initiation. As each member completes his
or her "work" with the madoule, he or she is expected to leave a
small financial offering. Following the adoration, a strict ac-
counting of the money is duly recorded by the treasurer. At this
time the president often makes a short speech, which may be of a
general philosophical nature or alternatively address some pressing issue before the society. It is at this time that any visiting
dignitaries—Bizango presidents, houngan, etc.—are introduced
to the members. Following the president's speech, any particular
business of the society is dealt with. In the séance described

above, for example, a child of a society member had inadvertently been the recipient of a magical spell—a trap—and it was only the Bizango president who could treat her. Once all the issues on the agenda have been addressed, the séance ordinaire generally takes on an intense but festive air, with the members dancing long into the night.

It is important to note that, despite all the lurid tales in the popular and ethnographic literature, the nocturnal gatherings of the Bizango are in fact solemn, even pious affairs that reveal, among other things, a strict hierarchical organization modeled at least superficially on French military and civil government.

The Séance Extraordinaire and the Annual Feasts

In addition to the regularly occurring entrainment, or séance ordinaire, there are at least two other occasions when the Bizango societies come together. First there is the annual *fête*, a yearly feast that I was not able to observe but that is said to occur in December or January. It is a highly secret affair, held at great expense and featuring many hundreds of guests from societies throughout the country. It is during these annual gatherings that the societies are said to perform their "sacrifices," a euphemistic term of uncertain meaning, which probably entail a magical ceremony believed to rejuvenate and invigorate the bands for the coming year.

A more regular occurrence, and one that I was able to attend, is the periodic *séance extraordinaire*, a major feast for which any number of societies come together to inaugurate a new society or to celebrate the anniversary of the founding of an established group. These are impressive gatherings attended by as many as four hundred Bizango members. The following notes were made after I attended the inaugural feast of an empress, and they describe the return of the secret procession from the countryside and its visit to the graveyard to salute Baron.

The tables around us began to buzz with the rumour of the returning procession, and within moments the entire courtyard was filled with anticipation. The president led us quickly into the peristyle which, already crowded when we had arrived, was by now bulging with members of the Bizango. In the distance, seen through gaps in the bamboo wall, the procession like an articulated serpent crawled over the hills—proceeding, halting, then moving again, slowly emerging out of the nether darkness of the night. Lanterns on either flank floodlit great swirls of chalky dust. You could hear the distant voices, the whistles, and the short barking commands driving the members back into line. The crack of the sisal whips kept time with the ponderous cadence of the march as the leaders paused to allow the coffin to sway like a pendulum hanging from the shoulders of the escort. To this fusion of red and black, the droning voices lent a certain uniformity, binding everyone present to the rhythms of the music:

> We come from the cemetery,
> We went to get our mother,
> Hello mother the Virgin
> We are your children
> We come to ask your help
> You should give us courage

A second song went as follows:

> The band is out, the society is out,
> Watch out mother who made me.
> The band's out, the society is out
> Mothers of Children
> Tie up your stomachs.

As the procession poured into the temple, clusters of lanterns at the entryway outlined the stern faces of the magnificently robed acolytes. First inside was the sentinel, who lept around the poteau mitan in a mock display of suspicious concern. Behind him walked a lone man carrying a rope, followed closely by the sacred coffin and its circle of retainers. As the bulk of the society squeezed into the room, the guests pulled back into an adjoining chamber until the enclosure swelled with red and black robes. Slowly the procession circled the poteau mitan, but there were so many that the members didn't walk so much as lean into each other, flesh to flesh, sending a single wave surging around the post. A tall, dazzling woman wearing a satin and spangled Edwardian dress and a buccaneer's hat complete with ostrich plumes took the center of the room. With slow sweeping gestures she orchestrated the entire movement while her face, half hidden beneath her hat, radiated perfect serenity, a look both world-weary and utterly calm.

The power of the moment was dreamlike. The sacred coffin rested on the red and black flag, caressed by flowers. The Sans Poel blew out the burning candles they had clasped to their chests and lay them in one of two velvet hats placed at the foot of the coffin. The majestic woman in the glittering robe moved at ease through the huddled members of her procession, nodding to each one. Whistles and conch shells echoed as a great shout arose.

"Twenty-one shots of the cannon in honour of the Executive President!" As the whip outside began to crack, the woman, her head and great hat tilting slightly like the axis of a globe, turned slowly back towards the base of the poteau mitan. She was the Empress, I now realized, and we were all gathered to celebrate the founding of her society. A man acting as a herald stepped forthrightly to her side.

"Silence! In a moment we . . ." he began, but the raucous excitement kept him from being heard. "Silence! People you are not in your houses! Be quiet!" The Empress raised an arm and the room fell silent.

"In a moment," the man continued, "we shall have the honour of presenting you with the attending Presidents." Then one by one as their names were called five Bizango Emperors stepped forward. The Empress, lifting her face to the light to reveal the finest of features—thin bones and skin drawn beautifully across high cheekbones—formally opened the ceremony (Davis 1985, 244–46).

The ceremony itself was structured precisely like the ordinary séance. The madoule was paraded and saluted; offerings were made; speeches followed, with each of the Bizango presidents being invited to address the assembly; and finally the gathering took on the festive air of the celebration, with the people dancing until dawn. What was particularly impressive and significant about the *séance extraordinaire* was its sheer scale, the evidence it offered of the networking of the different societies, and the content of the speeches themselves (see below), which explicitly acknowledged the political ideology of the Bizango and traced its roots directly to the colonial era and the maroon communities.

One of the startling observations that I made during the course of my research among the Bizango societies was the extent to which the members recognized and acknowledged their political role. The Bizango leadership explicitly traced the origins of the societies to the Haitian revolution and the prerevolutionary leaders of the maroon bands, in exactly the way that Michel Laguerre had proposed. There can be little doubt that the philosophy of the contemporary societies presents the Bizango as the guardians of peasant lifeways. This philosophy is exemplified in the following speech made by a Bizango leader and recorded at a *séance extraordinaire*, a gathering of five different societies on the night of 31 March 1984:

> My dear friends. Often on a day such as this you have seen me stand before you, and for me it is a joyous occasion for it allows a chance to welcome you and to share through my words a number of ideas and themes that mean so much to us all. Sadly, tonight my thoughts have escaped, my imagination has escaped, and this prevents me from yielding to my strongest desires. Still, I wish to thank all the guests for responding to the invitation of this morning.
>
> Brothers and sisters! It is today that we come together in a brotherly communion of thoughts and feelings. Feelings that are crystallized into the force of our brotherhood, the force that gives meaning to our feast of this night.
>
> Yes, we are talking about our Bizango institution, in the popular language, Bizango or Bissago. Bizango is the culture of the people, a culture attached to our past, just as letters and science have their place in the civilization of the elite. Just as all peoples and all races have a history, Bizango has an image of the past, an image taken from an epoch that came before. It is the aspect of our national soul.
>
> Bizango brings joy, it brings peace. To the Haitian people, Bizango is a religion for the masses because it throws away our regrets, our worries, problems, and difficulties.
>
> Another meaning of the Bizango is the meaning of the great ceremony at Bois Caiman. They fall within the same empire of thoughts. Our history, such moments, the history of Makandal, of Romaine La Prophetesse, of Boukman, of

Pedro. Those people bore many sacrifices in their breasts. They were alive and they believed! We may also speak of a certain Hyacinthe who as the cannon fired upon him showed no fear, proving to his people that the cannon were water. And what of Makandal! The one who was tied to the execution pole with the bullets ready to smash him but found a way to escape because of the sacrifice he did.

And so I tell you again and again that there was a moment in 1804, a moment that bore fruits, that the year 1804 bore the children of today. Thank you.

Direct homage to the maroon leaders—Makandal in particular—appears as well on the Bizango passports, the only written documents employed by the societies. These papers allow society members or, in rare instances, nonmembers to pass freely through the territories of rival bands. Generally they are sheets of official government stamped paper available for purchase at the Bureau des Contributions (Haiti's IRS). Beneath the stamp there are a prayer, several passwords, the names of the bearer, and the villages and society presidents who have agreed to honor the document. A passport obtained on the central plateau by the Roman Catholic priest Jean Kerboull reads:

> République d'Haiti, entièrement. Dieu le Père, Dieu le Fils, Dieu le Saint-Ésprit. Amen. 50 Librement au nom de M. et Mme. Franck Justin Lisine Maristre, recommandés par Me Calfour et Me Grand Chemin et Me Grandbois et par les oraisons Magnificat, Marie Animam meam, Christ Sancto. Amen. Chef des loas rebelles Roi Makandal, non pas Makandal fait homme, la nuit comme le jour. Feu, vent, tempête, arrête-toi. Amen. Recommandé par M. and Mme. Partout. 25 gourdes.

The contemporary Bizango leadership appear to have little doubt about their own political and philosophical heritage, and they clearly are conscious also of their current political authority. "Bizango," in the words of one president, "is just like a normal government. Everyone has their place. It is a justice." Another president, when asked whether the Bizango reaches into all parts of Haiti, responded:

> The Bizango doesn't reach, it is already there. You see, we are like stars. We work at night but we touch everything. If

you are poor, I will call an assembly to cover your needs. If you are hungry I will give you food. If you need work, the society will give you enough to start a trade. That is the Bizango. It is hand in hand.

There is one thing the society refuses to get involved in. You can do almost anything, and the society may let you off, but if you stick your mouth in government talk, you can forget it. The society says you must respect the grade of the chief of the law. You can't just seize office, you must deserve it. Go through elections and hear the voice of the people. If you like the government, then you'd best remember that all the King's dogs are Kings, even those doing evil. On the other hand, if a militia member [Tonton Macoute] is a real bother, one day his chief will call him in and tell him he's been transferred. We in the society don't want to harm him, but we too have our limits.

Yet, when asked whether the Bizango cooperates with the central government, this same informant replied indignantly:

The government cooperates with us. They have to. Imagine what would happen if some invaders landed in a remote corner of the Department of the Northwest. They would be dead before they left the beaches. But not by the hand of the government. It is the country itself that has been prepared for these things since ancient times.

The people in government in Port-au-Prince must cooperate with us. We were here before them, and if we didn't want them, they wouldn't be where they are. There are not many guns in the country, but those that there are, we have them.

This last statement is no idle boast if one is to judge by the zeal with which prominent national politicians, most notably François Duvalier, have courted the Bizango societies. The Duvalier revolution, often misrepresented in the Western press and remembered only for its later brutal excesses, began as a reaction on the part of the black majority to the excessive prominence of a small ruling elite that had dominated the nation politically and economically for most of its history. When Duvalier was first elected in 1957, he was unable to trust the army—by the end of his tenure in office there had been over a dozen attempted invasions or coups d'état—and so he created his own security force, the Volunteers for the National Security (VSN), or the Tonton Macoute as they came to be known. To date, however, nobody has adequately explained the genesis of the Tonton Macoute as a national organization, or the remarkable speed with which it was established and insinuated in virtually every Haitian community. An explanation may lie in the network of Bizango societies.

François Duvalier, a physician by training, was a keen student of Haitian culture. A published ethnologist (Denis and Duvalier 1936, 1944), he was in his youth a pivotal member of a small group who put out an influential journal called *Les Griots*, and in that journal's pages the germ of the Duvalier movement was sown. Though they were themselves scions of the elite, well educated and thoroughly urban, the intellectuals galvanized by *Les Griots* were responding to the humiliation of the American occupation and the flaccid acquiescence of their bourgeois peers. They did so by espousing a new nationalism that openly acknowledged the African roots of the Haitian people. The philosophy of the group was explicitly laid out in an early issue (October–December 1938) of the journal. "All our efforts," they wrote, "from independence to this day consisted in the systematic repression of our African heritage. . . . Our action should lead us to the need of a revalorization of this racial factor" (Duvalier 1968, 38). At a time when drums and other religious cult objects were being hunted down and burned and the peasants were forced to swear loyalty to the Roman Catholic church, the members of *Les Griots* declared that Vodoun was the legitimate religion of the people. It was a courageous stand, and it later earned Duvalier the support of the peasant society.

In the course of the 1957 election that brought him to power, Duvalier actively sought the endorsement of the houngan, and in certain sections of the country Vodoun temples served as his local campaign headquarters. With his success François Duvalier became the first national leader in almost a hundred years to recognize the legitimacy of the Vodoun religion and the right of the people to practice it. During his term in office he appointed houngan to prominent government offices. At least once he had all the Vodoun priests brought together at the National Palace (Rotberg 1971; Bastien 1966; Diederich and Burt 1967). And Duvalier himself was widely rumored to be a practicing houngan. It was an extraordinary transformation of official government policy. A year or two before the accession of Duvalier, Vodoun drums were still being burned; a year after, a Vodoun priest was serving in the national cabinet. In the Duvalier years the traditional political role of Vodoun that can be traced directly back to the revolutionary slave uprising was appropriated and, in the deepest sense, the "totality of the cult [became] an ideological symbol, part of the national political culture" (Laguerre 1984, 4).

François Duvalier knew that he was surrounded by enemies, and he recognized with equal clarity that his strength—and the ultimate power of any black president—lay within the traditional society. Throughout his time in office he worked openly to penetrate the network of social control that already existed within that society. He openly courted prominent houngan, and it is no coincidence that an individual such as my principal informant—a man both deeply religious and deeply patriotic—became the effective head of the Tonton Macoute for a full one-fifth of the country. Before Duvalier, blacks had limited access to public or government positions. In some cities there were parks where, by unwritten agreement, blacks were not permitted to walk. To men like my informant, Duvalier seemed like a savior. That was why, when I once asked him if he had had to kill many people during the early days of the struggle, he could reply sincerely, "I didn't kill any people, only enemies."

The work of Michel Laguerre has suggested that the secret societies are a "paramilitary group connected to the voodoo temples" (Laguerre 1984, 19), and there is little doubt that Duvalier's close contacts with the houngan put him directly in touch with the Bizango societies and their leaders. It is important to note that Duvalier was the first national president to take a direct, personal interest in the appointment of each *chef de section*. Remember that, in Haiti, the administrative structures of the national government do not carry any jurisdiction in the daily lives of the vast majority of Haitian peasants (see chapter 1). Instead, the government depends on a pivotal character, the *chef de section*, who serves as an intermediary between the traditional peasantry and the institutions of the metropolitan government. But the *chef de section* is himself a member of the peasantry, and the network of contacts he taps is the network within that society. The informal tribunals he brings together consist of the representatives of the peasantry. Therefore it was highly significant to discover in the course of my research that, in most instances, the *chef de* section is either a Bizango president or a prominent houngan or bokor, or both. One Bizango president summed up the relationship between the Bizango and the *chef de section* in this way:

> Of course the *chef de section* has his responsibilities. But since the society goes out at night, it keeps many things from happening. Many people who would have the idea of doing something, they think, "well, such and such a society is going out. I won't take the chance." Most wrongdoings are done at night. We work at night. We stop them. Anyway often the *chef de section* is a resident. Usually they're houngan or society presidents. For example, if you're going to such and such a region as a society, I must warn the *chef de section* that I'll be in his region. And he'll always agree to my going there since I'm helping him. The *chef de section* must know what's going on in his section. But if the society is going into a region to take someone, and the *chef de section* is told and he knows the culprit is guilty, he won't interfere. Anyway as I said most often the *chef de section* is a houngan or Bizango president. He walks by day, but by night he too changes his skin.

François Duvalier's exploitation of the institution of the *chef de section* reveals his perspicacious knowledge of the traditional society and indicates one means by which he attempted, with great success, to wield influence over the peasantry. The extent to which Duvalier penetrated the Vodoun society is perhaps best reflected in the fact that since his death he has been canonized as a Vodoun spirit (Laguerre 1984). This is an event that Duvalier himself might have anticipated. Even in life he came to be regarded as the personification of Baron Samedi, the guardian of the cemetery and a spirit particularly associated with the secret societies. In his own dress and public behavior, particularly the nasal twang in his voice, Duvalier appeared to affect that role quite deliberately; the ubiquitous black horn-rimmed glasses, the dark suit, and the narrow black tie show up time and again in old lithographs of the popular spirit.

In short, whatever his ultimate motives, François Duvalier succeeded in penetrating the traditional Vodoun society on a number of levels. In the capital the words Tonton Macoute and Vodoun priest became almost synonymous, and it was "almost impossible for one to be an influential voodoo priest without being a Tonton Macoute or for a voodoo church to be successful without being headed by a priest—Tonton Macoute" (Laguerre 1984, 23–24). By the same token, the leaders of the secret societies almost inevitably became powerful members of the Tonton Macoute, and if the latter was not actually recruited from the Bizango, the membership of the two organizations over-lapped to a significant degree. In the end, one might almost ask whether François Duvalier himself did not become the symbolic or effective head of the secret societies.

THE BIZANGO AS AN ARBITER OF SOCIAL LIFE

One of the enigmatic features of the Bizango as a Haitian institution is the stark contrast between its nefarious public image and the logical and apparently purposeful character of its actual functions. Alfred Métraux accurately reflected popular sentiment when he described the Bizango as "bands of sorcerers, criminals of a special kind" (Métraux 1972, 293). This conceptualization appears time and again in Haitian folklore, and it is one that even certain Vodoun priests insist upon. During the initial phase of my research, for example, one prominent houngan cautioned:

> Their ritual speaks the truth. Listen to the songs. What do they say? None of them say "give me life." And when they put the money in the coffin what do they sing? "This money is for the djab"—the devil—or "woman you have two children, if I take one you'd better not yell or I'll eat you up!" The songs have only one message—Kill! Kill! Kill! To do a good service in the Bizango you must do it in a human skull. And it can't be a skull from beneath the earth, it must be a skull they prepare. Their chalice is a human skull. What does this tell you?
>
> Let me tell you what will happen. When an outsider intrudes on the society, when he tries to enter the Bizango, he receives a *coup l'aire* or *coup poudre*. Do you want to see beasts fly? If you're lucky, they shall only frighten you and tie you to the poteau mitan while twenty Sans Poel with knives dance around you. On the side they'll have a pot of oil, with cooking meat floating on the surface. Only they'll have a finger in it, and you will not know if the meat comes from

your mother. Then they will judge you, and you pray the president says you're innocent (Davis 1985, 220).

In fact this perception of the secret societies is completely consistent with the character of the Bizango service as a religious rite. The religion of the Haitian people does not consist of a single uniform theology. On the contrary, what anthropologists have loosely termed Vodoun, or Vodoun religion, is actually a collection of diverse rites that ultimately trace their origins to different parts of Africa. The word voodoo comes from the Fon language of Dahomey (now Benin) and Togo and means simply "god" or "spirit." The peasants themselves do not call their religion Vodoun. Theirs is a closed system of belief, and in a world of few alternatives one either "serves the loa," the spirits, or one does not. Vodoun, from their point of view, refers to a specific event—a dance ritual during which the spirits arrive to mount and possess the believer. Yet even this concept is not universal, and there are many regions in Haiti, particularly in the south, where the word is hardly recognized.

If there is a general concept that covers the full range of religious practices in Haiti, it would be the notion of Guinée, of Africa, the mythical homeland. The peasants conceive of themselves as *ti Guinée*, the children of Guinée, and their religious aspirations are to "serve Guinée." Guinée, then, is the totality of the Haitian religious experience, and there are a few particularly knowledgeable and respected houngan who serve that totality, who are familiar with the entire range of the spiritual pantheon. Alternatively, and more commonly, a houngan serves a specific rite, or perhaps two, each consisting of a specific body of ritual that is carefully defined, circumscribed, and consistent. The nature of the rite—be it Rada, Nago, Ibo, Petro, Congo, Dahomey, etc.—depends on its provenance in Africa and on the specific developments that it has undergone in Haiti. Although today many hounfour, particularly in Port-au-Prince, serve more than one tradition—often both Rada and Petro, for example—there are places in Haiti that may be considered repositories of specific rites. Nan Souvenance in the Artibonite Valley, for example, serves Dahomey; its sister site, Nan Sucre, serves Congo; Ville o Camps serves Rada.

In this sense it is useful to recognize that the Bizango is itself a religious rite, and like any other it may be classified beneath the umbrella of Guinée. What distinguishes the Bizango, and what may earn it the disdain of certain houngan Guinée, is its heavy emphasis on magic. Of course, it is seldom possible to separate the religious aspects of Vodoun from the obvious magical components (see chapter 1). Certain rites, though, are infused with magical elements to a much greater extent than others. The range extends from the Rada, which is highly religious in nature, to the Petro, which is magico-religious, to the Bizango, which is almost strictly a magical practice. This progression accurately reflects the historical origins of each rite. Rada derives its name from the Dahomean center of Arada, and it has come to represent within Haiti the emotional stability and warmth of Africa, the hearth of the nation. By contrast, the spirits of the Petro are believed to have been forged in the steel and blood of the colonial era. They reflect all the rage, violence, and delirium that threw off the shackles of slavery. The spirits invoked, the drums, the dancing, and the rhythms are completely distinct. Whereas the Rada drumming and dancing is on beat, the Petro is offbeat, sharp and unforgiving, like the crack of a rawhide whip.

The Bizango is an extreme form of the Petro, and it is sometimes described as *Petro Sauvage*—the wild Petro. For example, the Bizango drums are those of the Petro, but they are played in part lying on their sides, thereby producing the penetrating sound of wood on wood so typical of Bizango music. Because of its position at one extreme of the spectrum of Vodoun rites, Bizango is in some senses the opposite of the Rada. If the latter represents the benign aspect of the faith, Bizango symbolizes unforgiveness. Rada stands for light and the normal affairs of humanity; Bizango occurs by night, in the darkness that is the province of the djab, the devil. In its very definition of itself, the Bizango projects a nefarious image, and it is this projection that has so infected the public mind in Haiti and ethnographic writings.

Viewed from within, however, the Bizango societies appear to have a benevolent function. For the initiates they represent a refuge of some importance, serving as an economic cushion, for example, during times of need. As one Bizango president commented, "the society that initiates someone should always be prepared to support him and his family in the event of a misfortune, social, economic, moral or other. When one falls, the society should be strong enough to pick the member up." The

offerings made during the nocturnal ceremonies become a resource available to all the society. The members receive spiritual
protection as well. Those who have been granted the secret of
the society receive a tattoo, a *garde* that is believed to offer
resistance to black-magic spells. Similarly, it is the secret societies that implant the spiritually endowed *bornes*, the iron spikes
found at the entryway to most compounds. The benevolence of
the Bizango affects all its members and their families and, as one
president said, "since almost everyone has some relative initiated, the Bizango becomes a shelter for all."

But if the Bizango society insulates its members from the
vicissitudes of life, its authority and power to do so are derived in
part from the harshness with which it sometimes levies sanctions
against those who transgress the societal codes. "For the sick and
the troubled," one Bizango president explained, "the society is a
wonderful thing, whether you have money or not. But it is only
good because it can be very bad. If you get into trouble with it, it
can be very hard on you." Yet by no means is the sanction of the
society invoked in the haphazard way generally described in
Haitian folklore. On the contrary, the imposition of social sanctions requires a complex judicial process complete with its own
set of checks and balances. For example, in popular belief the
Bizango sorcerers prey on innocent children, and it is common
for recalcitrant children to be admonished that their behavior
will lead to their being eaten by Sans Poel. In reality, children are
considered by the Bizango to be *ti les anges*, the little angels, and
completely beyond the societal sanctions. The ominous threat of
punishment at the hands of the Bizango is something that every
child grows up with, but it is less an actual possibility than it is
one aspect of an educative process that promotes a certain norm
of social behavior. The role of the Bizango in the socialization of
children is best summarized in the words of a Bizango leader:

> Bizango is a great religion of the night. "Order and Respect
> of the Night"—that is the motto, and the words speak the
> truth. Order because the Bizango maintains order. Respect
> for the Night? As a child what did your father teach you?
> That the night is not your own. It is not your time, and you
> must not encounter the Sans Poel because only something
> terrible can occur. Night belongs to the djab, and the eyes of
> the innocent must not fall upon it. Darkness is the refuge of

thieves and evildoers, not the children. It is not a child that should be judged.

Adults, of course, do fall within the range of the Bizango sanctions but, again, these are not invoked in either a random or capricious way. As one society member put it, "in my village you kill yourself. People don't kill you." Those who are taken in the night by the Bizango are not innocent victims but those who have committed some antisocial offense. The same informant put it this way: "Look, it's like this. I come here and you do something bad to me. Or let's take another example. If I'm at work and someone spreads some gossip, some rumor that's not true but that gets me fired. It's not right. So I arrive and I sell you to the Sans Poel. Because what you did was not right. You pass a rumor and you stop me from living. As we say, you oppose yourself to my eating, so I oppose myself to your living." "Selling someone to the society" (*vann oun moun nan société*) is a fundamental right of both members and nonmembers, and although at times some money may be exchanged, the expression is basically euphemistic, referring in fact to the first step of a complex process that includes informal tribunals, judgment, and possibly the direct application of sanctions by the society.

To exercise this right an individual need only contact the emperor, the founding president, and explain his or her case. The emperor, if he believes the incident is significant, will convene the executive leadership of the society, the Groupe d'État Majeur. Together they "weigh the balance," determining whether the complaint is warranted. If it is, they bring both the accused and the plaintiff before them. This may be done in two ways, which further reveal that for the Vodounist the boundary between the material and the immaterial, between the physical and the spiritual, is both fine and permeable.

The leadership may, through magic, judge only the spirits of the disputants. The mystical force of the society—the "escort"—casts a spell that causes both adversaries to fall ill, and then, just as death nears, it takes the *ti bon ange* of each individual. If one person's force is strong, if he or she is innocent, death is not possible. But the *ti bon ange* that is judged guilty will never return to its body, and the *corps cadavre* of that person will be found the next day in its bed with the "string of life cut." The innocent one will awaken and remember the experience only as a dream.

Alternatively, the Bizango leadership may elect to bring the adversaries together in the flesh, in which case they dispatch the *bourreau* and *chasseur* to seize physically the accused. The selling of an enemy to the society is never done casually, for if the accused is deemed innocent at the tribunal, then the plaintiff is guilty of spreading a falsehood, and he or she is punished.

The actual judicial process may be extremely complex and lengthy. One prominent emperor explained it this way:

> The Sans Poel is a group that must retrace "Order and Respect." A society cannot judge someone who hasn't directly affected or offended the society. They must wait until he attacks a member before they can work against that person. There may be a thousand people in the society. If someone does something wrong there will be a report. Say someone speaks against the society—well, he must be made to respect his mouth. So we all come together. Someone gets the feast organized—the rice, beans, sausage, rum— and they call the major members of the society aside. This is the council [the *conseil*]—the Groupe d'État Majeur—the president, ministers, one queen. We pass the person. Let's say I suggest so and so must die December 5. Others say November 5, others January 1. Once it's agreed upon we go to the emperor, in this case myself, who says alright how can we make this person respect the "Order and Respect for the Night." He must die immediately. So we mark the paper and he dies. If anyone disagrees the case can drag on. Yet every three months or so we'll have a séance for this. If we reach an impasse we make a formation of thirteen members. If seven say they don't want so and so to die, it passes and he is not harmed. This is how the Sans Poel works.

The delay that can occur between the initial accusation, the ultimate judgment, and the administration of the punishment serves a definite purpose, for it allows the accused to make amends by coming to terms with the family of the plaintiff. This possibility of retribution was made explicit by one Bizango emperor:

> The name and the description of the problem is before the society which passes you through a judgment. Because above all, in the Cannibal there must be justice. Some

people spend three years in agony, sick and dying because the judgment hasn't been pronounced. Everyone knows so and so is on the list. But it is like this because this is not a sacrifice, it is a justice.

The family of the sick one may hire a diviner to go out and find out what happened. He'll find out that the sick one has been sold to a society and he'll explain what must be done. Find out what she or he did and to whom and where and when. Then the diviner will go around and find out what society he was sold to. Eventually he'll find out. Then word gets through to the society and they assemble. They prepare four plates of food—*plates principales*. No matter what your situation is you must pay for the four plates. The four plates are the emperor, the queen, brigadier general, and the 4 ascariots. You see, it is not necessary to kill the person. What is important is to pass him under a tribunal of hardship until he is disgusted and worn out and thinks over what he did. He must face the justice.

This concept of selling someone to the society lies at the very foundation of the Bizango judicial process, and members and leaders alike are conscious of the transgressions for which a judgment might be invoked. One Bizango emperor listed the following offenses, which he actually codified as the "seven actions."

1. Ambition—excessive material advancement at the obvious expense of family and dependents
2. Displaying lack of respect for one's fellows
3. Denigrating the Bizango society
4. Stealing another man's woman
5. Spreading loose talk that slanders and affects the well-being of others
6. Harming members of one's family
7. Land issues—any action that unjustly keeps another from working the land

This list, which was endorsed by other Bizango presidents, reads like a character profile of Clairvius Narcisse and brings this discussion momentarily back to his case.

Clairvius Narcisse often fought with various members of his own family. He sired numerous children and then didn't support them. By neglecting these and other community obligations, he managed to save enough money so that his house was the first in the lakou to have the thatch roof replaced by tin. But although his profligate existence certainly offended his extended family, the dispute with his brother was basically a question of access to land; so serious a dispute between the Narcisse brothers would likely have involved arbitration by the Bizango society. My primary informant had suggested that it was Clairvius's uncle who actually requested that the tribunal be convened. We can only guess what might have occurred at that judgment, but several points would have been considered. The father of the two brothers was still alive at the time, and Clairvius Narcisse did not have any children recognized by the community. In Haiti, it is the custom that family landholdings are not divided up "among the first generation of heirs since younger brothers would not take it upon themselves to imply such disrespect of the senior ones as to demand that their tracts be split off" (Underwood 1964, 471). What's more, if heirs "insist on a formal division before the death of their elders, tradition brands them disrespectful and impertinent" (Métraux 1951, 22).

One of the Narcisse brothers was clearly wrong in terms of the proper code of conduct of Haitian peasant society. The most important obligation of the patriarch in Haiti is to keep "family resources intact in order to provide a start in life for children" (Underwood 1964, 470). This explicit emphasis on posterity presumably placed the childless, wifeless Clairvius in a less favorable position compared to his brother, who at the time had a large family to support. If Narcisse had, in fact, been in the right and had been zombified by the guilty brother, it is difficult to imagine that the secret society would have permitted that brother to live on in peace in the village for close to twenty years. Given the current chilly relationship between Narcisse and his family, it seems more likely that Clairvius was the guilty party—a conviction held by the majority of my informants in Haiti and reinforced by this extraordinary statement made by one Bizango emperor in Saint Marc: "Narcisse's brother sold him to a society in Caho. It was the seventh condition. It was the parent's land. He tried to take it by force. But all this doesn't mean the society is an evil thing. If someone inside your house betrays you, they deserve to die. But that doesn't make your house a bad place."

The possibility that the Bizango was implicated in the demise of Clairvius Narcisse was suggested by several other lines of evidence. For one, the actual range of punishments available to the Bizango consists of the same magical spells, powders, and supernatural entities available to any sorcerer in Haiti (see chapter 1). These include the *coup l'aire* (a magical spell that breaks the victim's equilibrium, causing misfortune and illness), the *coup nam* (a soul spell and a magical means of capturing the *ti bon ange*), the *coup poudre* (a powder spell, a magical powder that may cause illness and/or death), and the *l'envoi morts* (the sending of the death spirits). To administer these spells the society *bourreau* (executioner) sets "traps" in places the accused is known to frequent. A powder sprinkled in the form of a cross on the ground to capture the *ti bon ange* is one example of such a trap. Once caught, the victim can be saved only by the intervention of the society president, and that treatment can cost a great deal. Alternatively, the *coup poudre* may be applied directly to the victim. As Clairvius Narcisse himself explained: "The bokor sent for my soul. That's how it's done. There is the basin. It's full of water but they prick your skin and call the spirit and the water changes into blood."

The connection between the Bizango and zombification was emphasized by a number of society leaders. One president explained: "Sans Poel doesn't need to buy zombies. Each person they sacrifice they take his zombie . . . yes, since you have done a major offense they'll go and raise your body and make you work. They'll raise you in the cemetery. They'll make you sorry for your mouth, as generally this is done for people who talk too much. They'll pass near your family's place with you, so your family can hear you yelling. Often this happens in Saint Marc when they pass and you hear them yelling, 'Papa, papa, they're leaving with me.'" In another conversation a different Bizango president stated:

Every evildoer will be punished. It is as we sing:

> They kill the man
> to take his zombie
> to make it work
> O Sans Poel O
> They killed the man
> to take his zombie
> to make it work.

A third leader noted:

Of course societies can make their own zombies. Let's say they're going down the street, and they meet someone who's been talking wrong or is otherwise in a bad situation. They'll take him and make a zombie out of him. The person could be someone talking wrong, he could be the one who is going and speaking to the government, telling the state that such and such a society is doing this or that. The person hides but we will catch him.

There are two types of zombies. One is the *zombi éfface*—that is a spirit zombie which is like the wind. The other is like a person and they take him to do a judgment. They go get the body of it. It looks just like you. They do the judgment on this one. So there's one which is a person in flesh, the other which isn't. It is often used for *expéditions [l'envoi morts*, or death spirits]. The person or flesh zombie must have been killed by powders, but the *zombi éfface* can have been killed by anything. The *zombi éfface* is more precisely the spirit of a dead person that you send on someone. . . . But if that victim is innocent, he can't die from the death spirit. Poisons or *coup poudre*—right or wrong they kill.

The powder has many things . . . *crabe araigné* [tarantulas], sea worm and the sea toad [*crapaud la mer (Sphoeroides* sp.)] are essential for zombie powders. They also use *24 heures* ("24 hours"), which is an animal that kills in twenty-four hours. But the zombie doesn't really die. It hears everything you say but it can't speak. It slows you down. All the doctors think you're dead. It's like you are suffocating.

But it is not just anyone. There must be proof. If there is not concrete proof, you can give him a *coup l'aire*. They can make him ill, or even kill him, but to take him there must be proof.

The link between the powders and the secret societies is generally recognized within Haiti. One Bizango queen advised that if one wanted to learn the powders, "you best learn to walk at night." One of the popular songs to Simbi, the patron of the magical powders, goes:

Simbi en Deux Eaux
Why don't people like me?

Because my magical force is dangerous.
Simbi en Deux Eaux
Why can't they stand me?
Because my magical force is dangerous.
They like my magical force to fly the Sans Poel
They like my magical force to walk in
        the middle of the night.

Finally, the link between the secret societies and the creation of zombies is explicit in the following purportedly eyewitness experience of a prominent mambo (Vodoun priestess) in
Gonaïves. The Rara bands referred to in the account emanate
from the Vodoun temples during holy week and to a great extent
are owned and operated by Vodoun priests and composed of
secret society members (Laguerre 1984). The emergence of the
Rara bands at Easter represents the one occasion each year on
which the secret society publicly displays itself, appearing in
long, frenzied processions that weave through the streets absorbing idlers and growing longer and longer tails of dancers. The
leaders of the processions are all men, but they are dressed as
women in long satin gowns sporting lewd bustlines. Sweeping
across the head of the procession is a menacing figure, wielding a
sisal whip, flaying at the crowd. On the surface it is a symbolic
display, and no one is hurt. Nevertheless, Rara remains somehow
intimidating and subversive, an amazing and bizarre sexual inversion. It is no wonder or accident that by political decree the
militant bands traditionally have been forbidden to enter the
major cities. To be sure, the Rara bands serve more than a
recreational function. They distribute powders as sanctions, and
their songs are designed to blame and censure the bad behavior
of certain members of the community. It is this latter function
that is obviously referred to in this account:

> There was this fellow who lived near here named Anris.
> You'd really have to admit the man was evil. Before he died I
> once heard him describe all the people he had killed and
> there must have been fifty. One of them was a girl, Cilian,
> my own cousin and godchild of his mother. He had tried to
> take advantage of Cilian and when the young girl told his
> mother, she became furious. To take his revenge, he killed
> the young girl. Everyone knew it.
> One year at Easter there was a Rara band coming out of

*The posturing of a Rara band. Note the men dressed
in women's clothing.*

my mother's lakou. I was with my cousin Julian and another
named Marienne. We followed the band and danced until
reaching the Alexis crossroads, and then beyond all the way
to the cemetery of Marchand. The band was going all the
way to Mapou, planning on returning the next day, but we
were tired and so decided to go back home. Just as we came
back toward the cemetery we noticed this other band and as
it approached I saw my brother-in-law and a cousin. Just as
the band turned into the lakou, this fellow comes over to me
and tells me they have taken Anris. I looked in and recognized him with my own eyes. My cousins got frightened and
ran home. But I stayed and saw that they killed Anris.

The burial was Saturday or Sunday and the wake occurred on Monday. It was at first like any other with the *prêt
savanne* leading the last prayer and all the young girls are
flirting with their boyfriends when suddenly a man appears
and in a growling voice demands that the lights be turned
off. He was ignored at first and the people and *prêt savanne*
went about their business. When he screamed again, people
began to complain but then he screamed even louder and
himself ran about turning off the lights. No one tried to stop
him. He told nobody to leave. Then in the middle of the

wake who should be dragged into the room but Anris. Everyone screamed. The *prêt savanne* ran off. In the middle of the place. They had brought him. They'd made him a zombie.

In summary, it appears that the Bizango societies, working either directly or through certain bokor, may have a direct role in the creation of spirit and/or physical zombies. The creation of a zombie, or indeed the threat of zombification, is not imposed in either a random or a critical way. On the contrary, there appears to be a logical purpose to zombification, consistent with the heritage of the people and their need to protect that heritage. A zombie is not an innocent victim, but an individual who has transgressed the established and acknowledged codes of his or her society. The act of zombification represents the ultimate social sanction. When Clairvius Narcisse referred to those who had been responsible for his fate as the "masters of the land," those who "do as they please," he was only partially correct. The Bizango societies might well represent a potent political force in the Haitian countryside but they apparently do not act "as they please." Instead, they work within an established body of ritual and folk tradition which is designed, not to disrupt order and conformity, but to enforce it.

CONCLUSION

ETHNOBIOLOGY AND THE

HAITIAN ZOMBIE

Ethnobiology is the study of the relationship between man and his ambient flora and fauna. As an academic discipline, it has its roots in the numerous observations of explorers and traders, missionaries, naturalists, anthropologists, and botanists concerning the use of plants and animals by the seemingly exotic cultures of the world. It was born as much as anything from the coalescence of disparate field reports, and from its inception it has struggled to find the unifying theory innate to many more narrowly delimited scientific disciplines.

As a result ethnobiology has, at times, suffered from a lack of orientation and integration, and its traditional task of cataloging the uses of plants and animals has been criticized as lacking theoretical content. In part these criticisms have been valid. Ethnobiological data collected without reference to an intellectual problem may be eclectic to the point of inutility. Yet critics of the practice of ethnobiology generally overlook two important points. First, the compilation of raw information provides the foundation of any natural science, and without a basic inventory theoretical formulations are not possible. Second, ethnobiology remains, on one level, what it has always been—a science of discovery. Its contributions to the welfare of mankind have not been trivial. In the field of medicine alone, between 35 and 50 percent of the modern drug armamentarium is derived from natural products, and a majority of these compounds were first used as medicines or poisons in a folk context (Holmstedt and Bruhn 1983; Farnsworth and Morris 1976). Today, in an era marked by the massive destruction of diversity, not only of plants and animals but of human societies as well, basic biological exploration remains a vital and essential contribution of the ethnobiologist.

Moreover, critics of ethnobiology often ignore the considerable theoretical advances that the field has made. Increasingly, the old practice of ethnobiological discovery—of finding new plants or animals, labeling them according to the rules of binomial nomenclature, and incorporating their usefulness into modern society—has given way to an intellectual perspective that views both the organisms and their utilization as a metaphor for understanding the very cognitive matrix of a particular society (Berlin 1974; Berlin et al. 1966; Conklin 1954). This trend has resulted in sophisticated studies which, depending on the problem at hand, may concurrently employ a range of methodologies derived from subdisciplines of anthropology, phytochemistry, genetics, botany, zoology, and pharmacology; it is precisely this interdisciplinary orientation that allows the ethnobiologist to pose and answer questions that cannot be approached by narrower specialists.

The Zombie Project is a case in point. The taxonomic identification of the plant and animal ingredients in the poison and the knowledge of their toxicity lent credence to folk contentions that had been reported but overlooked by anthropologists. This discovery, in turn, led to an obscure biomedical literature which contributed considerable evidence to bolster the psychiatrists' conviction that Clairvius Narcisse had been a zombie. Preliminary laboratory tests presented evidence of the efficacy of the preparation. An anthropological perspective elucidated the process of zombification, which not only answered pharmacological questions (e.g. the significance of the "antidote") but raised what is arguably the most provocative issue—the connection between the secret Bizango societies and the zombie phenomenon.

In its conclusions, my research suggests that zombies of two forms exist, the *zombi astral* or *zombi éfface* and the *zombi corps cadavre*, both of which are emically believed to be created by a complex knowledge of magic. However, for the physical zombie to exist, a pharmacologically active folk toxin must be employed, and in revealing this material basis to the phenomenon I have sought to highlight the sorcerer's remarkable empirical knowledge of pharmacology. The bokor's repertoire includes a plethora of plant- and animal-based preparations. The critical ingredient in the zombie powders is almost certainly tetrodotoxin, a potent neurotoxin fully capable of pharmacologically inducing the prerequisite state of apparent death. The medical potential of tetrodotoxin is considerable. The ability of the drug to prevent generation of the action potential by specifically blocking the sodium channels while having no effect on the flow of potassium has made it an invaluable neurobiological tool for the study of nerve function (Kao 1983; Kao and Walker 1982). A possible role for tetrodotoxin in surgery has been suggested by laboratory experiments, which indicate that the drug is one of the few known compounds that induce hypotension without dramatically increasing intracranial pressure (Cottrell et al. 1983). Continuing investigations into the biological activity of other pharmacologically active constituents in the zombie preparation may lead to further discoveries of medical significance.

In examining the process of zombification, however, I have tried to emphasize that no cultural phenomenon can be reduced to pharmacology. Indeed, as a Western scientist seeking a folk preparation, I found myself swept into a complex worldview utterly different from my own—one that left me demonstrating less the chemical basis of a popular belief than the psychological and cultural foundations of a chemical event. It is this elaborate connection between spiritual belief, psychological predisposition, and pharmacology that underlies all peasant or indigenous practices involving psychotropic preparations.

In the end, what began as a search for an isolated folk toxin provided a context for addressing more general issues of some ethnographic significance. An examination of the sociological role of zombification within the peasant society, for example, outlined the political and legal dimensions of an unstudied symbolic belief system. The investigation touched upon a network of power relations that reaches to all levels of Haitian political life, and in so doing it shed light on many aspects of recent Haitian political history which have yet to be explained adequately—in particular, the meteoric rise under François Duvalier of the Tonton Macoute. Perhaps most important, by explaining zombification as a logical process within the context of traditional Vodoun society, I have attempted to demystify one of the most exploited of folk beliefs, and one that has been used in a nefarious way to denigrate an entire people and their remarkable and quite wonderful religion.

In the wake of the collapse of the Duvalier regime, the fate of

Vodoun and the parallel institution of the Bizango has been a matter of some concern and speculation. One of the immediate and significant consequences of the Duvalierization of the folk religion and the secret societies was the backlash that occurred after the revolution of 7 February 1986. Slogans appeared on the walls of the capital reading, "Down with Voodoo! Liberation of the Zombies!" (Bartley 1986). Protestant and Roman Catholic vigilante gangs ransacked Vodoun temples and killed an undetermined number of houngan. The exact nature of this backlash is, even today, difficult to assess. Initially it appeared to mark the beginning of yet another systematic antisuperstition campaign reminiscent of those that occurred periodically between 1930 and 1957. Recent observations, however, suggest otherwise. Many of the hounfour that were destroyed now appear to have belonged to houngan who, as members of the Tonton Macoute, had been especially abusive. It is possible, for example, to find intact and functioning temples in close proximity to the remains of those that were totally destroyed, which suggests that the attacks were directed less at Vodoun than at particular individuals. In the political vacuum that suddenly emerged after thirty years of despotic rule, many old private scores were settled. Nonetheless, the political strength and vitality of the Vodoun society is demonstrated by the inclusion of the folk religion in the new national constitution, which was formally adopted by the plebescite on 29 March 1987. In a precedent of historic significance, the constitution recognized Creole as an official language of the state, and it also acknowledged Vodoun as a legitimate religion and a vital part of the national patrimony. To what extent this libertarian spirit, nobly expressed in the constitution, will become manifest as effective public policy remains to be seen.

One thing is certain. Whatever the fate of the current constitution, the Vodoun church will continue to fulfill both a religious and political function, as it has since the colonial era. After all, a Vodoun ceremony catalyzed the successful slave revolt that led to independence in 1804 and, in the wake of the revolution, Vodoun leaders continued to serve as middlemen between the peasants and the emerging institutions of the urban political and economic elite. The secret societies created by the former slaves and maroons in the early nineteenth century had the expressed purpose of protecting the freedom and the land base of the peasantry. Moreover, these Bizango societies, by historical record, have responded directly and forcefully to diachronic changes in the institutions and politics of the central government. Secret societies are likely to have provided members of the secret police of Faustin Soulouque (1847–59), a Vodounist who became notorious for the ceremonies held in his palace (Leyburn 1941). Throughout the internecine political intrigue that placed no fewer than twenty-two heads of state in power between 1842 and 1915, secret societies were recruited by black military leaders in their struggle against the mulatto elite. During the military occupation by the United States (1915–34), the secret societies surfaced as a part of the Kako resistance movement, which grew into full-scale guerrilla warfare (Laguerre 1986). In the midst of the virulent antisuperstition campaign in the 1940s and 1950s, it was no doubt the Bizango societies that were behind the "unruly peasants [who, opposing the campaign,] threatened the political and economic security of Haiti" (Desmangles 1979, 6). François Duvalier, of course, brought all aspects of the Vodoun society into clearer view and provoked a dramatic resurgence of secret society activity (Hurbon 1979). Ironically, it was the Bizango that were in no small part responsible for the collapse of the government of Duvalier's son, Jean-Claude.

Unlike his father, Jean-Claude Duvalier distanced himself from the secret societies. His marriage to Michele Bennett, which was heralded by some as a rapprochement between the Duvalier partisans and the mulatto elite, was viewed by traditional society as a betrayal. Not only did Bennett represent one of the wealthiest and most exclusive families of the elite society, but one of her closest relatives had actually been implicated in an attempted coup against François Duvalier. In the months prior to the collapse of Jean-Claude's government, the secret societies withheld their support and actually organized the first protests against the regime. By the time the popular protests began in Gonaïves and then spread to Port-au-Prince, it was clear that Jean-Claude Duvalier had lost his support among the people. As Michel Laguerre reports: "The empty coffin seen carried on the hands of two protesters with a sign 'Jean-Claude Duvalier, you belong there' was an indication that a secret society wanted to punish him after he was found guilty by the council of elders. He was seen as having betrayed the promises made by his father by courting the local bourgeoisie at the expense of the secret societies" (Laguerre 1986, 19). According to press reports, it was a convocation of a group of Vodoun priests and Bizango leaders at the National Palace that ultimately persuaded Duvalier to step down and flee the country.

Today Duvalier is gone, and the current leaders of the country are struggling against the weight of two hundred years of Haitian history to create a democratic state. But whatever the outcome of the political debates in Port-au-Prince, Vodoun will survive. The members of the secret societies will "continue to function as an underground government with their emperors, kings, queens, presidents and cabinet ministers, army officers, soldiers and diplomats," and their leaders will continue to engage in local and national politics (Laguerre 1986, 19). As Michel Laguerre has cautioned, "most of the weapons—revolvers and rifles—they acquired as Tonton Macoutes have not been taken away from them. They are more equipped than ever to protect their own interests and those of their respective communities. In the forthcoming elections they will no doubt support candidates who are unwilling to persecute their organizations or who may even be sympathetic to their religious beliefs and practices. . . . From now on every constitutional president will need to have a functional knowledge of voodoo [*sic*] if he or she wishes to become a popular and successful leader among the Haitian masses" (Laguerre 1986, 19). That, perhaps, will be the most significant legacy of the Duvalier regime.

NOTE ON ORTHOGRAPHY

Orthography of the name of the Haitian traditional religion has been the source of some academic debate. The word *voodoo* is derived from a term in the Fon language of Dahomey (now Benin) and Togo that means simply "god" or "spirit." Many knowledgeable scholars, including Alfred Métraux and Michel Laguerre, refer to the folk religion as voodoo. Unfortunately, numerous sensational and inaccurate interpretations in the media—in particular, Hollywood films—have created a public conception of voodoo as a fantasy of black magic and sorcery. Other anthropologists, in an attempt to both highlight and avoid this stereotype, have substituted a number of terms such as *vodu*, *vodun*, *voudoun*, and *vodoun*. I have followed their lead because I feel, as I hope this book has shown, that the rich religion of the Haitian traditional society deserves to be recognized and that what we have come to know as voodoo bears little resemblance to it. I use the term *Vodoun* because, to me, it seems the most accurate phonetically. It is important to note, however, that the Haitian peasants themselves do not call their religion Vodoun. The term, from their point of view, refers to a specific event: a dance ritual during which the spirits arrive to mount and possess the believer.

There has also been considerable disagreement concerning the spelling of the term zombie. *Webster's* prefers *zombie*, the more familiar form, to *zombi*. My Oxford dictionary doesn't even list the word, which says something about the American fascination with Haiti since the occupation. Sources in the scholarly literature are mixed. Seabrook (1929) used *zombie*, as did Deren (1953). Métraux (1972), Huxley (1966), and Leyburn (1941), on the other hand, use *zombi*. I have simply added to the confusion, I must confess, by using *zombi* in a previous publication but returning in this book to the more conventional spelling, *zombie*. My reason for the change is simple enough. At one point academic precedent seemed to favor the spelling *zombi*, but I have found in the last two years that *zombie* is irrevocably engraved in the public vocabulary, and, in this instance, there seems to be little reason to contradict popular usage.

The word for the spirits of the Vodoun pantheon is *loa* and, following the precedent of virtually all previous writers, I have continued this spelling. Phonetically, however, the more accurate spelling is *lwa*, and at least one prominent researcher (Murray 1977) has used this form.

Finally, for the sake of clarity, I refer throughout the book to the "Vodoun society." This is a concept of convenience, and like this note on orthography, it reflects the views and concerns of an outsider looking in, not that of a believer surrounded by his or her spirit realm.

GLOSSARY

Abortifacient. An agent that causes abortions

Adoration. The song that accompanies the offering of money at ceremonies

Agwé. Vodoun loa; the spirit of the sea

Alkaloid. One of a large group of nitrogenous basic substances found in plants. They are usually very bitter and many are pharmacologically active.

Anodyne. A medicine that relieves pain

Anoxia. Absence of oxygen supply to tissue despite adequate perfusion of the tissue by blood

Anthelmintic. An agent that is destructive to worms

Anticholinergic. Blocking the passage of impulses through the parasympathetic nerves; an agent that blocks the parasympathetic nerves

Aphonia. Loss of voice due to functional or organic disorder

Arawaks. The indigenous inhabitants, at the time of the arrival of Columbus, of the island that became known as Hispaniola

Arrêt. Magical force invoked by the houngan for the protection of a household or compound of houses

Asphyxia. A lack of oxygen or excess of carbon dioxide in the body usually caused by interruption of breathing and which usually leads to unconsciousness

Asson. The sacred rattle of the houngan or mambo; a calabash filled with seeds or snake vertebrae and covered by a loose web of beads and snake vertebrae

Ataxia. Failure of muscular coordination

Autonomic nervous system. The portion of the nervous system concerned with the regulation of the cardiac muscles, smooth muscle, and glands; that part of the nervous system regulating involuntary action

Ayida Wedo. Vodoun loa whose image is the rainbow; mate of Damballah

Ayizan. Vodoun loa, patroness of the marketplace and mate of Loco

Bagi. Inner sanctuary of the temple, the room containing the altar for the spirits

Baka. An evil spirit, a supernatural agent of the sorcerers that often takes the form of an animal

Baron Samedi. Vodoun loa, the lord and guardian of the cemetery, represented there by a large cross placed over the grave of the first man to be buried there. Important spirit of the Bizango.

Bête Sereine. Animal of the Night, an appellation for the members of the Bizango societies. Literally, "serene beast."

Bizango. The name of the secret society; also connotes the rite practiced by the Shanpwel. The name is possibly derived from the Bissagos, an African tribe that occupied an archipelago of the same name off the coast of Kakonda, between Sierra Leone and Cape Verde.

Blanc. "White," but more precisely "foreigner" and, like the term *gringo* in parts of Latin America, not necessarily pejorative

Bokor. Although the word is derived from the Fon word *bokono*, or priest, in Haiti the bokor has come to represent the one who practices sorcery and black magic as a profession.

Buga. The toad *Bufo marinus*

Bourreau. The executioner, a rank in the Bizango societies said to be responsible for enforcing the decisions of the Groupe d'État-Majeur

Cacique. Term is still used in Haiti to refer to the pre-Columbian Amerindian rulers and divisions of the country.

Calabar bean. *Physostigma venenosum,* a climbing liana of the Leguminosae; a source of physostigmine

Calabash. A gourd used as a water container or ceremonial vessel

Canari. A clay jar that is used for sheltering the *ti bon ange,* and which is broken at funeral rites

Cannibal. A term for a secret society

Canzo. The ordeal by fire through which the adept passes into initiation

Cardiac glycoside. Any one of a number of glycosides occurring in certain plants that has a characteristic action on the contractile force of cardiac muscle

Carrefour. The crossroads; also a Vodoun loa and one associated with the Bizango, as well as the Petro rites

Cata. The smallest of the set of three Rada drums

Catarrh. Inflammation of a mucous membrane, particularly the air passages of the head and throat

Catatonic. Mental state relating to or marked by schizophrenia, characterized by symptoms such as stupor, catalepsy, or negativism

Chasseur. The hunter, a rank of the Bizango society

Chef de section. The appointed authority responsible for policing the *section rurale*

Cheval. The horse; in Vodoun parlance, the individual who is mounted by the spirit. From this term comes the metaphor for possession and the meaning of the title of Maya Deren's book *The Divine Horsemen.*

Christophe, Henri. The former slave, lieutenant of Dessalines, who ruled the northern half of Haiti from 1807 to 1820, when he took his own life

Ciguatera. A form of ichthyosarcotoxism marked by gastrointestinal and neurological symptoms due to ingestion of marine fish that store the toxin in their tissues

Clairin. Inexpensive clear white rum used commonly in Vodoun ritual

Concombre zombi. The vernacular name for *Datura stramonium*

Convoi. The name of a particular secret society

Corps cadavre. The body, the flesh, and the blood as opposed to the various components of the Vodoun soul

Coumbite. Collective labor party, generally for agricultural work

Coup l'aire. An air spell, a means of passing a magical spell that will cause misfortune and illness

Coup nam. A soul spell, a means of magically capturing the *ti bon ange* of an individual

Coup poudre. A powder spell, a magical powder that may cause illness and/or death

Creole. The language of the traditional Vodoun society

Cyanosis. A bluish coloration to the skin caused by lack of oxygen in the blood

Damballah Wedo. Vodoun loa whose image is the serpent, the mate of Ayida Wedo

Datura. A genus of plants in the potato family (Solanaceae)

Decoction. A medicine or other substance prepared by boiling

Dessalines, Jean-Jacques. Leading general under Toussaint L'Ouverture and the first president of independent Haiti from 1804 until his assassination in 1806

Dessounin. The ritual separating a dead person's *ti bon ange* and spirit, or loa, from the body

Diuretic. An agent that promotes the excretion of urine

Djab. The devil, a baka, a malevolent force

Dokte feuilles. The leaf doctor, herbalist healer

Dropsy. The abnormal accumulation of serous fluid in the cellular tissue or in a body cavity

Dysphagia. Difficulty in swallowing

Electrocardiograph. An instrument for recording the changes of electrical potential occurring during the heartbeat

Electroencephalograph (EEG). An apparatus for detecting and recording the electrical activity of the brain

Emic. An anthropological term denoting the view from within a particular cultural reality; a level of analysis that seeks primarily to elucidate the categories and rules as perceived by the members of the social group under study. Typically, the thrust of an emic analysis must be consistent with the tenets of local belief, and it is the informant who is the ultimate judge of the accuracy of the researcher's conclusions.

Empereur. A founding president of a Bizango society; also the titular leader of a number of different societies

Erythema. Name applied to redness of the skin produced by congestion of the capillaries, which may result from a variety of causes

Erzulie. A Vodoun loa, the spirit of love

Ésprit. The spirits or soul of the dead

Ethnobotany. In the broadest sense, the study of the interaction between people and plants, between human societies and their ambient natural vegetation

Ethnopharmacology. The science of drugs, particularly as related to the manipulation of natural products for medicines, narcotics, or poisons by traditional peoples in a folk context

Etic. An anthropological term that describes a second level of analysis in which the ethnographic observer is obliged not simply to understand how the informant sees his or her world, but to generate scientifically useful explanations to account for social and cultural phenomena

Expédition. A death spirit (see *l'envoi morts*), the act of sending a death spirit

Febrifuge. An agent that reduces body temperature in fever

Fugu. A genus of marine fish and the vernacular name for the fish containing tetrodotoxin that are served in Japanese restaurants

Fwet kash. A sisal whip

Gad (Garde). A protective charm, a tattoo that is physically applied to the skin at initiation to protect the individual from evil

Glucoside. A glycoside in which the sugar constituent is glucose

Glycoside. Any compound that contains a carbohydrate molecule (sugar)

Gourde. Unit of Haitian money worth twenty cents

Gout. A hereditary form of arthritis characterized by an excess of uric acid in the blood

Govi. The sacred clay vessels in which the spirits of the dead or the loa are housed

Grans Bwa. A Vodoun loa, the spirit of the forest

Gros bon ange. "Big good angel"; that aspect of the Vodoun soul shared by all sentient beings; one individual's part of the vast pool of cosmic energy

Groupe d'État-Majeur. Said to be executive leadership of the Bizango society

Guede. A Vodoun loa, the spirit of the dead

Guinée. Africa, or the mythical homeland; the land of the spirits

Hoodoo. A variation of the word *voodoo*, used commonly in the southern United States

Hounfour. The Vodoun temple, including the material structure and the acolytes who serve there. When used in opposition to peristyle, it refers to the inner sanctuary with the altar.

Houngan. Vodoun priest

Hounsis. Members of the société, or hounfour, at various levels of initiation. From the Fon language (*hu*—a divinity; *si*—a spouse)

Hyperhidrosis. Excessive perspiration

Hypertension. Persistently high arterial blood pressure

Hypostasis. Poor or stagnant circulation in a dependent part of the body or organ, as in venous insufficiency

Hypotension. Abnormally low blood pressure

Infusion. The product of the process of steeping a substance in water for the extraction of its medicinal principles

Intraepidermal. Within the epidermis

Intraperitoneal. Within the peritoneal cavity; the peritoneum being the membrane lining the abdominopelvic walls and investing the viscera

Invisibles, Les. Term for all the invisible spirits, including the loa

Ischemia. Deficiency of blood in a body part, due to functional constriction or actual blockage of a blood vessel

Lambi. Conch shell used as a trumpet

Langage. Sacred language used only in ceremonies of African origin

Legba. A Vodoun loa, the spirit of communication and the crossroad

L'envoi morts. The sending of a death spirit, one of the most potent of the dark acts in the repertoire of the bokor

Leopard Society. The secret society of the Efik of Old Calabar

Loa. The deities of the Vodoun faith

Loco. A Vodoun loa, the spirit of vegetation

Loup garou. The werewolf. The flying queen, or *reine voltige*, of the Bizango is said to be a *loup garou.*

Lutin. The spirit of a dead person who feels himself or herself mistreated or ignored and who returns to haunt the ungrateful descendants

Macandal, François. Mandingue slave born in Africa and believed to have been executed in 1758 for his part in a poison conspiracy; also, in contemporary Haiti, the name of a secret society

Macoute. Straw shoulder bag of the Haitian peasant

Madoule. The sacred coffin and symbol of the Bizango societies

Malfacteur. Evildoer, particularly an individual who specializes in powders

Maman. The mother, the largest of the three drums in the Rada battery

Mambo. Female Vodoun priestess

Manger moun. "To eat people," a euphemism for killing someone

Mapou. The sacred tree of the Vodoun religion, *Ceiba pentandra* of the botanical family Bombacaceae

Maroon. Fugitive slave, from Spanish root *cimarrón*, meaning "wild, unruly"

Mort bon Dieu. A call from God, a natural death

Myocardium. The middle and thickest layer of the heart wall

Mystères. The loa

Nam. Generic term derived from the French *âme*, or soul, and referring to the complete Vodoun soul, including *gros bon ange*, *ti bon ange*, and the other spiritual components

N'âme. The spirit of the flesh that allows each cell to function

Narcosis. A state of stupor, unconsciousness, or arrested activity produced by the influence of drugs.

Narcotic. A drug that dulls the senses and induces sleep

Nèg Guinée. A person of Africa, of the mythical homeland, of African descent

Obeah. A traditional religion of Jamaica which, like Haitian Voudon, is principally a distillation of West African beliefs and practices

Ogoun. A Vodoun loa, the spirit of fire, war, and the metallurgical elements; the blacksmith god

Ophthalmia. Severe inflammation of the eye or of the conjuntiva or deeper structures of the eye

Ordeal poison. A generic term used to describe the toxins employed by numerous indigenous groups throughout Africa as a means of determining guilt or innocence in traditional judicial proceedings. In many instances the folk preparations were also used as an instrument of execution.

Paquets Congo. A small sacred bundle containing magical ingredients that serves to protect a person against illness or evil; the closest object there is to the notorious and often misrepresented "voodoo doll"

Parasympathetic nervous system. The craniosacral portion of the autonomic nervous system

Parenteral. Absorption of a drug not through the alimentary canal, but rather by administration through some other route, as subcutaneous, intramuscular, intravenous, etc.

Paresthesia. An abnormal sensation, as of prickling of the skin

Percutaneous. Performed through the skin

Peristyle. The roofed, usually unwalled area where most ceremonies occur

Petro. A group of Vodoun loa traditionally said to be of American origin, now increasingly believed to be derived from Congolese rites

Pharmacology. The science of drugs and the study of the reactions and properties of drugs

Pharmacopoeia. A book describing drugs and their medicinal applications, or more generally a term used to describe the stock of drugs, medicinal or otherwise, possessed by a particular social group

Physostigmine. An alkaloid ($C_{15}H_{21}N_3O_2$) usually obtained from the ripe, dried seed of *Physostigma venenosum*. It is a cholinergic that functions as an anticholinesterase.

Pierre tonnerre. The thunderstones, said to be created by the spirits and thus imbued with mystical healing powers

Plaçage. A socially, if not legally, sanctioned relationship that brings with it a recognized set of sexual and economic obligations for both man and woman; a customary form of common-law marriage practiced for reasons of choice and economic necessity by the majority of the Haitian peasantry

Poro. A secret society among the Mende of Sierra Leone

Poteau mitan. The centerpost of the peristyle and the axis along which the loa rise to enter the ceremonies

Poudre (poud). Magical powder

Pouin (pwin). Magical protective power or force summoned to execute the will of the houngan

Président. The highest position below that of the emperor within the Bizango societies. Member of the Groupe d'État-Majeur

Pruritogenic. Capable of causing or tending to cause itching

Psychoactive. Designates a drug that has a specific effect on the mind

Psychogenic. Of intrapsychic origin; having an emotional, psychological origin

Psychopharmacology. The study of the actions of drugs on the mind

Psychotomimetic. A drug that produces manifestations resembling those of psychosis including visual hallucinations, distortions of perception, and schizophrenic behavior

Psychotropic. Exerting an effect on the mind, usually employed for drugs that affect the mental state

Pulmonary edema. An abnormal accumulation of fluid in the lungs

Purgative. Cathartic, particularly one that stimulates peristaltic action or that causes evacuation of the bowels

Rada. Vodoun rite; a body of loa, songs, and dances of Dahomean origin. Name derived from the town of Arada in Dahomey (now Benin)

Rara. Spring festival characterized by processions associated with particular hounfour or Bizango societies

Reine. The queen—high-ranking female position in the Bizango societies. *Première reine*, the first queen, is a member of the Groupe d'État-Majeur. Below her are the *deuxième reine* (second queen), *troisième reine* (third queen), *reine drapeau* (flag queen).

Reine voltige. The flying queen; also conceived of as a *loup garou*, or werewolf. The four *reines voltiges* carry the sacred coffin during the formal Bizango processions.

Saint Domingue. The French colony that later became Haiti

Sans Poel. Term used to refer to the secret societies; sometimes used interchangeably with Bizango, but more properly refers to the members of the Bizango, not the rite itself

Saponin. A group of glycosides widely distributed in plants and characterized in part by their property of forming a durable foam when their watery solutions are shaken

Sapotoxin. Any of various toxic saponins

Séance. The term used to describe the nocturnal gatherings of the Bizango

Seconde. The second or middle drum in the Rada battery of three

Secrétaire. The secretary; rank of the Bizango society

Section rurale. The fundamental administrative unit of local government in rural Haiti

Sentinel. The sentinel; rank of the Bizango society; the guard or scout who moves ahead of the processions and secures the entryway into the Bizango ceremonies

Servi loa. The term used by Vodoun acolytes to refer to their faith, "to serve the loa"

Serviteur. One who serves the loa

Sobo. Vodoun loa, the spirit of thunder

Société. A hounfour and its members, not to be confused with Bizango society

Soldat. The lowest rank in the Bizango society

Stomatitus. Inflamation of the oral mucosa due to local or systemic factors

Subcutaneous. Beneath the skin, as in subcutaneous injections

Superviseur. Rank of the Bizango society; said to be responsible for conveying messages between different society leaders in different regions of the country

Sympathetic nervous system. The thoracolumbar portion of the autonomic nervous system

Tetrodotoxin. A highly lethal neurotoxin ($C_{11}H_{17}N_3O_3$) present in numerous marine fish as well as other unrelated organisms. Ingestion results in malaise, dizziness, and tingling about the mouth, which may precede ataxia convulsions, respiratory paralysis, and death.

Thyrotoxicosis. A morbid condition resulting from overactivity of the thyroid gland

Ti bon ange. That aspect of the Vodoun soul said to be responsible for creating a person's character, willpower, and individuality

Ti Guinée. A child of Guinée, the mythical homeland; also used to refer to a member or offspring of the Vodoun society

Tonnelle. A thatch or corrugated tin roof improvised in the absence of a complete peristyle; a canopy beneath which ceremonies and dances occur

Tonton Macoute. From ton ton, or uncle, and macoute, the straw shoulder bag of the peasant. Name for the independent security forces established by François Duvalier

Topically active. Designates a chemical or pharmaceutical substance that may be applied effectively to the skin

Toussaint L'Ouverture. Former slave, revolutionary leader, general, and liberator, historically perceived as the Simon Bolívar of Haiti. He was betrayed by Napoleon and deported to France, where he died in 1803.

Uremia. Toxic condition caused by the presence in the blood of waste products normally eliminated in the urine

Vermifuge. An agent that expels worms or intestinal animal parasites

Vesication. The process of blistering

Ve-ve. Symbolic designs drawn on the ground with flour or ashes and intended to invoke the loa. Each spirit has a characteristic *ve-ve.*

Vlinblindingue. A name of a secret society (also vinbrindingue)

VNS. Acronym for the Volunteers for the National Security, the militia established by François Duvalier to protect his regime

Vodoun. The theological principles and the religious practice of the Haitian traditional society

Wanga. A magical charm used for selfish or malevolent intent, the magical weapon par excellence

Wété Mo Nan Dlo. "To take the dead from the water"; the ritual whereby the *ti bon ange* is reclaimed by the living and given a new form

Zombi astral. A zombie of the *ti bon ange*; an aspect of the soul that may be transmuted at the will of the one who possesses it

Zombi cadavre. The *corps cadavre, gros bon ange,* and the other spiritual components. A zombie of the flesh that can be made to work

Zombi éfface. Another term for the *zombi astral,* a zombie of the *ti bon ange*

Zombi jardin. A working zombie, a *zombi corps cadavre*

Zombi savanne. A former zombie, one who has been through the earth, become a zombie, and then returned to the state of the living

BIBLIOGRAPHY

Abel, J. J., and David I. Macht. 1911. "The Poisons of the Tropical Toad *Bufo aqua.*" *Journal of the American Medical Association* 56:1531–36.

Agiri, B. 1972. "The Ogboni among the Oyo-Yoruba." *Lagos Notes and Records* 3 (11): 50–59.

Akashi, T. 1880. "Experiences with Fugu Poisoning." *Iji Shimbum* 27:19–23.

Alger, N. 1974. "Comments." *Current Anthropology* 15 (2): 152–53.

Anand, B. K., and G. S. Chhina. 1960. "Investigations on Yogis Claiming to Stop Their Heart Beats." *Indian Journal of Medical Research* 49 (1): 82–89.

Anand, B. K., G. S. Chhina, and B. Singh. 1961. "Studies on Shri Ramanand Yogi during His Stay in an Airtight Box." *Indian Journal of Medical Research* 49 (1): 82–89.

Anonymous. 1884. "Burying Cholera Patients Alive." *The Lancet* 2 (23 August): 329.

Anonymous. 1898. "Premature Burial." *Journal of the American Medical Association* 29 (January 30): 273–74.

Anonymous. 1984. "Puffers, Gourmands, and Zombification." *The Lancet* (2 June): 1220–21.

Arensberg, C. 1954. "The Community Study Method." *American Journal of Sociology* 60 (2): 109–204.

———. 1960. "Discussion of Manner's Methods of Community Analysis in the Caribbean." In *Caribbean Studies*, pp. 92–98. *See* Rubin 1960.

———. 1961. "The Community as Object and Sample." *American Anthropologist* 63:241–64.

Asprey, G. F., and P. Thornton. 1953. "Medicinal Plants of Jamaica. Part 1." *West Indian Medical Journal* 2:233–52.

———. 1954. "Medicinal Plants of Jamaica. Part 2." *West Indian Medical Journal* 3:17–41.

———. 1955a. "Medicinal Plants of Jamaica. Part 3." *West Indian Medical Journal* 4:69–82.

———. 1955b. "Medicinal Plants of Jamaica. Part 4." *West Indian Medical Journal* 4:145–68.

Audain, J. J. 1886. Editorial in *Le Peuple* (23 January), Port-au-Prince.

Ayensu, E. S. 1978. *Medicinal Plants of West Africa.* Algonac, Mich.: Reference Publications.

———. 1981. *Medicinal Plants of the West Indies.* Algonac, Mich.: Reference Publications.

Bagnis, R., F. Berglund, P. S. Elias, G. J. Van Esch, B. W. Halstead, and

K. Kojima. 1970. "Problems of Toxicants in Marine Food Products. 1. Marine Biotoxin." *Bulletin of the World Health Organization* 42:69–88.

Barber, T. X. 1961. "Death by Suggestion: A Critical Note." *Psychosomatic Medicine* 23:153–55.

Barker, H. D., and W. S. Dardeau. 1930. *Flore d'Haiti*. Service technique du Department de l'Agriculture et de l'Enseignement Professionnel, Port-au-Prince.

Barker, H. D., W. S. Dardeau, A. Gomez, F. Kebreau, A. Severe, and J. G. Sylvain. 1930. *Identification des plantes d'Haiti pars leurs noms creole*. Bulletin no. 18, Department de Botanique, Port-au-Prince.

Barker, J. C. 1965. "Scared to Death." *British Medical Journal* (4 September): 591.

Barrau, J. 1957. "Le *Duboisia myoporoides R. Br.* plante médicinale de la Nouvelle-Caledonie." *Journal d'Agriculture Tropical et Botanique Appliqué* 4 (9/10): 453.

Barton, D., J. H. Fishbein, and F. W. Stevens. 1972. "Psychological Death: An Adaptive Response to Life Threatening Illness." *Psychiatry in Medicine* 3:227–36.

Bascom, W. 1939. "Secret Societies, Religious Cult Groups, and Kinship Units among the West African Yoruba." Ph.D. diss., Northwestern University.

Baskett, J. 1971 (orig. 1818). *History of the Island of St. Domingo from Its First Discovery by Columbus to the Present Period*. Westport, Conn.: Negro Universities Press.

Bastide, R. 1960. *Les religions Africaines au Brésil*. Paris: Presses universitaires de France.

Bastien, R. 1961. "Haitian Rural Family Organization." *Social and Economic Studies* 10:478–510.

———. 1966. "Vodoun and Politics in Haiti." In *Religion and Politics in Haiti*. Washington, D.C.: Institute for Cross-Cultural Research.

Beaglehole, J. C. 1961. *The Journals of Captain Cook*. Vol. 2, *Voyages of the Resolution and Adventure, 1772–1775*, pp. 534–35. Cambridge: Cambridge University Press.

Bellman, B. 1975. *Village of Curers and Assassins*. Paris: Mouton.

Benson, J. 1956. "Tetraodon (Blowfish Poisoning)." *Journal of Forensic Sciences* 1 (4): 119–25.

Berlin, B. 1974. *Principles of Tzeltal Plant Classification*. New York: Academic Press.

Berlin, B., D. Breedlove, and P. Raven. 1966. "Folk Taxonomies and Biological Classification." *Science* 154:273–75.

———. 1973. "General Principles of Classification and Nomenclature in Folk Biology." *American Anthropologist* 75 (2): 214–42.

Beverley, R. 1705. "The History and Present State of Virginia." In *Sacred Narcotics of the New World Indians*, pp. 130–32. *See* Schleiffer 1973.

Bierer, J. 1976. "Zombi." *International Journal of Social Psychiatry* 22 (3): 200–201.

Bonde, L. C. von. 1948. "Mussel and Fish Poisoning. 2. Fish Poisoning (Ichthyotoxism)." *South African Medical Journal* 22:761–62.

Bonsal, S. 1912. *The American Mediterranean*. New York: Moffat, Yard and Company.

Borison, H. L., L. E. McCarthy, W. E. Clark, and U. Radhakrishnan. 1963. "Vomiting, Hypothermia, and Respiratory Paralysis Due to Tetrodotoxin (Puffer Poison in the Cat)." *Toxicology and Applied Pharmacology* 5:350–57.

Bouder, H., A. Cavallo, and M. J. Bouder. 1962. "Poissons veneneux et ichtyosarcotoxisme." *Bulletin de l'Institut Océanique Monaco* 1240:1–66.

Bourguignon, E. 1959. "The Persistence of Folk Belief: Some Notes on Cannibalism and Zombies in Haiti." *Journal of American Folklore* 72 (283): 36–47.

———. 1976. *Possession*. San Francisco: Chandler and Sharp.

———. 1982. "Ritual and Myth in Haitian Voodoo." In *African Religious Groups and Beliefs*. Ottenberg 1982.

Boyé, L. 1911. "Intoxications et empoisonnements." In *Traité de pathologique, exotique, clinique et thérapeutique*, edited by C. Grail and A. Clarac, p. 387. Paris: n.p.

Brown, J. 1971 (orig. 1837). *The History and Present Condition of St. Domingo*. 2 vols. London: Frank Cass.

Brown, P. 1951. "Patterns of Authority in West Africa." *Africa* 21 (4): 261–78.

Bruhier-d'Ablaincourt, J. J. 1742. *Dissertation sur l'incertitude des signes de la mort et de l'abus des enterrements et des embauments précipités*. Paris: n.p.

Brutus, T. C., and A. V. Pierre-Noel. 1960. *Les plantes et les légumes d'Haiti qui guérissent*. 3 vols. Port-au-Prince: Imprimerie de l'Etat.

Burkhill, I. H. 1935. *A Dictionary of the Economy Products of the Malay Peninsula*. London: Crown Agents for the Colonies.

Burrell, R. J. W. 1963. "The Possible Bearing of Curse Death and Other Factors in Bantu Culture on the Etiology of Myocardial Infarction." In *The Etiology of Myocardial Infarction*, edited by T. N. James and J. W. Keys, pp. 95–100. Boston: Little, Brown and Company.

Butt-Thompson, F. W. 1929. *West African Secret Societies*. London: H. F. and G. Witherby.

Cabrera, L. "El Monte." Manuscript, n.d.

Cannon, W. B. 1942. "Voodoo Death." *American Anthropologist* 44:169–81.

Cappannari S., B. Rau, H. Abram, and D. Buchanan. 1975. "Voodoo in the General Hospital." *Journal of the American Medical Association* 232 (9): 938–40.

Carneiro, R. 1970. "Hunting and Hunting Magic among the Amahuaca." *Ethology* 10:331–41.

———. 1978. "The Knowledge and Use of Rain Forest Trees by the Kuikuru Indians of Central Brazil." In *The Nature and Status of Ethnobotany*, pp. 201–16. *See* Ford 1978.

Carnochan, F. G., and Adamson, H. C. 1938. *L'Empire des serpents*. Paris: Payot.

Carré. 1845. *De la mort apparente*. Thèse de Paris.

Castaneda, C. 1972. *The Teachings of Don Juan: A Yaqui Way of Knowledge*. New York: Ballantine Books.

Castellanos, J. "Historia del nuevo reino de Granado." In *Sacred Narcotics of the New World Indians*. *See* Schleiffer 1973.

Cawte, J. 1983. "Voodoo Death and Dehydration." *American Anthropologist* 83:420–42.

Chambers, F. 1983. *Haiti*. World Bibliographic Series, vol. 39. Oxford: Clio Press.

Chen, K. K., and H. Jensen. 1929. "A Pharmacognostic Study of Ch'an Su, the Dried Venom of the Chinese Toad." *Journal of the American Pharmaceutical Association* 23:244–51.

Chesneaux, J. 1971. *Secret Societies in China in the Nineteenth and Twentieth Centuries*. London: Heinemann.

Chilton, W. S., J. Bigwood, and R. E. Jensen. 1979. "Psilocin, Bufotenin, and Serotenin: Historical and Biosynthetic Observations. *Journal of Psychedelic Drugs* 11 (1–2): 61–69.

Clark, W. G., and B. A. Coldwell. 1973. "The Hypothermic Effect of Tetrodotoxin in the Unanaesthetized Cat." *Journal of Physiology* 230:477–92.

Clark, W. G., and J. M. Lipton. 1974. "Complementary Lowering of the Behavioral and Physiological Thermoregulatory Set-Points by TTX and Saxitoxin in the Cat." *Journal of Physiology* 238:181–91.

Clavigero, F. T. 1937. *The History of (Lower) California*. Translated and edited by S. E. Lake and A. A. Gray. Stanford: Stanford University Press.

Clune, F. J. 1973. "A Comment on Voodoo Deaths." *American Anthropologist* 75:312.

Coe, M. D. 1971. "The Shadow of the Olmecs." *Horizon* (Autumn): 66–74.

Collomb, H. 1976. "Death as a Determinant of Psychosomatic Syndromes in Africa." *Journal of the American Academy of Psychoanalysis* 4 (2): 227–36.

Comhaire, J. 1955. "The Haitian 'Chef de Section.' " *American Anthropologist* 57:620–24.

Comhaire-Sylvain, S. 1958. "Courtship, Marriage, and Plasaj at Kenscoff, Haiti." *Social and Economic Studies* 7:210–33.

———. 1961. "The Household at Kenscoff, Haiti." *Social and Economic Studies* 10:192–222.

Conklin, H. C. 1954. "The Relation of Hanunoo Culture to the Plant World." Ph.D. diss., Yale University.

Cooke, R. G. 1979. "Los impactos de las comunidades agricolas sobre los ambientes del tropico estacional: datos del Panama prehistorico." *Actas de IV Simposium Internacional de Ecologio Tropical* 3:917–73.

———. 1981. "Los habitos alimentarios de los indigenas precolombinos de Panama." *Academia Panamena de Medicina y Cirugia* 6 (1): 65–89.

Cottrell, J. E., J. Hartung, C. Capuano, S. Mermelstein, J. P. Griffin, and B. Shwiry. 1983. "Intracranial Pressure and Cerebral Blood Flow during Tetrodotoxin-Induced Hypotension." *Anesthesiology* 59 (3): A69.

Courlander, H. 1960. *The Drum and the Hoe: Life and Lore of the Haitian People.* Berkeley: University of California Press.

———. 1973. *Haiti Singing.* New York: Cooper Square Publications.

Courlander, H., and R. Bastien. 1966. *Religion and Politics in Haiti.* Washington, D.C.: Institute for Cross-Cultural Research.

Craige, J. H. 1933. *Black Baghdad.* New York: Minton, Balch and Company.

———. 1934. *Cannibal Cousins.* New York: Minton, Balch and Company.

Curtin, P. 1969. *The Atlantic Slave Trade: A Census.* Madison: University of Wisconsin Press.

Dalziel, J. M. 1937. *The Useful Plants of West Tropical Africa.* London: Crown Agents for the Colonies.

Daraul, A. 1961. *A History of Secret Societies.* New York: Citadel Press.

Davis, E. W. 1983a. "The Ethnobiology of the Haitian Zombi." *Journal of Ethnopharmacology* 9 (1): 85–104.

———. 1983b. "Preparation of the Haitian Zombi Poison." Harvard University, *Botanical Museum Leaflets* 29 (2): 139–49.

———. 1983c. "The Ethnobiology of the Haitian Zombi—on the Pharmacology of Black Magic." *Caribbean Review* 12 (3): 18–22.

———. 1983d. "Sacred Plants of the San Pedro Cult." Harvard University, *Botanical Museum Leaflets* 29 (4): 367–86.

———. 1985. *The Serpent and the Rainbow.* New York: Simon and Schuster.

Davis, J. H., and R. K. Wright. 1980. "The Very Sudden Cardiac Death Syndrome: A Conceptual Model for Pathologists." *Human Pathology* 11:117–21.

Debbash, Y. 1961. "La marronage: essai sur la désertion de l'esclave Antillais." *L'Année Sociologique* 3:2–112, 117–95.

———. 1979. "Le Maniel: Further Notes." In *Maroon Societies*, pp. 143–48. *See* Price 1979.

Debien, G. 1962. "Plantations et esclaves à Saint Domingue: Sucrerie Cottineau." *Notes d'Histoire Coloniale* 66:9–82.

———. 1966. "Le marronage aux Antilles françaises au XVIII siècle." *Caribbean Studies* 6 (3): 3–44.

———. 1979. "Marronage in the French Caribbean." In *Maroon Societies*, pp. 107–34. *See* Price 1979.

DeCandolle, A. 1885. *Origin of Cultivated Plants*. New York: D. Appleton.

Delbeau, J. C. 1969. "La médicine populaire en Haiti." Ph.D. diss., Université de Bordeaux.

Denis, L. 1963. "Médicine populaire." *Bulletin de Bureau d'Ethnologie d'Haiti* 4 (29): 37–39.

Denis, L., and D. F. Duvalier. 1936. "La civilisation haitiene: notre mentalité est-elle africaine ou gallo-latine?" *Revue Anthropologique* 10–12:353–73.

———. 1944. "L'évolution stadiale du vodou." *Bulletin de Bureau d'Ethnologie d'Haiti* 3:9–32.

Dépestre, R. 1971. *Change*. Violence II, no. 9. Paris: Seuil.

Deren, M. 1953. *Divine Horsemen: The Living Gods of Haiti*. London: Thames and Hudson.

Desmangles, L. G. 1977. "Baptismal Rites: Religious Symbiosis of Vodoun and Catholicism in Haiti." In *Liturgy and Cultural Religious Tradition*, edited by H. Schmidt and D. Power, pp. 51–61. New York: Seabury Press.

———. 1979. "The Vodoun Way of Death: Cultural Symbiosis of Roman Catholicism and Vodoun in Haiti." *Journal of Religious Thought* 36 (1): 5–20.

Dewisme, C. H. 1957. *Les zombis*. Paris: Edition Bernard Grasset.

Diederich, B. 1983. "On the Nature of Zombi Existence." *Caribbean Review* 12 (3): 14–17, 43–46.

Diederich, B., and A. Burt. 1967. *Papa Doc*. New York: McGraw-Hill.

Dieterlen, G. 1973. *La notion de personne en Afrique noire*. Paris: Editions C.N.R.S., no. 544.

Dobkin de Rios, M. 1974. "The Influence of Psychotropic Flora and Fauna on the Maya Religion." *Current Anthropology* 15:147–52.

Donner, E. 1938. "Togba, a Woman's Society in Liberia." *Africa* 11:109–11.

Dorjahn, V. 1982. "The Initiation and Training of Temne Poro Members." In *African Religious Groups and Beliefs*, pp. 35–62. *See* Ottenberg 1982.

Dorsainvil, J. C. 1934. *Histoire d'Haiti*. Port-au-Prince: Editions Henri Deschamps.

———. 1975. *Vodou et neurose*. Port-au-Prince: Editions Fardin.

Douglas, M., ed. 1972. *Witchcraft, Confessions, and Accusations*. London: Tavistock.

Douyon, E. 1965. "La crise de possession dans le Vaudou haitien." Ph.D. diss., University of Montreal.

Douyon, L. 1980. "Les zombis dans le contexte vodou et haitien." *Haiti Santé* 2 (1): 19–23.

Down, R. J. 1969. "The Medicial Significance of Shellfish and Blowfish Neurotoxins (Saxitoxin and Tetrodotoxin) as Suggested by Tests in Killifish." In *Food-Drugs from the Sea*, pp. 327–43. Proceedings of the Marine Technology Society.

Dubois, C. G. 1908. "The Religion of the Luiseño Indians of California." In *University of California Publications in American Archaeology and Ethnology*. Vol. 8, no. 5. Berkeley: University of California Press.

Dufra, E., G. Loison, and B. Holmstedt. 1976. "*Duboisia myoporoides*: Native Antidote against Ciguatera Poisoning." *Toxicon* 14:55–64.

Duncan, C. 1951. "A Case of Toadfish Poisoning." *Medical Journal of Australia* 2 (20): 160–67.

Dunham, K. 1969. *Island Possessed*. Garden City, N.J.: Doubleday.

Dunstheimer, G. 1972. "Some Religious Aspects of Secret Societies." In *Popular Movements and Secret Societies in China*, edited by J. Chesneaux, pp. 23–28. Stanford: Stanford University Press.

Duvalier, F. 1968. *Oeuvres essentielles: Elements d'une doctrine*. Vol. 1. Port-au-Prince: Presses Nationales d'Haiti.

Eastwell, H. D. 1982. "Voodoo Death and the Mechanism for Dispatch of the Dying in East Arnhem, Australia." *American Anthropologist* 84:5–18.

Editorial. 1971. "Scared to Death?" *Annals of Internal Medicine* 74:789–90.

Eisenbruch, M. 1983. " 'Wind Illness' or Somatic Depression?: A Case Study in Psychiatric Anthropology." *British Journal of Psychiatry* 143:323–26.

Eldridge, J. 1975. "Bush Medicine in the Exumas and Long Island Bahamas: A Field Study." *Economic Botany* 29 (4): 307–32.

Eliade, M. 1959. *Initiation rites, société sécretes, naissance mystique: Essai su quelques types d'initiation*. Paris: Gallimard.

Elkington, A. R., P. R. Steele, and D. D. Yun. 1965. "Scared to Death." *British Medical Journal* (7 August): 363.

Emboden, W. 1972. *Narcotic Plants*. New York: Macmillan.

Engel, G. L. 1968. "A Life Setting Conducive to Illness." *Annals of Internal Medicine* 69 (2): 293–300.

————. 1971. "Sudden and Rapid Death during Psychological Stress—Folklore or Folk Wisdom?" *Annals of Internal Medicine* 74:771–82.

————. 1976. "Psychological Factors in Instantaneous Cardiac Death." *New England Journal of Medicine* 294:664–65.

Evans-Pritchard, E. E. 1937. *Witchcraft, Oracles, and Magic among the Azande*. Oxford: Clarendon Press.

————. 1965. *Theories of Primitive Religion*. Oxford: Oxford University Press.

Fabing, H. S., and J. R. Hawkins. 1956. "Intravenous Bufotenin Injection in the Human Being." *Science* 123:886–87.

Faine, J. 1937. *Philologie creole*. Port-au-Prince: n.p.

Farmer, A., and W. F. Falkowski. 1985. "Maggot in the Salt, the Snake Factor, and the Treatment of a Typical Psychosis in West African Women." *British Journal of Psychiatry* 146:446–48.

Farnsworth, N. R., and R. W. Morris. 1976. "Higher Plants—the Sleeping Giant of Drug Development." *American Journal of Pharmacy* 147 (2): 46–52.

Fletcher, M. R. 1895. *One Thousand Buried Alive by Their Best Friends*. Boston: n.p.

Flier, J., M. Edwards, J. W. Daly, and C. Myers. 1980. "Widespread Occurrence in Frogs and Toads of Skin Compounds Interacting with the Ouabain Site of Na+, K+ ATPase." *Science* 208:503–5.

Fluckiger, F. A., and D. Hanbury. 1879. *Pharmacographia: A History of the Principal Drugs of Vegetable Origin Met within Great Britain and British India*. London: Macmillan.

Folkard, R. 1884. *Plant Lore, Legends and Lyrics*. London: n.p.

Fontenelle, J. 1834. *Recherches médico-légales sur l'incertitude des signes de la mort*. Paris: n.p.

Ford, R. I., ed. 1978. *The Nature and Status of Ethnobotany*. Museum of Anthropology, no. 67. Ann Arbor.

Forde, D., ed. 1956. *The Efik Traders of Old Calabar*. London: Oxford University Press.

Forster, G. 1777. *A Voyage Round the World*. London: White, Robson, Elinsley, Robinson.

Fouchard, J. 1981. *The Haitian Maroons*. New York: Edward W. Blyden Press.

Franck, H. A. 1920. *Roaming through the West Indies*. New York: Blue Ribbon Books.

Franklin, J. 1970 (orig. 1828). *The Present State of Hayti*. Westport, Conn.: Negro Universities Press.

Frazer, J. G. 1927. *The Golden Bough*. New York: Macmillan.

Frobenius, L. 1913. *The Voice of Africa*. 2 vols. London: Hutchinson and Company.

Fry, A. 1965. "Scared to Death." *British Medical Journal* (4 September): 591.

Fuhrman, F. A. 1967. "Tetrodotoxin." *Scientific American* 217 (2): 61–71.

Fukuda, T. 1937. "Puffer Fish Poison and the Method of Prevention." *Nippon Iji Shimpo* 762:1417–21.

———. 1951. "Violent Increase of Cases of Puffer Poisoning." *Clinics and Studies* 29 (2): 1762.

Fukuda, T., and I. Tani. 1937a. "Records of Puffer Poisonings. Report 1." *Kyushu University Medical News* 11 (1): 7–13.

———. 1937b. "Records of Puffer Poisonings. Report 2." *Iji Eisei* 7 (26): 905–7.

———. 1941. "Records of Puffer Poisonings. Report 3." *Nippon Igaku Oyobi Kenko Hoken* (3258): 7–13.

Furst, P. 1972. "Symbolism and Psychopharmacology: The Toad as Earth

Mother in Indian America." In *XII Mesa Redonda-Religion en Meso-america*. Mexico: Sociedad Mexicana de Antropologia.

———. 1974. "Comments." *Current Anthropology* 15 (2): 154.

———, ed. 1972. *Flesh of the Gods: The Ritual Use of Hallucinogens*. New York: Praeger.

Gaillard, C. 1923. "Recherches sur les poissons représentés dans quelques tombeaux egyptiens de l'Ancien empire." *Mémoires de l'Institut Français d'Archéologie Orientale* 51:97.

Gaillard, R. 1982. *Charlemagne Peralte le Caco*. Port-au-Prince: Imprimerie Le Natal.

Gannal, F. 1890. *Mort apparente et mort réelle*. Paris: Muzard et fils.

Garcia Barriga, H. 1974. *Flora medicinal de Colombia*. Bogotá, Colombia: Instituto de Ciencias Naturales.

Gardner, W. J. 1873. *History of Jamaica from Its Discovery by Christopher Columbus to the Present Time*. London: E. Stock.

Githens, T. S. 1949. *Drug Plants of Africa*. African Handbook 8. Philadelphia: University of Pennsylvania Press.

Glascock, A. P. 1983. "Death Hastening Behavior: An Explanation of Eastwell's Thesis." *American Anthropologist* 85:417–20.

Gluckman, M. 1944. "The Logic of African Science and Witchcraft: An Appreciation of Evans-Pritchard's *Witchcraft Oracles and Magic among the Azande*." *Human Problems in British Central Africa* 1:61–71.

Goe, D. R., and B. W. Halstead. 1953. "A Preliminary Report of the Toxicity of the Gulf Puffer *Spheroides annulatus*." *California Fish and Game* 39:229–32.

Golden, K. M. 1977. "Voodoo in Africa and the United States." *Journal of Psychiatry* 134 (12): 1425–27.

Golin, S., and E. Larson. 1969. "An Antidotal Study on the Skin Extract of the Puffer Fish *Spheroides maculatus*." *Toxicon* 7:49–53.

Gomez, E. 1982. "Voodoo and Sudden Death: The Effects of Expectations on Health." *Transcultural Psychiatric Research Review* 19:75–92.

Gomez, E., and N. Carozos. 1981. "Was Hexing the Cause of Death?" *American Journal of Social Psychiatry* 1 (1): 50–52.

Gonsalves, A. D. 1907. "Peixes veneosos de Bahia." *Gazette Medical da Bahia* 38 (10): 441–52.

Goodman, L. S., and A. Gilman. 1970. *The Pharmacological Basis of Therapeutics*. 4th ed. London: Macmillan.

Greene, W. A., S. Goldstein, and A. J. Moss. 1972. "Psychosocial Aspects of Sudden Death." *Archives of Internal Medicine* 129:725–31.

Habekost, R. C., I. M. Fraser, and B. W. Halstead. 1955. "Observations on Toxic Marine Algae." *Journal of the Washington Academy of Science* 45 (4): 101–3.

Hadwen, W. R. 1905. *Premature Burial—and How It May Be Prevented*.

London: Swan Sonnenschein and Company.

Hall, R. B. 1929. "The Société Congo of the Ile à Gonave." *American Anthropologist* 31:685–700.

Hall, R. C. W., B. Pfefferbaum, E. R. Gardner, S. K. Stickney, and M. Perl. 1978. "Intoxication with Angel's Trumpet: Anticholinergic Delirium and Hallucinosis." *Journal of Psychedelic Drugs* 10 (3): 251–53.

Halstead, B. W. 1951. "Poisonous Fish—a Medical Military Problem." *Res. Rev. U.S. Navy NAVEXOS* (P-510): 10–16.

———. 1958. "Poisonous Fishes." *Public Health Report* 73:302–12.

———. 1978. *Poisonous and Venomous Marine Animals of the World*. Princeton, N.J.: Darwin Press.

Halstead, B. W., and N. C. Bunker. 1953. "The Effect of Commercial Canning Process upon Puffer Poisoning." *California Fish and Game* 39 (2): 219–28.

Halstead, B. W., and D. S. Schall. 1955. "A Report on the Poisonous Fishes Captured during the Woodrow G. Krieger Expedition to the Galapagos Islands." In *Essays in the Natural Sciences in Honor of Captain Allan Hancock*, pp. 147–72. Los Angeles: University of Southern California Press.

Hamblin, N. 1979. "The Magic Toads of Cozumal." Paper presented at the 44th annual meeting of the Society for American Archaeology, Vancouver, B.C.

Hamburger, J. 1966. "Some General Considerations." Paper delivered at the Ethics in Medical Progress Ciba Foundation Symposium, Churchill.

Hansen, H. A. 1978. *The Witch's Garden*. Santa Cruz, Calif.: Unity Press.

Harley, G. W. 1944. *Notes on the Poro in Liberia*. Peabody Museum Papers, vol. 19, no. 2. Cambridge: Harvard University.

Harner, M. 1973. *Hallucinogens and Shamanism*. Oxford: Oxford University Press.

Harris, M. 1979. *Cultural Materialism*. New York: Vintage Books.

Harris, W. T., and H. Sawyer. 1968. *The Springs of Mende Belief and Conduct*. Freetown: Sierra Leone University Press.

Hartmann, F. 1895. *Buried Alive*. Boston: n.p.

Hashimoto, Y. 1979. *Marine Toxins and Other Bioactive Marine Metabolites*. Tokyo: Japan Scientific Societies Press.

Hedberg, I., O. Hedberg, P. Madati, K. Mshigeni, E. N. Mshir, and G. Samuelsson. 1983. "Inventory of Plants Used in Traditional Medicine in Tanzania. II. Plants of the Families *Pilleniaceae-Opiliaceae*." *Journal of Ethnopharmacology* 9:105–28.

Hellmuth, N. M. 1974. "Comments." *Current Anthropology* 15 (2): 155–56.

Herbert, C. C. 1961. "Life-Influencing Interactions." In *The Physiology of Emotions*, edited by A. Simon, C. C. Herbert, and R. Strauss, p. 190. Springfield, Ill.: Charles C. Thomas.

Herskovits, M. J. 1938. *Dahomey*. 2 vols. New York: J. J. Augustin.

————. 1975 (orig. 1937). *Life in a Haitian Village*. New York: Alfred A. Knopf.

Hill, A. F. 1952. *Economic Botany*. New York: McGraw-Hill.

Hobsbawn, E. J. 1959. *Primitive Rebels: Studies in Archaic Forms of Social Movements in the Nineteenth and Twentieth Centuries*. Manchester, Eng.: Manchester University Press.

Holmstedt, B. 1972. "The Ordeal Bean of Old Calabar: The Pageant of *Physostigma venosum* in Medicine." In *Plants in the Development of Modern Medicine*, edited by T. Swain, pp. 303–60. Cambridge, Mass.: Harvard University Press.

Holmstedt, B., and J. G. Bruhn. 1983. "Ethnopharmacology: A Challenge." *Journal of Ethnopharmacology* 8:251–56.

Hooker, J. D. 1855. *Himalayan Journals: Notes of a Naturalist in Bengal, the Sikkim and Nepal Himalayas, the Khasia Mountains*. London: John Murray.

Horowitz, M. M. 1971. *Peoples and Cultures of the Caribbean*. New York: Natural History Press.

Horton, R. 1967a. "African Traditional Thought and Western Science. Part 1." *Africa* 37 (1): 50–71.

————. 1967b. "African Traditional Thought and Western Science. Part 2." *Africa* 37 (1): 155–87.

Hunter, J. D. W. 1965. "Scared to Death." *British Medical Journal* (18 September): 701.

Hurbon, L. 1972. *Dieu dans le Vaudou haitien*. Paris: Payot.

————. 1979. "Sorcellerie et pouvoir en Haiti." *Archives de Science Sociales des Religions* 48 (1): 43–52.

Hurston, Z. N. 1981. *Tell My Horse*. Berkeley, Calif.: Turtle Island.

Huxley, F. 1966. *The Invisibles*. New York: McGraw-Hill.

Icard, S. 1897. *La mort réelle et la mort apparente*. Paris: Alcan.

Ishihara, F. 1918. "Über die physiologischen Wirkungen des Fugutoxins." *Mitt. Med. Fak. Univ. Tokyo* 20:375–426.

Iwakawa, K., and S. Kimura. 1922. "Experimentelle Untersuchungen über die Wirkung des Tetrodontoxins." *Arch. Exp. Pathol. Pharmacol.* 93 (4–6): 305–31.

Jacques, C. 1945. "*Duboisia myoporoides*." *Revue Agricole*, Chambre d'Agriculture, Nouvelle Calédonie (January): 5408–9.

Jahn, J. 1961. *Muntu: An Outline of the New African Culture*. New York: Grove Press.

James, C. L. R. 1963. *The Black Jacobins*. New York: Random House.

Jedrej, M. C. 1976a. "Structural Aspects of a West African Secret Society." *Journal of Anthropological Research* 32 (3): 234–45.

————. 1976b. "Medicine, Fetish, and Secret Society in a West African Culture." *Africa* 46 (3): 247–57.

Johnson, N. A. 1974. "Zombies and Other Problems: Theory and Method in Research on Bilingualism." *Language Learning: A Journal of Applied Linguistics* 24:105–33.

Jones, G. I. 1956. "The Political Organisation of Old Calabar." In *The Efik Traders of Old Calabar*, pp. 116–57. *See* Forde 1956.

Kaempfer, E. 1906. *The History of Japan (1690–1693).* Translated by J. Scheuchzer. Glasgow: Maclehose.

Kao, C. Y. 1966. "Tetrodotoxin, Saxitoxin, and Their Significance in the Study of Excitation Phenomenon." *Pharmacological Reviews* 18 (2): 997–1049.

————. 1983. "New Perspectives on the Interaction of Tetrodotoxin and Saxitoxin with Excitable Membrane." *Toxicon*, suppl. 3: 211–19.

Kao, C. Y., T. Suzuki, A. L. Kleinhaus, and M. J. Siegman. 1967. "Vasomotor and Respiratory Depressant Action of TTX and Saxitoxin." *Archives Internationale de Pharmacodynamie et de Thérapie.* 165 (2): 438–50.

Kao, C. Y., and S. E. Walker. 1982. "Active Groups of Saxitoxin and Tetrodotoxin as Deduced from Actions of Saxitoxin Analogues on Frog Muscle and Squid Axon." *Journal of Physiology* 323:619–37.

Karsten, R. 1935. *The Headhunters of Western Amazonas.* Helsingfors Societas Scientiarum Fennica. Commentationes Humanarum Litterarum, vol. 2, no. 1.

Kastenbaum, R., and R. Aisenberg. 1972. *The Psychology of Death.* New York: Springer Publications.

Katz, J. J. 1973. "Interpretive Semantics Meets the Zombies: A Discussion of the Controversy about Deep Structure." *Foundation of Language* 9 (4): 549–96.

Kawakubo, Y., and K. Kikuchi. 1942. "Testing Fish Poisons on Animals and Report on a Human Case of Fish Poisoning in the South Seas." *Kaigun Igakukai Zasshi* 31 (8): 30–34.

Kelley, T. 1983. *The Zombie.* New York: Samuel French.

Kennedy, A. B. 1982. "Ecce Bufo: The Toad in Nature and Olmec Iconography." *Current Anthropology* 23 (3): 273–90.

Kerboull, J. 1973. *Le vaudou-magie ou religion.* Paris: Editions Robert Laffont.

————. 1977. *Voodoo and Magic Practises.* N.p.: Barrie and Jenkins Communica.

Kiev, A. 1961. "Spirit-Possession in Haiti." *American Journal of Psychiatry* 118 (2): 133–38.

————. 1962. "Psychotherapy in Haitian Voodoo." *American Journal of Psychotherapy* 16 (3): 469–76.

————. 1972. *Transcultural Psychiatry.* New York: Free Press.

Kim, Y. H., G. Brown, H. S. Mosher, and F. A. Fuhrman. 1975. "Tetrodotoxin: Occurrence in Atelopid Frogs of Costa Rica." *Science* 189:151–52.

Kimura, S. 1927. "Zur Kenntnis der Wirkung des Tetrodongiftes." *Tohoku*
Journal of Experimental Medicine 9:41–65.

Kirk, R. 1974. "Zombies v. Materialists." *Aristotelian Society Supplementary*
48:135–52.

———. 1977. "Reply to Don Locke on Zombies and Materialism." *Mind*
86 (342): 262–64.

Knab, T. n.d.(a). "Narcotic Use of Toad Toxins in Southern Veracruz."
Manuscript.

———. n.d.(b). "The Life History of Mad Juan—a Case of Drug Induced
Schizophrenia." Manuscript.

Kristos, K. 1976. *Voodoo*. Philadelphia: J. P. Lippincott.

Lachman, S. J. 1982–83. "A Psychophysiological Interpretation of Voodoo
Illness and Voodoo Death." *Omega* 13 (4): 345–60.

Lacombe, R. 1977. *La république d'Haiti*. Paris: La Documentation Française.

Laguerre, M. 1973a. "The Place of Voodoo in the Social Structure of
Haiti." *Caribbean Quarterly* 19 (3): 36–50.

———. 1973b. "The Failure of Christianity among the Slaves in Haiti."
Freeing the Spirit 2 (4): 10–24.

———. 1974a. "Voodoo as Religion and Political Ideology." *Freeing the*
Spirit 3 (1): 23–28.

———. 1974b. "Ecological Approach to Voodoo." *Freeing the Spirit* 3 (1):
3–12.

———. 1976a. "Belair, Port-au-Prince: From Slave and Maroon Settle-
ment to Contemporary Black Ghetto." In *Afro-American Ethno-History in*
Latin America and the Caribbean, edited by N. E. Whitten, 1:26–38.
Washington, D.C.: Latin American Group.

———. 1976b. "The Black Ghetto as an Internal Colony: Socioeconomic
Adaptation of a Haitian Urban Community." Ph.D. diss., University of
Illinois.

———. 1977. "The Festival of Gods: Spirit Possession in Haitian Voodoo." *Freeing the Spirit* 5 (2): 23–35.

———. 1978. "Ticouloute and His Kinfolk: The Study of a Haitian
Extended Family." In *The Extended Family in Black Societies*, edited by
D. Shinkin, pp. 407–45. Paris: Mouton.

———. 1980a. *Voodoo Heritage*. Sage Library of Social Research, vol. 98.
Beverly Hills: Sage.

———. 1980b. "Bizango: A Voodoo Secret Society in Haiti." In *Secrecy*,
edited by S. K. Tefft. New York: Human Science Press.

———. 1982. *The Complete Haitiana: Bibliographic Guide to the Scholarly*
Literature, 1900–1980. Millwood, N.Y.: Kraus International Publications.

———. 1984. "Voodoo and Politics in Contemporary Haiti." Paper delivered at symposium New Perspectives on Caribbean Studies: Toward the 21st Century. Research Institute for the Study of Man and the C.U.N.Y., 28 August–1 September 1984.

———. 1986. "Politics and Voodoo Still a Potent Combination in Haiti." *Wall Street Journal*, 18 April 1986, p. 19.

Lahav, P. 1975. "The Chef de Section: Structure and Functions of Haiti's Basic Administrative Institution." In *Working Papers in Haitian Society and Culture*, 4:51–81. *See* Mintz 1975.

Lalone, R. C., E. D. Devillez, and E. Larson. 1963. "An Assay of the Toxicity of the Atlantic Puffer Fish *Sphoeroides maculatus*." *Toxicon* 1:159–64.

Laroche, M. 1976. "The Myth of Zombi." In *Exile and Tradition*, edited by R. Smith, pp.44–61. Halifax, N.S.: Longman and Dalhousie University Press.

Larsen, N. P. 1925. "Fish Poisoning." *Queen's Hospital Bulletin* 2 (1): 1–3.

———. 1942. "Tetrodon Poisoning in Hawaii." *Proceedings of the 6th Pacific Science Congress* 5:417–21.

Larson, E., L. R. Rivas, R. C. Lalone, and S. Coward. 1959. "Toxicology of Western Atlantic Puffer Fishes of the Genus *Sphoeroides*." *The Pharmacologist* 1 (2): 70.

Larson, E., R. C. Lalone, and L. R. Rivas. 1960. "Comparative Toxicity of the Atlantic Puffer Fishes of the Genera *Sphoeroides*, *Lactophorys*, *Lagocephelus*, and *Chilomycterus*." *Federation Proceedings* 19 (1): 388.

Leber, A. 1927. "Über Tetrodonvergiftung." *Arb. Trop. Grenzgebiete* 26:641–43.

Legerman, C. J. 1971. "Kin Groups in a Haitian Market." In *Peoples and Cultures of the Caribbean*, pp. 382–90. *See* Horowitz 1971.

Leon, R. 1959. *Phytotherapie haitienne: Nos simples*. Port-au-Prince: Imprimerie de l'Etat.

Leonard, A. G. 1906. *The Lower Niger and Its Tribes*. London: Macmillan.

Les P. Missionaires du T. S. Redempteur. 1943. *Haiti Flore Medicinale*. Port-au-Prince: Monastère Saint Gerard.

Lester, D. 1972. "Voodoo Death: Some New Thoughts on an Old Phenomenon." *American Anthropologist* 74 (3): 386–90.

Lewin, L. 1920. *Die Gifte in der Weltgeschichte*. Berlin: J. Springer.

———. 1931. *Phantastica: Narcotic and Stimulating Drugs, Their Use and Abuse*. New York: E. P. Dutton.

Lewis. G. 1977. "Fear of Sorcery and the Problem of Death by Suggestion." In *The Anthropology of the Body*, edited by J. Blacking, pp.111–43. London: Academic Press.

Lewis, M. G. 1843. *Journal of a West Indian Proprietor Kept during a Residence in the Island of Jamaica*. London: n.p.

Lex, B. W. 1974. "Voodoo Death: New Thoughts on an Old Explanation." *American Anthropologist* 76 (4): 818–23.

Leyburn, J. G. 1941. *The Haitian People*. New Haven. Conn.: Yale University Press.

Little, K. 1948. "The Poro as an Arbiter of Culture." *African Studies* 7 (1): 1–15.

———. 1949. "The Role of the Secret Society in Cultural Specialization." *American Anthropologist* 51:199–212.

———. 1951. *The Mende of Sierra Leone*. London, n.p.

———. 1965. "Political Function of the Poro. Part 1." *Africa* 35 (4): 349–65.

———. 1966. "Political Function of the Poro. Part 2." *Africa* 36 (1): 62–71.

Locke, D. 1976. "Zombies, Schizophrenics, and Purely Physical Objects." *Mind* 85:97–99.

Lockwood, T. E. 1979. "The Ethnobotany of Brugmansia." *Journal of Ethnopharmacology* 1:147–64.

Loederer, R. A. 1935. *Voodoo Fire in Haiti*. New York: The Literary Guild.

The London Times, 28 February 1970.

Long, E. 1774. *History of Jamaica*. London, n.p.

Lowenthal, I. 1978. "Ritual Performance and Religious Experience: A Service for the Gods in Southern Haiti." *Journal of Anthropological Research* 34 (3): 392–415.

Lown, B., J. V. Temte, P. Reich, C. Gaugham, Q. Regestein, and H. Hai. 1976. "Basis for Recurring Ventricular Fibrillation in the Absences of Coronary Heart Disease and Its Management." *New England Journal of Medicine* 294 (12): 623–29.

Lown, B., R. Verrier, and S. Rabinowitz. 1977. "Neural and Psychologic Mechanism and the Problem of Sudden Cardiac Death." *American Journal of Cardiology* 39:890–902.

Lown, B., R. Desilva, P. Reich, and B. Murawski. 1980. "Psychophysiologic Factors in Sudden Cardiac Death." *American Journal of Psychiatry* 137 (11): 1325–35.

Lynn, W. G. 1958. "Some Amphibians from Haiti and a New Subspecies of *Eleutherodactylus schmidti*." *Herpetologica* 14:153–57.

MacCormack, C. 1979. "Sande: The Public Face of a Secret Society." In *The New Religions of Africa*, edited by B. Jules-Rosette. Norwood, N.J.: Ablex Publishing.

McHenry, L. E., and R. C. W. Hall. 1978. "Angel's Trumpet: Lethal and Psychogenic Aspects." *Journal of the Florida Medical Association* 65 (3): 192–96.

MacKay, G. E. 1880. "Premature Burials." *Popular Science Monthly* 6 (19): 389–97.

MacKenzie, C. 1971 (orig. 1830). *Notes on Haiti*. 2 vols. London: Frank Cass.

MacKenzie, N. 1967. *Secret Societies*. New York: Collier Books.

Magid, A. 1972. "Political Traditionalism in Nigeria: A Case Study of Secret Societies and Dance Groups in Local Government." *Africa* 42 (4): 289–304.

Mak, L. F. 1981. *The Sociology of Secret Societies*. Kuala Lumpur: Oxford University Press.

Maniget, L. F. 1977. "The Relationship between Marronnage and Slave Revolts and Revolution in St. Domingue-Haiti." In *Comparative Perspectives on Slavery in New World Plantation Societies*, edited by V. Rubin and A. Tuden, pp. 420–38. Annals of the New York Academy of Sciences, vol. 292. New York: The Academy.

Mant, A. K. 1968. "The Medical Definition of Death." In *Man's Concern with Death*, edited by A. Toynbee, pp. 13–24. London: Hodder and Stoughton.

Marano, L. 1982. "Windigo Psychosis: The Anatomy of an Emic-Etic Confusion." *Current Anthropology* 23 (4): 385–412.

Marcelin, M. 1949. *Mythologie vodou*. Port-au-Prince: Les Editions Haitiennes.

Mars, L. P. 1945. "The Story of Zombi in Haiti." *Man* 45 (22): 38–40.

————. 1947. *La lutte contre la folie*. Port-au-Prince: Imprimerie de l'Etat.

————. 1977. *The Crisis of Possession in Voodoo*. Berkeley, Calif.: Reed, Cannon and Johnson.

Mathis, J. L. 1964. "A Sophisticated Version of Voodoo Death: Report of a Case." *Psychosomatic Medicine* 26 (2): 104–7.

Matsuo, R. 1934. "Study of the Poisonous Fishes at Juluit Islands." *Nanyo Gunto Chihobyo Chosa Ronbunshu* 2:309–26.

Mauss, M. 1926. "Éffet physique chez l'individu de l'idée de mort suggerée par la collectivité (Australie, Nouvelle-Zelande)." *Journal de Psychologie Normale et Pathologique* 23:653–69.

Maximilien, L. 1945. *Le vodou haitien*. Port-au-Prince: Imprimerie de l'Etat.

————. 1982. *Le vodou haitien—rites radas—canzo*. Port-au-Prince: Editions Henri Deschamps.

Mbiti, J. 1969. *African Religions and Philosophy*. Garden City, N.Y.: Anchor Books.

Mennesson-Rigaud, O. 1958. "La role du vaudou dans l'independance d'Haiti." *Présence Africaine* 18/19:43–67.

Métraux, A. 1946. "The Concept of Soul in Haitian Vodu." *Southwestern Journal of Anthropology* 2:84–92.

————. 1951. *Making a Living in the Marbiel Valley (Haiti)*. Occasional Papers in Education 10, UNESCO.

————. 1953. "Médecine et vodou en Haiti. *Acta Tropica* 10 (1): 28–68.

————. 1971. "Cooperative Labor Groups in Haiti." In *Peoples and Cultures of the Caribbean*, pp. 318–39. *See* Horowitz 1971.

————. 1972. *Voodoo in Haiti*. 2d ed. New York: Schocken Books.

Meyer, K. F., H. Sommer, and P. Schoenholz. 1928. "Mussel Poisoning." *Journal of Preventive Medicine* 2:365–94.

Michenfelder, J., and R. A. Theye. 1973. "Cerebral Protection by Thio-
pental during Hypoxia." *Anesthesiology* 39 (5): 510–17.

Middleton, J. 1973. "Secrecy in Lugbara Religion." *History of Religions* 12
(4): 299–316.

Milton, G. W. 1973. "Self Willed Death or the Bone Pointing Syndrome."
The Lancet 1:1435–36.

Mintz, S. 1966. Introduction to *The Haitian People*, by J. Leyburn. 2d ed.
New Haven, Conn.: Yale University Press.

———. 1971. "The Caribbean as a Socio-cultural Area." In *Peoples and
Cultures of the Caribbean*, pp. 17–46. *See* Horowitz 1971.

———. 1972. Introduction to *Voodoo in Haiti*. *See* Métraux 1972.

———. 1975. *Working Papers in Haitian Society and Culture*. New Haven,
Conn.: Antilles Research Program, Yale University.

Mira, F. 1939. "Psychiatric Experience in the Spanish War." *British Medical Journal* 1 (17 June): 1217–20.

Montalvo-Despeignes, J. 1976. *Le droit informal haitien*. Paris: Presses
universitaires de France.

Moral, P. 1961. *Le paysan haitien*. Paris: G. P. Maisonneuve et Larose.

Moreau de Saint-Mery, M. L. E. 1958. *Description topographique, physique,
civile, politique, et historique de la Partie française de l'Isle de Saint Domingue*. 2 vols. Paris: Librairie Larose.

———. 1979. "The Border Maroons of Saint-Domingue: Le Maniel." In
Maroon Societies: Rebel Slave Communities in the Americas, pp. 135–42.
See Price 1979.

Moritz, A. R., and N. Zamcheck. 1946. "Sudden and Unexpected Deaths
of Young Soldiers." *Archives of Pathology* 42:459–94.

Morton-Williams, P. 1960. "The Yoruba Ogboni Cult in Oyo." *Africa* 30
(4): 362–74.

Moscoso, R. M. 1943. *Catalogus Florae Domingensis*. Part 1. New York:
L and S Printing.

Mosher, H. S., F. A. Fuhrman, H. D. Buchwald, and H. G. Fischer. 1964.
"Tarichatoxin-Tetrodotoxin: A Potent Neurotoxin." *Science* 144:1100–
1110.

Mullin, C. A. 1923. "Report on Some Polychaetous Annelids; Collected
by the Barbados-Antiqua Expedition from the University of Iowa in
1918." *University of Iowa Studies in Natural History* 10 (3): 39–45.

Murphy, W. 1980. "Secret Knowledge as Property and Power in Kpelle
Society: Elders vs. Youth." *Africa* 50: 193–207.

Murray, G. F. 1976. "Women in Perdition: Ritual Fertility Control in
Haiti." In *Culture, Natality and Family Planning*, edited by J. F. Marshall
and S. Polgar, pp. 59–78. Chapel Hill: University of North Carolina
Press.

———. 1977. "The Evolution of Haitian Peasant Land Tenure: A Case

Study in Agrarian Adaptation to Population Growth." Ph.D. diss., Columbia University.

———. 1980. "Population Pressure, Land Tenure, and Voodoo: The Economics of Haitian Peasant Ritual." In *Beyond the Myths of Culture*, edited by E. B. Ross, pp. 295–321. London: Academic Press.

Murray, G. F., and M. Alvarez. 1975. "Haitian Bean Circuits: Cropping and Trading Maneuvers among a Cash Oriented Peasantry." In *Working Papers in Haitian Society and Culture*, pp. 85–126. *See* Mintz 1975.

Narahashi, T., J. W. Moore, and W. R. Scott. 1964. "Tetrodotoxin Blockage of Sodium Conductance Increase in Lobster Giant Axons." *Journal of General Physiology* 47:965–74.

Newberg, L. A., and J. Michenfelder. 1983. "Cerebral Protection by Isoflurane during Hypoxemia or Ischemia." *Anesthesiology* 51 (1): 29–35.

Nicholls, D. 1970. "Politics and Religion in Haiti." *Canadian Journal of Political Science* 3 (3): 400–414.

Nixon, W. 1965. "Scared to Death." *British Medical Journal* (18 September): 701.

Noguchi, T., and Y. Hashimoto. 1973. "Isolation of Tetrodotoxin from a Goby *Gobius criniger.*" *Toxicon* 11:305–7.

Noniyama, S. 1942. "The Pharmacological Study of Puffer Poison." *Nippon Yakubutsugaku Zasshi* 35 (4): 458–96.

Oliver-Bever, B. 1983. "Medicinal Plants of Tropical West Africa. III. Anti-Infection Therapy with Higher Plants." *Journal of Ethnopharmacology* 9:1–83.

Ottenberg, S. 1971. *Leadership and Authority in an African Society*. Seattle: University of Washington Press.

———. 1972. "Humorous Masks and Serious Politics among Afikpo Ibo." In *African Art and Leadership*, edited by D. Fraser and H. M. Cole, pp. 99–121. Madison: University of Wisconsin Press.

———. 1982a. "Boy's Secret Societies at Afikpo." In *African Religious Groups and Beliefs*, pp. 170–84. *See* Ottenberg 1982c.

———. 1982b. "Illusion, Communications, and Psychology in West African Masquerades." *Ethos* 10 (2): 149–85.

———, ed. 1982c. *African Religious Groups and Beliefs*. Meerut, India: Archana Publications.

Parkes, C. M., C. B. Benjamin, and R. G. Fitzgerald. 1969. "Broken Heart: A Statistical Study of Increased Mortality among Widowers." *British Medical Journal* (22 March): 740–43.

Parrinder, G. 1961. *West African Religion*. London: Epworth Press.

Parsons, E. C. 1928. "Spirit Cult in Hayti." *Journal de la Société des Americanistes de Paris* 20:157–79.

Pattison, E. M. 1974. "Psychosocial Predictors of Death Prognosis." *Omega* 5 (2): 145–60.

Peng, G. F., L. Wang, and Y. H. Wang. 1921. *Biological Dictionary*. Shang-hai: Chung Hua Book Company.

Peters, C. E. 1965. "Société mandingue." *Revue de la Faculté d'Ethnologie* 10:47–50.

Phisalix, M. 1922. *Animaux venimeux et venins*. 2 vols. Paris: Masson et Cie.

Pierre, R. 1978. *Les zombis en furie*. Port-au-Prince: Ateliers Fardin.

Plonson, C. 1974. *Vaudou, un initié parle*. Paris: Jean Dullis Editeur.

Plotkin, D. 1979. "Land Distribution in Lowland Haiti Community: The Case of Ca-Ira." Manuscript.

Pocchiari, F. 1977. "Trade of Misbranded Fish: Medical and Public Health Implications." *Annali dell'Instituto Superiore di Sanita* 13:767–72.

Pradel, J., and J. Casgha. 1983. *Haiti: la république des morts vivants*. Paris: Editions du Rocher.

Price, R., ed. 1979. *Maroon Societies: Rebel Slave Communities in the Americas*. Baltimore: Johns Hopkins University Press.

Price-Mars, J. 1928. *Ainsi parla l'oncle*. Port-au-Prince: Imprimerie de Compiegne.

———. 1938. "Lemba-petro, un culte secret." *Revue de la Société d'Histoire et de Geographie d'Haiti* 9 (28): 12–31.

Prince, R. 1985. "Comments." *Transcultural Psychiatric Research Review* 22 (4): 190–94.

Rahe, R. H., and E. Lind. 1971. "Psychosocial Factors and Sudden Cardiac Death: A Pilot Study." *Journal of Psychosomatic Research* 15:19–24.

Rahe, R. H., L. Bennett, and M. Romo. 1973. "Subjects' Recent Life Changes and Coronary Heart Disease in Finland." *American Journal of Psychiatry* 130:1222–26.

Rees, W. D., and S. G. Lutkins. 1967. "Mortality of Bereavement." *British Medical Journal* (4): 13–16.

Richardson, B. W. 1893. "Fish Poisoning and the Disease 'Siguatera.' " *Asclepiad* 10:38–42.

Richardson, J. 1861. "On the Poisonous Effects of a Small Portion of the Liver of a *Diodon* Inhabiting the Seas of Southern Africa." *Journal of the Linnaean Society* 5:213–16.

Richter, C. P. 1957. "On the Phenomenon of Sudden Death in Animals and Man." *Psychosomatic Medicine* 14:191–98.

Rigaud, M. 1953. *La tradition voudou et voudou haitien: Son temple, ses mystères, sa magie*. Paris: Editions Niclaus.

———. 1970. *Secrets of Voodoo*. New York: Arco.

———. 1974. *Ve-Ve*. New York: French and European Publications.

Rigaud, O. 1946. "The Feasting of the Gods in Haitian Vodu." *Primitive Man* 19 (1/2): 1–58.

Ritchie, J. M. 1975. "Binding of Tetrodotoxin and Saxitoxin to Sodium

Channels." *Phil. Trans. R. Soc. London B.* 270:319–36.

Robb, G. L. 1957. "The Ordeal Poisons of Madagascar and Africa." Harvard University, *Botanical Museum Leaflets* 17 (10): 265–315.

Roberts, J. M. 1972. *The Mythology of the Secret Societies*. New York: Scribners.

Robinson, P. F., and F. J. Schwartz. 1968. "Toxicity of the Northern Puffer *Sphoeroides maculatus* in the Chesapeake Bay and Its Environs." *Chesapeake Science* 9 (2): 136–43.

Rotberg, R. 1971. *Haiti: The Politics of Squalor*. Boston: Houghton Mifflin.

———. 1976. "Vodoun and the Politics of Haiti." In *The African Diaspora: Interpretive Essays*, edited by M. L. Kilson and R. I. Rotberg, pp. 342–65. Cambridge, Mass.: Harvard University Press.

Roumain, J. 1942a. "Contributions a l'étude de l'ethnobotanique precolombienne des Grandes Antilles." *Bulletin Bureau d'Ethnologie de la République d'Haiti* 1:13–71.

———. 1942b. *A propos de la campagne antisuperstitieuse*. Port-au-Prince: Imprimerie de l'État.

———. 1975. *Quelques moeurs et coutumes des paysans haitiens*. Port-au-Prince: Imprimerie de l'État.

Rubin, V., ed. 1960. *Caribbean Studies: A Symposium*. Seattle: University of Washington Press.

Rubin, V., and R. Schaebel. 1975. *The Haitian Potential*. New York: Columbia University Press.

Sabom, M. B. 1982. *Recollections of Death—A Medical Investigation*. New York: Simon and Schuster.

Safford, W. 1920. "Daturas of the Old World and New: An Account of Their Narcotic Properties and Their Use in Oracular and Initiatory Ceremonies." In *Annual Report of the Smithsonian Institute*. Washington, D.C,: Government Printing Office.

St. John, S. 1884. *Hayti or the Black Republic*. London: Smith, Elder and Company.

Savtschenko, P. N. 1882. "A Case of Poisoning by Fish." *Medits Pribav. Morsk. Sborniku*. 9:55–61.

Schleiffer, H. 1973. *Sacred Narcotics of the New World Indians*. New York: Hafner Press.

———. 1979. *Narcotic Plants of the Old World*. Monticello, N.Y.: Lubrecht and Cramer.

Schmidt, H. 1971. *The United States Occupation, 1915–34*. New Brunswick, N.J.: Rutgers University Press.

Schultes, R. E. 1970. "The New World Indians and Their Hallucinogenic Plants." *Bulletin of the Morris Arboretum* 21:3–14.

———. 1979. "Ancient Gold Pectorals from Colombia: Mushroom Effigies." *Botanical Museum Leaflets* 27:5–6, 113–42.

Schultes, R. E., and A. Hofmann. 1979. *Plants of the Gods.* New York: McGraw-Hill.

———. 1980. *The Botany and Chemistry of Hallucinogens.* 2d ed. Springfield, Ill.: Charles C. Thomas.

Schwartz, C. J., and W. J. Walsh. 1971. "The Pathological Basis of Sudden Death." *Progress in Cardiovascular Disease* 39:97–102.

Seabrook, W. B. 1929. *The Magic Island.* London: George G. Harrap and Company.

See, W. 1880. "The Extreme Rarity of Premature Burials." *Popular Science Monthly* 17:527.

Sharon, D. 1978. *Wizard of the Four Winds.* New York: Free Press.

Sheumack, D. D., M. E. H. Howden, I. Spence, and R. J. Quinn. 1978. "Maculotoxin: A Neurotoxin from Venom Glands of the Octopus *Hapalochlaena maculosa* Identified as Tetrodotoxin." *Science* 199:188–89.

Shipp, R. L. 1974. *The Puffer Fishes (Tetraodontidae) of the Atlantic Ocean.* Ocean Springs, Miss.: Publications of the Gulf Coast Research Laboratory Museum, no. 4.

Simmel, G. 1906. "The Sociology of Secrecy and the Secret Societies." *The American Journal of Sociology* 11 (4): 441–98.

Simmons, D. C. 1956a. "Efik Divination, Ordeals, and Omens. *Southwest Journal of Anthropology* 12:223–28.

———. 1956b. "An Ethnographic Sketch of the Efik People." In *The Efik Traders of Old Calabar*, pp. 1–26. *See* Forde 1956.

Simpson, G. E. 1940a. "The Vodun Service in Northern Haiti." *American Anthropologist* 42:236–54.

———. 1940b. "Haitian Magic." *Social Forces* 19:95–100.

———. 1941. "Haiti's Social Structure." *American Sociological Review* 6 (5): 640–49.

———. 1942a. "Loup Garou and Loa Tales from Northern Haiti." *Journal of American Folklore* 55 (218): 219–27.

———. 1942b. "Sexual and Familial Institutions in Northern Haiti." *American Anthropologist* 44 (2): 655–74.

———. 1943. "Traditional Tales from Northern Haiti." *Journal of American Folklore* 56 (222): 255–65.

———. 1945. "The Belief System of Haitian Vodoun." *American Anthropologist* 47 (1): 37–59.

———. 1948. "Two Vodun Related Ceremonies." *Journal of American Folklore* 61 (239): 49–53.

———. 1951. "Acculturation in Northern Haiti." *Journal of American Folklore* 55 (218): 219–27.

———. 1980. *Religious Cults of the Caribbean: Trinidad, Jamaica, and Haiti.* Caribbean Monograph Series, no. 15. San Juan: Institute of Caribbean Studies. University of Puerto Rico.

Simpson, K., ed. 1965. *Principles and Practise of Medical Jurisprudence.* London: Churchill.

Smith, M. G. 1960. "The African Heritage in the Caribbean." In *Caribbean Studies. See* Rubin 1960.

———. 1965. *The Plural Society in the British West Indies.* Berkeley: University of California Press.

Snow, L. F. 1974. "Folk Medicinal Beliefs and Their Implications for Care of Patients." *Annals of Internal Medicine* 81:82–96.

———. 1975. "Voodoo Illness in the Black Population." In *Culture, Curers and Contagion,* edited by N. Klein. Novato, Calif.: Chandler and Sharp.

Sofowora, A. 1982. *Medicinal Plants and Traditional Medicine in Africa.* Chichester, Eng.: John Wiley and Sons.

Spradley, J. P. 1970. *Participant Observation.* New York: Holt, Rinehart and Winston.

Stevenson, M. 1915. *Ethnobotany of the Zuni.* 30th Annual Report of the Bureau of American Ethnology. Washington, D.C.: Government Printing Office.

Sylvain, G. 1901. *Fables creoles.* Port-au-Prince: n.p.

Taft, E. 1938. *A Puritan in Voodooland.* Philadelphia: The Pennsylvania Publishing Company.

Tahara, Y. 1896. "Über die Giftigen bestandheile des Tetrodon." *Congr. Internat. Hyg. Demog.* 8 (4): 198–207.

Tani, I. 1940. "Seasonal Changes and Individual Differences of Puffer Poison." *Nippon Yakubutsugaku Zasshi* 29 (1/2):1–3.

Taylor, N. 1965. *Plant Drugs That Changed the World.* New York: Dodd, Mead and Company.

Thompson, J. E. S. 1970. *Maya History and Religion.* Norman: University of Oklahoma Press.

Thompson, R. F. 1983. *Flash of the Spirit.* New York: Vintage Books.

Tingling, D. C. 1967. "Voodoo, Root Work, and Medicine. *Psychosomatic Medicine* 29 (5): 483–90.

Torda, T. A., E. Sinclair, and D. B. Ulyatt. 1973. "Puffer Fish (Tetrodotoxin) Poisoning: Clinical Record and Suggested Management." *The Medical Journal of Australia* 1:599–602.

Tsuda, K., and M. Kawamura. 1952. "The Constituents of the Ovaries of Globefish. VII: Purification of Tetrodotoxin by Chromatography." *Journal of the Pharmacological Society of Japan* 72:771–72.

Tu, Y. C., T. T. Tu, T. L. Wu, C. H. Ling, and C. C. Hsu. 1923. *Zoological Nomenclature.* Shanghai: Commercial Press.

Turner, W. J., and S. Merlis. 1959. "Effect of Some Indole Alkylamines on Man." *Archives of Neurology and Psychiatry* 81:121–29.

Underwood, F. W. 1964. "Land and Its Manipulation among the Haitian Peasantry." In *Explorations in Cultural Anthropology,* edited by W. Goodenough, pp. 469–82. New York: McGraw-Hill.

Vaisrub, S. 1959. "Brain and Heart—the Autonomic Connection." *Journal of the American Medical Association* 234:1959.

Verdcourt, B., and E. C. Trump. 1969. *Common Poisonous Plants of East Africa*. London: Collins.

Vietmeyer, N. D. 1984. "The Preposterous Puffer." *National Geographic* 163 (2): 260–70.

Wallace, R. K., and H. Benson. 1972. "The Physiology of Meditation." *Scientific American* 226 (2): 84–91.

Warner, W. L. 1941. *A Black Civilization: A Social Study of an Australian Tribe*. New York: Harper and Brothers.

Watson, L. 1974. *The Romeo Error*. London: Hodder and Stoughton.

Watt, J. M., and M. G. Breyer-Brandwijk. 1962. *Medicinal and Poisonous Plants of Southern and Eastern Africa*. 2d ed. Edinburgh, Scot.: E. and S. Livingston.

Webster, H. 1968. *Primitive Secret Societies*. New York: Octagon Books.

Weckman, G. 1970. "Primitive Secret Societies as Religious Organizations." *International Review for the History of Religions* 17:83–94.

Wedgewood, C. 1930. "The Nature and Function of Secret Societies." *Oceania* 1 (2): 129–45.

Weil, A. T. 1972. *The Natural Mind*. Boston: Houghton Mifflin.

————. 1980. *The Marriage of the Sun and the Moon*. Boston: Houghton Mifflin.

————. 1983. *Health and Healing*. Boston: Houghton Mifflin.

Wieland, H., and R. Alles. 1922. "Über des Giftstoff der Krote." *Berl. Deut. Chem. Gesellsch.* 55:1789.

Williams, E. 1971. "The Origin of Negro Slavery." In *Peoples and Cultures of the Caribbean*, pp. 47–74. *See* Horowitz 1971.

Wimpffen, F. 1817. *A Voyage to Saint Domingo*. London, n.p.

Wintrob, R. M. 1973. "The Influence of Others: Witchcraft and Rootwork as Explanations of Behavioral Disturbances." *Journal of Nervous and Mental Disease* 156 (5): 318–26.

Wirkus, F., and T. Dudley. 1931. *The White King of La Gonave*. Garden City, N.Y.: Garden City Publishing Company.

Wittkower, E. D. 1964. "Spirit Possession in Haitian Vodun Ceremonies." *Acta Psychotherapeutica et Psychosomatica* 12:72–80.

Wolf, S. 1967. "The End of the Rope: The Role of the Brain in Cardiac Death." *Canadian Medical Association Journal* 97:1022–25.

Wolff, K., ed. 1950. *The Sociology of Georg Simmel*. Glencoe, Ill.: Free Press.

Wong, W. 1976. "Some Folk Medicinal Plants from Trinidad." *Economic Botany* 30:103–42.

Wood, H. A. 1963. *Northern Haiti: Land, Land Use, and Settlement*. Toronto: University of Toronto Press.

Woodward, R. B. 1964. "Structure of Tetrodotoxin." *Pure Applied Chemistry* 9:49–74.

Wrong, D. H. 1968. "Some Problems in Defining Social Power." *American Journal of Sociology* 73 (6): 673–81.

Yano, I. 1937. "The Pharmacological Study of Tetrodotoxin." *Fukuoka Med. Coll.* 30 (9): 1669–1704.

Yasumoto, T., and C. Y. Kao. 1986. "Tetrodotoxin and the Haitian Zombie." *Toxicon* 24:747–49.

Yokoo, A. 1950. "Chemical Studies on Globefish Poison. III. Separation of Spheroudin." *Journal of the Chemical Society of Japan* 71:590–92.

Young, P. J. W. 1965. "Scared to Death." *British Medical Journal* (18 September): 701.

Zahan, D. 1960. *Société d'initiation Bambara, le N'Domo, le Kore.* Paris: Mouton.

———. 1979. *The Religion, Spirituality, and Thought of Traditional Africa.* Chicago: University of Chicago Press.

Zuesse, E. M. 1985. *Ritual Cosmos: The Sanctification of Life in African Religions.* Athens: Ohio University Press.

Zug, G. R. 1979. *Bufo marinus: A Natural History Résumé of Native Populations.* Washington, D.C.: Smithsonian Institution Press.